The People's Constitution

The path to empowerment of Australians in a 21st century democracy

BRONWYN KELLY

AF584904

The People's Constitution: The path to empowerment of Australians in a 21st century democracy
Copyright © Bronwyn Kelly, January 2023
Bronwyn Kelly asserts her right to be known as the author of this work.
ALL RIGHTS RESERVED.
No part of this publication may be reproduced, stored in a retrieval system, or transmitted in any form by any means, electronic, mechanical, photocopying, recording or otherwise, without the prior consent of the author, except in the case of brief quotations embodied in critical articles and reviews.

A catalogue record for this work is available from the National Library of Australia

Cover design and photo by Bronwyn Kelly
Cover Photo: The path to parliament,
Canberra, Australia

Printed by Kaligraphic Print, Sydney

About *The People's Constitution*

This book offers the people of Australia a comprehensive proposal for a new type of constitution for their Commonwealth, a constitution in which they will have a role beyond mere voting and by which they can be empowered for the first time to take a rightful place in their own governance. It is designed to give them a practical means of forming a new, more productive and transparent partnership with those they elect and thereby to re-create their political systems and the nation itself as a fully open, participatory democracy.

In this new democratic arrangement, Australians can exercise a rightful share of power principally to express their sovereign will as a nation. The current Australian Constitution makes no place for the expression of this will. In the people's constitution, however, the people of Australia are offered a practical, well organised means to express their sovereign will in a coherent way and to offer that as new terms of trust to those they elect to positions of power.

The People's Constitution is set at a turning point in the history of democracy and in our understanding of how state sovereignty may be ethically arranged and made stable. It canvasses the history of Australia's capacity for effective governance since the current Constitution was first adopted in 1901 and examines the usefulness of the arrangement of power made possible under it, not just in relation to today's political challenges but also in relation to the capacity of these arrangements to help Australians meet the challenges of the future. Some of these challenges – including climate change and war – are potentially existential in their dimensions. Acknowledging the precariousness of our future, this book asserts that the type of democratic sovereign state made possible by Australia's current Constitution offers Australians insufficient capacity to safely navigate their future. It suggests that the capacity of their democracy can be sufficiently strengthened if a place is made in the Constitution for the people to state their values as a nation, reach agreement with each other on human rights and obligations, and access rights to express their will for the future.

Transition to a people's constitution also offers Australians their first chance to exercise the fundamental human right of self-determination – that is, the right by virtue of which all peoples of the world can freely determine their political status and freely pursue their economic, social and cultural development. This right has been acknowledged in international law as central to every individual's and every nation's capacity to realise a decent future of wellbeing and security, and it is a right that the First Nations peoples of Australia currently consider to be central to their future. They have emerged from their tragic experience of dispossession declaring something that is fundamental to all humanity. In the Uluru Statement from the Heart they have declared that when they have power over their destiny their children will flourish.

Accordingly, Aborigines and Torres Strait Islanders have called upon Australians to walk together with them in a movement of *all* Australian people for a better future. In addition to an Indigenous Voice in the Constitution, they are calling for a coexistence of sovereignties based on justice and self-determination. This book strongly supports those calls and indeed suggests that a positive response to them in any forthcoming referendum on a constitutionally enshrined Indigenous Voice offers all Australians substantial benefits. But to capture those benefits it will be necessary to re-build our 120-year-old Constitution so that it empowers all Australians to have a Voice.

In the 21st century, across the Western world, the whole concept of sovereignty has been undergoing a transformation. It has been shifting, slowly but steadily, from a *supposition* that sovereignty is something granted to a government by the consent of a willingly submissive people, to a *proposition* that it is something to be shared by people who can exercise self-determination in political equality. That shift implies the need for a shift in the Australian Constitution. This is a paradigmatic shift but it is also entirely feasible if Australians build a *people's* constitution.

As they approach the question of whether they may wish to become a republic, this book argues that an Australian people's constitution would make such a decision truly meaningful and empowering by enabling them to describe the sort of republic they wish to become and the place they can rightfully take within it to increase the chances that all their children will flourish.

About the Author

Bronwyn Kelly

Dr Bronwyn Kelly is an Australian researcher and writer on public policy, specialising in long term integrated planning for Australia's society, environment, economy and democracy and in systems of governance for nation states. She is the Founder of Australian Community Futures Planning (ACFP), a research entity providing assistance to Australians in planning a better future for themselves and for future generations.

Prior to founding ACFP Dr Kelly was a public sector professional for thirty years in the Senior Executive Service of state and local government in New South Wales (1984-2014). Her experience traversed government sector reform, policy development, profitable management of government commercial trading enterprises, utilities operation, environmental and scientific management and integrated long term community strategic planning. She held senior positions in Sydney Water, Australian Water Technologies, the NSW Government Cabinet Office, and was a senior policy advisor to a state government minister in NSW. As a Director of Corporate and Technical Services in local government for fifteen years, she pioneered innovative and best practice implementation of Integrated Planning & Reporting – a legislated form of community futures planning operating in local government in several states of Australia.

Dr Kelly is the author of *By 2050: Planning a better future for our children in 21st century democratic Australia*, the major essay "Prospects for journalism, the free information market and democracy in Australia under the ACCC's News Media Bargaining Code", and a range of media articles on public policy, Indigenous recognition, climate change, government sector ethics, and democracy. She is also the lead author on Australia's first long term integrated community futures plan, *Australia Together*, co-author of *The State of Australia 2022: End of Term Report, 46th Parliament of Australia* and creator/presenter of several videocast series including *The State of Australia in 2020*, *The State of Australia 2022*, *Snapshots from Australia Together*, and the five-part lecture series, *What is National Integrated Planning and Reporting?* These publications are accessible at the Australian Community Futures Planning website: www.austcfp.com.au

Dr Kelly's PhD is from Sydney University, 1985, in History of Systems of Thought. Her Doctoral thesis was *The Textual Mandate: the authorisation of the logic of deterrence in western philosophy since Descartes*, an exploration of humanity's fear of death and extinction in the nuclear age. She was also an Honorary Professional Fellow at the University of Technology Sydney's Institute for Public Policy and Governance from 2014 to 2021.

Acknowledgement

The author acknowledges the Traditional Owners of the lands on which we live and work across Australia and pays respect to Elders past, present and emerging. I and my family recognise and celebrate the extraordinary contribution that Aboriginal and Torres Strait Islander peoples have made through millennia to all aspects of Australian life, culture and the environment.

We acknowledge that sovereignty has never been ceded and support the claims of the Uluru Statement from the Heart in full.

For those that each of us love.

CONTENTS

The ultimate, hidden truth of the world is that it is something we make, and could just as easily make differently.

David Graeber

When we have power over our destiny our children will flourish.

Uluru Statement from the Heart

The birds they sang at the break of day,
Start again I heard them say.

Leonard Cohen, *Anthem*

Introduction – Inviting Australians to take power over their destiny

Sydney, July 2022

This book is an invitation to all Australians to take up positions of rightful power within their democracy. It calls on them to choose to exercise much greater influence in their own governance and control over their own future than they have been able to exercise to date. And it offers them a way to exercise that greater level of control, both as individuals and collectively as a nation, by establishing a place for themselves in the central, defining statement of the nation – the Australian Constitution.

Fundamentally this is a book about power, how it is arranged and distributed in the early 2020s in our form of democracy under our Constitution. And it is about how a new Australian Constitution may be written to change that arrangement so that power is shared in a more fully democratic and inclusive sovereignty, one in which we the people have agency and, through that agency, more control over not just our destiny but our prospects for survival.

As an invitation it has been inspired by another far more remarkable one issued to all Australians in 2017 by its First Nations peoples – the Uluru Statement from the Heart.[1] This Statement stands as perhaps the most gracious invitation that has ever been offered by an invaded nation to an occupying nation. After no less than 230 years of decimation – to the point of attempted genocide – the impact of which is yet to be fully internalised in the Australian

---

[1] Uluru Statement from the Heart, 2017, https://ulurustatement.org/the-statement/.

national soul, it is astonishing that First Nations, having not only survived but come together (and having done so without extinguishing their own diversity), can still muster the generousity to invite the invaders to

> walk with them in a movement of the Australian people for a better future.[2]

The magnanimity of the invitation that is the Uluru Statement from the Heart bespeaks a magnificent Indigenous culture that has sprung from the Australian continent. And as time has passed in the 21st century, more and more Australians have come to recognise this marvel of survival and are seeking to know and understand the Aboriginal and Torres Strait Islander civilisation. They are seeking to find the source of such resilience and grace and the culture which has enabled that combination. The fact that they cannot find that civilisation or its peoples in their own Constitution is being recognised as a gaping hole in the soul of the nation – a blankness in the heart that blights the possibility of genuine social cohesion and perhaps even survival itself.

Non-Indigenous Australians are learning more and more from Aborigines and Torres Strait Islanders about survival, as well they might when knowledge of how to survive in a brutal climate may soon turn out to be the only thing between them and extinction. There is a growing awareness that opportunities to exploit the land – on the rapacious, unsustainable industrial scale that Europeans have come to depend on – may in future not be available or productive enough for survival if climate change is not stopped. But alongside that fear there is a growing acknowledgement that Indigenous knowledge of sustainable land management may offer a potential lifeline. At least, such knowledge may cushion us somewhat against the effects of climate change if it is internalised in our land use and marine management before the planet heats by more than 1.5 degrees Celsius above pre-industrial revolution temperatures.

For Indigenous Australians though, it may be that there can be no real confidence that their cultural practices in relation to land and

---

[2] View the Uluru Statement from the Heart in full in Appendix 1.

conservation would be sufficiently acknowledged if their culture and they themselves are not acknowledged in the central founding document of the nation. This surmise on my part may be merely the presumption of a white woman of Celtic and European background whose ancestors may well have played a part in Aboriginal dispossession and who, regardless of any confirmation of invidious participation in such dispossession, continues to benefit from the whole sorry history. But logic would dictate that if First Nations are calling not just for recognition in the Constitution but recognition in the form of a Voice designed to give them control over their own destiny, then they have concluded through their bitter experience that a substantive rather than merely symbolic form of recognition is absolutely essential to their survival. And by extension, non-Indigenous Australians should logically infer that a substantive form of Indigenous recognition in the Constitution is a condition precedent not just to national redemption for the crimes of the past but to our broader destiny as a unified nation – one with a viable future.

The Uluru Statement from the Heart is built on a fundamental assumption that until First Nations have a substantive Voice in the statement that constitutes the nation, they will not have power over their own destiny and their children will not flourish. The kernel of faith in the Uluru Statement, proclaiming that

> when we have power over our destiny our children will flourish,

resounds with the sharpest logic. Indeed, how could it be otherwise? How could any individual or nation really flourish without power, particularly the power of self-determination?

Few communities on earth could claim to know more than Australia's Aborigines about what it is really like to live without even a vestige of that sort of power – what it is like to live as the dispossessed, the unentitled, the racially segregated, derided and disadvantaged, the culturally suppressed, the voiceless. But anyone may discern from the evidence that is in plain sight that the social breakdown and individual trauma caused by such total powerlessness is deep and intergenerational in its effects.

Powerlessness does not enable, it destroys. And absolute powerlessness destroys absolutely.

Against this background it is clear that the Indigenous Voice is what any human group under threat will seek to design in their polity when "the torment of [their] powerlessness" reaches a crisis point. It is what any sane and reasonable but powerless minority community will inevitably design when, living in an ostensibly democratic country, its members protest that the benefits of that democracy have not been equitably extended to them and that this inequality itself has reached such proportions that their powerless community and everything it rests on are on the brink of a crisis, the "dimensions" of which are existential and "tell plainly of the structural nature of [their] problem".[3]

Structured as reasonably as the call for an Indigenous Voice is, there is nothing that could justify a refusal to enshrine such a Voice in our Constitution. It is the minimum of the justice that is required. But the whole Australian nation would also be doing itself a huge favour by enshrining the Indigenous Voice. It would be giving itself the chance to start again, this time establishing a nation without the faults of its original founding. The call for an Indigenous Voice was a long time coming, but when it came – in such a reasonable and, at the same time, profound form – it caused a watershed, a unique moment of potential transformation for the entire nation. The scope of this watershed might not yet be fully apparent but it offers much more than a reprieve or absolution for those who benefitted unjustly from colonisation. More than a symbolic recognition and the possibility of amends, it offers non-Indigenes a model for enshrining a voice of their own, a voice that can give them greater control over their destiny and enable their children to flourish, a power of self-determination that can be shared in such a way as to enable us to establish the nation we *all* want, rather than the one that has been foisted on us all by its encoding in the current Constitution.

That latter nation – the one created in 1901 at Federation – was remarkable and munificent in its own way. But it was also racist,

[3] Uluru Statement from the Heart. See Appendix 1.

exclusive, and extremely jealous of sharing power with those it had charged with responsibility for selecting representatives in the national parliament. The creation of Australia as a representative democracy was a great day and a dreadful day all at once, not just for Aborigines and Torres Strait Islanders but for all Australians. The chosen identity of a white Australia has sealed all our fates from that day to this, if only because no racist elements of the Constitution have since been expunged and no further powers have been conferred on Australians to help them escape that fate of exclusion from determining their own future. Nothing has changed in the Constitution to help them overcome their own voicelessness. In this sense the Indigenous call for a constitutional Voice serves to awaken all other Australians to the founding disempowerments of our nation – disempowerments which came down with exponential force on First Nations peoples, but which also beset all those seemingly empowered by representative politics.

The fate imposed on Australians in 1901 is not inescapable, especially now that First Nations have given us a model for how it might be escaped. Having made the nation once at Federation, there is nothing stopping Australians from remaking it, bearing in mind that one of the best features of the Constitution was that it reserved power to remake it entirely to "the people", albeit only after the parliament might let them conduct referendums for the purpose. But even that limitation can change. It can change very much for the better if we establish a new type of democratic constitution – one in which the people are acknowledged as the source of sovereignty.

To establish a basis for that particular change this book will first examine the best and worst of the current Australian Constitution. This will be done by observing it not from the point of view of an elected parliamentarian or High Court judge (in other words not from the point of view of someone who is already empowered by the Constitution) but from the perspective of an elector – of someone who takes for granted the best of the system, in that for the present at least she is able to vote,[4] but who knows that when she votes she is doing nothing more than giving away power and giving it away entirely without conditions. Through this prism the Constitution will be reviewed from the perspective of an awareness of the limits of mere representative democracy – a system which tends strongly to preserve power only for those who already have it and who make laws which reinforce their power, and only their power.

In place of that sort of democracy, a new Constitution will be proposed which can enable transition to a fully participatory democracy, creating a fairer and much wider spread of power arranged through an orderly process – a constituted process to impart for the first time a significant and rightful share of power to the people of Australia. This will give a share of power to those who to date have been acknowledged in the Constitution as nothing more than the group whose vote is required to elect their governors and whose relevance and control is lost entirely as soon as they have discharged that duty.

In short, Australia's current power arrangements will be reviewed here from the perspective of the powerless but also in contemplation of the degree and type of power the Australian people will need, as a minimum, to secure not just whatever future they may deeply desire but their very survival as a civilisation. Taking into account our vulnerability to imminent loss or even annihilation in the face of climate change, particularly as it is combined now with other existential threats (pandemics, natural resource depletion, biodiversity extinctions, unsustainable consumption patterns, global economic inequality and structural collapse, and possible nuclear war), this analysis will posit that while it is vital to look to First Nations for wisdom about survival – since no race has done it better than them – it is equally vital to learn from them about how powerlessness itself can pose an existential threat and that without a voice in our own governance our prospects for survival – as individuals, as

[4] The right to vote is not enshrined in Australia's Constitution and is therefore precarious. See Chapter 6 for more details. Also George Williams and Daniel Reynolds, *A Charter of Rights in Australia,* UNSW Press, NewSouth Publishing, Sydney, 2017, Chapter 3 – Our rights under the law, page 46.

cultures, as a nation – may well amount to zero. Non-Indigenes will be pushed to the brink, just as Indigenes have been.

This may seem shocking but there it is. It is not incomprehensible and it is not far-fetched. Such a fate is at least as likely as not, and therefore, ignoring or denying it would amount to insanity – a bent more towards suicide than survival. However, the good news is that the means of making that fate less likely are entirely in our hands. Not only do we have the technology and the wealth, we also have the capacity to reorganise our governance and the way we distribute power to avert this fate. We have the capacity to cooperate with other nations and to use our democracy to its fullest scope so that it delivers an entirely different destiny, not just mere survival in a diminished form but a viable and fulfilling future for individuals and the nation as a whole.

Of course the degree of difficulty in reorganising our governance so that we can establish viability as a species into the future is likely to be greater than the degree of difficulty associated with using technical and financial solutions. The will to power in humans is so ingrained that it will not be easily shared by those that have it. But unless power is spread more widely as a force for inclusion, there is every likelihood that our current consumption patterns – those which suit the already powerful – will simply outstrip the capacity of the planet to sustain us. In particular the world is likely to emit far more in greenhouse gases than we should emit if we wish to hold planetary temperature increases below 1.5 degrees Celsius. We may stave off global heating for a little while via technology but to nowhere near the degree necessary to prevent temperature increases above 2° Celsius – increases which will irreversibly lock in either our annihilation or at least destroy what Noam Chomsky has called

> *organised* human life on earth.[5] [Emphasis added.]

[5] Noam Chomsky: "The Future of Organized Human Life is at Risk Thanks to GOP's Climate Change Denial", Interview with Democracy Now Independent Global News, YouTube, 6 November 2018, https://www.youtube.com/watch?v=0t-YiZGEtaQ

In Chomsky's view – and he is not alone – if the planet heats by more than 2° Celsius our prospects will be, at worst, total extinction and, at best, total chaos. Either way, and even if he is only half right, it won't do to ignore the problem and it won't solve the problem if we simply rely on the will of the rich and powerful, their technological and financial approaches, and their exclusionist control. Inclusive power arrangements – and by this I mean *fully* inclusive – will have far greater capacity than the current exclusive power systems to enable Australians to bring all necessary solutions to bear on the problem.

Inclusive power arrangements are not possible in our representative democracy under Australia's current Constitution. It will need to be rearranged to favour new systems which give all Australians a voice and the Indigenous Voice provides inspiration for this. As we learn about survival in a harsh land from First Nations, we can also learn about the fuller array of solutions from them – solutions derived by people who were driven to the brink of extinction but who have come back from that brink asserting that self-determination – power over one's own destiny – is essential to survival.

Powerlessness negates our existence in all its essentials – physical, emotional, and social. Powerlessness kills. Powerlessness consigns any of us left standing to shorter and emptier lives in more miserable circumstances than we should otherwise expect in an enlightened, technologically advanced, wealthy society. Australia's Indigenes are proof of this. Shared power on the other hand can be entirely enabling. It is essential if we are to make our own lives fulfilling but, as First Nations have now shown, this can only obtain if power is arranged so that each voice counts for more than it does in our current democracy. This book aims to show how we can re-arrange power to that end.

The structure of this book

This book plots a path to empowerment of Australian citizens in their democracy by alteration of the Constitution. Broadly, the path can be charted by:

- insertion of a new preamble and an extra chapter into the current Constitution; and
- a range of smaller consequential alterations and amendments to existing chapters.

The additional preamble and chapter will function as the means of inserting the Australian people into the Constitution – thereby establishing it as the Australian *people's* constitution. The additions would have the effect of increasing shares of power held by the Australian people in democracy such that, as electors, they will have power beyond their current limited role as mere voters. They would also clarify the *location* of the sovereign will, transferring it from the current sovereign to the people but within a system of checks and balances that reduces the potential for abuse of power by any party empowered by the Constitution, including the parliament, the governor-general, the executive government, the states, the territories, the judicature, and the people themselves.

Specifically, the additions are also designed to enable the Australian people to *express* their sovereign people's will, first by stating their values as a nation, secondly by enshrining their human rights, and thirdly by establishing a right to create a national people's voice alongside an Indigenous Voice. Additions enabling the people to express their will are considered throughout the book to be essential to the democratic process by which sovereignty, and any use of power it implies, may be legitimately authorised. It is a fundamental premise of this book that sovereignty – especially sovereignty within a democracy – cannot be rightly defined as the property of a monarch or an elected parliament, much less an exclusive property which once attained requires no further explication. Sovereignty in that definition enshrines powerlessness for the people and as such defeats democracy. Accordingly, the book works on a different definition of sovereignty – namely, that it is the product of the people's will and can be neither legitimised nor authorised unless and until the people have expressed that will.

The additions of a new preamble and a people's chapter are offered to create a means by which the people of Australia may assemble themselves to express that sovereign will in the form of terms of trust which they may issue to those they elect and to which the elected should swear to be faithful and bear true allegiance. In this new arrangement of democracy, the power to determine the national interest and the power to make laws to promote it are separated, whereas currently those two powers are conflated into one body – the parliament. In the separation the people would be accorded their rightful, primary role of determining the national interest and the elected parliaments and governments would retain their respective legislative and executive roles. In the new system of rightfully shared powers, the parliament would essentially be offered something it currently does not have – a guidance system about the will of the people (their description of their best interests). This guidance system can enable the parliament to work together with any and all Australians to chart a safe course to the better future we genuinely desire.

The smaller alterations and amendments, of which there are only four, would in the main have the function of reducing the capacity for abuse of power by individuals or institutions already empowered under the Constitution.

In effect, none of these additions or smaller amendments would reduce the primacy of federal parliament's role as the maker of laws for the Commonwealth of Australia. Nor would they reduce the role of the executive government or change the distribution of powers as it operates now between the parliament, the executive government, the states and the judicature. They would simply provide a clearer context in which the powers of these entities may and may not be exercised consistent with the people's sovereign will.

However, insofar as the additions and alterations may effect a change in the *location* of the sovereign will – namely from the British Crown, where it now exists, to the Australian people – they will have the effect of changing the powers of the Crown and/or its representative relative to the powers of all other parties enabled by the new Constitution. They will also have the effect of clarifying the power of the prime minister in relation to decisions on war.

For these purposes, the book is divided into three parts.

Part 1 – From representative democracy to a people's democracy: finding the path to empowerment of Australians

Chapter 1 – The limits of Australia's representative democracy

Chapter 1 explains the rationale behind the suggested new preamble and extra chapter in the Constitution, first by exploring the history and characteristics of Australia's current representative democracy, and then by examining the past performance of that political structure and its capacity to deliver wellbeing and security for Australians in the future. It examines how power is distributed *exclusively* now and why it needs to be distributed *inclusively* if we are to prosper as a free nation.

Chapter 1 also suggests that a key factor affecting the need for a new inclusive power system has arisen from the fact that Australia's First Nations have called for a coexistence of sovereignties. The conclusion is that if an Indigenous Voice is to have the best chance of actually working to the benefit of Aborigines and Torres Strait Islanders, it will be necessary not just to enshrine the Indigenous Voice in the Constitution but to revise the Constitution itself so that it can support a sufficiently powerful voice for both Indigenous and non-Indigenous Australians. This is the minimum necessary for a coexistence of viable sovereignties.

Chapter 2 – Setting a path to power for the people

Chapter 2 begins to set out how Australia can step away from the merely representative system of governance we call a "democracy" and jump up to a fuller, genuine mode of democracy – a participatory democracy. It examines the failure of Western models of democracy which are confined to representative government, looking closely at America's experience as a key example of the drawbacks of exclusivity in governance. With those lessons learned it then begins to examine how Australia can avoid those failures by using a different model for a new democracy – a model which is inspired by the proposal for a First Nations Voice in the Constitution and which can be built on to create Australia as a fully inclusive democracy.

The proposal to rescue a better democracy for Australia is essentially to chart a path to empowerment of the Australian people in their Constitution. Chapter 2 begins to scope how this may be achieved if the Constitution is rebuilt by Australians so that it defines for the first time:

- what the nation stands for;
- what we value;
- what we regard as inalienable rights; and
- what we envisage as the necessary minimum capacity to:
    - design our preferred future – our willingly shared destiny, and
    - determine our preferred path towards it.

It scopes the design a new democratic public square in which the Australian people can organise their voice. It also introduces discussion of how this public square can be organised in a single space on the internet. This is a mechanism for a public square which will allow democracy to thrive on a wider scale than has been possible to date.

Chapter 2 concludes with a discussion about whether Australia is ready for this new type of democracy in which diverse voices have a greater say about the future of the country and how different they may want it to be from the past. It suggests that Australians of the 2020s are ready to build a people's constitution and can expect to be successful in remaking their nation if, and only if, they start all over again, this time with a constitution which makes space for all their voices and enables them to express their sovereign people's will.

Part 2 – Constituting a nation according to a people's sovereign will

Chapter 3 – Finding a place to start

Chapter 3 begins by examining where best to start if we are to create an inclusive democracy – one in which diverse people and cultures can efficiently and meaningfully participate and hold those they elect to account. The discussion suggests that because so much has changed in our nation's attitudes and circumstances since the Constitution was framed in 1901, that document is now largely discordant with the values that might be expected in a multicultural, gender equal, universally enfranchised, class conscious but relatively wealthy society.

Chapter 3 also sets out how the current Australian Constitution is geared to *override* the people's will. It concludes by suggesting that if Australia is to escape its ineffective power system and start again as a strong nation ready for 21st century challenges, it will need to do more than apply piecemeal amendments to the Constitution.

Chapter 4 – Essentials for a start as a new nation

Chapter 4 sets out the scope of the task of establishing the Australian people's constitution. It discusses how difficult or easy this transformation of our power arrangements may be for both the electors and the elected and whether, if it is to be successful in providing the nation with a new start, the Constitution will require minor alteration or more extensive additions and alterations.

The chapter works on the assumption that it is necessary to inject the people of Australia into their own Constitution so that they can establish fairer shares of power. In this new arrangement, the people will still have the *final* say, as they do now on, *who* ought to govern, but they will also have the *first* say on *what* those they elect may and may not do with the power they are being given.

The chapter introduces the essential elements of this new type of constitution. As a minimum these include mechanisms and processes that will enable and indeed require Australians to:

- build a statement of their values as a society;
- enshrine human rights and obligations in law along with a process for conferring and protecting rights;
- enshrine a system or process which will lift the voice of Australians to a level of coherence at which their will can be understood and actively fulfilled by the elected; and
- freshly describe some mechanisms for reduction of abuse of power.

These are the essential elements of the guidance that elected parliamentarians need and that the electors need if they are to start again as a nation.

Chapter 5 – Essential No. 1: Building a statement of Australian national values

Chapter 5 lays the foundation for a public debate about the first essential additional element in a people's constitution – a *Statement of Australian Values*. It explores research about the attitudes of Australians on things that matter to them as both individuals and as a society. The purpose is to compile a draft list of values that Australians can consider in any exercise to build a new preamble in the Constitution.

The discussion also poses the view that a specific values statement authorised by the people will change the parameters of power for the elected by setting out the overarching terms of trust between electors and the elected. Once these terms are in place, the electors are entitled to expect that laws will accord with their values, not undermine them. This is a whole new way of authorising power, one which places the public interest and purpose of the nation at the heart of the Constitution. No longer will the Constitution focus solely on the process for *who* might be elected; it will also describe *what* they are elected for – the overarching purpose of the nation, the value of it, and the reason why we wish in the 21st century to persist with the agreement we made 120 years earlier to "unite in one indissoluble Federal Commonwealth".

Chapter 5 ends with a proposed starting draft of a Statement of Australian Values for insertion as a preamble in a people's constitution. This is based on the voices of Australians as they have expressed their preferences for and against various values in surveys and commentary in the 21st century. The starting draft is offered as a contribution to community deliberations, an opportunity for which may arise if a new constitutional convention is established.

Chapter 6 – Essential No. 2: Enshrinement of human rights in an Australian people's constitution

Chapter 6 lays the foundation for the second essential additional element in a people's constitution – a *National Agreement on Human Rights and Obligations*. It begins by setting out a history of how rights have been withheld from Australians even though Australia is a signatory to several treaties which have established our rights in international law and even though official Australian policy statements support the principle that these rights are universal, indivisible, inherent (as the birthright of all human beings, enjoyed by all simply by reason of their humanity rather than granted or bestowed), and inalienable (in the sense that they cannot be given up or taken away).

The chapter examines how Australian governments have displayed only a sporadic willingness to extend human rights to Australians and to be held accountable for abuses of those rights. It traces a connection between that reluctance of successive federal governments to grant equal rights to Australians and an increasing pattern of abuse by state and federal governments of the rights of many Australians and other people.

Discussion centres then on how the increasing tendency to abuse those rights has arisen from three main cultural mindsets, each of which has been destructive of the freedoms and liberties that Australians clearly value. The three most destructive mindsets are suggested as:

- the perceived need to counter threats of terrorism;
- the desire to thwart native title claims; and

- the desire of Australian governments to build support for war.

The chapter sets out how these mindsets are promoted to convince Australians that they are necessary for protection of their rights, prosperity and freedoms but have instead come to function as a threat to our human rights and freedoms. Inasmuch as the Constitution itself makes no place for human rights, and does not even safely enshrine the right to vote, Australians are defenceless against the increasing pattern of abuse of their rights by governments. They are living without protection of their rights in law and have no means of holding governments to their obligations to ensure Australians can enjoy the full benefit of the rights conferred in international treaties, particularly the right to self-determination.

Accordingly, Chapter 6 proposes a new system for enshrining human rights and obligations in the Constitution and it assesses both the risks and benefits that may arise from that. Important benefits include that the reform process will:

- enable *all* Australians to exercise the right of self-determination and by virtue of that right to freely determine their political status and freely pursue their economic, social and cultural development – something that no Australian can do now; and
- enable Australia to reset the Constitution itself so that it is more likely to be capable of supporting a coexistence of sovereignties and a stable treaty with First Nations.

The proposed new system for enshrining human rights and obligations in the Constitution, via a *National Agreement* rather than a Bill or Charter, is predicated on the principle that the Australian People are the sovereign source of power in their own land and therefore they, and not their parliaments, are the legitimate authority for purposes of determining that human rights shall be lawful in Australia. In this context the chapter proposes that Australians should consider making a *National Agreement* to confer on themselves and each other equally all the human rights already available to them under international law but denied to them in domestic law because of the Constitution's silence on rights.

Chapter 7 – Essential No. 3: A process for expression of the Australian people's national voice

Chapter 7 lays the foundation for the third essential element of a people's constitution – a National People's Voice. The concept of this voice stems from the realisation that in our current arrangement of democracy, where we hand over power in elections without instructions, we lose our voice as soon as we have voted.

The chapter sets out how a National People's Voice is most likely to be expressed in the form of a statement about what Australians want to achieve as a nation in the *future* – what they wish to *become* in national character. More specifically, the National People's Voice is envisaged as a fundamental right. The proposal is that:

- the people of Australia shall be enabled to exercise a right to express their sovereign will for the future of their society, environment, economy and democracy; and that
- expression of this sovereign will for the future shall take the form of a collaboratively assembled and regularly monitored and reviewed, integrated plan for the wellbeing and security of all Australians over the longer term (up to 30 years); and that
- for purposes of assisting the people in orderly composition of their National Voice, there shall be an Independent Commission for National Engagement and Integrated Planning.

It is suggested that this Commission will be fully independent of the parliament, the executive government and any corporate entities.

The overarching intention of the proposal is to help Australians, in all their diversity, establish a stronger relationship of mutual trust and respect with the federal parliaments they elect. For that purpose the chapter concludes that it is the right to express the national voice that must be enshrined in the Constitution rather than any particular statement of aspirations for the future that may arise from the process of expression of that voice. The chapter envisages that the right to a national people's voice would be justiciable but the voice itself would not be binding on any government. The intention is to install sufficient but not overweening power for the people in the Constitution in such a way as to ensure that they can express their will without undermining the system of representative government. Instead it should enhance the capacity for responsible behaviour in that system.

Chapter 8 – Essential No. 4: Priority constitutional amendments for an inclusive democracy

Chapter 8 discusses a selection of four amendments that are fundamental to the protection of Australia's democracy and should be applied regardless of whether Australians accept the need for a people's constitution, a republic, or a constitutionally enshrined Indigenous Voice.

The chapter considers how democracies are in decline world-wide and that some communities in Australia have already tried to circumvent the decline of their own democracy by establishing an array of mechanisms for strengthening democratic processes at the local level. These include citizens' juries and processes for co-design of individual policies by citizens and politicians. It is noted that these processes have excellent potential to re-empower those Australians fortunate enough to get the opportunity to participate. But those opportunities tend to arise ad hoc and because there is no overarching plan in which any piecemeal local democratic decisions can be assessed, there is only a limited potential for national benefit overall.

In response, it is suggested that the support that federal politicians need most from the Australian people can best be organised by the inclusive reforms outlined in Chapters 5, 6 and 7. However, these reforms would be more effective if accompanied by some other more localised reforms to the mechanics of the election system, the powers of the governor-general and prime minister and the power of the parliament to make laws based on race.

Part 3 – The path to empowerment of the Australian People

Chapter 9 – Processes for engagement on and adoption of The People's Constitution

Chapter 9 discusses the democratic processes by which Australians might alter their Constitution. It examines potential obstructions to those processes and suggests options for overcoming these obstructions. It also highlights the fact that time is running out for Australians to secure their rights and freedoms and to secure their future safety in the face of climate change and global conflict.

Chapter 10 – The possibilities of a new democracy under a people's constitution

Chapter 10 summarises the benefits to Australia that can arise from a people's constitution that is structured to enshrine political equality by enshrining values, rights, obligations, and voices (including an Indigenous Voice and a national people's voice). It outlines how and why it is essential to re-write the Constitution along these lines to add more capacity for "responsible government" onto the current system of merely representative government, and why a rightful share of power should be accorded to the people alongside the shares of power held by the federal parliament and executive government, the judicature, the states and the governor-general. Benefits include a safer passage to a sustainable future where wellbeing and security are reliably available to all, and the possibility of a stable coexistence of sovereignties based on self-determination. It outlines how power can be distributed to enable diverse people and groups of people to find a way to live and prosper together.

Part 1 – From representative democracy to a people's democracy: finding the path to empowerment of Australians

Chapter 1 – The limits of Australia's representative democracy

After 120 years of our constitution as a federation of states, Australians might assume we live in a free and open democratic society. Indeed, annual surveys by Freedom House[6] tell us that we do. But if that is so, we live there precariously because our Constitution makes almost no provisions for our freedoms and is unique among democracies in having no charter of human rights. As constitutional law experts George Williams and Daniel Reynolds have observed:

> Australia is the only democratic country in the world without a national charter of rights. Indeed among all nations (democratic or not), very few lack a charter. Apart from Australia, the only other such nations are the Vatican City (a theocratic monarchy) and Brunei (an authoritarian sultanate with a record of human rights abuses).[7]

Because this charter of rights is absent in our Constitution, Australia's version of representative democracy provides its people with nothing in terms of self-determination – a human right which, as I will show, is an essential mechanism of freedom and wellbeing. But even if a charter of rights were to be inserted into Australian law, this

---

[6] Freedom House rates people's access to political rights and civil liberties in 210 countries and territories through its annual Freedom in the World report. Australia ranks as a "Free" society in the index with a score of 95/100 in 2022. Australia's score dropped steadily from 98/100 between 2017 and 2022. Countries achieving a score of 100/100 in 2022 were Finland, Norway and Sweden. New Zealand achieved a score of 99/100. The United States' score was 83/100. https://freedomhouse.org/countries/freedom-world/scores

[7] George Williams and Daniel Reynolds, *A Charter of Rights in Australia,* UNSW Press, NewSouth Publishing, Sydney, 2017, Chapter 1 – An absence of human rights, page 21.

would not of itself turn our democracy into one in which each person is equally free to determine their political status and freely pursue their economic, social and cultural development. This is because representative democracies, especially if they tend towards exclusion of the voices of their members, have a way of shaving off the rights and freedoms to which people may assume they are entitled. Regardless of the countries in which they might be established, representative democracies do not come as an unalloyed gift. They can and often do create far more subjection than liberty.

In Australia's case this subjection is magnified relative to liberty, not just because of an absence of rights but because our Constitution provides very little in protection from abuse of power. While those who are fortunate enough to be counted among the elected in our parliaments may protest that the Constitution and laws made under it will protect the electors by prescribing and limiting the conditions on which power may be exercised, the fact remains that the Constitution and all other laws are themselves made exclusively by those elected to power. This is especially dangerous when the Constitution itself does not state that those we elect to power are responsible to the people and does not stipulate values and principles by which the powerful may make laws.

In the absence of those values and principles, parliaments can and do make laws which, insofar as they create inequalities before the law, are horribly unjust and immoral and which can and do allow abuses of power most Australians would not think possible in our enlightened society. In constitutions that are silent on values (like Australia's), the "rule of law" – about which Western leaders boast, and which some have of late taken to baselessly asserting is available only in a democracy – is not primarily disposed to protect we, the electors. Inasmuch as it exists at all, which some would say is doubtful, it is set up to protect the elected. Under the so-called rule of law, the elected may do anything that is not made illegal by their laws. They *are* the law and are therefore above it – no less so than the autocratic governments they accuse of not respecting the rule of law.

In the 21st century, multi-party parliaments, no less than one-party states, have generally displayed a stubborn reticence to make laws which might bind them in ways they do not wish to be bound. This is perhaps most evident in Australia in the refusal in 2020 of elected members of both major parties (Labor and Liberal/National) to establish a binding Code of Conduct for federal parliamentarians.[8]

They have also not refrained from *unmaking* laws which bind them in ways they no longer wish to be bound. In Australia's case this is perhaps most evident in amendments made to the Migration Act in 2004 which allowed for the indefinite detention of stateless people[9] and detention of children in appalling conditions in

---

[8] See the Australian Senate Finance and Public Administration Legislation Committee's Report on the National Integrity (Parliamentary Standards) Bill 2019: In 2020, Labor, Liberal and One Nation senators rejected legislation proposed by The Greens for a binding Code of Conduct for federal parliamentarians. They also rejected proposals to establish an independent parliamentary standards commissioner and even an advisor on ethical issues. This Committee rejected consideration of the most basic instruments of ethics in a modern democracy including straightforward proposals of the bill for: a commitment to uphold democracy and respect others regardless of background; a requirement to declare and avoid conflicts of interest; a prohibition on using their position for profit; and a prohibition on parliamentarians accepting any gift, hospitality or other benefit where there is an actual or perceived conflict of interest. They also rejected provisions requiring: the responsible use of influence of the position of parliamentarian; proper use of public resources; standards for personal conduct; a prohibition on the use of confidential information to further private interests; and a requirement that post-retirement activities not take improper advantage of any office held as a parliamentarian. They would have none of this written into laws that would apply to them. National Integrity (Parliamentary Standards) Bill 2019 – Parliament of Australia (aph.gov.au)

[9] See Al-Kateb v Godwin [2004] HCA 37, (2004) 219 CLR 562, High Court (Australia). In this case the High Court determined that amendments to the Migration Act did lawfully allow indefinite detention, and that the Act was not unconstitutional. This ruling pertained "even though the detention was recognised as arbitrary, [and] contrary to Article 9 of the International Covenant on Civil and Political Rights. … The Court held Parliament had sufficiently expressed its intention that children could be detained, notwithstanding that their detention ran foul of human rights principles." John von Doussa QC, President, Human Rights and Equal Opportunity Commission, "Why We Need An Australian Bill of Rights – a joint forum", University of South Australia, 7 December 2005

immigration facilities in contravention of human rights treaties to which Australia was, and still is, a signatory. Little wonder that trust in Australian governments has dropped during the 21st century.[10] When Australians see what ruthless governments are prepared to do to other people's children, many will instinctively fret about what such governments may do to their own. They fret all the more (and trust all the less) when they see the unstinting efforts of some governments to deny the right of the young to a sustainable future in the face of climate change.[11]

Finally, Australian governments have not refrained from making new laws which limit or even extinguish any power the people may have had (or thought they had) in terms of basic civil and political rights. Between 2002 and 2021 Australian governments enacted more than 80 pieces of legislation limiting freedom of expression, freedom of assembly and protest, freedom of information, freedom of the press, whistleblower protections, rights to open trial and the presumption of innocence, rights to not be detained without charge, rights to privacy, and the public's right to know of possible misconduct and illegal conduct by elected parliamentarians and government officials.[12] Citing "national security" as a justification,

---

accessible at https://www.humanrights.gov.au/about/news/speeches/why-we-need-australian-bill-rights-joint-forum

[10] Between 2007 and 2019, an average of 32% of Australians thought the government in Canberra could be trusted almost always or most of the time, compared to an average of 66% who said it could be trusted only some of the time or almost never. Trust improved during the Covid-19 pandemic in 2020 but deteriorated again in 2021. See Scanlon Foundation Surveys, Mapping Social Cohesion 2020, SC2020 Report Final.pdf (scanloninstitute.org.au) and Mapping Social Cohesion 2021, Mapping_Social_Cohesion_2021_Report_0.pdf (scanloninstitute.org.au).

[11] In 2022, the federal minister for the environment, Sussan Ley, successfully appealed against a high-profile court decision that found she had a duty of care to protect young people from the climate crisis when assessing fossil fuel developments. Adam Morton and Tamsin Rose, "Sussan Ley does not have duty of care to protect young from climate crisis, appeal court rules", The Guardian, 15 March 2022.

[12] For summaries of many of the assumed rights that were attacked in this legislative program see Bronwyn Kelly, *By 2050: Planning a better future for our*

this legislative program was a full-on assault on powerless Australians and therefore on democracy itself – since a democracy isn't a democracy if citizens have no civil powers or rights. In place of our hitherto relatively open democracy this massive legislative program entrenched a coercive and secret state,[13] one denying conventions on rights to equality before the law. The program reduced almost every right that may have been taken for granted by Australians under the International Covenant on Civil and Political Rights.[14] No quarter was given to the Australian people in this 20-year onslaught on their freedom to determine whether such legislation would safeguard their democracy by striking a reasonable balance between genuine national security concerns and the public's right to know when the government is and is not acting in the public interest.

These instances of parliamentary power in lawmaking – an autocratically sovereign power, in the sense of being absolute, exclusive, and reductive of human rights – are not isolated. The lawmaking system which is governed by Australia's Constitution is infused through and through with opportunities for federal parliaments to undermine it and to do so with little if any need for recourse to the Australian people and sometimes without any need to submit to effective check by those other entities established under the Constitution – namely, the states and the judicature – that were meant to act as checks on the unreasonable or unintended use or concentration of power.

Over the 120 years of the Australian Constitution's life, laws and policies have been changed by the federal parliament, some of which in effect allow for complete reversals of arrangements made under

---

children in 21st century democratic Australia, March 2020, Chapter 8 – Subsection: Checking for Threats to Democracy. By 2050: Planning a better future for our children in 21st century democratic Australia eBook : Kelly, Bronwyn: Amazon.com.au: Kindle Store

[13] For a history of the transformation of Australia to a secret state see Brian Toohey, *Secret: The making of Australia's security state*, Melbourne University Press, 2019, especially Part 7 – Liberty Lost.

[14] International Covenant on Civil and Political Rights, 1966, http://www.austlii.edu.au/au/other/dfat/treaties/1980/23.html

the Constitution as they were intended in 1901. This is not of itself always harmful. In a way, it could be considered a strength of the Constitution that it has allowed the nation more easily to move with the times, respond to emergencies, or give effect to reasonable and more efficient re-distributions of power. For instance, it has been possible to centralise the power to collect income tax, gradually taking it away from the states and settling it solely in the Commonwealth. This and other redistributions have been possible by negotiation between those parties who have power under the Constitution (i.e., the executive government of the Commonwealth, the federal parliament, the governor-general, the judicature and the states – notably not the people), without amendment to the Constitution itself. Indeed so much has changed without the need for amendment of the Constitution that it is as if there is (and always was) very little in it that lawmakers couldn't get around, should they so wish.

That so much has changed in the arrangement of powers, without the need for change in the Constitution itself, should give electors the tip that something might be amiss with it. It might look miraculously prescient or cleverly flexible but equally it can look as though it is structured so that the permission of the people is not necessary to achieve almost any change that the powerful may desire. It is also likely that there is now very little in it that actually reflects the way we really operate as a sovereign power in the 21st century. It doesn't even mention basic institutions such as the office of prime minister, cabinet (let alone the recently invented "National Cabinet"), universal suffrage or democracy. In fact the creation in 2020 of the "National Cabinet" and the "National Covid-19 Coordination Commission" (the latter complete with confidentiality protections as if its unelected corporate sector members had the status of cabinet ministers) were living examples of how new institutions can easily be created and can even be stacked with corporate stakeholders whose conflicts of interest (compared to the national interest) need not be made clear.[15] So the Constitution does

---

[15] Establishment of the "National Covid-19 Coordination Commission" in March 2020 enabled proposals and funding transfers to the private sector to support the

not authorise or protect the institutions we might assume are central to organised democracy and stable government (like an elected prime minister) and at the same time it doesn't prohibit the creation of institutions which could (and do) easily threaten democracy. It certainly doesn't prohibit unrestrained corporate power, which in today's transnational corporate world we are increasingly coming to recognise as a direct threat to national democracies.

As such, it should be all the more alarming that one type of power the Constitution *does* permit is an autocratic power that may be exercised by the governor-general. The Constitution enshrines the notably unelected governor-general not just as a symbolic head of state but as an ultimately powerful decider on laws, on the tenure of governments, parliaments and particularly prime ministers, and even to some extent on military enablement and war. More than that, should she or he choose, a governor-general is permitted (and/or not prohibited) by the wording of the Constitution to exercise mysterious unspecified powers – the so-called "reserve powers"[16] – that are not even granted to the queen or king under British law.[17] When Queen Victoria signed the Australian Constitution into law, she herself had nothing like the power that she vested in the governor-general.

Morrison government's preferred "gas-led recovery" from the pandemic recession. It enabled diversion of funding away from investment in renewable energy and markedly increased subsidies, grants and profits for fossil fuel corporations, contrary to the interests of Australians. Last accessed July 2022.

[16] See Australian Government Solicitor, *Australia's Constitution with Overview and Notes by the Australian Government Solicitor*, page v. foi-2021-017.pdf (pmc.gov.au): "There is a small number of matters (probably only four) in relation to which the Governor-General is not required to act in accordance with Ministerial advice. The powers which the Governor-General has in this respect are known as 'reserve powers'." Argument persists over whether the reserve powers actually exist (since they are not spelled out) but it is generally thought that they do. Famously the reserve powers were called upon by governor-general John Kerr in 1975 to dismiss Labor Prime Minister Gough Whitlam and appoint Liberal Party Opposition Leader Malcolm Fraser as a caretaker prime minister in his place. What are reserve powers? - Parliamentary Education Office (peo.gov.au)

[17] See Helen Irving, *Five Things to Know About the Australian Constitution*, Cambridge University Press, New York, 2004, page 81: "The Queen herself has no reserve powers."

Literal readings of constitutional provisions involving the powers of the governor-general establish quite clearly that Australia is not a democracy. We may call it that but our laws do not make it so. And the fact that we have elections means nothing. Despite what Freedom House may assume, elections – even free and fair ones – do not a democracy make. In law and in reality, Australia is nothing more or less than a constitutional monarchy. It is a sovereign state which might be crudely but not inaccurately described as a Hobbesian state – the type of state conceived by Thomas Hobbes in 1651 in his seminal work, *Leviathan*, the so called "modern state" in which all power is turned over willingly and in full by the people to a sovereign who shall decide for them as the ultimate authority.[18]

In Thomas Hobbes' view, that sovereign was preferably a single person. In later versions of that state the sovereign frequently became a parliament. In Australia's case though, while the parliamentary model was selected, strange and even scary remnants of the all-powerful (single) sovereign were nevertheless retained and so, by virtue of our Constitution, 21st century Australians have a state with the equivalent of a monarch with even more potential autocratic control than a British queen or king, and who can certainly defy convention to override parliamentary power. That type of modern state is not a democracy; it is anything but. In the circumstances it should not be surprising that the word "democracy" is not used anywhere in Australia's Constitution.

The fact is there is almost no resemblance between the way the Constitution actually says sovereignty can operate in Australia and the way modern Australians may have come to assume it is or will be operated – that is, as a supposed free and open democracy where

---

[18] Thomas Hobbes, *Leviathan: or the matter forme and power of a commonwealth ecclesiastical and civil*. First published in 1651, *Leviathan* posed the concept of the modern state in which individuals cede power to a sovereign to decide all things necessary for their governance in exchange in the main for protection from the ravages of wars which arise when diverse individuals act in accordance with the "state of nature". The modern state was conceived by Hobbes as a form of governance capable of releasing people from lives that are "solitary, poore, nasty, brutish, and short."

their voices can count. In summary, the Australian Constitution might not be unfairly labelled as nothing more than an antiquated mess that we have learned to ignore and work around. In the case of centralisation of taxing powers this may not be too dangerous. But the Constitution's relevance to our lives and its influence over our political and governance arrangements has, decade by decade, been slowly unravelled, so much so that by 2004 eminent constitutional lawyer, Helen Irving, was able to publish a book called *Five Things to Know About the Australian Constitution*,[19] in which she disclosed that two of the five things we need to know are that "the Constitution does not say what it means" and "the Constitution does not mean what it says". It might be funny were it not for the fact that two of the other three things to know are that "the Constitution fails to say things that might be important" and "the Constitution says certain things that contradict each other". In the circumstances it could not be argued that it is unfair to call the Australian Constitution "a mess", and quite a dangerous one from the point of view of providing sufficient checks and balances in the distribution of powers necessary to underpin a sound, fair and stable democracy.

While it persists as a mess, the Australian Constitution is functioning to ensure not only that the people are locked out of participation in their own governance but that laws can be (and are being) made which would be taken by most 21st century Australians to be abhorrent to them and to democracy itself. A graphic example of this was distilled for Australians in 1998 in the High Court's judgement in relation to the validity of the Hindmarsh Island Bridge Act.[20] That judgement was remarkable not merely because it ruled against the Indigenous plaintiffs who had asserted that the Act establishing the Bridge was invalid, but because it did not refute the Commonwealth's contention that there is a "races power" (section 51 (xxvi)) in the Constitution which enables "Nazi race laws" to be

---

[19] Helen Irving, *Five Things to Know About the Australian Constitution*, Cambridge University Press, New York, 2004.

[20] Kartinyeri v Commonwealth (1998) 195 CLR 337, summarised in the Agreements, Treaties and Negotiated Settlements Project, ATNS. https://database.atns.net.au/agreement.asp?EntityID=8423

made, including for instance laws banning people from working in certain professions or from attending particular schools, on the grounds of race. In this case, the federal Solicitor-General, Gavan Griffith QC, had unapologetically argued before the Court that the races power "is infused with a power of adverse operation", meaning it can be used to discriminate against a race as easily as in favour of a race; and more than that, the High Court "could do nothing about it".[21]

In the end, the High Court split on the issue of whether the races power could be used to adversely discriminate against a race and the question remains unresolved (thanks once again in large part to the lack of values and principles in the Constitution). But the Hindmarsh Island Bridge Act was upheld, indicating that the Constitution allows that Indigenes can certainly be discriminated against and, even worse (if that's possible), that the power of the parliament, at least when it comes to its right to embed and legitimise racism, may not be constrained by the judiciary. When this judgement in relation to the application of the races power under section 51 (xxvi) is set alongside consideration of racist powers embedded in Section 25 of the Constitution – headed "Provisions as to races disqualified from voting" – Australians might be well justified in taking fright that there is still a power in the Constitution to exclude a citizen from voting on the basis of race, and that the withdrawal of the right to vote may also not be constrained by the judiciary. No race, even a white one, is protected by the Australian Constitution from the possible loss of voting rights. So much for the comfort and dependability of our representative democracy.

In its essential disregard for human rights and for the will of the people who, under its terms, have no other choice than to consent to

---

[21] For explication see George Williams and Daniel Reynolds, *A Charter of Rights in Australia,* UNSW Press, NewSouth Publishing, Sydney, 2017, Chapter 4 – Why doesn't Australia have a charter of rights?, page 77: "In this case, the federal government argued that the Commonwealth has the power to pass laws that discriminate against Australians on the basis of race. ... The Court split on whether the races power can still be used to discriminate against Indigenous or other peoples. This fundamental question remains unresolved."

be governed by this system of representation, the Australian Constitution is disposed to shift power away from the people and towards an unaccountable tiny few. This is obviously an arrangement jealously guarded by those who manage to seize power, but this should not deter us from the need to re-balance the way power may be rightly shared. However, if the people of Australia are to increase their capacity to exercise a greater share of power – a rightful share – within their system of representative democracy, it is as well to understand more about where power can and does disproportionately accumulate under the current Constitution. In the next sections I will sketch out the sort of overweening power it makes possible and suggest a new arrangement for a fairer sharing of power where abuse by any elites who capture the state may be moderated.

Where power now resides, unrestrained

Australians may not in the main be familiar with their Constitution but those that have some knowledge of it would probably assume that there are checks and balances built into it that are intended to moderate abuses of power. They might assume that the High Court will moderate the parliament if it tends to excess. But in terms of changes to powers and the sorts of laws that can be made, the Constitution is no longer effective as a moderator, if it ever was. It is the law governing the topics and areas in which the different levels of parliaments (state or federal) shall be able to make laws and in some cases it limits how laws may and may not be made; but in that capacity it is pre-disposed at its worst to allow the making of laws which are racist and discriminatory and which thereby distribute power unfairly or take it away entirely. It is designed in such a way as to embed inequality – particularly inequality before the law – and plainly to trash cultural values on the basis of race, no matter how dearly values of equality may be held or how necessary they may be for social cohesion in Australia's multicultural society. Had women been considered a threat to power, the Constitution may well have been designed to trash cultural values on the basis of gender too. But since the designers were obsessively afraid of non-whites and entirely unafraid of women, the questions of embedding inequality for them

– or even a mention of them – didn't arise. Tussles over power that have arisen since 1901 have therefore left room for equality before the law on the basis of gender, but not on the basis of race. In both sorts of tussles, however, the Constitution really only facilitated power for one group – and it wasn't women or non-whites.

Although it will not seem so – because, of the 44 referendum questions put to Australians to amend their Constitution since 1901, only eight have been approved by the people – tussles over power, in constitutional matters at referendums or in the Courts or in the legislature or in federal-state negotiations, have tended to result in shifts of power away from the people and upwards to the federal parliament and federal executive government. Australians may have tried to stop the gradual concentration of power towards the top of the political chain by rejecting referendum proposals which appear as attempts to shift it upwards, but in the main they have failed. It is a major problem at the heart of the Constitution that it facilitates or at least leaves the way open for more centralisation than devolution of power. In these tussles it is the federal parliament and executive government that have generally emerged victorious, drawing more power into themselves and further away from the possibility of interference from or moderation by both the people and other parties to the Constitution (particularly the states).

The concentration of power in the federal parliament and executive government is of course not simply a result of a messy Constitution. It has also arisen from coincidental deals between the elected and non-elected powers which dominate our capitalist society – namely large private corporations and, particularly in Australia, a heavily concentrated corporate news media. But it is the Constitution that has allowed these deals to build up so that, as exchanges of power, they are dirtier and more exclusive by the year.

It is now not an indefensible proposition to say, as American President Joe Biden did in 2022, that media mogul Rupert Murdoch is "the most dangerous man in the world",[22] inasmuch as he might

[22] US President, Joe Biden, quoted in Jonathan Martin and Alex Burns, *This Will Not Pass: Trump, Biden and the Battle for America's Future*, Simon and Schuster,

represent the apogee of unelected and entirely unaccountable power. It is not unreasonable because he is a person who exercises inordinate influence with no corresponding obligation to act in the national interest. And President Biden is not the only world leader to articulate the danger posed by Murdoch (and his soon to be imposed dynastic "heir and successor", son Lachlan). Former Australian Prime Minister Kevin Rudd, in his testimony to a Senate inquiry into media diversity in Australia in 2021, also asserted that Rupert Murdoch now holds governments in fear and trembling:

> Everyone's frightened of Murdoch. They really are. There's a culture of fear across the country. ... The truth is as prime minister I was still fearful of the Murdoch media beast. ... When did I stop being fearful? Probably when I walked out of the building in 2013. ... No one should be frightened of Murdoch, but can I tell you, he's a frightening kind of guy, because of the power he wields.[23]

This is testimony to which we should give credit. Those, like Kevin Rudd, who have worked at the centre of power will know who holds it – and in the 21st century it isn't them.

A later Australian Prime Minister, Scott Morrison, may have put another view about where power lies. In his view it lies in a place he insists it shouldn't – in the United Nations. Hence he inveighed in 2019 against the UN, characterising it (unconvincingly) as "an unaccountable internationalist bureaucracy ... demanding conformity rather than cooperation on global issues".[24] And in laying that charge against the UN, Morrison appointed himself to a mission to counter the said unjustifiable hegemony, asserting that:

> Only a national government, especially one accountable through the ballot box and the rule of law, can define its

---

May 2022, reviewed by Martin Pengelly in "Biden finds Murdoch 'most dangerous man in the world', new book says", The Guardian, 4 April 2022.

[23] Kevin Rudd, quoted by Daniel Hurst, "Kevin Rudd says Australian politicians 'frightened' of 'Murdoch media beast' in Senate inquiry", The Guardian, 19 February 2021.

[24] Scott Morrison, "In Our Interest", Speech to the Lowy Institute, 2019, The 2019 Lowy Lecture: Prime Minister Scott Morrison | Lowy Institute

> national interests. We can never answer to a higher authority than the people of Australia.

The posturing here implied that the UN was demanding some sort of ignominious "conformity" from sovereign nations rather than peaceful cooperation and therefore the UN was demanding that nations surrender their sovereignty. This assertion denied the plain fact that when Australia became a member of the United Nations it signed on to become part of an organisation whose charter included:

> Article 2.1: 'The Organization is based on the principle of the sovereign equality of all its Members'; and
>
> Article 2.7: 'Nothing contained in the present Charter shall authorize the United Nations to intervene in matters which are essentially within the domestic jurisdiction of any state or shall require the Members to submit such matters to settlement under the present Charter'.[25]

In short, the UN has never demanded "conformity" of its members or by its members to anything other than what they have freely agreed to. It has never sought to drag power away from its member nations. If anything, the UN Charter works the other way around: in signing onto it, freely, members simply agree that for purposes of maintaining international peace and security (and only those purposes) they will act "in conformity with the principles of justice and international law".[26] Again, no ceding of sovereignty is required. Power does not reside with the prejudicially described "unaccountable internationalist bureaucracy" of the UN and we have no need of Mr Morrison's attempts to defend us against its purported encroachments. This is not to say that power does not reside with other internationalist bureaucracies that are far more unaccountable and powerful than the UN, such as the International Monetary Fund, the World Bank and other economic agencies of (or controlled by) the US government. It's just that it doesn't reside where Mr Morrison

---

[25] "Charter of the United Nations and Statute of the International Court of Justice", San Francisco, 1945, Article 2. uncharter.pdf

[26] "Charter of the United Nations and Statute of the International Court of Justice", San Francisco, 1945, Article 1. uncharter.pdf

claimed. The UN only has the power its members freely give it. By contrast, US controlled economic institutions exercise coercive power wherever they can. As a range of economic historians have documented, a Washington-centred and controlled consensus emerged in the 1970s and 1980s as:

> the liberalisation policy agenda prescribed to (imposed on) developing countries by Washington-based institutions such as the IMF, the World Bank and the economic agencies of the US government. This included fiscal austerity, trade liberalisation, deregulation of financial and labour markets, and privatisation of state enterprises. As argued by Joseph E. Stiglitz and Jagdish Bhagwati, among others, from the 1970s onwards the IMF (and other Washington-based institutions) effectively morphed into tools of US economic imperialism.[27]

That is internationalist power in full swing and it entirely marginalises the UN.

Of course, Mr Morrison's speech conveniently ignored all of this. Instead he attempted to propel a popular discourse at the time that national sovereignty and democratic values would be surrendered if Australia cooperated with nations like China, a discourse which in turn ignored the plain fact that our domestic interests will inhere in global agreements being amicably reached, especially with China which is now Australia's biggest trading partner by far. In an irretrievably globalised world those domestic interests cannot be furthered otherwise than by cooperation and indeed by a particular and rather limited type of conformity, namely, conformity to international law – the thing Australia pledged in 1945 to uphold under the Charter of the United Nations and Statute of the International Court of Justice.[28] Nevertheless, the Morrison speech was an attempt to reject the need to abide by the very rules Australia had worked hard as a UN Member to set up after World War II. But it

---

[27] William Mitchell and Thomas Fazi, *Reclaiming the State: A progressive vision of sovereignty for a post-neoliberal world*, Pluto Press, London, 2017, page 73.
[28] "Charter of the United Nations and Statute of the International Court of Justice", San Francisco, 1945. uncharter.pdf

also functioned as cover for the real unaccountable power Mr Morrison was seeking to elevate – corporate power. In the 2020s it is plain for all Australians to see (since nobody bothers to hide it) that multinational corporations and moguls – plutocrats – now wield overwhelming control in global and domestic markets and over parliaments, and do so without admitting obligations either to conformity to law or cooperation on global issues, and certainly without admitting any obligation to a national interest, democratic values or, for that matter, humankind.

Given the extent of corporate power in Australia and world-wide, it is not unreasonable to conclude that there is a kind of misanthropy or aggrieved insanity in Scott Morrison's encouragement of Australians to distrust, not corporations, but governments and the United Nations as he did again in 2022 after the demise of his government. Addressing a group of Pentecostal faithful in Perth he loudly preached that:

> We don't trust in governments, we don't trust in the United Nations, thank goodness.[29]

In effect, once he had been deposed from the power vested in the national government – a power he had sought to elevate in 2019 – Mr Morrison recanted his thereto dearly held belief that "we can never answer to a higher authority than the people of Australia", and newly proclaimed that we must never answer to a lower authority than "god". In doing so he was doing nothing less than attempting to build support for, and legitimise in advance, any actions that may be taken by an individual or community to undermine duly elected governments. At the same time he was surely doing nothing less than enjoining people to disregard any obligations of conformity to international law, to agreements we have made and to covenants our governments have signed under the auspices of the UN (such as the United Nations Framework Convention on Climate Change or the International Covenant on Civil and Political Rights), as though human laws must be subordinate to some sort of divine law, as though the

---

[29] Scott Morrison quoted by Josh Butler, "'We don't trust in governments' or UN, Scott Morrison tells Margaret Court's Perth church", The Guardian, 18 July 2022.

laws we make by international agreement mean nothing, as though a democracy must give way to a theocracy, and as though we should aspire to becoming a state subject to church rule.

In plain sight on that day in Perth Scott Morrison was discouraging peaceful cooperation with other nations. Incanting that god (his god presumably) was the only legitimate authority and that "god's kingdom will come" to overthrow mere earthly governments, Morrison "called on worshippers to put their faith in religion above other institutions like government".[30] This sermon, published as it was beyond the walls of the church building, called out to people to withdraw from cooperation in international institutions, to disregard "the importance of the role [that Morrison himself grudgingly acknowledged] they play", to assert church (*his* church) over the state, to invalidate anything arising from the secular state (which Australia is), and to put their faith in no institution of cooperation built by humankind.

Although Morrison's speech seemed to champion the establishment of Australia as a theocracy, his preaching could have no other effect than to give free rein to the only power likely to be left standing if all his wishes were to be miraculously granted and "fallible", "earthly"[31] governments were swept away – corporate power.

In the sweep of history, this is a kind of madness that began with capitalism itself but which reached a zenith when neoliberalism began to remove all restraints on the potential excesses of capitalism by its focus on de-regulation and free markets. In order to encourage corporations to invest, corporations operating in the capitalist empires of the British and the Dutch were given rights in the 17th century to limit their liability to the amount of their investment and

---

[30] Josh Butler, "'We don't trust in governments' or UN, Scott Morrison tells Margaret Court's Perth church", The Guardian, 18 July 2022.

[31] Scott Morrison, "'We don't trust in governments', Scott Morrison tells Margaret Court's Perth church", YouTube, 19 July 2022: "If you are putting your faith in those things [governments and the UN] like I put my faith in the lord, you are making a mistake. They're earthly, they are fallible."

nothing more.[32] In other words, with the introduction of "limited liability" corporations were released from liability for the funds of any other investor (such as governments, taxpayers and depositors in their banks) and for the risks and injuries associated with their corporate activities. As such, corporations worldwide can now shunt all risk away from themselves and keep all profits to themselves. This limitation of liability has been slowly and legally extended by unscrupulous corporations who have played with rules designed to constrain them appropriately, with varying degrees of success through history. For instance, corporations gained so much influence during the American Civil War that, shortly before his death, Abraham Lincoln lamented what he saw happening with the following "resounding prophecy":

> Corporations have been *enthroned*. ... An era of corruption in high places will follow and the money power will endeavor to prolong its *reign* by working on the prejudices of the people ... until wealth is aggregated in a few hands ... *and the Republic is destroyed*.[33] [Emphasis added.]

In short Lincoln anticipated the demise of America's Republic as a state in which supreme power is held by the elected representatives of the people, and its replacement with a corporate monarch. He also anticipated the means by which the replacement would be achieved – by media moguls "working on the prejudices of the people".

Despite Lincoln's fears, the rules in America were boosted further in corporations' favour in 1886 when the Supreme Court designated corporations as "persons" entitled to the protection of the 14th Amendment.[34] The 14th Amendment to the US Constitution was enacted to give equal rights to former slaves enfranchised after the Civil War. In summary it stated that "No State shall make or

---

[32] Jeremy Lent, *The Patterning Instinct: A Cultural History of Humanity's Search for Meaning*, Prometheus Books, New York, 2017, Kindle edition, page 493.

[33] Abraham Lincoln, quoted by Jeremy Lent, *The Patterning Instinct: A Cultural History of Humanity's Search for Meaning*, Prometheus Books, New York, 2017, Kindle edition, page 494.

[34] Jeremy Lent, *The Patterning Instinct: A Cultural History of Humanity's Search for Meaning*, Prometheus Books, New York, 2017, Kindle edition, pages 494-5.

enforce any law which shall abridge the privileges or immunities of citizens of the United States." No such rights to status as humans have been extended to corporations in Australia's Constitution (yet). But even so, with the rise of neoliberalism – i.e., largely unregulated capitalism – multinational corporations have come to fully rival governments in strength in Australia and almost everywhere else in the world. They have attained sovereign status and may be the only player left standing with that status – or at least they will be if the constitutions of democratic nations are not reset to prevent the overreach of their power. If corporations are not to be "enthroned" permanently, as Lincoln feared, the people of nation states will need to re-design constitutions that ensure they are not afforded human status, and indeed status *over* humans.

We tend to think of corporations as being comprised of human beings, who by extension must be capable of ethics, empathy and care for others and a basic willingness to behave well and lawfully. But they are actually inhuman, abstract, almost untraceable entities with a single focus of maximising financial returns. Their will is amorphous but entirely alien to humans. As renowned author and cultural historian Jeremy Lent has observed, large multinational corporations are:

> theoretically immortal, cannot be put in prison … and are not constrained by the laws of any individual country. … With equivalent rights to human beings [in America] but with the incalculable advantage of their superhuman powers, corporations have literally taken over the world. They have grown so massive that fifty-three of the largest hundred economies in the world are corporations. Along with their vast power, corporations have imposed on the world a set of values, arising from their overriding objective to maximize financial returns, at odds with many intrinsic human values.[35]

Corporations are therefore the equivalent of countries we can't find. There are people behind them, of course, but not people we can get

---

[35] Jeremy Lent, *The Patterning Instinct: A Cultural History of Humanity's Search for Meaning*, Prometheus Books, New York, 2017, Kindle edition, page 495.

hold of, much less draw into a system of conformance to laws which protect the public interest. Their "values" are utterly inhuman and they in no way identify with the public interest. This makes it all the more irresponsible for a former prime minister of an advanced sovereign nation like Australia to disparage rather than honour the office Australians granted to him and to encourage his congregation not to trust an institution like the United Nations which was established to ensure that countries can seek each other out physically for purposes of cooperating to build a secure future for all mankind, not just a few plutocrats. It is not just irresponsible, it is insanity to disparage the value of human cooperation, especially at a time when the world as we know it is unlikely to survive *unless* humans cooperate.

In this sweep of history we have washed up in a place where the power exercised by concentrated corporate media and neoliberal hegemony in 21st century Australia is far greater than any power we the people may exercise within our Constitution to control any excesses of an elected executive government or parliament. Corporate power has grown so mighty that Australians might be justly frightened of it – so wholly unaccountable as it is. Many have expressed a desire to rein it in, including the 500,000+ people who in 2020 signed the petition launched by former Australian Prime Minister Kevin Rudd calling for a royal commission into the Murdoch media empire and its dominance of the Australian news market. Other types of corporate power are also – and not a minute too soon – coming under fire, including the power of multinational giants to evade tax, the power to increase corporate profits while suppressing the shares of wealth that are being returned to Australians, the power to privatise taxpayer-owned assets, the power to monopolise markets via the forced introduction of laws and policies which are inherently anti-competitive in their effect,[36] the power to outlaw

---

[36] The laws introduced in 2020 to establish the "News Media Bargaining Code" and the National Competition Policy are essentially anti-competitive. See Bronwyn Kelly, "Prospects for journalism, the free information market and democracy in Australia under the ACCC's News Media Bargaining Code", September 2020, https://www.austcfp.com.au/_files/ugd/2b062e_4741dfca603c41fdb05326d9688

industrial action, and the power of international weapons manufacturers to skew national budgets away from essential services and trap Western nations into seemingly endless debt and war. All of these corporate powers now need to be reined in.

Regardless of whether Rupert Murdoch is really the most dangerous man in the world, the fact that a US president can, in a moment of candour, single him out as such is indicative of a societal awakening to the inordinate power of corporations. Murdoch has become a synecdoche for burgeoning, destructive power – power that is monstrous and out of control. He has become the image of it in all its ugliness. In Australia that sort of power is out of control in large part because of the total inadequacy of a Constitution that passively grants – because it does not disallow – grossly disproportionate power to an unelected few at the same time as it provides no possibility that such power can be reined in by the people (or, for that matter, by the judicature and the states). Australia's Constitution leaves Australians defenceless against the abuse of power and the exercise of it in a manner that is contrary to the public interest. So in the next section I will begin to sketch the better arrangement of power that will be necessary – and soon – if we are to improve our defences against the misuse of power but also to strengthen the capacity of our democracy to help us secure a better future.

Where power should reside – and soon

In the context of the above rendition of power arrangements in Australia and how abuses are now so unfortunately unrestrained by the Constitution, it is apparent that the founding document of our representative democracy is broken, although as I will show, several parts of it are salvageable and in fact are essential to retain, including aspects of its features of representative government, federalism and

---

84aea.pdf. For an insight into how Australia's National Competition Policy is anti-competitive see Australian Community Futures Planning, "What is National Integrated Planning & Reporting? – Episode 3", YouTube, (view from 35 minutes, 45 seconds.)

judicial review. Generally though, it is useless in its current form for what is likely to be a dearly held wish of Australians. I mean it is quite useless if we genuinely wish to retain Australia as a democratic state. The Constitution is bereft of capacity to rein in corporate power. But that is only its second biggest weakness. The bigger problem with it is that it has no capacity to create the necessary participation in democracy that all Australians will need if they are to build a democracy worth the name and to navigate the future safely.

That latter incapacity – to enable inclusive participation of the kind necessary to ensure Australians can build the future they prefer, a future that will secure them and their wellbeing in terms they accept and plan for as a minimum – that is a more serious or at least higher priority problem than the incapacity to rein in corporate power. This is because Australians will not be able to shave off the excesses of corporate power anyway unless they first establish a system empowering themselves in two new ways.

Given the excesses of corporate power, it is tempting to give priority to pursuing systems which might neuter corporate power as fully as possible. But it would probably be dangerous to assume that a power system could be or would be constituted to wipe it out entirely. What is required instead – or rather, simultaneously – is a new specification of the process by which power may be shared with and exercised by the people in an orderly manner. That process must function as both a negative force and a positive force in the democracy:

- On the negative side it must enable efficient vigilance by the people against surges of unreasonable power (wherever and whenever they may arise).
- On the positive side it must enable the people to set the agenda for their future – to establish the specifics of their will.

So it must be a double power. It must clip back the potential for excesses of power (corporate, political, legal, civil and theocratic) and at the same time positively enable specification of a new future – a new will of the people that is sufficiently intelligent and intelligible to override the will to inordinate power, whenever and wherever it may emerge.

Australia's Constitution is singularly inadequate for these purposes, which means it is singularly inadequate to the task of securing our future. It is also inadequate at an incredibly inconvenient moment – an unprecedented moment in history when the world has about a decade left to prevent irreversible, catastrophic global heating. I have only touched thus far on a small number of the myriad problems afflicting Australia's democracy, or what's left of it, that stem directly from our broken Constitution and the weakened, fragile democracy it has left us with. As the book unfolds I will explore more. But it must be said at the outset that continued neglect of the mess at the centre of the statement that defines our birth as a federation will risk the complete loss of the nation as we have come to know it (or think we know it) in a post-World War II world.

In large part, between 1945 and 2001, that Australian nation came to complacently proclaim – to assume, to take it for granted – that it was free, democratic, tolerant, welcoming, multicultural, fair, equal in its offers of opportunity, committed to some level of social security and dignity for anyone in need, committed to universal health care, generous in its international citizenship and responsibility, respectful of laws both domestically and in the international rules based order, and possessed of "golden soil and wealth for toil" – or to put it less poetically, possessed of resources and prospects for continuing per capita prosperity that may be the envy of the world.[37] But if this is how Australians might have thought of their country – if this is how we in the majority might have characterised our particular exceptionalism – none of those positive

[37] These are only my words for how Australians may have characterised their nation prior to 2001 and how they are still likely to describe it positively in 2022. Still, they are not at all out of kilter with words that have been used by 21st century Australian governments, whenever they have felt the need to make new citizens understand the culture they will be required to fit into. See Australian Government Department of Home Affairs, "Life in Australia: Australian values and principles", Commonwealth of Australia 2020, page 4. Life in Australia - English (homeaffairs.gov.au)

features of a possible Australian identity could be taken for granted after 2001, a year that one author has aptly described as "the year everything changed".[38]

Once the threat of catastrophic international terrorism barged in on our sense of security on 11 September 2001, nothing was the same or could be the same again. Coming as it did coincident with the threat that climate change poses to our security, and hot upon the heels of the threat that neoliberalism had begun to pose to our chances of reducing economic and social inequality, that moment in 2001 crystalised a picture of a world that was even more unsafe than it must have seemed when atomic bombs were dropped on Japan in 1945 and the world settled fearfully into a Cold War that lasted more than thirty years. In that period the world lived with the threat of extinction by nuclear war. Then in 1989, the Cold War ended and Western nations proclaimed that the "end of history"[39] had been reached and that in the wash-up of the long ideological war between capitalism and communism, capitalism had triumphed as the soundest means of humankind's salvation. Capitalism as a religion had been vindicated and the faithful rejoiced. Indeed they gloated, to the extent that American exceptionalism blew out to maniacal proportions into an extremism that suggested the United States was not only the greatest nation in the world but the one entitled to rule the world using any and all means to contain any challenging power that might threaten that entitlement, a fully imperialist power

---

[38] Phillipa McGuinness, *The Year Everything Changed: 2001*, Vintage Books Australia, 2018.

[39] The "end of history" is a phrase coined by Francis Fukuyama in 1989 (notably before the fall of the Berlin Wall) which was later co-opted by triumphalists in Western liberal democracies as proof of the ascendancy of Western political systems over others. Fukuyama spent decades attempting to clarify that he was not celebrating the end of the Cold War and the triumph of the West but was simply suggesting that the modern liberal state was for a time the only power system left standing after the ravages of 20th century wars and economic blocks, notwithstanding the enduring worries still inherent in liberal democratic forms of government. See David Runciman, *Confronting Leviathan: A history of ideas*, Profile Books, 2021, Chapter 12 – Fukuyama on History.

entitled to invade, interfere with or override the sovereignty of any other nation.

By the 2020s, however, it was obvious that not only had the threat of annihilation by nuclear disaster reared back up again, other possibly more potent sources of extinction had reared up too – chief among them being climate change, pandemics and over-consumption which has the potential to result in biodiversity collapse and attendant human extinction. So far from having achieved a benign "end of history" – a place where we could peacefully settle, comfortable at last in the assumption that capitalist liberal democracy is the most munificent political arrangement – it emerged that a far more atrocious end to history, one of our own making, had simply been brewing unrestrained and was now taking perceptible shape as an imminent perfect storm of existential threats.

Humans will hope of course that there is still time for our species to avert this crisis. And there is resourcefulness in humans that could still, even in 2023, be organised to avert or attenuate the disaster. But no democracy, least of all Australia's, is yet well-organised enough to unleash that resourcefulness to the extent necessary to head off the crisis in time. Once post-industrial planetary temperature increases surge over the 1.5° Celsius mark – a mark which on current patterns of consumption the world is likely to reach before 2030, if not by 2025 – resource scarcity is likely to start a cascade of global conflict over what little there is left in natural resources to sustain life. And to the extent that this is likely to be a conflict some corporates will seek to profit from, it may be expected that they will consider it very much in their interests to stoke it.

This may seem alarmist but it is not at all unrealistic. Most Australians know and accept that climate change is the biggest threat to our future wellbeing and security[40] and most sense that even if the

---

[40] In 2021, 75% of Australians in the Australia Institute's "Climate of the Nation" poll reported that they were "concerned about climate change"; 82% were "concerned climate change will result in more bushfires, more droughts and flooding, and animal and plant species extinction"; 82% "supported a phase-out of coal fired power stations"; 69% thought "Australia should set targets and implement domestic action to limit global warming to 1.5-2°C and achieve net

threats are not as significant as they seem, the last thing we should do is ignore them.[41] The "lucky country"[42] we may well be; but every time a new natural disaster piles up on top of the all too recent previous disasters, it is harder not to wonder if that luck has run out. And every time the Intergovernmental Panel on Climate Change releases yet another report on how close the world is to irreversible over-heating, it is harder to deny a premonitory sense that the world is edging far too close for comfort to extinction. The challenge is unprecedented and we are unprepared. Noam Chomsky is not alone in giving expression to that sense when he intones, as he did in June 2022,

> We are at a unique moment in human history. Decisions that must be made right now will determine the course of future history if there is to be any human history, which is very much in doubt. There is a narrow window in which we must implement measures to avert cataclysmic destruction of the environment, measures that are quite feasible.[43]

It is shocking to hear words like "if there is to be any human history, which is very much in doubt", or that we are on a path to

---

zero emissions"; 67% thought "Australia should be a world leader in finding solutions to climate change"; and 63% preferred Australia's economic recovery to be primarily powered by renewables, while only 12% preferred it to be powered by gas. 211013-Climate-of-the-Nation-2021-WEB.pdf (australiainstitute.org.au). In 2021, in the ABC's Australia Talks survey, 63% of Australians reported that "climate change is a major problem" and 68% said "we are handling climate change poorly". Australia Talks, one of the nation's biggest social surveys, is back for 2021. Here's how it works - ABC News

[41] In 2022 the Lowy Poll reported that 60% of Australians agreed with the statement that "Global warming is a serious and pressing problem. We should begin taking steps now even if this involves significant costs." Attitudes to global warming - Lowy Institute Poll

[42] In 1964, Donald Horne penned the phrase: "Australia is a lucky country run mainly by second-rate people who share its luck." The first half of the phrase became famous; the second part is frequently forgotten. *The Lucky Country*, Penguin Books, 1964.

[43] Noam Chomsky, Speech to the American Solar Energy Society 51st annual conference, University of New Mexico, June 21, 2022, https://www.youtube.com/watch?v=ZkjJfTsXffY

"destroy organised human life on earth"[44] or that "Earth's sixth mass extinction event is underway".[45] Still more shocking is the prospect that this time the extinction may include us. But the prospect is no less real for being shocking and unprecedented. The full weight of science is behind it. To deny it we would need to believe fully in miracles and fully against all evidence. We would have to deny rationality not just in part but completely. We would also have to deny a shared morality that obliges humans to care for one another and an instinct to do all things necessary to care for our children and the natural world that is the only thing that can sustain them. We would have to be inhuman, like a corporation.

Of course, since few Australians would admit of such inhumanity in their character either as individuals or as a nation, there is a prospect that not only is there time to reverse the path to extinction but there is the will to take that path, a will to live that is ingrained and irrepressible in human nature. This is a path that cannot be taken, however, if arrangements are not changed to give more power – much more power – to the people to determine what should be rightfully lawful and what should not, what should be created as a society, and what should be created as a future for that society. That necessary quantum of power can only be attained by Australians if they have a voice in their own governance. But as our particular democracy is currently arranged, we have no such voice.

We have a vote (for now) but a vote is not a voice, not by a long shot. It is certainly not a voice which articulates exactly what we want to build as a future in terms of wellbeing and security, let alone build as a core of acknowledged societal values which will bind us together strongly enough while we attempt to do something else that is unprecedented – namely, to transition to a place where two sovereignties, that of First Nations and the sovereignty that we

---

[44] Noam Chomsky, "The Future of Organized Human Life Is at Risk Thanks to GOP's Climate Change Denial", YouTube, 6 November 2018. Noam Chomsky: The Future of Organized Human Life Is At Risk Thanks to GOP's Climate Change Denial - YouTube

[45] Damian Carrington, "Earth's sixth mass extinction event under way, scientists warn", The Guardian, 11 July 2017.

currently call the Crown, can coexist, and productively enough to ensure the survival of both. This coexistence is central to the call for Voice, Treaty and Truth in the Uluru Statement from the Heart. In fact First Nations assert that the coexistence is there already, because their sovereignty has never been ceded. This is undeniable.

Even so, a coexistence of sovereignties between First Nations and the Crown – either as a verbal assertion or on paper in law – is not of itself an enabling instrument of the sort of power that can be accurately characterised as self-determination, the form of sovereignty called for in the Uluru Statement. The call from Uluru is for

> a better future for our children based on justice and self-determination.[46]

As yet, the path has not been mapped out between wherever we are now and that destination of self-determination, although the means by which First Nations compellingly suggest we travel there is by a Makarrata Commission and an Indigenous Voice in the Constitution. But it is that sort of power, and only that sort, that can give us the measure of control we need over our lives if we are to lead them in the manner each one of us determines to be meaningful and fulfilling.

To live a life like that, we first need to attain a minimum level of secure wellbeing; but that is only a beginning. To attain fulfilment – to make life itself worth living, or as Hobbes might put it, to permanently escape the "state of nature" in which the condition of man is "solitary, poore, nasty, brutish, and short" – there is another more fundamental need, one which has been deemed in international covenants to be obviously vital to life. It shows up as Article 1 in *both* the International Covenant on Civil and Political Rights and the International Covenant on Economic, Social and Cultural Rights:

> All peoples have the right of self-determination. By virtue of that right they freely determine their political status and

[46] Uluru Statement from the Heart. See Appendix 1.

freely pursue their economic, social and cultural development.[47]

The fact that this is the first Article in both Covenants is testimony to just how fundamental self-determination is to existence – in quantum and quality. In effect, human life is both meaningless and potentially non-existent without it. But that sort of power does not yet exist in law for anyone in Australia. It is a power that has been assumed to be essential by nations (including Australia) acting in cooperation at the UN since at least the 1960s, but in reality it has been withheld from Australians by every government since.

Australia has ratified both UN Covenants granting self-determination as a right and has therefore agreed to make them part of our domestic law. But while laws have been passed in a few areas, such as freedom from discrimination on the basis of race, these laws have sometimes been enacted in such a way as to enable their rescission or suspension whenever a government may find them inconvenient. Just such a suspension occurred under the Racial Discrimination Act in 2007 to enable the Howard Government to mount the Northern Territory Intervention[48] and send troops and public servants into remote First Nations communities without consultation, ostensibly in order to impose solutions for protection of children from domestic abuse – in short to impose on Indigenous families a "solution" they would not dare to impose on whites. Suffice to say, the Howard government trashed human rights legislation to no good end in this case. The Intervention was mounted on the grounds of protecting Aboriginal families and children, although clearly the motivation was entirely political with the Howard government wishing to appear "responsible" and "caring" via paternalistic intrusion. But in reality the Northern Territory Intervention was a new order of state sanctioned cruelty. Tragically, it led directly to Aboriginal children being alienated from their

---

[47] Article 1, International Covenant on Civil and Political Rights and International Covenant on Economic, Social and Cultural Rights, 1966.

[48] The Northern Territory Intervention was enacted under the Northern Territory National Emergency Response Act 2007. NORTHERN TERRITORY NATIONAL EMERGENCY RESPONSE ACT 2007 (NO. 129, 2007) (austlii.edu.au)

families "at unprecedented rates" and their young languishing in detention "in obscene numbers".[49] In effect it re-instituted another age of stolen generations.[50]

It speaks volumes that Australia has never ratified another UN declaration of human rights in which self-determination is fundamental – the United Nations Declaration on the Rights of Indigenous Peoples (UNDRIP).[51] Under Article 3 of this Declaration:

> Indigenous peoples have the right to self-determination. By virtue of that right they freely determine their political status and freely pursue their economic, social and cultural development.

Australian governments have claimed to support this, but not only was Australia one of four countries to vote against the UNDRIP in 2007 (while 144 voted for it), no federal government has since seen fit to affirm any of the rights listed in the Declaration as something they are bound to observe in law, even though the government withdrew its objections to the UNDRIP in 2009.[52] The Australian Capital Territory did amend its Human Rights Act 2004 in 2016 to make specific reference to rights under Articles 25 and 31 of the UNDRIP[53] but, in the main, no law has been enacted by the federal parliament in Australia to implement the above International Covenants (or the UNDRIP) either in full or with respect to their

---

[49] Uluru Statement from the Heart. See Appendix 1.

[50] Jacynta Krakouer, Indigenous X, "The stolen generations never ended – they just morphed into child protection", The Guardian, 17 October 2019. In 2021 AIHW reported that, "18,900 Indigenous children were in out-of-home care as at 30 June 2020, 11 times the rate for non-Indigenous children." AIHW Media Release, 18 May 2021. Rate of children in out-of-home care remains stable - Australian Institute of Health and Welfare (aihw.gov.au)

[51] United Nations Declaration on the Rights of Indigenous Peoples, 2007. DRIPS_en.pdf (un.org)

[52] Australian Government Attorney-General's Department, International Human Rights System webpage, last accessed 3 August 2022: "The Australian Government also supports the United Nations Declaration on the Rights of Indigenous Persons- external site as a non-legally binding document." International human rights system | Attorney-General's Department (ag.gov.au)

[53] Australian Capital Territory, Human Rights Act 2004, Clause 27.

clauses on self-determination. As eminent constitutional lawyers have pointed out:

> This leaves Australia in breach of its obligations under international law.[54]

This therefore is the legal framework into which First Nations are now seeking to insert a Voice. It is a neglected framework singularly ill-suited for sustaining a form of sovereignty capable of giving First Nations enough power over their destiny to ensure their children will flourish. The reality is that unless that sovereignty comes with a lawful acknowledgement of self-determination as a right *for everyone* and with a mechanism that allows everyone to exercise it in full, then so far from (at last) attaining a constitutional acknowledgement of their sovereignty, First Nations may risk embedding an impotent form of it, just as Australians did when they first assented to a constitutional monarchy. This does not mean any Australian has an excuse to pull back from enshrining an Indigenous Voice in the Constitution. On the contrary, a failure to enshrine the Voice would be likely to lead to a situation that risks First Nations' sovereignty in full.[55] It is quite likely that First Nations will not keep their sovereignty *unless* they have a Voice in the Constitution. But it does mean that all Australians – Indigenous and non-Indigenous – should be aware of how far we still need to go to bestow on ourselves the sort of sovereignty that can only arise with self-determination. This is the potent sort of sovereignty we need, as opposed to the impotent sort. Further discussion on this issue and on the ways to embed a viable co-existence of sovereignties in the Constitution is provided in Chapters 5, 6 and 7.

---

[54] Williams and Daniel Reynolds, *A Charter of Rights in Australia,* UNSW Press, NewSouth Publishing, Sydney, 2017, page 19.

[55] Dispute over the risk of ceding sovereignty arose in 2022, championed by Greens Senator Lidia Thorpe. Olivia Day, "Lidia Thorpe accused of refusing to 'accept the advice' on the Indigenous Voice to Parliament (msn.com)", Daily Mail, 8 November 2022. The weight on opinion would suggest that a Voice in the Constitution would not cede sovereignty but would offer the possibility of a "meaningful expression of sovereignty".

The Indigenous Voice itself may provide some new institutional arrangements whereby Aboriginals will have a say in laws which affect them and therefore a significantly greater measure of self-determination than they have now. But if models of a First Nations Voice developed and published in 2021 in the Final Report of the Indigenous Voice Co-design Process[56] are anything to go by, this new Voice may be all too easily side-stepped if it is not backed up with a parallel recognition in the Constitution of fundamental human rights. As designed in that particular report, an Indigenous Voice will oblige the government and parliament to seek the advice of an institutional "*National* Indigenous Voice" on (unspecified) issues which "overwhelmingly relate to Aboriginal and Torres Strait Islander people". But it will not oblige the government or parliament to heed that advice or even be transparent about its reasons for its decisions. That particular model for an Indigenous National Voice would therefore impose no genuine accountability on the parliament or executive government, regardless of the degree to which the parliament might reject the advice of the National Indigenous Voice and thereby directly harm the legitimate interests of Indigenous and all other Australians. There is no reciprocity in the arrangement – no respect is required on the government's part. While the Voice Co-design Process managed to increase the government's obligations for transparency in the suggested model for a National Indigenous Voice – at least it increased transparency on any consultation conducted for bills to be considered by parliaments – the model nevertheless provided that "all elements [of a bill/act of parliament] would be non-justiciable, meaning that there could not be a court challenge and no law could be invalidated based on whether there was alignment with the consultation standards or transparency mechanisms."[57] Self-

---

[56] Australian Government, National Indigenous Australians Agency, "Indigenous Voice Co-design Process: Final Report to the Australian Government", July 2021, Indigenous Voice Co-design Process Final Report to the Australian Government (niaa.gov.au). See also Bronwyn Kelly, "On Australia Day we must proclaim an Indigenous Voice to Parliament", John Menadue's Pearls and Irritations, 26 January 2022.

[57] "Indigenous Voice Co-design Process: Final Report to the Australian Government", July 2021, page 18.

determination this is not. A promise of genuine justice in lawmaking it is not.

Such a model for an Indigenous National Voice, if implemented without parallel reconstruction of the Constitution, may therefore be likely to do little more than give Australia's Indigenes a Voice with one hand and take it back with the other, especially if an untrustworthy government is installed. No doubt it will increase the influence of First Nations peoples, but only until political considerations get in the way again, just as they did when the Howard government thought it would be politically expedient to completely remove any powers for local Indigenous communities in remote areas and subject them to another militarised intrusion. So if an inclusive Australia wishes to give an Indigenous Voice the best chance of actually working, it will be necessary not just to enshrine a First Nations Voice in the Constitution but to revise the Constitution itself so that it can support a sufficiently powerful voice for both Indigenous and non-Indigenous Australians. This is the minimum necessary for a coexistence of viable sovereignties.

Australia's First Nations are ahead of the rest of Australians in knowing full well that this powerful voice – the type of voice that is more specific and influential than a vote, the voice that should be heeded – is the one that is essential if their children are to flourish. They have the vote, but still their children are "alienated from their families at unprecedented rates" and "languish in detention in obscene numbers".[58] This is why they have sought to enshrine an Indigenous Voice in the Constitution and why that call is utterly reasonable and sensible. They know, better than other civilisations, that it is a matter of life and death. They are ahead of non-Indigenes in their knowledge of the vital necessity of self-determination via a powerful Voice. They are ahead of the rest in knowing that power should reside with we the people – and soon, before we are all overwhelmed by a planetary fate we cannot control.

All of this implies that Australia's Constitution needs to be altered to vest power in all its peoples – Indigenous and non-Indigenous.

---

[58] Uluru Statement from the Heart. See Appendix 1.

However, it does not imply that all power should be vested *exclusively* in the people or that their accession to power, particularly the power of self-determination, should disable the better features of representative democracy where order should be maintained and abuses of power should be prevented through a system of separations of power. The safer and far more productive arrangement of democracy would be one where power itself is understood to be divisible, in the sense that there are different types of power that may be distributed among partners to the democracy. A safer arrangement would assign the power to characterise the sovereign will to the people. They would assume the role of sovereign currently assumed by the monarch in our Constitution but retain the advantages of the current system of representative democracy where the federal parliament and executive government, the judicature, the states and (if preferred) a governor-general or other nominal head of state share other types of power in an arrangement similar to the current distribution but preferably with less room for abuse of those powers.

In one sense this would not be a significant departure from the role of the people in the current Constitution because they already have the last word on what it says (inasmuch as they are the only ones who can confirm amendments by referendum). But insofar as it will give the people of Australia their first opportunity to specify their sovereign will, it will be a paradigm shift in the structure of Australia's democracy. This is not to say that the shift will be disruptive of peace and order. Quite the contrary. Insofar as it offers the electors and elected their first opportunity to specify their roles and responsibilities to each other more clearly than they can under the current Constitution, it lays a foundation for sincere mutual respect.

In pursuit of that better relationship between the people of Australia and those they elect, it is the project of this book to frame the essentials of a new constitution – *the people's constitution*. These essentials are designed to enable Australians to add their voices to their votes and thereby establish the better arrangement of power that they so desperately need within their democracy.

While this better arrangement of democracy is not intended to be an overthrow of either the current Constitution or those institutions that currently exercise power exclusively under its terms, it is nevertheless a paradigmatic shift in the way Australians have been used to operating within their democracy and in the way they are likely to assume democracy itself generally works. As such it is important to understand the full scope of the task of shifting from the current arrangement to the one that would pertain under an Australian people's constitution. This will require an examination of the sort of democracy we have now, its weaknesses and the risks it poses both to our sovereignty and our capacity for self-determination. That is the subject of the next chapter.

Chapter 2 – Setting a path to power for the people

With the election of the Labor Party to government in Australia in 2022, the chances that First Nations will succeed in a referendum enshrining a Voice for them in the Constitution have been significantly increased. It will be a truly joyful moment when it arrives, hopefully before 2025. Research shows that a majority of Australians in 2021 were in favour of enshrining an Indigenous Voice in the Constitution and there is every reason to think that (barring churlish obstruction by any petulant parliamentarians jealous of sharing power) a referendum on that question will succeed.[59]

But as shown above, the particular Constitution in which we may enshrine a Voice for First Nations is itself incapable of giving effect to a Voice sufficient to ensure their children will flourish. Even if, in the process of the referendum, the parliament sees fit to delete the races powers from the Constitution and/or clarify that laws can be made for the Aboriginal race which discriminate in favour of them (not against them), this would be only the first step towards giving them enough power over their destiny to ensure their children will flourish. It would be an extremely important step but still only the first one. And even if they navigate their way safely through a referendum process to establish the Voice in an institutional form that may satisfy

---

[59] In the Australian Election Study surveys conducted by the Australian National University, around three-quarters of voters were prepared to support a change to the Constitution to recognise Indigenous Australians in both 2016 and 2019. Ron Levy and Ian McAllister, "Our research shows public support for a First Nations Voice is not only high, it's deeply entrenched", The Conversation, 9 December 2021. Our research shows public support for a First Nations Voice is not only high, it's deeply entrenched (theconversation.com)

(at least as a start), what Australian Indigenes would find is that they have simply landed in the same place that all Australians have been stuck in since 1901 – and have been even more firmly stuck in since 2001 – a place of powerlessness in relation to those who still can, and do, act without restraint under the Constitution and who admit no obligation to the future of the people of Australia, let alone to the future we might prefer. The races power might be ditched in the process of enshrining a Voice for First Nations – come the day! But this would in no way leave the path free to establish a voice sufficient for the degree of self-determination – that is, the degree of *power* – all Australians will need if we are to outrun the perfect storm of existential threats I discussed in Chapter 1 before that storm overwhelms us. If the decade of coalition government from Abbott to Morrison shows us anything – the period now commonly and justly referred to as "the lost decade" – it demonstrates with alarming clarity how useless our democracy can become if it is left in the hands of those determined to frustrate the wider interests of the nation for narrow sectional, corporate and political interests. That lost decade is the precautionary fact that impels the need for change in the distribution of power I am arguing for here.

To achieve the required level of self-determination it will be necessary to lift the power of *all* Australians well above the level of the essentially voiceless. In short, it will be necessary to step up from the merely representative system of governance we call a "democracy" and jump up to a fuller, genuine mode of democracy – participatory democracy. Such a jump is entirely feasible but it is not possible with a constitution which gives no power to the people and creates no framework, processes or institutions to ensure that their power will be respected and enduring. Nor will it be possible unless the Constitution is rebuilt so that it defines for the first time what the nation stands for, what we value, what we regard as inalienable rights, and what we envisage as the necessary minimum capacity to design our preferred future – our willingly shared destiny – and determine our preferred path towards it.

At its heart, that necessary minimum capacity can only be secured if *all* Australians are empowered with a voice. And to be powerful, that voice must be vested in Australians in a particular form. It must be enshrined in the Constitution as a right of access to an ongoing process which can continuously enable the people to drive the nation via the safest paths toward a future in which every single one of us may find a place to survive and flourish in all our diverse essentials. In short it must be a voice that makes the people's sovereign will clear.

A constitution with that sort of capacity is likely to spark a significant transformation in the arrangement of power as it prevails now in the modern Hobbesian state. In essence, the people will no longer be relegated to mere subjects of the Crown (or any other unitary sovereign – say, a parliament or executive government operating in disregard of the public interest). Nor may their will be subverted to or by the decisions of the Crown. Instead, the sovereign will emanates from the people, and the parliament is charged as a servant of their will – a will they can give voice to by expressing their values, rights and aspirations. That voice is essentially pluralist and yet integrated – the many in the one. This makes it very different to the sovereign voice permitted in the modern Hobbesian (Australian) state – a voice which should be described as the one over the many, like the state represented in the frontispiece of *Leviathan*.[60]

Throughout this book I will elaborate on this proposed new arrangement of power and sovereignty and the type of voice necessary to establish and stabilise it. But for the moment it is simply necessary to say that the process for expressing that voice must be enabled in the Constitution.

The path to that sort of powerful voice for a people's will has never yet been trod in a Western democracy. But Australia has actually been warming up to it for at least half a century. In 1967, Indigenous Australians sought to be counted as Australians in the census and this resulted in the most resounding referendum Yes vote since Federation. Almost 91% of Australians voted Yes to proposals to extend a power to the Commonwealth to make laws for Aboriginals and to count them as Australians. Ironically, this change

---

[60] Frontispiece of *Leviathan*, See Appendix 2.

was achieved by deleting mention of Aboriginals from the Constitution, meaning that at the very moment they could finally be counted they were also expunged from the Constitution itself. Nevertheless, the result was an unambiguous endorsement that Australians want an inclusive society and have wanted it for a long time.

There is still a long way to go to be free from racism. So in that sense there is still a long way to go before everyone might be willing to accept that everyone else should have a voice. Indeed, Australians are still steeped in the habit of assuming that if they are to get what they need and want, their voice must rise above if not delete all others – in other words their voice must be politically successful at the ballot box and must overwhelm the diverse voices of others. In this arrangement the result at a ballot box ejects the legitimate agendas and basic needs of large swathes of the population. However, this happens only because people have not found a way yet to assemble their diverse voices in an orderly manner so that they can each be heard. They have certainly not found a way to do this on a national scale and in such a way as to make it unnecessary for majorities to exclude the voices of minorities. They have not found a way to organise a new national democratic open forum – what some proponents of democracy would call a "public square" – where voices can actually be heard (as opposed to merely expressed) and integrated into a coherent statement of inclusive will that supports the diversity of our needs.

In the age of the internet, however, the means of organising the public square on a national scale has arrived. Never has there been a more completely open platform on which any person may seek out what they need and want to know for free, and express any opinion they may have for free. The voices we and our politicians get to hear may no longer be selected or dismissed by gatekeeper publishers and journalists. That has created the space for virtual community engagement in which voices can specify their objectives for the governments they elect. Instead of being confined to the national voting process, in which we basically give *carte blanche* and a blank cheque to politicians to do what they like, voices can introduce specificity about the national will. People can set the direction of the nation so that it is inclusive, rather than leave it to those who have the money to buy governments.

Of course, we may feel the internet is not a suitable place for this process. After all, it has been an impersonal, dehumanising and divisive force in communications. But if organised properly, a space could be created on it to enable the building of a full, genuine, open democracy, one which can work to produce what we might come to recognise as a re-humanised agenda. Probably, the internet is the only space where such an agenda can be built *by* the people so that it works efficiently and effectively on a national scale *for* the people.

Scaling up to a participatory democracy

At this point it is probably wise to ask what we might gain in the form and strength of our democracy if we establish a new central public square on the internet on a national scale. Can democracy be organised at a national level so that it provides each of us with the practical possibility of more efficient and effective involvement in our own governance? To answer that, it will be helpful to step back and consider what democracy was always meant to be about and then assess whether a new open forum will deliver a better form of democracy – one that is genuinely inclusive because it is efficient and accessible by all.

The type of large scale, open democratic forum that I have suggested here can be usefully compared and contrasted with the much smaller public square that operated at the dawn of democracy in Athens, an open space and political system which obliged all those enfranchised to contribute to public debate (notably *before* voting) and to take their turn in administration of a public office. This inclusive form of duty and active participation in governance was the original intention of Athenian democracy and it worked well for a time because it was applied on a small scale (only property owning men were enfranchised and the city itself was small geographically and in population). But expansion of that fledgling model of democracy so that it may operate on a wider scale has hitherto been a challenge that no government has been willing to step up to. As populations and territories expanded over the centuries, they instead developed alternative concepts of self-rule, none of which found a way to efficiently assemble power, territory and sovereignty on a large, fully inclusive – that is, fully democratic – scale. Democracy did not scale up. In fact Western governments as they designed constitutions have displayed a history of fear of democracy, spurred no doubt by the fear that power is fleeting and that the few who have it must be eternally vigilant against the many who do not. Fear of "the mob", as it has been called, has kept democracy at bay for centuries.

Sometimes this fear has been spoken of, sometimes not. In the making of the American Constitution, for instance, the founders displayed no will to create a democracy and designed a system which could have no other effect than to keep it at bay. In that case, sovereignty was instead quite deliberately encoded as a republic:

> The United States shall guarantee to every State in this Union a Republican Form of Government, and shall protect each of them against Invasion; and on Application of the Legislature, or of the Executive (when the Legislature cannot be convened) against domestic Violence.[61]

As it is framed in the US Constitution, that "Republican Form of Government" is decidedly not a democracy. It makes space for nothing like the open discourse of the Athenian square. It is pure Hobbes – a state in which the monarch has simply been re-dressed as a system of "representative government", one in which "the people" have no more power than they had before, except to say who shall speak and decide for them. It is a monarchy without a monarch, a vote without a voice. That system merely decides who shall govern, not what they should govern for. It is the opposite of a democracy – not government of the people by the people for the people, but rather government of the people by an authority that decides for itself what government will be for – and that, in the case of the president, has no accountability to the people beyond what he might

[61] The Constitution of the United States of America, 1787, Article 4, Section 4. constitution_pdf2 (constitutioncenter.org)

freely choose. The US president's only accountability is to uphold the American Constitution. It is to uphold nothing other than the thing that gives him power. Insofar as that Constitution grants some rights and liberties to the American people it might appear to be as democratic as might be necessary for "a new nation conceived in liberty, and dedicated to the proposition that all men are created equal".[62] But while that new nation has "endured" as Lincoln at Gettysburg hoped it would, it has not lived up to its promise, particularly in terms of equality.

Indeed, the people of America gained relatively little in terms of enduring rights or "secure Blessings of Liberty"[63] in exchange for surrendering power completely. As payment for giving up hope of a voice, the Republic really only offered them one thing – protection from "Invasion" and "domestic Violence" (meaning civil war). Again, this is pure Hobbes. This is not to say the Americans had a choice about the type of state they could build at the time. Any other, less autocratic option would have exposed them to potential annihilation at birth. It would have robbed them of the means of organising their defence from the primary threat of military invasion. There was a point to the Hobbesian state in America in the 18th century – a compelling point which might be summed up as "organise civilly or die".

As it turned out, the republic that the United States built as a modified form of the modern state certainly worked to help protect them from external invasion. It did not work at all to protect them from internal invasions – states plundering each other and killing on an unprecedented scale as they did only a few decades later. But insofar as it compelled the formation of a Union capable of averting the perceived external existential threat as the new nation's fragile

---

[62] US President Abraham Lincoln, The Gettysburg Address, 19 November 1863.

[63] Preamble to The Constitution of the United States of America, 1787: "We the People of the United States, in Order to form a more perfect Union, establish Justice, insure domestic Tranquility, provide for the common defence, promote the general Welfare, and secure the Blessings of Liberty to ourselves and our Posterity, do ordain and establish this Constitution for the United States of America." Op. Cit.

and vulnerable independence was declared, the modern Hobbesian style of state was a triumph in the US.

In the process, however, democracy was necessarily sacrificed to defence considerations. There were remarkable attempts to establish the United States as at least a partial democracy by encoding human rights into the Constitution and by establishing a system of separations, checks and balances in power. But the human rights applied only to a select few and the checks and balances were often flouted. Accordingly as the centuries rolled on, America eventually calcified into a form of the state where the originally intended "general Welfare"[64] of the people is almost entirely subordinated to considerations of defence and the military. Just about everything today in the American polity is geared to enable war at the will of that sovereign state and the result is that:

> The US has never had a decade without war. Since its founding in 1776, the US has been at war 93 per cent of the time. ... The US has launched 201 out of 248 armed conflicts since the end of World War II.[65]

The modern American state, inasmuch as it remains in its original "republican form", largely unamended, appears to offer the people of America very little in wellbeing and security today beyond what may be achieved by almost continuous war. The United States has achieved its primary aim of secure existence but at the expense of just about everything that makes existence worthwhile for many millions of its people. It is a great state, but a failing one particularly in terms of inequality of income, wealth and wellbeing, and that failure will accelerate if America refuses to lift its system of representative government up to a more inclusive democracy. A state

---

[64] Preamble to The Constitution of the United States of America, 1787. Ibid.

[65] John Menadue, "Is war in the American DNA?", John Menadue's Pearls and Irritations, 2 January 2018 and "Our dangerous ally could drag us into war with China", 3 August 2022. See also the multiplicity of websites fact checking this statistic including Washington's Blog at https://www.globalresearch.ca/america-has-been-at-war-93-of-the-time-222-out-of-239-years-since-1776/5565946 and Freakonometrics at https://freakonometrics.hypotheses.org/50473, last accessed 6 August 2022.

cannot achieve government of the people by the people for the people if it does not grant the people a reasonable share of power. A vote does not do that; nor will it until it becomes a voice.

America is unlikely to comprehend all that at this late stage of its calcified republic. It could, in theory, still scale up to a more open participatory democracy in time to deal with critical issues at the national level in relation to securing wellbeing for its people but there is little evidence of a will in that direction or comprehension of a need. As such, America's capacity to lead the free world on the international stage and to prove that its form of democracy is the best is likely to be severely diminished. Australia, however, has the benefit of an example before it of a proposition from its First Nations which in effect is seeking to place voices above – or, at least, before – votes and is thereby offering a model of democracy that I will argue can deliver the freedoms, wellbeing and security we want more reliably than the current American model.

It might be said that two different models for the future of our democracy are on offer here. One is the American model – a model to which many Australians will look if they are keen to improve the capacity of their democracy but which they are likely to find has not delivered either wellbeing or security to its people. I would suggest this failure stems at least in part from the exclusivity of the republican form of government in the US Constitution. Despite its emphasis on rights and freedoms, it is essentially still designed to exclude many of the voices of Americans. By contrast, the other model that is inspired by the First Nations Voice offers Australia the potential to scale up to a full, strong, enabling democracy – the sort that can only arise from a significant increase in participation by people not in politics or at the ballot box but in national direction setting and specification of a coherent will. In other words it inspires us to consider the benefits that may arise from including the voices of all Australians in our democratic processes.

It is important to understand the differences between these two models particularly insofar as they offer quite different possibilities for Australia's future as an independent sovereign nation whose people will have a greater capacity for self-determination than they do now. In the early 2020s, independence in sovereignty is very much at risk in Australia due to federal government preferences for a tightened alliance with the United States for defence purposes and a simultaneous preference not to involve the Australian people in any decision on defence or the extent of strategic alliances. The newly elected Labor government in 2022 was keen to engage in conversations with Australians on wellbeing and an Indigenous Voice but not on defence and independence in sovereignty. I will argue in this book that it is essential for Australians to be able to maintain their independence as a nation and to be involved as fully and openly as they wish in all strategic decisions on defence, alliances and war. However, our democracy needs to be adjusted to allow for this involvement and to ensure that we make the right types of adjustments we first need to examine the sort of democracy we have now. We need to examine its weaknesses and the risks it poses both to our sovereignty and our capacity for self-determination. Is our current form of democracy, in which we have no effective voice beyond voting, capacious enough to ensure that the Australian people can secure their future as an independent sovereign nation? In the next sections I will argue that it is not and that a choice of an inclusive model of democracy will offer far greater control over our future security than would be possible compared to versions of democracy that allow for far too much exclusion. I will explain this using America's model of democracy as a point of reference and will suggest that, notwithstanding all its strengths in promoting liberty and liberality, it should not be used as a model for the optimum arrangement of governance for Australia, especially if stability, security, and sovereignty in decision-making are key national objectives.

Our democracy now – Australia's capacity for independent sovereignty

Australia is no less (or more) a representative government than America and as such is no less (or more) a democracy than America. Neither nation is the liberal democracy it boasts of being and both are entirely vulnerable as stable and peaceful democracies whenever their respective systems of representative government are undermined – or to put that more accurately, whenever their respective representative systems do not work well enough to hold the nation together. As I write this in July 2022, that is a breakdown that is playing out in plain sight in America where a new, intense friction has grown up between "representative government" and "democracy", as though these two terms that we frequently use to characterise Western liberal forms of governance are no longer interchangeable.

Since the spectacular assault on the US Capitol on 6 January 2021, and the subsequent stubborn refusal of many millions of Americans to accept the election result as a valid basis for the peaceful handover of democratic governance,[66] it is clear that a large part of American society no longer assumes that free election of representatives is a system to be relied on as the basis of formation of a democratic government. This should function as a warning to other democracies that unless they establish something more than a system of representative government, they will not be able to build confidence in democracy as the best means of achieving stable governance that is capable of promoting the wellbeing and security of all. As I said in Chapter 1, elections do not a democracy make, and it is the same with representative government. Something more must be added to it to make sure that as a representative system it translates into responsible, responsive and, indeed, accountable government. Until that extra capacity is added, any form of Western democracy is likely to be too stunted to be serviceable for purposes of delivering wellbeing and too prone to exposing nations to risk in defence and security.

---

[66] Polling in America about the validity of the US presidential election in 2020 suggests that "The number of people overall who believe the election was fraudulent has hovered around 35% since November 2020." This implies that around 100 million Americans may hold the view that the 2020 presidential election was stolen from Donald Trump. The Poynter Institute, Politifact, 30 January 2022. PolitiFact | No, most Americans don't believe the 2020 election was fraudulent

In Australia's case, the warning about America's now rather stunted form of democracy should be amplified, because for defence and security purposes we have chosen to ally our state to America's. This made sense after World War II but in the 21st century it simply means we have allied our state to what has turned out to be a very unstable democracy and possibly one that is on the brink of failure as a nation capable of demonstrating decent world leadership for those who desire freedom. America is a country which asserts that *its* democracy – even in its most limited form where elites and sectional interests have achieved exclusive control by gaming the system of representative government – is the only form of governance worth having, regardless of whether it suits the cultural preferences of other sovereign nations. In the Biden era this sort of hyperbole has come to dominate American National Security Strategies in statements which assert that American democracy "is the only way to ensure that people are truly able to live lives of dignity and freedom".[67]

By and large, Australians have bought into this idea of democratic America, and, by and large, we have been comfortable with America taking the role of international leader for democratic, free nations. But there is ample evidence that America's democracy has not assured many millions of its people a life of dignity and freedom. That has not stopped successive American administrations, in a slavish subscription to this idea of American exceptionalism, from carrying on what amounts to a messianic crusade to export their preferred form of governance to all other nations, imposing it on them whether they like it or not. Nor has it stopped America from violating the sovereignty of dozens of other nations since World War II by political and military interference. In this overreach, America has been dragging Australia into dependency on an ally that is itself unstable. This makes it all the more important for Australia to design its democracy so that it is less vulnerable to the sort of weaknesses affecting America's and more reliable for purposes of maintaining our sovereignty as an independent nation, one less easily dragged into

---

[67] President Joseph Biden, The White House, Washington, "National Security Strategy", October 2022. Biden-Harris Administration's National Security Strategy.pdf (whitehouse.gov)

another's wars. This will require Australia to build a new model of democracy – one which is not reduced to mere electioneering for selection of representatives but which, in addition to and *before* election processes, allows the people to speak for themselves.

This new model of democracy should insert an extra step into our current processes for electing representatives. Before we elect them, we the people must first work together to set down in writing a description of the preferred character and values of our nation and scope the policy agenda that will be necessary for realisation of that preferred national character. In short, we the people of Australia should learn to provide instructions to those we elect about the nation we are trying to build and that they are being elected to deliver by ethical application of the powers we vest in them in elections. In this new arrangement, democracy should come to be recognised not as an end in itself – like some sort of religion headed by an idolised god that purports to hold all the answers or a holy grail that promises eternal life – but as a means to quite a different end of national security and wellbeing for all. Clearly America's withered form of democracy is not delivering wellbeing and security and as such we would be well advised not to model our governance system on theirs.

Fortunately Australia's democracy can be rescued – as long as we don't yoke it to a value system which is not our own. That would imperil Australia as an independent sovereign nation as I will explain.

Australians might assume they share common values of freedom and liberal democracy with America and on that basis we may have assumed that American democracy is safely consonant with our values and that it is therefore safe to align ourselves with the US for purposes of defence. Indeed in the 2010-2020 decade Australia began not so much to align itself as to shackle itself to the US corporate/state defence establishment. We have been skating towards surrendering sovereignty in military operations and war powers and closing off the option of remaining neutral in confrontations between superpowers. No doubt this is in response to our having perceived an incessant pattern since World War II of ruthless intrusion by America into the sovereignty of other nations[68] and a fear by the major Australian political parties (Labor and Liberal/National) that should the US choose to effect regime change in Australia, they will. As Brian Toohey has reported, US foreign intervention is a matter of congressional record:

> The New York Times Magazine reported on 13 September 1976 that congressional investigations had shown that the CIA, 'in some 900 foreign interventions over the past two decades, has run secret wars around the globe and has clandestinely dominated foreign governments so thoroughly as to make them virtual client states'.[69]

Nevertheless, Australia's mainstream political leaders have continued to deepen their connections with what former Prime Minister Malcolm Fraser called this "dangerous ally".[70] They

> are undeterred by the fact that the US has been involved in an astonishing number of wars and has repeatedly overthrown governments in defiance of international norms laid down at the founding of the United Nations.[71]

America's unconscionable behaviour has had almost the full measure of its intended intimidating effect on Australia's governments. At the time of writing (2022), it was arguable that we were approaching a point where we may be fully locked into a defence arrangement with America that will make it impossible for us not to follow them into wars which are in no way in Australia's interest and which in fact expose Australia as a target for conventional or nuclear attack. The arrangements that were being

---

[68] For a history of the brutality and violence of regime changes effected by the United States since World War II, see Brian Toohey, *Secret: The making of Australia's security state*, Melbourne University Press, 2019, especially Chapter 28 – What to do about a bellicose ally.

[69] Brian Toohey, *Secret: The making of Australia's security state*, Melbourne University Press, 2019, page 236.

[70] Malcolm Fraser with Cain Roberts, *Dangerous Allies*, Melbourne University Publishing, 1 May 2014.

[71] Brian Toohey, *Secret: The making of Australia's security state*, Melbourne University Press, 2019, page 199.

made under AUKUS (the security pact with the UK and America announced in 2021) may, if they are fully executed, even go so far as to lock Australia into paying for a significant part of the American defence establishment and its aggression programs while simultaneously leaving us with no capability to manage our own defence.

Nevertheless, in 2022 the ink was not dry on AUKUS. It was still possible to abandon AUKUS and even the ANZUS treaty, since the former did not yet irretrievably bind us and the latter never bound us to follow America into its wars anyway. We could still claim the full measure of sovereignty, at least as far as it pertains to decisions on defence and war. But the opportunity for genuine independence in both defence and sovereignty was fast closing.

There is never a good time for a nation to sacrifice its sovereignty but in the early 2020s Australia was doing exactly that at the worst possible time – at a time when the friction between representative government and democracy in America was itself skating dangerously close to civil war proportions, and dangerously away from the only feature of democracy that their republic might have sought to retain, namely the peaceful transfer of power after an election without the need for involvement of, or takeover by, the military.

The friction, indeed the severance of the connection in America's republic between representative government and democracy, was on view for all to see in the House committee investigating the 6 January 2021 attack on the Capitol. When Congresswoman Liz Cheney asked former National Security Advisor to President Trump, General Michael Flynn, "Do you believe in the peaceful transition of power in the United States of America?", the General pleaded the Fifth Amendment, exercising his right under the Constitution not to answer.[72] Such a refusal by a high ranking powerful member of the military (retired but still active) to answer whether he might support

---

[72] "Gen. Mike Flynn pleaded the Fifth when asked about Jan. 6 insurrection | Jan. 6 hearings" https://www.youtube.com/watch?v=Oyg60yZhdy0 Under the Fifth Amendment to the US Constitution, a witness in a criminal proceeding may not be compelled "to be a witness against himself".

a fundamental tenet of both representative government and democracy – be it in a republican or other constitutional mode – surely sounds an alarm that America's political, civil and military arrangements had reached a deep crisis. Australia in the decade to 2022 was therefore yoking itself to a state whose representative democracy was coming apart.

Of course, we could have always foreseen that it might come apart. Structured as it was – a monarchy without a monarch – parts of America's form of democracy made it fragile from the beginning. Like any modern state in the Hobbesian vein, it was designed to fend off civil war, the "war of all against all". But barely a few decades elapsed before it was plunged into the most catastrophic civil war of modern times. As I have said, the sacrifice of its chance of democracy for the sake of security in defence made sense in 1787 but Americans were not compensated for their sacrifice. They ended up with neither a democracy nor security.

One major cause of the degeneration into America's war of all against all is that the American Constitution provided no place for all – no place for slaves, Indigenous peoples, women, or migrants. It was exclusionist. Many of these limitations were eventually overcome and a trend towards inclusion did emerge, albeit very slowly and haltingly. But if in the 21st century the United States is sliding once again towards internal civil unrest of possible war proportions, it is evident that the Republic is no longer structured well enough to deliver peace and stability. As such it would be remiss of Australians not to establish a defence capacity that is fully independent of America. It is therefore now time to imagine how we might exercise our independence and sovereignty more fully in matters of defence. But this can only happen if we find a way of organising an orderly public square and establishing that space so that democracy can function in Australia to overcome the obvious failures on display in other democracies today – most worryingly, perhaps, in American representative government and its incapacity now to function as a government of "we the people", rather than as a militarised autocracy. There is no other place where that public square might be organised than on the internet.

In 2022 in Canberra, the public square in which our voices may seek an audience has been almost totally confined to the four walls of parliament. It is not an open square at all, especially when only corporate lobbyists have parliament house passes and when there is no constitutional basis making the government responsible to the people. The internet is the only space big enough, open enough and connected enough to facilitate a full, genuine democracy on a national scale. Now that the internet exists, there is nothing (yet) stopping Australians from organising a space on it to develop and express their coherent will. What they can't yet do is impress that will, whatever it may be, on their parliaments. They can't assert their will as the highest authority. They cannot articulate the guiding intention of the nation. That requires not just a new public square but a new Constitution – The Australian People's Constitution.

If Australians wish to build their nation so that it becomes a truly independent sovereignty – one that can withstand the worst of the various pressures that might be (and are routinely) placed on them by more powerful nations – then a constitution that gives governments the means and the confidence to fend off modern attacks on our sovereignty is essential. Australians and indeed modern states are not accustomed to assuming that constitutions can be effective in that regard, even though their purpose is to do nothing more and nothing less than confirm sovereignty. But that is only because of the way modern nations assume constitutions can be and should be designed.

Australia's current Constitution, so designed, gives the people no power to fend off external pressures. But a people's constitution, structured properly, can significantly increase the chances of retaining the sovereignty that actually will suit the Australian public interest in the 21st century – the sovereignty we freely choose to confer on ourselves rather than the sovereignty a foreign power may tolerate in its own preferred interest. In the remainder of this book I will expand on how this capacity can be established in a well-designed people's constitution and how that type of constitution can enable an orderly and productive functioning of the new type of open public square I have suggested – a space where the people of Australia can assemble themselves to use orderly democratic processes to express their sovereign will.

Towards The People's Constitution

Scott Morrison was right when he said a government "can never answer to a higher authority than the people of Australia." Of course, he said that right thing for all the wrong reasons and then recanted anyway; so his insincerity might tend to discredit his original proposition (although it really only discredits his motivation). But fundamentally, if the people of any nation are intent on establishing a genuine democracy, then the proposition that the people are the highest authority on the subject of the sovereign will should be irrefutable. Be that as it may, it is not possible to establish the people as the highest authority on the sovereign will if they are not enabled by their constitution to do anything other than give all that authority away, and specifically, if they are not enabled to state what is permitted by their authority and what is not, what is desirable in their laws, and what is essential for their wellbeing, security, and future. They need two things to do that: an open but well organised public square and a constitution which gives them the positive and negative force I spoke of above. They need a force which gives them at least equal power with those they elect and much more than the corporations they do not.

At first glance, this might seem like an impossible, unrealistic, impracticable, foolishly idealistic and naïve suggestion. Doubtless, sceptics and cynics will respond with claims that anyone who might consider exploring it simply doesn't understand how politics works. But this is merely a blind, an illusion put about by the powerful to disguise the plain fact that politics itself doesn't work. If it did, the world – the West equally with the East – would not be in such dire straits. At this stage of history, when the time to save our planet and species is short, understanding how politics works is far less important than understanding why it doesn't and then setting up improvements to our system of democracy to overcome the weaknesses of politics. There are myriad reasons why politics in

Australia at least doesn't work but chief among them is that it refuses to accord each voice some status, it refuses to capitalise on human diversity, it refuses to act as a full democracy. A well organised space on the internet can be assembled to enfranchise all those voices.

In its infancy, of course, the internet is chaotic. It is also currently causing as much harm and division as it is advancement and inclusion. Thus far, the voices it has enabled clang around in a cacophony. The din is extraordinary. Little wonder that the few decent politicians left standing are unable to hear any of these voices (unless those voices have a lobbying pass to Parliament House), much less discern a coherent will amid the confusion. But the reality is that it is not technically or procedurally difficult at all to arrange that space, keep access to it open, and to equip participants with skills and capacity to build a coherent voice.

Through the centuries, since Athenian democracy first rose and fell, we have been unable to conceive of a system in which the many might speak as one and still retain a space for diversity in that voice. We have been confined to settling for a system that is a distant second best – a system where, in the absence of common ground, a political and often unsatisfactory compromise must be reached before we can solve even the easy problems. Those compromises inevitably exclude someone from a legitimate recognition or equality. Sometimes (oftentimes) they exclude whole genders, whole races, whole underclasses, whole biological communities, whole future generations. This system of politics – a system in which failure is inherent – has pertained through the ages precisely because common ground is almost always absent when it is needed. At the national level in a big country it is mostly non-existent. If it turns up at all, it is nearly always too late. To make matters worse, politics is arranged these days so that vested interests work to ensure common ground never emerges unless they want it to.

Of course it is not only nefarious powerplays that prevent us from finding common ground. The diversity of human beings ensures its absence just as surely as the venality of the powerful. Given that, it might be smart to stop looking for it and to extract ourselves from political systems which, after all, do nothing more than insist on exclusion, building in winners and losers. If we can arrange a system in which the many can speak as one and still retain a space for diversity, it could at least be supposed that we will have nothing to lose. This book will argue that this is now a practical possibility and that in any case it is an opportunity no sane society should discard before they try it.

As I have already said, there has been a readiness for this among everyday Australians for at least 50 years. We have simply lacked the means to achieve it (until now). We have not lacked the will. The will was boosted in 1975 when Australia's only constitutional crisis shocked everyone with the sacking of a Prime Minister by a Governor-General – a Prime Minister who had not lost the confidence of the House of Representatives and who by the will of the Australian people had been elected to government only 18 months before.

The crisis resulted in wave of calls for a "democratic constitution". Recognising that we don't have such a thing, eminent Australian historian Manning Clark wrote in 1977 that the Australian Constitution was part of the "powerful, dread, dead hand of the past".[73] He predicted that Australians who want their own distinctive society – a "society in which there is social justice and planning" – would respond, not by tinkering with the federal Constitution but by building an entirely new one themselves:

> What will probably happen will be that the people, having come up against a brick wall, and finding from bitter experience they cannot climb over that wall, will do the sensible thing and walk around it, or face the other way, and ignore it. The people will make changes in other walks of life: they *will acquire or capture a voice* in deciding the conditions under which they want to live in the schools, in the universities, in the workshop, in the factory, on the sporting field. ... Australians have now created their own literature, their own schools of painting, their own music, their own

[73] Manning Clark, Essay on "The People and the Constitution" in Sol Encel, Donald Horne and Elaine Thompson (eds.), *Change the Rules: Towards a democratic constitution*, Penguin, Ringwood Victoria, 1977, page 19.

> drama. The time has now come for Australians to create their own political institutions. The time has come to end our period of political cringing and create institutions related to the spirit of the place, the past, and an independent present. Then the people might turn to deal with that anachronism of contemporary Australia, the federal Constitution. This time they will not draft a British or a Yankee Constitution. This time, having at last liberated themselves from their own barbaric past, having shed the last vestiges of colonialism, and provincialism, they will at long last have the faith in their power to make their own history. *This time the people will draft their own constitution*.[74] [Emphasis added.]

In the ensuing decades, the will to do as Manning Clark imagined may have subsided, but only temporarily. It has been sparked into life once again by a concentration of crises in climate change, massive biodiversity losses, social injustice, increasing inequality, the barbarity of racism and religious conflict, the failure of capitalism in its unregulated forms, the inhumanity of corporations and the military industrial complex, and the vision of the retreat of democracy across the Western World. And with the onset of Covid-19, the will to transfer our governance onto a transparent, ethical foundation – to reset the economy onto a sustainable footing and thereby reduce inequality – has blossomed once again. But this time it has blossomed because Manning Clark's brick wall has suddenly been understood as the limit of our existence – not a brick wall on which was painted the mere dead hand of the past, but a brick wall marking the limit of our future, the end of our story, or at least the end of our story as we might prefer it to be. This picture painted on the wall was one of the end of all our wellbeing and security.

Having arrived at that wall, it might be reliably assumed that the will to live, the instinct to survive, will kick in, at least for enough of us, and that this will drive us to organise safe paths to a future, as

---

[74] Manning Clark, Essay on "The People and the Constitution" in Sol Encel, Donald Horne and Elaine Thompson (eds.), *Change the Rules: Towards a democratic constitution*, Penguin, Ringwood Victoria, 1977, pages 19-20.

Manning Clark might have said, by acquiring or capturing a voice in deciding the conditions under which we want to live. This is a new type of sovereign voice – an arrangement of power where instead of voting to establish a parliament that will decide for us, we decide for ourselves. We hand over power still, but this time with instructions about what it may be used for – to what end – and what the minimum obligations of elected parliaments will be to us, to we the people. We set down the terms of trust that will govern a new relationship of mutually respectful obligation between the electors and the elected. This arrangement of power has not hitherto been possible. But it is now an entirely practical possibility.

Almost fifty years on from the constitutional crisis of 1975, Australians are expressing not just a will to live but a will to control how to live with wellbeing and fulfilment, since what is life worth otherwise? That is a display of a higher order demand for power, one that can rise above the limitations of the modern Hobbesian-style state. This level of demand has inevitably arisen over the last 120 years from the introduction of universal education, from the enlightenment that comes from free access to knowledge, and from a general awareness that *none* of our lives need to be solitary, poor, nasty, brutish or short and that science and human cooperation can now ensure that we escape that fate. We need no longer be confined to it as we were in the past. We need no longer be driven, powerless, into the barbarity of the war of all against all. That said, it is logical that we will be confined to the barbarity of the past if we continue to rely on the barbarity of past systems of governance. This in turn implies the need for an entirely fresh start.

Starting again

In supporting the call for a First Nations Voice in the Constitution, Australians are signalling that they are looking for a way to start again, to shuffle off the past, including the guilt of the nation's founding. Starting again, from an entirely new position about who should share power in our system of government if it is to be truly democratic, is in reality the only way to go around the wall – "the only sensible thing" as Manning Clark might have put it. To do otherwise is to deny life as the fundamental impulse and choose murder and suicide. It is to deny the community of humankind.

For some, that new start is to put their faith in their god and distrust all earthly things like governments and people. Others might choose to put their faith in capitalism or whatever ideological prescription comes to hand. But history has shown that our future is what *we* make it. It is determined by *us* and is most reliably made to our liking when *we* specify the values by which it should be made. That is where any decent democratic constitution – a constitution for humankind – should logically start.

Australia's Constitution of 1901 started by "humbly relying on the blessing of Almighty God",[75] a starting position that effectively ruled out the possibility and value of relying on each other. The architecture of the Constitution reinforced that exclusion and division by dispensing with the scale of human agency necessary to enable self-determination. That necessary scale can only be attained in a "we the people" constitution. And since we have nothing like that sort of constitution, the only way to get it is to start again.

As Australians are likely to say Yes to the invitation from First Nations to "walk with them in a movement of the Australian people for a better future", there is perhaps no better time to build a constitution with an architecture capable of supporting the Australian people to design and take charge of that better future. Part 2 of this book offers a way for Australians to accept the invitation in the Uluru Statement from the Heart in such a way as to truly empower them and then to ensure that all our children will flourish.

[75] Preamble to the Commonwealth of Australia Constitution Act, 9 July 1900: https://www.aph.gov.au/constitution

Part 2 – Constituting a nation according to a people's sovereign will

Chapter 3 – Finding a place to start

If Australia is to start again, where does it start?

There are several places we could start from. For instance, we could start with the current Constitution and examine what's good and bad about it in the context of the values of today's society and the nation we have inherited and modernised since 1901. We could ask how well it reflects our current values. And we could look at how well it reflects our actual arrangements for our governance as they are now.

Were we to undertake that exercise we would find that the Constitution is discordant with today's values, including the values that might be expected in a multicultural, gender equal, universally enfranchised, class conscious but relatively wealthy society. We would find that as far as multiculturalism goes, the Constitution is racist. On gender equality, it is silent and women are as absent from mention in at as Aborigines. On suffrage, it is still back with the dark ages, incapable as it is of comprehending anything beyond the rule of old, white men of limited religious (i.e., solely Christian) persuasion. On distribution of wealth, it contemplates little more than the need to protect claims on the "Colonies of Australia" as "possessions of the Queen",[76] and to "admit" (such is the royal largesse) those possessions formally into her "Commonwealth". In that respect we would find it disregards what we know now – that the continent was possessed by Britain on deeply dubious legal premises (even by the standards in international law of the day), inasmuch as it rested on

---

[76] Preamble to the Commonwealth of Australia Constitution Act, 9th July 1900: "... whereas it is expedient to provide for the admission into the Commonwealth of other Australasian Colonies
and possessions of the Queen" https://www.aph.gov.au/constitution

an assumption now acknowledged by the High Court to be false, namely that Australia was an unsettled continent, *terra nullius*, before colonisation. As Henry Reynolds has demonstrated, from at least the 1850s onward "the legal foundations of the colony were unsound and remain so to this day". Possession of the continent as a British property was "an act of theft on a truly heroic scale".[77]

As such, were we to assess the legitimacy of the nation's constitution at Federation as a British colonial possession, we would be faced with a chasm of difference between the unquestioning representation of the rightness of the annexation of Australia by Britain in the Constitution and what today's courts have acknowledged in law since 1992, when:

> despite themselves the High Court judges in the Mabo case changed property law forever and intimated that the traditional doctrine relating to sovereignty might eventually have to change as well.[78]

Since the Mabo[79] judgement, which established that native title survived the British claim of sovereignty, and the Wik judgement[80] four years later, which established that pastoral leases also did not extinguish pre-existing native title, the gap between the basic false premise of the nation as it was taken for granted in the Constitution and the truth about a pre-existing sovereignty which has never been ceded, is now a gap too wide to ignore. It is also unlikely that a gap that wide could be bridged by piecemeal amendments to the Constitution. Confined as it is to the single-sovereign model of the Hobbesian modern state, a few amendments to existing chapters would be insufficient to accommodate more than one sovereignty –

---

[77] Henry Reynolds, *Truth-Telling: History, Sovereignty and the Uluru Statement from the Heart*, NewSouth Publishing 2021, pages 63 and 46.

[78] Henry Reynolds, *Truth-Telling: History, Sovereignty and the Uluru Statement from the Heart*, NewSouth Publishing 2021, page 12.

[79] High Court of Australia, Mabo v Queensland (No 2) ("Mabo case") [1992] HCA 23; (1992) 175 CLR 1 (3 June 1992)

[80] High Court of Australia, Wik Peoples v Queensland ("Pastoral Leases case") [1996] HCA 40; (1996) 187 CLR 1; (1996) 141 ALR 129; (1996) 71 ALJR 173 (23 December 1996)

either an Indigenous sovereignty that "coexists with that of the Crown" as called for in the Uluru Statement from the Heart, or a sovereignty of the people that is capable of establishing self-determination. It simply isn't designed for that purpose. If the Constitution is to be made capable of supporting a coexistence of sovereignties, its capacity will need to be amplified beyond its current framework for distribution of power.

Finally, were we to undertake an assessment of how well the Constitution reflects our current arrangements for power-sharing and governance, we would find multiple mismatches between what it says about the powers of the federal parliament and executive government, the governor-general, the states and the judicature and what actually pertains in the arrangement of power now. There are multiple sections that can no longer be active but are still retained. They sit there like strange ghosts of regimes past.

For instance, the Constitution originally provided for appeals from the High Court and state courts to the British Privy Council but this was abolished in 1986 without amendment to the Constitution itself. It also still provides that the queen or king, under Section 1, "is part of the Parliament" and that, under Section 61, the

> executive power of the Commonwealth is vested in the Queen [or King] and is exercisable by the Governor-General as her [or his] representative.[81]

In the wording, a sovereign of what is now a foreign country still presides over lawmaking in Australia. In 2022 most Australians would assume she or he (as the case may be) is merely a figurehead who does not exercise any executive power. But as far as the Constitution goes, she or he still retains that power and this applies despite the fact that in 1931 under the Statute of Westminster, Britain unilaterally revoked its sovereign power to enact laws that applied in Australia. Britain tried to shake us off as "a dominion subject to its laws", and in reality did, particularly once World War II came around,

[81] See Australian Government Solicitor, *Australia's Constitution with Overview and Notes by the Australian Government Solicitor*, page v. foi-2021-017.pdf (pmc.gov.au)

the Japanese invaded Singapore, and the King's Australian subjects were deserted. But at least as far as the Constitution was concerned Australia was still not prepared to fully cut the apron strings. We retain these remnants of past colonial ties even as we promote ourselves as a proud, independent country.

These are just a few examples of how Australia's Constitution has become irrelevant to how we live, how we govern ourselves, how we think of our country today and how we describe our values.

Since the Constitution is so plainly out of date, we might assume then that all we need do to make a new beginning as a nation is simply to bring the Constitution up to date. But to opt for that method of "starting again", we would have to assume that our current governance arrangements are desirable and perfectly useful in their current form. We would have to assume that the system as we have it arranged now works, and that it works for us.

Let me not waste time here: there are no grounds to suggest that the system works for us and that Australians would assume that it does. As income and wealth inequality in Australia have widened and our natural environment has been plundered and trashed, far too many people have seen that our political system does not work for them and have called for change. They have suggested a myriad of reforms, most notably of:

- the senate (with some wanting to abolish it and others wanting to expand it);
- the transparency and openness of government proceedings and information;
- the transparency of lobbying and disclosure of conflicts of interest;
- voting systems and electoral laws;
- political donations;
- ministerial standards, codes of ethics, corruption prevention and investigation;
- the financial arrangements between the different levels of government;

- the war powers of the parliament (or more accurately, the lack of them); and
- the distribution of powers between the Commonwealth, the states, their parliaments and executive governments, the governor-general, the courts and the territories.

And that is all before we get to reforms people want in the Constitution itself, such as inclusion of a charter of rights and a wider role for people in participation on policy that affects them (for example, an Indigenous Voice, and a people's voice through citizens' assemblies or juries). Both the political system as we operate it now and the Constitution are grand failures in terms of meeting our minimum expectations for wellbeing and security. They have brought us to the brink of social, environmental and economic crisis. We are wealthy at the national level but not secure as individuals, families or local communities.

In the context of the success rate of our political system it therefore makes no sense to assume that the only thing we need to do is update the Constitution so that it "means what it says" and "says what it means". That approach might look like a practical option. Indeed, as Helen Irving has pointed out:

> The Constitution could say what it means and mean what it says (if we wanted it to).[82]

She goes on to explain:

> The Constitution belongs to the Australian people, but it is almost impossible to understand by the majority of people without detailed guidance. This is not inevitable. If we want a new Constitution, we can achieve it by means of referendum. We can alter parts, or we can alter the whole thing. We could change its words – to make it say what it means and mean what it says – without changing anything else about it. We could keep the same Constitution, by changing the

[82] Helen Irving, *Five Things to Know About the Australian Constitution*, Cambridge University Press, New York, 2004, page 108.

> Constitution. Indeed, if we re-wrote it, we could finally have the Constitution we really have.[83]

But why would we want to have "the Constitution we really have"? Why would we want that if it enshrines a political and governance system that hasn't been working? Doubtless there are some aspects of our governance system worth retaining because they do in fact work reasonably well if they are used well and in good faith. The system of "responsible government" for instance works well when used well:

> The principle of 'responsible government' ... is basic to our system of government and ... underlies our Constitution. Under this principle, the Crown (represented by the Governor-General) acts on the advice of its Ministers who are in turn members of, and responsible to, the Parliament. It is for this reason that section 64 of the Constitution requires Ministers to be, or become, members of Parliament.[84]

This contrasts sharply with the American system where the cabinet members are not elected to congress (they are the captain's pick – that is, they are appointed by the president) and are therefore not accountable to congress, which means they cannot be held accountable by the people at the ballot box (although they can of course be held accountable by the American courts – sometimes).

So if we compare the US system with the Australian system of responsible government there are undoubted advantages in the Australian system at least in terms of the dual regard ministers in executive governments might accept that they should have to both electors and the courts. The logic of Australia's system is that if the members of the executive government are also elected members of parliament then the executive has a higher degree of responsibility and accountability back through the parliament to the people and the

---

[83] Helen Irving, *Five Things to Know About the Australian Constitution*, Cambridge University Press, New York, 2004, page 116.

[84] See Australian Government Solicitor, *Australia's Constitution with Overview and Notes by the Australian Government Solicitor*, page v. foi-2021-017.pdf (pmc.gov.au)

people have somewhat more control over how governments administer Commonwealth institutions and services.

This is all good in theory, but it can only work if the Constitution compels the elected to use the system of responsible government well and in accordance with the public interest. Decidedly, Australia's Constitution does not do that. For a start, the oath of office that must be taken by all those elected to parliament under Section 42 of the Constitution in no way requires them to use the system of responsible government well, let alone for purposes of the public good. The "public good" or the "public interest" is not even articulated in the Constitution and the only purpose of the oath of office is to compel elected members to

> bear true allegiance to Her Majesty Queen Victoria, Her heirs and successors according to law.[85]

This doesn't even require those we elect to support the Constitution, let alone Australians. In summary, while the system of responsible government offers an advantage over the American system, it negates that by not charging elected parliamentarians with an obligation to the electors – not one single obligation.

This could of course be ameliorated, at least to some extent, by an amendment to the Constitution along the lines suggested by the Australian Republican Movement (ARM) in their "Australian Choice Model"[86] for a referendum to make Australia a republic, released in January 2022. The ARM has suggested that the current oath should be replaced with an oath requiring members of parliament and an Australian head of state to swear that:

---

[85] Commonwealth of Australia Constitution Act, 9th July 1900, section 42. The Australian Constitution – Parliament of Australia (aph.gov.au)

[86] Australian Republican Movement, The Australian Choice Model webpage, https://republic.org.au/policy

> I will be loyal to the Commonwealth of Australia and the Australian people whose Constitution and laws I shall uphold.[87]

This is a move in the right direction and if it turns out to be all that Australians are offered then it would be a positive increment of change that should not be rejected by people wishing to increase the accountability of their governors to them. But the new oath and a range of other equally worthy amendments suggested by the ARM are confined largely to:

- setting the rules and system for electing heads of state from among the Australian people;
- crimping the powers of heads of state in relation to assenting to laws; and
- narrowing the occasions when they can exercise power as a head of state without the advice of the Executive Council (Cabinet).

These are vital amendments for the Constitution of a supposedly independent nation. But even if we assented to these amendments, we would still only have a Constitution that at best superficially requires the elected to be "loyal to the Australian people" and the "Commonwealth". A generous interpretation of what the word "Commonwealth" might mean in the context of a useful constitutional oath might be the "public welfare, general good or advantage"[88] – what began in the 15th century as the "common weal" but what today we would call "wellbeing". But it is more likely to mean something other than the people and their interests, perhaps just a federation of states. As such, this sort of oath would be superficial because it would provide no guidance (specific or even non-specific) on *what the elected should be loyal to*, no terms on which power may be rightly exercised, no indication of what

---

[87] Australian Republican Movement, The Australian Choice Model: Proposed Amendments to the Australian Constitution, January 2022, page iii. CAB+Australian+Republic+Constitution.pdf (squarespace.com)

[88] Wikipedia webpage, "Commonwealth", https://en.wikipedia.org/wiki/Commonwealth, last accessed 9 August 2022.

"wellbeing" even means for us. Moreover, Australians would have no more in terms of human rights, no greater agency or utility in their own Constitution and governance than they do now, and no greater capacity and power to build the nation they want for the future.

A constitution that does not say what the people of the nation freely value and what they want their commonwealth to become is fairly useless both to electors and the elected. For the elected, were they to swear an oath to be "loyal to the Commonwealth of Australia and the Australian people whose Constitution and laws [they] shall uphold", what would it even mean? Loyal to what? Who knows? Who can say – if, after all, the people of Australia themselves have not said what is the essential purpose of their coming together in an indissoluble commonwealth, if they have not said what matters to them, and what type of society they want the elected to be loyal to?

And whose Constitution is it anyway? If it is anybody's Constitution it is the property of the current nominal sovereign, King Charles III, or perhaps his Governor-General. It may be considered the property of the people, inasmuch as they are the only ones who can amend it. But at the same time it is not their property, especially insofar as they cannot exercise their sole right to amend it without the permission of the parliament, and even then it can only be amended in terms agreeable to the parliament. It is certainly not the people's constitution, inasmuch as they are not even mentioned as having a role in it beyond casting a vote and their needs and will are not reflected in it. It is not the people's and can't be theirs until they are recognised in it as a party to be respected and accorded a fair and rightful share of power.

Likewise, the laws made under it are not "their" laws. Indeed it presumes far too much to claim that laws made by a form of state, in which all power has been given away by the people to a sovereign decider, will be laws to which the people of today would necessarily subscribe of *their* own free will. It might have been reasonable to assume that laws made with a fresh Constitution in the first decade after 1901 were the people's laws, but not now. Laws being made in the 21st century are not distinguished for instance by the rights, freedoms and liberties they grant to Australians. Since 2001, they have been distinguished by the rights, freedoms and liberties they have taken away. Nor is the government obliged in any way to the people when making laws on annual budgets, taxation, or even representation. In that regard, the elected have no obligation to provide for the wellbeing of the people. Their only obligation is to provide for the "indissoluble Federal Commonwealth under the Crown"[89] – that means the state, the queen's or king's Commonwealth, not the people's common weal. The Constitution provides strictly for a sovereign state, not a sovereign people, let alone a plural sovereignty.

In effect, the Australian Constitution is designed to *override* the people's will. Their voice is deliberately excluded. Accordingly, once those we elect attain power (as long as they attain it in accordance with the process for "representative government"[90] laid down in the Constitution), they are not constrained from making and remaking the law entirely as they see fit and those laws are usually to reinforce their power, not to share it. The Constitution really has nothing in it that constrains lawmaking to the will of the people, once they have discharged their obligation to elect someone to represent them – to speak for them and thereby to silence them, to extinguish their voice or at least to make it irrelevant to the final decision process.

That is the rub with "representative government". It is simply a mechanism to replace the will of the people with the will of the

---

[89] Preamble to the Commonwealth of Australia Constitution Act, 9th July 1900: "WHEREAS the people of New South Wales, Victoria, South Australia, Queensland, and Tasmania, humbly relying on the blessing of Almighty God, have agreed to unite in one indissoluble Federal Commonwealth under the Crown of the United Kingdom of Great Britain and Ireland, and under the Constitution hereby established: ... " https://www.aph.gov.au/constitution

[90] See Australian Government Solicitor, *Australia's Constitution with Overview and Notes by the Australian Government Solicitor*, page v. foi-2021-017.pdf (pmc.gov.au): "Another fundamental principle which underlies the Constitution is that of 'representative government' – that is, government by representatives of the people who are chosen by the people. Consistently with this principle, sections 7 and 28 of the Constitution require regular elections for the House of Representatives and the Senate, and sections 7 and 24 require members of the Commonwealth Parliament to be directly chosen by the people."

sovereign. That is its point. Its point is to create order and safety from war by replacing what Hobbes might have called a mass of competing parts (presumably incapable of anything but strife) with a single sovereign (or sovereign entity such as a parliamentary government) who shall decide without reference to or any further restriction by the people. Its point is to nail down a flimsy assumption that the voices of the people in their incessant strife will inevitably imperil them. It is to hammer into unquestioned, almost biblical, scripture that order and peace can only be attained if all the people cede all the power to a single sovereign who then will speak for all on what counts as peace and what does not.[91] It's a failure of course, since peace has never eventuated from the great modern Western states.

No Western society has yet tested whether humans are capable of something other than strife. At least, they have not established political and governance arrangements that would enable societies to experiment with systems built on an assumption that the members of a nation (and individual nations for that matter) can work together in an inclusive diversity to achieve a peaceful coexistence and thereby secure our wellbeing and future as we might prefer to express and experience it. At present all the governance arrangements in both autocratic and democratic societies are geared for the opposite purpose of excluding the voice of the people in fashioning peace and their preferred destiny. Australia's Constitution is no exception. In that context it will take a lot more than a referendum every now and then to make a Constitution that is an instrument of the state into a Constitution that is an instrument of the people.

This is not to say that incremental amendments are worthless. But we can also contemplate the possibility and advantages of an entirely new constitution. As Helen Irving has pointed out, "We can alter parts, or we can alter the whole thing." It's just that altering parts is likely to deliver less power than we the people need if we wish to build a future of wellbeing and security for all. To the extent that

---

[91] See David Runciman, *Confronting Leviathan: A history of ideas*, Profile Books, 2021, Chapter 1 – Hobbes on the State: *Leviathan* (1651).

any piecemeal changes, such as amendments to replace the governor-general with an Australian head of state, contribute to the modernisation and independence of our nation, they can be a good place to start. But if the exercise is reduced to one that will merely bring the Constitution into line with the way our state apparatus and power system works now, then we should not expect much in the way of rights, freedoms, liberties, national maturity, social capacity, or power. If in establishing Australia as a republic we are hoping to gain independence, it will be a fairly muted form of independence – one with significant limitations in terms of strengthening our democracy. It will be powerful in its symbolism and give a boost to our view of ourselves as a nation prepared to stand on its own two feet. That is worth quite a lot. But otherwise it will simply reinforce the power system almost exactly as it is now. It will simply transfer sovereignty from Westminster to Canberra.

If the object is to build a new type of sovereignty, one that is plural – the many in the one, instead of the one over the many – then we will need more than piecemeal changes which in reality are likely to have little or no effect on our capacity to secure our future wellbeing, and which will do little more than reinforce the sort of top-down, exclusive, colonial power system that appears to have now brought the world to the brink of disaster.

In short, adapting an out-of-date Constitution so that it reflects and even more deeply entrenches a proven ineffective power system is not the best starting point. It will not help a nation start again. If the exercise is to build a constitution which still doesn't enable the people to express their sovereign will, it will be a largely useless exercise for purposes of making a new start. And this will pertain regardless of whether Australia becomes a republic.

I would reiterate that this does not mean Australia should not become a republic, much less overthrow systems of representative democracy. But if we contemplate that at this moment in our history, and indeed in human history itself, a new start for the nation is vital to our survival and wellbeing, and that the moment for that new start must be sooner rather than later, then there are things that are essential to that start and the speed with which we might bring it about. In the following chapters I will cover those essentials.

Chapter 4 – Essentials for a new start as a nation

In Chapter 2 I spoke of the nation's need to step up from the merely representative system of governance we call a "democracy" and jump up to a fuller, genuine mode of democracy. But how big is that jump likely to be? What are the essential things we need to install in the Constitution and how feasible will it be to achieve that?

If the objective of all this is to give people power, to make them the source of their own sovereignty, then, granted, the required jump looks to be enormous and we might question its feasibility. Indeed, from one perspective it seems to be a reversal of everything we have assumed about effective arrangements of power for hundreds of years – comfortable arrangements to which we have subjected ourselves in the belief that they are the most likely to lead to stability, even though the weight of evidence is that they support all manner of destabilising forces and it is by no means certain that current power arrangements in modern states, including states that claim to be democratic, work effectively to control those destabilising forces. But regardless of whether the modern state is viewed as a failure or not in terms of stability, flipping it on its head or, to be more accurate, adjusting roles and relationships in it so that a parliament becomes a servant to the will of the people expressed in their voice, that is clearly a big jump, especially if you happen to be among those who might fear losing some power, or might be explicitly required to exercise it for purposes other than your own.

However, from another perspective, a people's constitution is not a big jump, either for the electors or the elected. Indeed for many of the elected it could be a relief – a release from the endless, exhausting, adversarial argument to which they subject themselves (willingly but not always enjoyably or productively) and from the often vicious pressure of lobbyists and corporate vested interests. I will expand on that later.

For the moment, though, this is the important point: if the objective is to create fairer shares of power – with the people having not just the final say as they do now on *who* ought to govern, but the *first* say on *what* those they elect shall do with that power – then that is a considerably smaller jump. Our existing democratic arrangements can quite easily accommodate that sort of alteration to the Constitution. From that perspective the task at hand is not to effect some sort of radical overthrow of the system of governance that inheres in the modern state. Instead it is to create a new type of relationship between the electors and the elected. It is to:

- create the means by which electors can issue coherent instructions and guidance to the elected and to others empowered with a statutory role under the Constitution (such as the High Court or a head of state);
- create the means of orderly expression of the people's sovereign will, and the terms of trust that will govern a new relationship of mutual obligation and respect between the electors and the elected;
- place any necessary limits on what power may be used for and what it may not; and
- give a voice – a prevailing voice – to those who at the moment are limited to and silenced by their vote.

This new relationship requires both the elected and the electors to enter into a new understanding about their respective roles in the current process. The greatest shift will be required by the elected since they will for the first time be required to admit that the electors have a role in governance of their own nation and in setting its direction, and that this role goes way beyond the mere process of voting. The elected will be required to give full, unqualified assent to the principle that they are elected to do what Australians want, not what they themselves want, or lobbyists want, or even what the majority of their particular constituency wants (if it disables policies that are in the national interest as defined by the people). That will be very tough for the elected, addicted to power and accustomed to evasion of accountability as many of them are. It will be especially difficult insofar as the elected will be required to govern for *all* Australians, not just their electorate (if they are a member of the house of representatives) or their state or territory (if they are a senator). But beyond that, a shift that admits the electors into a powerful role in their own governance will not of itself undermine or negate the power of the elected. If anything it has more potential to verify their power – because it gives the people a mechanism for checking the degree to which it has been exercised in accordance with their specific will and is therefore legitimate.

A lesser or should I say, less reluctant, shift will be required by the electors. The challenge for them will be to learn how to integrate their voices and build a coherent set of instructions for the elected. That challenge might be summarised like this: the electors will need to channel the voices they have always raised – in activism and protest, in think tanks and in universities, in unions and in the public service, in families and local community groups, in charities and churches – into a participatory integrated national planning and direction setting process. I will explain this in more detail later in Chapter 7 but in general it should be noted here that if Australians are to be able to speak coherently, they will need to build that voice in the form of a long term integrated national plan, setting out what they want to create as a nation in terms of their preferred society, environment, economy and governance. The framework for this is already available and in use in Australia and indeed has been legislated at the level of local governance in several states. It is not a difficult framework for communities to understand or use, but if electors are to have a voice they will need a process for orderly development of this voice to be enshrined in the Constitution.

The above suggested new arrangement of power does not change the location of a nominal "head of state" or the location of various types of power shared currently by the parliaments (legislative), the executive government (administrative) and the judicature (determinations in legal disputes). No big jump of that kind is required at all. The new arrangement merely changes the location of the sovereign *will*, vesting it explicitly in the people. In this arrangement it is a plural will that is sovereign, not a king's, queen's, parliament's or government's arbitrary will. So this is nothing like an attempt to shift power from one bunch of people (usually a political party) to another bunch of people. In fact it has no bearing on that at all because the democratic process in this type of constitution still requires elections and a hand-over of power from the electors to the elected. The only thing that is changing – or rather, being added in – is that terms of trust are being specified for the elected. The people are being given the means to define their will, in writing.

That might look like a big change and conceptually it is. But even so, it does not require big, impossible procedural changes. It can be achieved by inserting a small number of elements into the Constitution, two of which are not radical or new, inasmuch as they have been popularly called for in recent decades. Those two are a statement of national values and a statement of human rights. The other elements of required constitutional change relate to establishing an enshrined voice for all, a mechanism to support development of that voice (namely, the national planning and direction process I spoke of above) and mechanisms for preventing undue influence in elections, corruption in governance, abuse of power (including through discrimination), and unauthorised ceding of sovereignty in international economic and defence transactions.

The combination of those additions and alterations to the Constitution may appear to some to be an inversion of the relationship between the elected and the electors. But this is incorrect. It is more accurate to say that it will replace the current hierarchical relationship with a more productive partnership of equals, one which in itself has much more potential to create the stability that Western societies have always craved but which has never yet arisen from the arrangement of power we have relied on. More than that, though, this new arrangement, for the first time, offers Australians the possibility of unprecedented fully inclusive social cohesion and therefore a greater degree of control over their destiny. It can be structured to function as the double power I spoke of in Chapter 1:

- a negative force enabling vigilance by the people against surges of unreasonable internal and external power or corruption; and
- a positive force enabling the people to set the agenda for their future – to establish the specifics of their will.

If we can build a new constitution incorporating these things – and we can – what we will find is that for the first time Australians can define:

- what the nation stands for,
- what we will and will not go to war for,
- what we value,
- what we regard as inalienable rights,
- what we envisage as the necessary minimum capacity to design our preferred future – our willingly shared destiny,
- what paths we are prepared to take to make that preferred future a reality, and
- what paths we want to avoid.

In that regard a new constitution is going to be all about ensuring we have the power to decide *what* we want – including what we want to *become* as a nation – and the means of confirming and conveying that will to parliaments. *Who* we want to govern us will become a secondary consideration, as it should be.

For the last 230 years we – the electors and the elected – have trundled along without that kind of guidance system. We defined what we wanted to *be* in 1901, but to date we have entirely skipped the process of defining what we want to *become*. However, very few Australians paying attention to the troubles of the world and at home would be likely to assume it is safe to trundle on through the 21st century with no guidance system and not even any idea of a preferred safe destination. Any constitution worth its salt needs to give its nation a process for that, a process for moving with the times, anticipating the future, defining where we want to go, what we want to avoid and the identity we want to share, adapting to what we can't change, designing whatever change we deem vital, and leading the way to an enabling form of democracy.

This will require more than a few piecemeal amendments and a review mechanism for the Constitution, although doubtless a compulsory mechanism of regular review by the people is also necessary. At the outset, though, it will require Australians to:

- build a statement of their values as a society;
- enshrine human rights and obligations in law along with a process for conferring and protecting those rights;
- enshrine a system or process which will lift the voice of Australians to a level of coherence at which their will, particularly for the future, can be understood and actively fulfilled by the elected; and
- freshly describe some of the limits to power for those we elect and some new systems for preventing corruption of elections.

These are the essential elements of the guidance that elected parliamentarians need and that the electors need if they are to start again as a nation. The next chapters set out how each of these can be built into Australia's Constitution.

Chapter 5 – Essential No. 1: Building a statement of Australian national values

In its release of "The Australian Choice Model", the Australian Republican Movement acknowledged that more work needed to be done on the Constitution beyond installing an Australian head of state. Accordingly, they appointed a "Constitutional Advisory Body", a panel that included several of Australia's most eminent constitutional law experts to draft amendments that could demonstrate how their Australian Choice Model could be incorporated into the existing Constitution. The panel suggested the need to include a new "preamble" but stated that:

> The wording of such a preamble would be a matter of much reflection, and we did not attempt to draft one."[92]

No suggestions were made as to why a new preamble was considered necessary. Nevertheless, we might assume that something new at the front of the Constitution is required, if only because the Constitutional Convention in 1998, formed to consider whether Australia should become a republic, resulted in a Communique from the Convention to the Parliament suggesting the need for a statement of Australian values.[93] This in turn resulted in the design of a new preamble to the Constitution which was put to a

---

[92] Australian Republican Movement, The Australian Choice Model: Proposed Amendments to the Australian Constitution, January 2022, page iv. CAB+Australian+Republic+Constitution.pdf (squarespace.com)

[93] For the wording of the Communique of the 1998 Convention on the Australian Constitution see Professor Mark McKenna, "First Words: A Brief History of Public Debate on a New Preamble to the Australian Constitution 1991-99", Parliament of Australia, Research Paper 16, 1999-2000 accessible at https://www.aph.gov.au/About_Parliament/Parliamentary_Departments/Parliamentary_Library/pubs/rp/rp9900/2000RP16#The. Last accessed 30 August 2022.

referendum in 1999 alongside a question regarding becoming a republic with a president appointed by a two-thirds majority of the federal parliament.[94]

> It is a matter of history that neither question on the referendum succeeded. In the majority, Australians rejected the preamble and the idea of becoming the proposed type of republic.

In the case of the new preamble, the failure stemmed largely from the fact that the process for its development was simply too exclusive to succeed. Had the preamble been developed by genuine consultation consistent with the intentions of the Communique, this may have resulted in our first statement of agreed national values. As it happened though, the requested preamble was effectively hijacked in several ways. In the end it was devised by a single person, the then Prime Minister John Howard. This version discarded significant aspects of the intention of the Convention as expressed in its Communique.

However, if we accept the proposition that a statement of values should be included as an overarching preamble providing a new context for the Constitution – a context which is about what Australians and the Australian nation stand for in constituting themselves as a federation, not what Britain stood for in 1901 – then what values should we espouse as a 21st century nation? If we were starting from scratch, with a clean slate, what national character would we desire? Could we agree on this?

In essence I would contend that we can. And to say that we cannot is to deny that people can coalesce around principles of any sort, when obviously they can and do if they are given the opportunity. Indeed in 1998 at the Constitutional Convention the delegates begged to be given the chance. On the first day of the Convention the then Chairman of the Australian Republican Movement, Malcolm Turnbull, put the following proposal:

---

[94] Australian Electoral Commission, 1999 Referendum. https://www.aec.gov.au/elections/referendums/1999_referendum_reports_statistics/1999.htm

> We believe that the preamble should be amended. If it is to remain a statement of history, then it should pay appropriate regard and respect to Aboriginal history ... The preamble should also affirm our commitment to those core political values which define our nation.[95]

After initially being surprised by this proposal, the delegates responded with alacrity to the possibility of being able to describe the values of the nation. As the University of Sydney's Professor Mark McKenna, a consultant to the Australian Parliament for the Convention, documented in 2000:

> In the days that followed, this [Mr Turnbull's] sentiment received almost unanimous support, while debate surrounding the preamble attracted some of the most inspiring and unusual speeches of the Convention. For many delegates, the preamble had become an essential and defining element of the future republic. Delegates in favour of writing a new preamble employed language which, only a decade earlier, would have been applied rarely to the Australian Constitution. A list of phrases used by Convention delegates as metaphors for the preamble proves revealing:
>
> - 'a new beginning'
> - 'a euphonic useful and uniting statement of fact'
> - 'a moral imperative'
> - 'a moral charter'
> - 'a mission statement'
> - 'a vision statement'
> - something to 'tell us who we are'
> - something to 'believe in'
> - a document to 'reinvigorate the national narrative'
> - 'the things we hold dear'

---

95 Professor Mark McKenna, "First Words: A Brief History of Public Debate on a New Preamble to the Australian Constitution 1991-99", Parliament of Australia, Research Paper 16, 1999-2000 accessible at https://www.aph.gov.au/About_Parliament/Parliamentary_Departments/Parliamentary_Library/pubs/rp/rp9900/2000RP16#The. Last accessed 30 August 2022.

- 'a welcome mat', and
- 'the lymph gland'.

> This catalogue of sometimes clumsy poetic images also included words such as 'truth', 'meaning', 'origins', 'values', 'aspirations', 'hopes', 'ownership', 'inclusion', 'heritage', 'spirituality', 'desires', 'feelings', 'justice', 'equality', 'cohesion' and 'settlement'. For the first time, Australians were imagining their constitution as a civic creed.
>
> Much was being asked of a preamble at the Convention. Some wanted a creation myth, some a myth of nationhood. Others wanted a statement of historical truths or a democratic covenant, some kind of antidote to the breakdown of traditional systems of belief and traditional institutions, an alternative to 'crass materialism', a document in which the people would 'belong'. Unlike the flawed and grimy world of day-to-day partisan politics, many delegates hoped that a new preamble would be a means of lifting politics above cynicism and corruption. It should be something to revere – a tablet of stone to cherish. At times, it seemed as if the Convention was witnessing a profound change in the republic debate – a shift from pragmatism to poetry. Although many delegates who spoke in favour of a new preamble believed the preamble should be justiciable, they mentioned this rarely, preferring instead to couch their arguments in emotive language.[96]

What is encouraging about the 1998 Constitutional Convention is that when given the opportunity, the delegates to that Convention, who came from a wide array of backgrounds and opinions, political and non-political, were excited by the exercise of imagining what Australia can become and rallied to the concept of expressing values for our society in evocative language. They came together on this *and in just two days*. And many of them even thought a preamble of national values should be justiciable – in other words it should be used to determine whether laws which undermine those values are

---

[96] Professor Mark McKenna, Ibid.

unconstitutional. If elites from such different partisan and ideological backgrounds (as the delegates were) can coalesce so quickly on this – as though there is a ready acceptance of the existence (somewhere) of a common instinctual set of values that we must define in order to create the possibility of a nation – then there is no reason why the Australian people could not articulate their preferred national character. In any case, it is plainly unhealthy, indeed downright dangerous to blunder on with a Constitution which mentions nothing in regard to what binds us together as a nation – what we commonly stand for or agree is good. On that basis, the following sections canvass the history of how the debate about Australian values has been framed at various levels in the 21st century by various governments and various pieces of research on the values of the nation compared to the values of individual Australians. This is an essential input to any forthcoming debate about what values might and/or should be included in a People's Constitution – one capable of coherently expressing the aspirations of such a diverse nation.

How have Australian values been defined over time?

Hitherto, Australians have not been good at sitting down together to define what we truly value. In the absence of an inclusive consultation process for this purpose we have instead tended to let governments frame those values for us. For its part the conservative government of the 2013-2022 period responded by developing a statement of our values, but mainly for the purpose of describing its version of them to visa applicants. This version was set out by the Australian Government's Department of Home Affairs in "Life in Australia: Australian Values and Principles"[97] in 2020 (although these values were in development by the Department before 2018). Accordingly, anyone seeking an Australian visa (temporary or permanent) is required to sign the Department of Home Affairs' "Australian Values Statement" as follows:

---

[97] Australian Government, Department of Home Affairs, Life in Australia: Australian values and principles, 2020. Life in Australia - English (homeaffairs.gov.au)

I understand that Australian society values:

- respect for the freedom and dignity of the individual;
- freedom of religion (including the freedom not to follow a particular religion), freedom of speech, and freedom of association;
- commitment to the rule of law, which means that all people are subject to the law and should obey it;
- parliamentary democracy whereby our laws are determined by parliaments elected by the people, those laws being paramount and overriding any other inconsistent religious or secular 'laws';
- equality of opportunity for all people, regardless of their gender, sexual orientation, age, disability, race, or national or ethnic origin;
- a 'fair go' for all that embraces:
    - mutual respect;
    - tolerance;
    - compassion for those in need;
    - equality of opportunity for all;
- the English language as the national language, and as an important unifying element of Australian society.

I undertake to conduct myself in accordance with these values of Australian society during my stay in Australia and to obey the laws of Australia.[98]

Despite the apparent importance of these values, the Australian government has never sought to check that these are the values we actually hold. Based on research in such programs as the Australian National University's "Australian Values Study 2018",[99] it is very likely that as a majority we do highly value some of these things,

---

[98] Australian Government, Department of Home Affairs, Life in Australia: Australian values and principles, 2020, page 5, Ibid.

[99] Australian National University, Social Research Centre, Australian Values Study: Australia's Voice in the World Values Survey, 2018, https://www.srcentre.com.au/ausvalues

particularly parliamentary democracy[100] and freedom of religion (as distinct from religion itself, which in the majority we no longer hold in high value,[101] particularly in our daily lives). Other studies suggest we hold some of the other values listed by Home Affairs and some other quite different values. The University of Western Australia (UWA), for instance, ran a study in 2018[102] called "The Values Project" to ascertain whether Australians hold the values espoused on their behalf by Home Affairs. In a survey of 7,000 Australians they found that we most highly value:

- "benevolence" – expressed as the welfare of people who are close to us;
- "security" – expressed as the safety and stability of society, relationships and self, as well as national security; and

---

[100] The Lowy Poll shows consistent support among Australians for democracy as the preferable form of government. Natasha Kassam, Lowy Institute Poll 2021, page 20. lowyinsitutepoll-2021.pdf (lowyinstitute.org)

[101] Australian National University, Social Research Centre, Australian Values Study: Australia's Voice in the World Values Survey: "The percentage of Australians who consider God 'not at all important' in their life is increasing. In the 1981 World Values Survey, 14 per cent placed themselves in this category, compared to 35 per cent in 2018. At the opposite end of the scale, the percentage replying that God is 'very important' in their life has declined from 25 per cent to 17 per cent between 1981 and 2018 (after increasing slightly in 2005). Similarly, more Australians are describing themselves as atheists, and fewer are describing themselves as religious. In 1981, only five per cent of Australians identified as atheist, compared with 20 per cent in 2018. The number of 'religious people' has fallen from 57 per cent of the population to 37 over that same period." Australian Values Survey 2018 - web.pdf (srcentre.com.au). Census data show a significant, continuous decline in the importance of religion, especially Christianity, to Australians since 1966. In the 2021 Census the number of Australians identifying as non-Christian or no religion outnumbered Christians for the first time. On current trends it is very likely that in the 2026 Census, Australians identifying as having no religion will fully outnumber both Christians and other religions. Australian Bureau of Statistics, Census 2021, Cultural Diversity, https://www.abs.gov.au/statistics/people/people-and-communities/cultural-diversity-census/2021

[102] University of Western Australia, What do we value? – How our values influence everyday behaviours, Centre for Human and Cultural Values, 2019. Values-Report-Final-2019-SM.pdf (whatdowevalue.com.au)

- "societal universalism" – expressed as understanding, appreciation, tolerance and protection for the welfare of all people, including strangers and those we don't know.[103]

According to the researchers, "People who value universalism (societal) attach great importance to equality, social justice, tolerance, wisdom and peace in the world."[104] These results paint a picture of Australians as compassionate, fair, socially oriented (as opposed to individually self-centred) and concerned for the welfare of all. In particular, they show we value peace in the world. For Australians, it seems that harmonious relationships (in the family, nationally and internationally), and the personal safety such relationships make possible, matter more than straight down the line individualism, sectarianism, isolationism, and assertion of nationalist virtue or supremacy.

This paints a picture of Australians as a more inclusive nation than Home Affairs has implied. Peace inside or outside Australia doesn't rate a mention at Home Affairs. Nor does harmony of relationships and common welfare. In other words social cohesion and inclusion, wellbeing, and responsible international citizenry are not front and centre for Home Affairs. Their version of the "fair go" does not include fair outcomes or fair sharing of benefits. On the contrary, it is geared more to embed growth in inequality and social stratification. This is evident in its heavily biased assertion that, "What someone achieves in life should be a result of their hard work and talents."[105] – an assertion which entirely fails to mention the contribution that societies – those organised to work together – make to an individual's capacity to "achieve in life". Indeed, insofar as the

---

[103] University of Western Australia, The Values Project webpage, 2018 https://www.thevaluesproject.com/blog/what-are-australian-values/, last accessed 10 August 2022.

[104] University of Western Australia, The Values Project webpage, 2018 https://www.thevaluesproject.com/blog/what-are-australian-values/, last accessed 10 August 2022.

[105] Australian Government, Department of Home Affairs, Life in Australia: Australian values and principles, 2020, page 7. Life in Australia - English (homeaffairs.gov.au)

Home Affairs statement starts with the "freedom and dignity of the individual" and finishes without mentioning a word like "society" (or "the environment" for that matter), it might as well have been written for Margaret Thatcher's England ("There is no such thing as society."[106]) of the 1980s rather than today's Australia.

By the same token, Home Affairs' preferred value of "commitment to the rule of law" is not ranked highly at all by the respondents in the University of Western Australia study. Only 1% of Australians reported that they regarded "conformity", defined as "adherence to rules, laws and obligations", to be their most important value.[107] And "equality of opportunity" rates no mention in the UWA study, although "equality" itself does. There is a clear difference in the values espoused on our behalf by Home Affairs and the descriptions of values respondents have offered to the UWA when it comes to equality. Home Affairs confines comment on equality to "equality of opportunity" and the "fair go" and doubtless Australians highly value those things.[108] But they are fundamentally different values to the actual equality of "all people, regardless of their gender, sexual orientation, age, disability, race, or national or ethnic origin". They are also quite different to the value of fairness in justice and equality before the law. In the Home Affairs statement, the "fair go" is an economic consideration, not a matter of social justice or fairness in the legal system.

---

[106] Margaret Thatcher: "And who is society? There is no such thing! There are individual men and women and there are families and no government can do anything except through people and people look to themselves first." https://www.keepinspiring.me/margaret-thatcher-quotes/

[107] University of Western Australia, What do we value? – How our values influence everyday behaviours, Centre for Human and Cultural Values, 2019, page 40. Values-Report-Final-2019-SM.pdf (whatdowevalue.com.au). However, it is interesting to compare this to a study by Next25 done in the first year of Covid-19 which reported that 76% of Australians thought "Honouring, respecting, and maintaining the rule of law" was important. Next 25 Navigator Social Research Report 2021 page 14. Next25_Navigator_2021_Report_Version1.1.pdf

[108] See Havas Labs Australia and YouGov, "Australian National Values in 2022". This study demonstrates that equal opportunity for all is rated as the most strongly held value by Australians in 2022. https://hosthavas.com/australian-national-values. Apply direct to Havas Labs if this URL fails.

It's very subtle, but the Home Affairs value statement promotes an impression of Australians as more focussed on individual achievement and getting ahead than they are on collective effort, societal cooperation, communal wellbeing (wellbeing for all, regardless of differences in income, wealth, class, individuality, identity, culture or disability) and shared prosperity. The UWA study refutes this, reporting that among the things that matter *least* to Australians are the goals of:

- attaining social status, and control or dominance over people and resources;
- personal success and demonstrating one's competence according to social standards; and
- showing respect, commitment and acceptance of the customs and ideas of traditional culture or religion.[109]

Quite apparently, we are an increasingly irreligious nation and irreverent of authority in general. Irreverence for pomposity and the "tall poppy" has long been ingrained in the "larrikin" element of the Australian character and since the 1960s has been accompanied by a solid trend towards secularity. It would seem that more Australians are determining their moral codes in a secular and humanistic framework and not with exclusive reference to religious beliefs. And based on the results of other surveys this irreverence may have been reinforced in the 21st century by perceptions of the dishonesty of politicians and their lack of integrity – a value that Australians clearly hold but which is entirely absent from Home Affairs' "Australian Values Statement".

The results of the UWA study line up closely with results of a detailed study conducted in 2003 by the Christian Research Association and NCLS (National Church Life Survey) Research. This

[109] University of Western Australian, The Values Project, 2018 https://www.thevaluesproject.com/blog/what-are-australian-values/, last accessed 10 August 2022.

study, called "Exploring What Australians Value"[110] might be considered outdated but the results on the desire for peace are very similar to the UWA study. The Christian Research Association NCLS study concluded that:

> The value most strongly affirmed by the Australian population as a whole was a world at peace.[111]

Bearing in mind the date of this report it might be assumed that the high value placed on world peace is a reflex of the commencement of Australia's involvement in the Iraq war, a highly unpopular (and to many, an immoral) decision by the Howard government. But the analysis actually relates to a 1998 study, the "Australian Community Survey" by Centre for Social Research at Edith Cowan University and NCLS, which predates the war and in fact is reflective of attitudes at the height of the period of America's rise as the perceived successful unipolar custodian of world peace and freedom after the end of the Cold War. This indicates that regardless of variations in the fractiousness of international relations and the prevalence of war, a desire for peace is constant among Australians across time. Since the end of World War II, it is probably our most consistent and enduring value. This ought not to be surprising given the very obvious close relationship between the threat of war and threat to our personal safety and survival.

Other results in the NCLS Australian Community Survey (1998) line up closely with the UWA study (2018). Although the studies are twenty years apart, the values of peace in the world, equality and social justice are at the top of both lists. And personal success, ambition, social recognition, religious and spiritual devotion, conformity, tradition, wealth and seeking power and control over others and resources are at the bottom of both lists. The highly valued things are the same in both studies, as are the least valued things.

---

[110] Philip Hughes, Sharon Bond, John Bellamy and Alan Black, The Christian Research Association and NCLS (National Church Life Survey) Research, Exploring What Australians Value, Openbook Publishing, 2003 https://cra.org.au/wp-content/uploads/2021/09/Exploring_Values-1.pdf

[111] Exploring What Australians Value, Ibid., page 11.

Neither set of results lines up with the Home Affairs version of what Australians value. Nor, apparently, do the results of a more recent privately funded study by Havas Labs, a division of the marketing firm Havas Australia Creative Group, line up as an ethos with the values espoused for Australians in the Home Affairs statement. The Havas Labs study, "Australian National Values in 2022", analysed sources from the Commonwealth Government, the Australian Bureau of Statistics, citizenship tests, media, research papers, and popular culture to compile a list of 25 "collective national values".[112] It sheds a good deal of light on the difference between the understanding Australians have of values we ostensibly hold as a nation – "what our nation is meant to value by convention"[113] – and what we personally value as individuals. It examines the ranking accorded to the 25 different values in terms of their importance to individuals and it compares this to what we assume to be the values that are stereotypically promoted as "Australian".

The study makes two very important observations about Australian values that are highly relevant if we are to attempt to create a preamble in a new Constitution that properly captures the sense of something as nebulous as "values". The first observation is that we are diverse:

> No two Aussies are the same. There really is no such thing as the average Australian.[114]

The data show that different cohorts of respondents rank values generally recognised as Australian quite differently to the way they rank the same values in terms of their personal priority. They place a greater or lesser importance on each of the 25 values depending on their stage of life (whether they have children under 18 living at home), location, gender, place of birth, income, and their generation

---

[112] Havas Labs Australia and YouGov, "Australian National Values in 2022", page 5, Op. Cit. https://hosthavas.com/australian-national-values

[113] Havas Labs Australia and YouGov, "Australian National Values in 2022", page 7, Ibid.

[114] Havas Labs Australia and YouGov, "Australian National Values in 2022", page 15, Ibid.

(older/younger). One of the more striking differences in values occurs between older and younger generations:

> Older generations conform to values in the national Australian stereotype, but these values face potential extinction with newer generations taking on a different value set. In a few short years, Australia could be seeing nationalism, tradition, and mateship receding in favour of a more intellectual, sustainable, progressive mindset which favours arts and culture.[115]

Nevertheless, we share values promoting wellbeing and in 2022 are "harking back to better times":

> An overwhelming majority of Australians lament how our values have changed in the last 5-10 years. They share fears that we're becoming more selfish, less communally-minded, and fundamentally changed as a country.[116]

Clearly, we perceive that times have been better and we connect features of this decline – inequality, poorer health, environmental degradation, economic decline – with the perceived rise of a value set held (or thought to be held) by Australia as a nation that is less human- and eco-centric than we would prefer it to be as individuals:

> Australians feel negative about how our values as a nation have changed, but we're at a turning point. As a nation of individuals, we're looking forward to a future caring for the environment and our fellow Aussies. Above all, we want to dial up the 'fair go' more than anything.[117]

In summary, the Havas study indicates that while we are diverse we are nevertheless unified in having "a new hope for a more

---

[115] Havas Labs Australia and YouGov, "Australian National Values in 2022", page 8, Ibid.

[116] Havas Labs Australia and YouGov, "Australian National Values in 2022", page 8, Ibid.

[117] Havas Labs Australia and YouGov, "Australian National Values in 2022", page 8, Ibid.

compassionate, sustainable and tolerant future with a fair go at its heart".[118]

The second important observation of the Havas Labs study is that while we differ across demographic groups on some values, we nevertheless seem to coalesce as a significant majority to differ with the stereotypical view of Australian "national" values – especially insofar as this stereotype resembles the narrow view and priority order of our values as expressed by the Department of Home Affairs. Our personal views of the relative *importance* of the 25 values studied by Havas Labs does not line up with our view of what is most important in the values ostensibly held by the nation (at least as they might be expressed by Home Affairs). The following table shows how in the Havas Labs study we rank the values we assume are typically held as "national" values, compared to how we rank those values in our personal value set:

Havas Labs & YouGov – Australian National Values in 2022	
Importance ranking for values in the national context	**Importance ranking for our values as individuals** (change in ranking compared to national values)
1. Equal opportunity	• Honesty (🡅3 places)
2. Freedom	• Freedom (no change)
3. Mateship	• Equal opportunity (🡇2 places)
4. Honesty	• Compassion (🡅3 places)
5. Security	• Work ethic (🡅2 places)
6. Rule of law	• Security (🡇1 place)
7. Work ethic	• Mateship (🡇4 places)
8. Physical health & fitness	• Physical health & fitness (no change)
9. Nationalism	• Tolerance (🡅7 places)
10. Resilience	• Rule of law (🡇4 places)
11. Compassion	• Sustainability (🡅4 places)
12. Connection to the land	• Resilience (🡇2 places)
13. Benevolence	• Responsibility for others (🡅1 place)
14. Responsibility for others	• Egalitarianism (🡅3 places)

[118] Havas Labs Australia and YouGov, "Australian National Values in 2022", page 8, Ibid.

Havas Labs & YouGov – Australian National Values in 2022	
Importance ranking for values in the national context	**Importance ranking for our values as individuals** (change in ranking compared to national values)
15. Sustainability	• Connection to the land (⬇3 places)
16. Tolerance	• Benevolence (⬇3 places)
17. Egalitarianism	• Tradition (⬆1 place)
18. Tradition	• Nationalism (⬇9 places)
19. Innovation	• Progressiveness (⬆1 place)
20. Progressiveness	• Creativity (⬆4 places)
21. Achievement	• Intellectualism (⬆4 places)
22. Art & culture	• Innovation (⬇3 places)
23. Entrepreneurship	• Achievement (⬇2 places)
24. Creativity	• Art & culture (⬇2 places)
25. Intellectualism	• Entrepreneurship (⬇2 places)

From this comparison it is clear that what we perceive as important in national values is *relatively* unimportant to us as individuals; and vice-versa – what is important to us personally is *relatively* unimportant to the nation, or at least we think it has become so. We value compassion and tolerance much more highly than we think the nation does. We also more highly value sustainability, creativity, intellectualism, honesty and egalitarianism. And vice versa, we value nationalism a lot less than we think the nation does. We also place significantly lower value on the rule of law and mateship. The only things we value to the same extent as the nation – that is in the same order of relative importance – are freedom and physical health and fitness. The following graph puts the above results into a picture to show how we have come to perceive a divergence between our personal values and assumed national values:

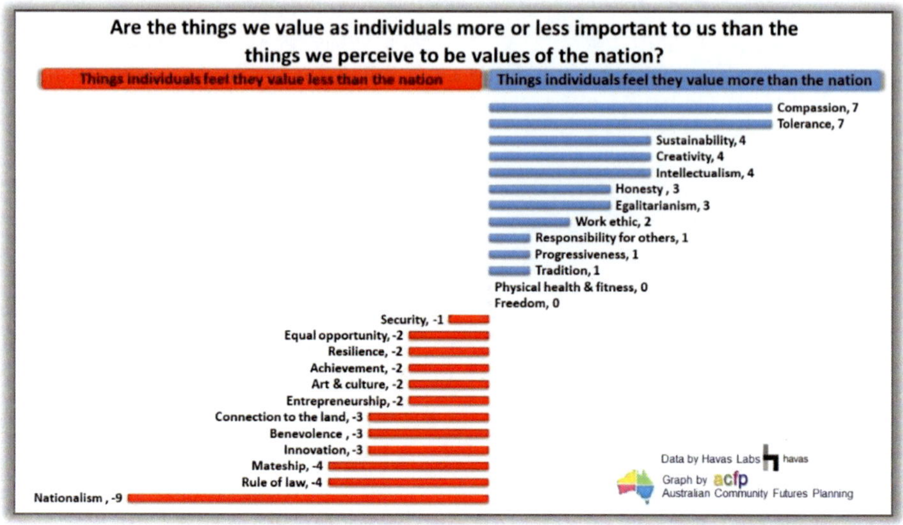

This is not to say that Australians don't value nationalism, the rule of law and mateship. They do, but their priority has fallen while other things have surged forward in our consciousness of their importance. If any readers happen to have felt at some stage in the decade to 2022 that they have woken up in another country – one in which they feel they no longer belong – this might explain why. It is because we believe the stereotypical national Australian values, (particularly nationalism – with all its overtones of racial superiority and detriment to the interests of other nations) are no longer our own most highly cherished values as individuals. If all these studies are sound (and there is no reason to deem them unsound), then in terms of what apparently matters most to *us* (social cohesion, wellbeing, and peaceful coexistence in domestic and international relationships), we have diverged from what seems to matter most to the nation. Or rather, we have diverged from what we have been *told* matters most to the nation by a fearful, conservative, unimaginative, uncooperative and increasingly pugnacious government (the one that created the Department of Home Affairs).

As Havas Labs sees it:

> We're lovers not fighters. While rule of law, nationalism, and security are key to our national values, they drop in importance for individuals when thinking about the values

> that are important to them as people. Instead, compassion and tolerance are held in high esteem by individuals, contrary to not being a part of our national value set.[119]

Inasmuch as research organisations are now drawing conclusions along lines that suggest the people of Australia want to become something more than the stereotype of the "Aussie" character that prevailed in the 20th century (one based predominantly on mateship, the fair go, and freedom), it is apparent that the Home Affairs "Australian Values Statement" is actively attempting to drag us in a jingoistic direction, which is contrary to our 21st century stated preference. The Home Affairs Statement promotes Australian values as narrow, insular and homogenous, as though stability arises from uniform conformance to rules even while professing that we are "free" (to be non-conformist). But the evidence is that Australians do not characterise themselves in such narrow terms. This is evident when we examine the breadth – or rather narrowness – of values promoted by Home Affairs and compare them to the far wider spectrum of values we exhibit and consider important, a comparison shown in the following table:

Values as individuals in order of stated importance (Havas Labs study)	Values covered by Home Affairs in their "Australian Values Statement"
1. Honesty	Not mentioned
2. Freedom	Mentioned
3. Equal opportunity	Mentioned
4. Compassion	Mentioned for some
5. Work ethic	Not mentioned
6. Security	Not mentioned
7. Mateship	Not mentioned
8. Physical health & fitness	Not mentioned
9. Tolerance	Mentioned
10. Rule of law	Mentioned
11. Sustainability	Not mentioned
12. Resilience	Not mentioned
13. Responsibility for others	Not mentioned

[119] Havas Labs Australia and YouGov, "Australian National Values in 2022", page 7, Ibid.

Values as individuals in order of stated importance (Havas Labs study)	Values covered by Home Affairs in their "Australian Values Statement"
14. Egalitarianism	Not mentioned
15. Connection to the land	Not mentioned
16. Benevolence	Mentioned for some
17. Tradition	Not mentioned
18. Nationalism	Not mentioned
19. Progressiveness	Not mentioned
20. Creativity	Not mentioned
21. Intellectualism	Not mentioned
22. Innovation	Not mentioned
23. Achievement	Not mentioned
24. Art & culture	Not mentioned
25. Entrepreneurship	Not mentioned

In this analysis only five of the top ten values for individuals rate a mention by Home Affairs and of the remaining fifteen values only one rates a partial mention. And to the extent that Home Affairs mentions "compassion" and "benevolence", it is highly discriminatory as to whom it might extend this compassion and benevolence. Home Affairs is simply not on the same plane as Australians when it comes to the values listed in the Havas Labs study, or the ANU, UWA and Christian Research Association/NCLS studies for that matter. As the self-appointed framer of our national values, it is clear that Home Affairs could not care less about most of what really matters to Australians. Little wonder that cynical responses to the Home Affairs Statement filter through the internet, like the wonderfully incisive parody of "Australien Values" by Juice Media in 2021.[120]

In effect the Home Affairs Statement reduces Australians to less than they obviously want to be – much less. It is an insult to Australians particularly in terms of their benevolence and desire to ensure the wellbeing of all. In part this reduction of the Australian character to meanness and insularity arises from the fact that the

[120] Juice Media "Australien Values", YouTube, 25 March 2021. Honest Government Ad | Australien Values - YouTube

Home Affairs statement is designed with immigrants as the target audience. Its purpose is to make it clear to immigrants that they will be expected to behave in accordance with rules which may well not apply in their country of origin (especially if it is a religiously intolerant, autocratic, non-English speaking country with a heavily stratified class system or one that discriminates against women). It is designed with the chief purpose of "maintaining an orderly, free and safe society" during influxes of immigration. This is of course reasonable. But otherwise it says little more to visa applicants than that if they want to stay in Australia and ensure their visa (or even their citizenship) is not revoked, they must conform to the "rule of law" and not make a loud fuss when someone (especially an elected government) says something they disagree with or a law is made which discriminates against them.[121] In other words, applicants must not engage in civil disobedience or protest, because laws are in fact now quite restrictive in terms of rights to free speech and activism. In the early 2020s, when the Australian government invites immigrants to become citizens, it is not offering as much in the way of freedom as it did in the late 20th century. And it says nothing whatsoever about the values that should be taken as a guide to immigrants on how, through their diversity, they can make the best contribution to the nation as a whole.

Indeed as far as freedom and diversity are concerned, people applying for Australian citizenship would be under no illusion that they are being asked to pass through a door that will close quite tightly behind them for good – a door which attempts to lock them away from their ancestry (and possibly close living relatives), culture, beliefs and values, or at least to lock them away from as much of those values as may not align with the narrow array of values of a white Australia. It is particularly focussed on locking them away from profession or demonstration of those values. This is evident in the preference of the Home Affairs Statement for the English language as "an important unifying element of the Australian society".

[121] For example, a law which allows a Home Affairs Minister to remove them from the community and detain them and their children indefinitely in immigration facilities (jails) when no crime has been committed.

A language of course has unifying power. But an implicit refusal to accommodate diverse languages is unlikely to be conducive to "unity" in a multicultural nation, especially when in census results (in 2021) 27.6% of Australians report being born overseas and 48.2% report having a parent born overseas.[122] In 2021, almost half of the Australian population was a first or second generation migrant and over 5.6 million people spoke a language other than English at home. "850,000 (852,706) of this group reported that they do not speak English well or at all."[123] Nor is a refusal to encourage immigrants to value their first language *alongside* English likely to be conducive to ensuring that diversity can be capitalised on as the strength that it is. And if policies of education funding simultaneously act as a discouragement to Australians to learn another language, this will compound the incapacity of the nation to capitalise on diversity while adding nothing to a project of "unity".

Insisting that applicants for citizenship will sign a statement that says

> I undertake to make reasonable efforts to learn the English language, if it is not my native language,[124]

is probably an efficient means of getting new citizens to get a job and conform to the approved social norms and laws. But given the sheer volume of immigration to Australia, it is not likely that a program of disregard for multilingual origins is likely to be the quickest way to get Australians to "unite". It might function well, albeit very slowly, if the intention is to create a homogenous kind of unity for Australian society but, oddly enough, this is not Home Affairs' stated intention. On the contrary, their intention is that:

---

[122] Australian Bureau of Statistics, "2021 Census: Nearly half of Australians have a parent born overseas", media release, 28 June 2022. 2021 Census: Nearly half of Australians have a parent born overseas | Australian Bureau of Statistics (abs.gov.au)

[123] Australian Bureau of Statistics, "2021 Census: Nearly half of Australians have a parent born overseas", media release, 28 June 2022, Ibid.

[124] Australian Government, Department of Home Affairs, Life in Australia: Australian values and principles, 2020, page 5, Op. Cit.

> Within the framework of Australia's laws, all Australians are able to express their culture and beliefs and to participate freely in Australia's national life.[125]

If that is indeed the objective then Home Affairs has picked the wrong language strategy to achieve it. It is actually very difficult to maintain a culture, let alone express it, if you do not also maintain the language that underpins it. Just ask Australia's Indigenous nations who have lost connection to their culture through loss of their languages. And a failure to actively support a multilingual basis to a significantly multicultural society like Australia's would not be conducive to what the Howard government, for instance, regarded as the key to "national unity".

In 2003, the Howard government released a policy statement on multiculturalism, framed in the context of security concerns about the threat of terrorism that arose after the September 11 attacks on America in 2001. It was titled "Multicultural Australia: United in Diversity"[126] and it sought (initially) to promote values of "diversity, understanding and tolerance in all areas of endeavour". But because it was informed by security concerns, this statement changed the way multiculturalism – or more specifically, *diversity* – was being characterised and valued. Diversity was still at least superficially viewed as a strength, but overtones were introduced which newly marked it out as a threat, particularly to "community harmony".[127] "Diversity management"[128] was introduced as a new concept within an essential program to ensure diversity continued to be "productive" for businesses and the economy. This effectively subjugated the objective of "community harmony" to the objectives of business owners and capital. Harmony was no longer so much an

---

[125] Australian Government, Department of Home Affairs, Life in Australia: Australian values and principles, 2020, page 8, Ibid.

[126] Commonwealth of Australia, "Multicultural Australia: United in Diversity", 2003. cover.cdr (multiculturalaustralia.edu.au)

[127] Commonwealth of Australia, "Multicultural Australia: United in Diversity", 2003, page 7, Ibid.

[128] Commonwealth of Australia, "Multicultural Australia: United in Diversity", 2003, page 9, Ibid.

objective in its own right – something polyphonic to be enjoyed in and of itself as the ultimate source of wellbeing and security. It was viewed more as a means of production and private profit. Its value was defined in terms of the economic benefit to be derived rather than in terms of the happiness and assurance of personal safety that can only be derived from living in a harmonious community. Polyphonic harmony was supplanted by a preference for monotonal unison.

It was subtle, but the policy shift set Australians aside. They were no longer the central purpose of their own nation. Nor was community cohesion a primary value. It was relegated as a secondary concern. And outwardly, to immigrants, the new policy posture could instead be quite accurately paraphrased as: "Australia is a multicultural nation because we rely on immigration and the 'economic benefits of diversity',[129] but once you become a citizen your diversity will need to be managed (if not stamped out), lest it interfere with the central purpose of the nation – namely, economic development."

On the face of it, this policy shift would have been and still could be viewed as an essential and prudent shift in the circumstances. It could be just what nations do instinctively when the world becomes more frightening as it did in 2001. But Australians lost something. It affected their attitudes to racial differences – shifting them more towards a fear of "the other". It also created the sense that diversity must be suffered rather than enjoyed – hence the repetition of the word "tolerance" by John Howard and the deletion of the word "appreciation" in relation to races and cultures. In the context of statements by John Howard such as,

> We will decide who comes to this country and the circumstances in which they come,[130]

---

[129] Commonwealth of Australia, "Multicultural Australia: United in Diversity", 2003, page 3, Ibid.

[130] Prime Minister John Howard, "Launch of a Stronger Tasmania Policy", released 2 November 2001. Transcript 12332 | PM Transcripts (pmc.gov.au)

the new multicultural policy could not be mistaken as promoting diversity over conformity. Instead it promoted a culturally homogenous unity, fearfully suppressive of difference.

The 2003 Howard government statement, "Multicultural Australia: United in Diversity", was misnamed. Nevertheless it served the government's purposes quite well by helping to spearhead a revision of the process for acquiring citizenship and a new process for governmental design of Australian values. In turn this led to some to-ing and fro-ing in statements about Australian values, with a new multicultural "statement" being released in 2017 under the prime ministership of Malcolm Turnbull. The new statement, called "Multicultural Australia: United, Strong, Successful",[131] dropped mention of "diversity" from the title, although some gestures towards valuing diversity were maintained in the body of the statement. However, these were reframed to give the greater "emphasis" to "our unique national identity and the importance of being an integrated and united people",[132] a twist of policy stance which favoured a homogeneity of the Australian character over heterogeneity.

Interestingly, the 2017 statement promoted a value of equality, albeit in a limited form as equality for "men and women", not for other genders, age groups or races. And it promoted the view that

> Ours is a society founded on a liberal-democratic tradition in which the fundamental rights of every individual are inviolable.[133]

However, these gestures towards equality, freedom and human rights were feeble and insincere. In the case of the "inviolable" rights of every individual, they post-dated a program of violations of human rights both in legislation and treatment of refugees. Nor did they

---

[131] Australian Government, "Multicultural Australia: United, Strong, Successful – Australia's Multicultural Statement", 2017. Multicultural Australia: Australia's multicultural statement (homeaffairs.gov.au)

[132] Australian Government, "Multicultural Australia: United, Strong, Successful – Australia's Multicultural Statement", 2017, page 4, Ibid.

[133] Australian Government, "Multicultural Australia: United, Strong, Successful – Australia's Multicultural Statement", 2017, page 9, Ibid.

inspire a reversal of this legislation. Not surprisingly, these professions of government commitment to equality and human rights were short-lived and in the 2020 Home Affairs "Australian Values Statement" they are conspicuous by their absence. Instead we are served up an English language policy which is unlikely to serve a society where diversity is appreciated, other than as a means of production. And even there, it is just as likely to be counterproductive since it will limit the capacity of immigrants to bring the full benefits of their diversity to bear on decisions about how they can make the best contribution to both society and the economy.

In the decades since Howard's "United in Diversity" statement, the national failure to support a multilingual society has created more leverage points for disunity than harmony. This is evident in the annual results of the Scanlon/Monash Index of Social Cohesion which show a solid trend of decline in cohesion since the establishment of the Index in 2007.[134] Nor has the failure to adequately support a multilingual society done much to ensure that businesses can capitalise on diversity. In the 2020s, narrow linguistic capacity not only marginalises large numbers of immigrants and Indigenous Australians but cuts successive generations of both migrants and non-migrants off from understanding the subtle differences between Australian culture and others. It walls Australians in rather than letting them roam free to explore the diversity of other nations' (particularly Asian nations') approaches to life, liberty and the pursuit of happiness. And to the extent that it suppresses Indigenous languages it is a particularly inhumane severance of their connection with ancestors. When compounded with the loss of their lands,

---

[134] The Scanlon Monash Index of Social Cohesion has aggregated responses to 18 questions in surveys of Australians since 2007. It "measures attitudes within the five domains which conceptualise social cohesion: belonging, worth, social justice, political participation and acceptance of diversity". The aggregate results show Australia's social cohesion has declined as an average of the five domains from a starting point of 100 in 2007 to 88 in 2021. The Index rose above 100 only once in the period, in 2009. Thereafter, the trend in cohesion was one of decline. https://scanloninstitute.org.au/mapping-social-cohesion-2021/ Last accessed 20 August 2022.

preferment of the English language is nothing more than an attempt to kill Indigenous cultures stone dead.

Over the decade to 2020, diversity was slowly squeezed out of multicultural statements with the result that the Home Affairs "Australian Values Statement" is not a friendly welcome mat. It is as unfriendly as the Border Force Guards and Australian Federal Police who brandish guns in airports and has as little capacity to create social cohesion as might be expected in a country where it represents the first image of Australians that migrants get. We might hope that migrants will eventually be able to tell the difference between what the government *says* Australians value and what they really value. But otherwise our official welcome says little more than that our professed tolerance is quite strictly limited – more limited than should be expected in an ostensibly "free" country – and that our compassion and benevolence are even more limited than our tolerance. It says nothing about the wider character of the nation particularly insofar as Australians value honesty, ethical behaviour, integrity, and are highly appreciative of diversity – a trait clearly exhibited in decades of strong support for multiculturalism.

According to the Scanlon Foundation, an organisation that has independently surveyed social cohesion annually for more than a decade in Australia, between 2013 and 2021 an average of 83% of Australians agreed or strongly agreed with the statement that "multiculturalism has been good for Australia".[135] However, that sense of appreciation of multiculturalism has declined somewhat, a decline that can be attributed almost entirely to the changes in government attitudes to diversity that I have discussed above. Between 2007 and 2017 Australians indicating a sense of rejection and reporting experience of discrimination "because of [their] skin

---

[135] Andrew Markus, The Scanlon Foundation, "Mapping Social Cohesion 2021" and "Mapping Social Cohesion 2020". SC2020 Report Final.pdf (scanloninstitute.org.au). Data on this question in these reports is in line with data in the Australian Bureau of Statistics' "General Social Survey 2020" which reported that 85.4% of Australians "agree that it is a good thing for society to be comprised of different cultures". General Social Survey: Summary Results, Australia, 2020 | Australian Bureau of Statistics (abs.gov.au)

colour, ethnic origin or religion" more than doubled, from 9% to a high of 20% in 2017. An average of 18% of Australians reported racial discrimination over the five years to 2021.

This is coincident with the rise of the Home Affairs Department and propagation of a discourse that promotes social exclusion more than inclusion. It is a discourse that professes "tolerance" but in reality, barely tolerates difference and freedom. It is also a discourse which dangles the "fair go" in front of visa applicants but does not actually offer it. Nor does it suggest how the fair go might be obtained, nor the cruelty with which it is often denied to "those in need" – just consider, for example, the Robodebt scandal[136] and the discriminatory imposition of the Cashless Welfare Card[137] on remote, predominantly Indigenous communities.[138] To top it all off, this discourse gives no hint of how social cohesion is really preferred and achieved in Australia and as such it provides no guidance as to how immigrants may make a contribution consistent with that value. The "Australian Values Statement" is therefore little more than a divisive and quite repressive instrument. It is an instrument incapable of helping immigrants best determine how their particular cultural distinctiveness can enhance the cohesion and vitality of Australian society.

Taking all this into account it is impossible to see how the "Australian Values Statement" could function as a basis for a national value set that might suffice for a people's constitution. It simply does not speak of our values as we have spoken of them in our responses to surveys over the years. To the extent that it supports freedom and

---

[136] See Wikipedia, Robodebt Scheme webpage, https://en.wikipedia.org/wiki/Robodebt_scheme last accessed 23 August 2022.

[137] See Wikipedia, Cashless Welfare Card webpage, https://en.wikipedia.org/wiki/Cashless_Welfare_Card last accessed 23 August 2022.

[138] See Australian NGO Coalition, Australian Human Rights Scorecard for Australia's Third Universal Periodic Review, April 2020, page 4: "The Cashless Debit [Welfare] Card racially discriminates with 81% of compulsory recipients being Aboriginal and Torres Strait Islander Peoples." Australia's Human Rights Scorecard: Australia's 2020 United Nations UPR NGO Coalition Report | Human Rights Law Centre (hrlc.org.au)

democracy, the "Australian Values Statement" is indicative of a narrow band of tenuous concepts we might value, but in these respects it is ill-expressed and even grotesquely twisted. For instance, it confines democracy to "parliamentary democracy whereby our laws are determined by parliaments elected by the people, those laws being paramount and overriding any other inconsistent religious or secular 'laws'".[139] This is cover for the autocracy of elected executive governments that impose laws that suit them, not a democracy for the people whose laws are derived consistent with their will. It is cover for an elitist system in which rules and laws are often actually arbitrary, temporary and discretionary precisely because they are not made under the auspices of a constitution which sets out the ethical and social principles by which laws may be made (it simply sets out how the lawmakers shall be selected). It is cover for a system that, quite regardless of parliament, could easily (and does) replace most of the values we strongly prefer with values we do not. To the extent that it locates sovereignty in the will and fiat of an elected "government" rather than in the people's will expressed to a diverse parliament, this representation dignifying Australia's democracy as "parliamentary" is false. It misrepresents parliamentary power as though it is inherently democratic, when it is not. It implies that the people have capacity to place restrictions on what laws shall and shall not be made, when in fact they are excluded from any such power.

There is no doubt that Australians prefer democracy (however it might be characterised) to autocracy. But this does not mean they want to live in a democracy that is merely masquerading as one. Australia's democracy is skating more towards rather than away from features of autocratic rule (seen particularly in lawmaking that is heavily contrary to the public interest, driven by a state that is seemingly beholden to or even held hostage by corporations and international neoliberal financial institutions[140]). Having said that, the

---

[139] Australian Government, Department of Home Affairs, Life in Australia: Australian values and principles, 2020, page 5, Op. Cit.

[140] For multiple examples of laws made at the behest of corporations contrary to the public interest under the Coalition governments of 2013 to 2022 see

Australian system has not yet lost its impetus towards social cohesion to the extent seen in American democracy. To some extent, our system of responsible government (where the executive government must be elected) has slowed down our slide towards a complete break between representative government and democracy. This is providential in that there is still time to correct the slide.

In part, the slide can be corrected if we bring the system into line with the people's values, not those of a particular government. This will require a statement of values to be inserted into a new people's constitution as the leading expression of the will of the people. I say "leading" expression because there are other essential elements to a new constitution which will contribute to a fuller expression of the will of the people and I will discuss these in the next two chapters. For the moment it is simply necessary to say that a statement of the people's values needs to be inserted into the Constitution as the overarching expression of the people's will in terms of the character of the nation they want to build.

This values statement must provide the focal point of guidance to parliaments, executive governments and the High Court in determining whether laws made by the parliament are "constitutional" – that is to say, rightly made according to a set of principles the people have endorsed rather than arbitrarily made according to the will of the elected. In short, the values statement must be justiciable. The Australian people must be confident it will be used to hold governments accountable for acting in line with the people's sovereign will, not the government's or even the parliament's will. This is the start of how we the people can change the location of the sovereign will and thereby make self-determination possible. It is only the start but it is the essential platform for determining the legitimacy of laws – that means their

---

Australian Community Futures Planning, The State of Australia in 2020, video series, Episode 4, Part 3, Corporate Irresponsibility, You Tube, The State of Australia in 2020 - Episode 4 Part 3 - YouTube. See also Australian Democracy Network, "Confronting State Capture", February 2022, https://australiandemocracy.org.au/statecapture

legitimacy in terms of whether they truly serve the public interest and the cohesion of a diverse society.

Selecting Australian values for a people's constitution

If Australia is to insert a new preamble into a new people's constitution (or even into the current Constitution), and if that preamble is to be about national or, shall we say, socially oriented values rather than purely personal ones, what values might be selected that will actually reflect those of a 21st century Australian society?

There is a cross-over, of course, between what we value personally as individuals and what we value as a society; but if we are to build a constitution that has a national focus, the primary task will be to build a preamble which foregrounds values that are oriented somewhat more toward the social than the strictly personal and which thereby offer us the best chance to describe the nation we want to build through our new Constitution.

Building a preferred, socially oriented value set

Taking all of the above into account about "Australian values" since the end of the 20th century, and considering the differences between values expressed for us by governments and values expressed by the people of Australia, it is clear that whenever 21st century Australians have been asked about what they value in their lives and nationally, they have freely declared their preferences and have been reasonably consistent on key social orientations, particularly towards peace, communal wellbeing and safety, freedom, honesty and rejection of inequality. Obviously, governments in the decade to 2022 did not listen to those answers, otherwise they would not have developed statements of values which so pointedly diverge from what we say we value. This divergence can be seen in summary as follows:

The divergence between what Home Affairs claims Australians value and what we have reported as our values	
Home Affairs "Australian Values Statement" ***I understand that Australian society values …***	**The values of Australian society as expressed by Australians**
• respect for the freedom and dignity of the individual;	We value the individual, but not above society.
• freedom of religion (including the freedom not to follow a particular religion), freedom of speech, and freedom of association;	We value tolerance of differences in religious belief but do not highly value religion itself, and certainly not as a priority above freedom of speech and association.
• commitment to the rule of law, which means that all people are subject to the law and should obey it;	We value the rule of law but not laws made through unethical governance. We do not value bad laws – those made contrary to the public interest, those that limit human rights, or those that are discriminatory.
• parliamentary democracy whereby our laws are determined by parliaments elected by the people, those laws being paramount and overriding any other inconsistent religious or secular "laws";	We value genuine, open democracy, not sham democracy. (Confidence in the value of "parliamentary democracy" is at risk under the current Constitution because it provides no basis for trust that laws made by the parliament will be geared to service genuine democracy, the other values we hold, or the public interest.[141])
• equality of opportunity for all people, regardless of their gender,	We value equality of opportunity but also a fair distribution of benefits and the principle of equality of genders,

[141] See Australian National University, Social Research Centre, Australian Values Study: Australia's Voice in the World Values Survey, 2018: "Although Australians remain supportive of the concept of democracy and broadly satisfied with how the political system is operating, their confidence in specific political organisations continues to fall. Very few Australians express confidence in the country's political parties, and that number is declining even further. In 2018, 27 per cent of Australians report having 'no confidence at all' in political parties. No more than one per cent of Australians has expressed having 'a great deal' of confidence in parties in any of the four times the question has been asked since 1981." Australian Values Survey 2018 - web.pdf (srcentre.com.au)

The divergence between what Home Affairs claims Australians value and what we have reported as our values	
Home Affairs "Australian Values Statement" ***I understand that Australian society values …***	**The values of Australian society as expressed by Australians**
sexual orientation, age, disability, race, or national or ethnic origin;	races and generations. We are distinctly dissatisfied with the growth in inequality[142] and inequity between current and future generations.[143]
• a 'fair go' for all that embraces mutual respect, tolerance, compassion for those in need and equal opportunity for all;	We value the fair go but it must be a fair go for all, not just for some. We value compassion but for all, not just for some. We also value tolerance (but a preference for positive appreciation of diversity would serve other objectives of inclusion better and enable us to capitalise on diversity).
• the English language as the national language, and as an important unifying element of Australian society.	We value the English language but not to the exclusion of other languages (including Indigenous languages).

The above table illustrates that if governments actually asked Australians about their values – instead of simply dictating those values to them – they would as a minimum write a distinctly broader, more socially oriented and inclusive values statement, one focussed on the actual quality of life and social cohesion that Australians aspire to rather than the narrow, ideologically driven disposition to which the "values" in the left-hand column are confined. It would describe a character that is more diverse and less self-centred.

---

[142] The ABC's Australia Talks survey in 2019 reported 76% of Australians agree that the gap between rich and poor is too large. Australia Talks - Find out where you fit, and how you compare to other Australians in 2021 - ABC. Australia Talks - Find out where you fit, and how you compare to other Australians in 2021 - ABC

[143] See Next25, Next 25 Navigator Social Research Report 2021 pages 5 and 15: This study reported that "Only 34% of Australians say government is taking future generations into account" but that this value was important to 70% of Australians. https://www.next25.org.au/navigator

Home Affairs has a tin ear when it comes to listening to what Australians really value as a society and in several cases does not even touch on the things we hold most dear, such as peace, security and wellbeing. But the answers about what Australians value in their society are fully evident, if only we care to look and listen. And because Australians have been so forthcoming, we can without further ado begin to assemble a picture of those preferences by examining the results of the three main studies mentioned above by the Christian Research Association/NCLS, UWA and Havas Labs, summarised in the following table:

Where do Australians begin to cohere in their values? Important socially oriented values identified by Australians in the 21st century			
Values as a society	**Importance ranking**		
	1998-2003 Christian Research Association / NCLS	**2018 University of WA**	**2022 Havas Labs**
Peace	**Top**	**Top**	Not asked
Honesty	**Top**	Not asked	**Top**
Safety, security, stability	Mid-level	**Top**	**Top**
Equal opportunity	Not asked	**Top**	**Top**
Benevolence and compassion	**Top**	**Top**	**Top**
Wellbeing for all	Not asked	**Top**	**Top**
Social harmony and appreciation of diversity	Not asked	**Top**	Mid-level
Equality and egalitarianism	**Top**	**Top**	Mid-level
Social justice	**Top**	**Top**	Not asked
Freedom	**Top**	Mid-level	**Top**
Protecting the environment	**Top**	Mid-level	**Top**

There is a high degree of concurrence here about what Australians value most. And the values that consistently rise to the top of the prioritised lists (if Australians are asked about them) are quite obviously all socially oriented rather than personally driven. We set these above more individually focussed values such as personal success, hedonism, personal beliefs and the pursuit of power. Community is clearly valued, and there is a sense in which we recognise community cohesion – that is, togetherness – as a prerequisite for personal happiness and individual life satisfaction.

Beyond this, the results in these studies show a strong preference for a peaceful and inclusive society rather than a country focussed on war and exclusion. In the clear preference for "honesty", they also suggest a strong preference for ethics and integrity; and we might reasonably take that to mean ethics in all relationships, in governance and in corporate responsibility. In fact, if we look around at other evidence of whether there is support for ethics and integrity in our lives, governance and corporate dealings, we will see the support is there in abundance. It is especially obvious in the results of the 2022 federal election which saw independent "Teal" candidates, campaigning on the basis of integrity in governance (as well as climate change and gender equality) sweep into parliament in unprecedented numbers, displacing Liberal Party candidates who were perceived to be associated with an unethical government (as well as gender discrimination and failure on climate change). Australians would obviously be distinctly unhappy living in a country where we could not trust each other and our governments. And this is what they demonstrate when they push honesty to the top of their list of values.

The above three studies, however, did not canvass the views of Australians on some other key values. For instance, none of them asked if we value democracy. But based on the results of the Australian National University's study in 2018 and annual Lowy Institute polls (both mentioned above), we so obviously do. Nor did they ask about whether we value Australia's First Nations, a value we have clearly demonstrated in growing support for enshrinement of an Indigenous Voice in the Constitution. Nor did they ask whether we value some other things that are inherently and extremely important for purposes of nation building such as:

- universal human rights;

- a human-centred and environmentally sustainable economy;
- meaningful and fulfilling work;
- the contributions and dignity of everyone (regardless of employment status, disability and working life stage);
- expansion of the mind and human creative capacity (that is, education valued for its own sake and information access that is unobstructed);
- scientific intelligence and research capacity;
- future generations and intergenerational equity;
- resilience (meaning preparedness for crises and an ability to overcome challenges and setbacks without social breakdown or an increase in inequality);
- fairness and ethics in foreign and domestic trade and finance;
- decency, humanity, cooperation and integrity in our international citizenry;
- independence in national sovereignty; and
- the planet, its ecosystems and species diversity.

Nor were we asked one of the most important questions of all, the one central to our capacity to live a fulfilling life – one worth living: we have not been asked whether we value self-determination through a voice in our own governance.

Of course just because these three or four studies haven't asked Australians about these values does not mean we have not supplied the evidence of their importance and our understanding of their centrality to our existence. The very fact that I can raise them is indicative of their having been raised time and time again in discussions about our fears for the future and what we do not want to lose. And since they are very likely to resonate with Australians at least as very important elements of the picture of the nation we want to build and are very likely to feature positively in such a picture, they should at least be assembled as key planks of a new draft of Australian values so that we can then step back and survey the possibilities. If we assemble all these societal values the first draft would be likely to contain the following:

- peace;
- honesty, integrity and ethics in all relationships, in governance and in corporate responsibility;
- safety, security and stability;
- open democracy where laws and policies serve the public interest;
- universal human rights;
- social harmony and appreciation of diversity;
- Aboriginal and Torres Strait Islander peoples, including their culture, heritage, and wellbeing;
- reconciliation with First Nations, truth telling, treaty and recognition of the centrality of their role in both our nationhood and our survival on this continent;
- the sovereignty of First Nations, their ancestral tie to the land, and the coexistence of that sovereignty with that of all Australians;
- the right of First Nations to a Voice in the Constitution;
- equality and egalitarianism (for genders, ages, races, and those of diverse sexual orientation, disability, national and ethnic origin, cultural heritage, religious persuasion, and wealth);
- wellbeing for all (including physical, mental and societal health and happiness);
- benevolence and compassion;
- equal opportunity for all;
- social justice (meaning fair outcomes for all, fair sharing of national wealth, fair sharing of the burden and benefit of taxation, fair access to services, and equality before the law);
- freedom (particularly freedom of speech, expression, information, peaceful assembly and association, protest, choice in life path and partner, travel, belief, religion, secularity and atheism, political communication, freedom of

the press, and freedom from discrimination, unlawful or arbitrary detention, political persecution, fear and want[144]);

- expansion of the mind and human creative capacity (that is, education valued for its own sake and information access that is unobstructed);
- scientific intelligence and research capacity;
- resilience (meaning preparedness for crises and an ability to overcome challenges and setbacks without social breakdown or an increase in inequality);
- protection of the natural environment;
- the planet, its ecosystems and species diversity (for their own sake, not just for human benefit but in recognition of the essential inter-dependency of all living things);
- future generations and intergenerational equity;
- a human-centred and environmentally sustainable economy;
- meaningful and fulfilling work;
- the contributions and dignity of everyone (regardless of employment status, disability and working life stage);
- fairness and ethics in foreign and domestic trade and finance;
- decency, humanity, cooperation and integrity in our international citizenry;
- independence in national sovereignty; and
- self-determination through a voice in our own governance.

This list is a first draft and is not meant to be exclusive. And the order in which these values have been placed is not meant to be restrictive or indicative of greater or lesser importance. It is more useful to assume that each one is simply a necessary attribute of the national character (or what some would call the national identity) – a

[144] The Universal Declaration of Human Rights, adopted by the United Nations General Assembly in 1948, declared that "the advent of a world in which human beings shall enjoy freedom of speech and belief and freedom from fear and want has been proclaimed as the highest aspiration of the common people". Australia was one of the eight nations involved in drafting the Universal Declaration of Human Rights. https://www.un.org/en/about-us/universal-declaration-of-human-rights

character which is in turn the one most likely to ensure our longevity and happiness as both individuals and a community. If these values are shared and understood as essential to us (even though we may each value them in different orders of importance), if they are agreed as necessary to the overall picture of what we stand for, then they can give us a strong chance of creating and securing the particular future we prefer. In fact if we try to create a future without knowing what we stand for, chances are it would not turn out as we prefer at all.

Checking that the value set will help Australians build the society they want

Having lined these values up this way, we might imagine that a nation that succeeds in enshrining these as values we truly and freely share, but also succeeds in creating a governance system conducive to living these values, would be an amazing place to live. It would be a place full of positive hope for everyone. But just to check that this is the sort of national character – the societal value set – that will best serve our shared purpose of building the future we might really want, we could imagine this character in reverse. We could imagine what our future would look like if we *don't* select these values. This reverse imagining is always a useful exercise in helping people select preferred values because it so quickly reveals the direction in which nations will travel if they fail to commit to these values or adopt an opposite value set and character.

The following table therefore juxtaposes the probable preferred values of Australians with their antithesis. It is provided to help Australians in discussions to confirm their preferred national character – one we might coalesce around in a preamble to the first people's constitution:

Imagining a different value set – What society would we build?	
Probable preferred Australian national values. The focus is towards …	**Values in reverse. The focus would be towards …**
• Peace.	• War. • Militarism in the civil space.
• Honesty, integrity and ethics in all relationships, in governance and in corporate responsibility.	• Unethical behaviour – particularly damaging in lawmaking. • Enabling corporate theft, corruption in governance (private and public), entrenchment of the secret state and collapse of trust in parliaments, executive governments and democracy itself.
• Safety, security and stability.	• Destabilisation and exposure to risk, particularly climate and economic risk. • Exposure to political instability. • Exposure to domestic, civil and international violence.
• Open democracy where laws and policies serve the public interest.	• Secrecy and inaccessibility to vital information. • Laws which serve sectional interests.
• Universal human rights.	• Autocracy, tyranny or at the very least reduced participation in democracy. • Denial of freedoms. • Denial of human dignity. • Denial by governments of their obligation to protect human rights.
• Social harmony and appreciation of diversity.	• A restoration of white Australia and economic decline (due to a failure to capitalise fully on diversity). • Civil unrest driven by narrow and divisive ideologies.
• First Nations:	• A restoration of white Australia (including cultural and physical

Imagining a different value set – What society would we build?	
Probable preferred Australian national values. The focus is towards …	**Values in reverse. The focus would be towards …**
○ Aboriginal and Torres Strait Islander peoples, including their culture, heritage, and wellbeing; ○ reconciliation with First Nations, truth telling, treaty and recognition of the centrality of their role in both our nationhood and our survival on this continent; ○ the sovereignty of First Nations, their ancestral tie to the land, and the coexistence of that sovereignty with that of all Australians; and ○ the right of First Nations to a Voice in the Constitution.	decimation of Aboriginal and Torres Strait Islander peoples). • Continued immaturity in the national character, continued denial of the legal and ethical faults in the nation's founding. • Continued injustice for the theft of a continent and stolen generations. • Continued denial of the possibility of a coexistence of sovereignties. • A refusal of reconciliation and recognition. • A denial of the right of Indigenous Australians to a Voice in the Constitution.
• Equality and egalitarianism (for genders, ages, races, and those of diverse sexual orientation, disability, national and ethnic origin, religious persuasion, and wealth).	• A restoration of stratified authoritarianism, particularly white male dominated and religious patriarchy. • Wealth for the few, not for the many. • Rights for some, not for all.
• Wellbeing for all.	• Wellbeing for some or none.
• Benevolence and compassion.	• Cruelty.
• Equal opportunity for all.	• Discrimination. • Increasing inequality. • The fair go for some, not all.
• Social justice (meaning fair outcomes for all, fair sharing of national wealth, fair sharing of the burden and benefit of taxation, fair access to services, and equality before the law).	• Inequality in distribution of burden and benefits. • Inequality before the law. • Denial of human rights, particularly economic, social and cultural rights.
• Freedom (particularly freedom of speech, expression,	• Forbidding self-expression, access to information,

Imagining a different value set – What society would we build?	
Probable preferred Australian national values. The focus is towards ...	**Values in reverse. The focus would be towards ...**
information, peaceful assembly and association, protest, choice in life path and partner, travel, belief, religion, secularity and atheism, political communication, freedom of the press, and freedom from discrimination, unlawful or arbitrary detention, political persecution, fear and want).	association and assembly, protest, movement (travel), positive contributions to a better future, a choice on what to read, study and where to work, a choice on who we love and a choice in what we believe. • Embedding discrimination. • Unjust detention and trial in secret (as opposed to open court). • Engendering fear. • Withholding the necessities of life, including food, shelter and connection.
• Expansion of the mind and human creative capacity (that is, education valued for its own sake and information access that is unobstructed).	• Insularity, narrowness of thought, suppression of creativity, inhumanity, and susceptibility to fake news.
• Scientific intelligence and research capacity.	• Denial of facts, susceptibility to misinformation, economic contraction, shorter life expectancy, poorer health and unchecked climate change.
• Resilience (meaning preparedness for crises and an ability to overcome challenges and setbacks without social breakdown or an increase in inequality).	• Survival of the fittest. • Development of a dog-eat-dog value set. • Rejection of long term planning in favour of short term interest. • Complacency and reliance on luck.
• Protection of the natural environment.	• Unsustainable resource exploitation and attendant economic collapse. • Loss of connection to the land.
• The planet, its ecosystems and species diversity (for their own sake, not just for human benefit	• Climate disaster, potential species annihilation (including

Imagining a different value set – What society would we build?	
Probable preferred Australian national values. The focus is towards …	**Values in reverse. The focus would be towards …**
but in recognition of the essential inter-dependency of all living things).	human and civilisation extinction).
• Future generations and intergenerational equity.	• Destruction of the future of our children.
• A human-centred and environmentally sustainable economy – one that works for, rather than debases, people, and one that conserves scarce natural and human resources and maximises the efficiency of labour.	• Abdication of the responsibility to establish a sustainable economy. • Preferring an economic structure that is inherently incapable of delivering our preferred quality of life and necessary wellbeing (that is preferring a neoliberal economic strategy that has been proven to be unsustainable, has diverted wealth away from the poorest towards the rich and has unnecessarily imposed involuntary unemployment and austerity). • An economy that debases people, squanders and destroys scarce natural and human resources and minimises the efficiency of labour.
• Meaningful and fulfilling work.	• Drudgery – a life unfulfilled. • Declining productivity. • Abdication of the responsibility to ensure full employment. • Abdication of responsibility for the economic restructuring that will be required as technology and artificial intelligence replace human labour.
• The contributions and dignity of everyone (regardless of employment status, disability and working life stage).	• Devaluation of unpaid working-age contributions (such as households caring for children, the aged and the disabled).

Imagining a different value set – What society would we build?	
Probable preferred Australian national values. The focus is towards …	**Values in reverse. The focus would be towards …**
	• Devaluation of the unemployed and other welfare sector funded citizens (such as aged pensioners). Disregard of the importance of demand from this sector as a source of stimulus for a thriving and sustainable economy. • Devaluation of certain essential occupations, including nursing, aged care, childcare, cleaning and teaching.
• Fairness and ethics in foreign and domestic trade and finance.	• Global economic inequality (upon which would follow global economic decline).
• Decency, humanity, cooperation and integrity in our international citizenry.	• Mass population displacement (instead of growth in the sustainability of developing nations). • Inhumanity in treatment of refugees. • Cessation of cooperative research.
• Independence in national sovereignty.	• Dependence on unreliable alliances, conscription to the imperial aims of global powers, accession to other nations' wars, and exposure of the home front to inadequate defence. • Isolating Australia from connection with the Asian region. • Surrender of sovereignty.
• Self-determination through a voice in our own governance.	• Autocracy, denying the participation of Australians in their own democracy. • Reinstatement of autocratic governance characteristic of the Hobbesian modern state.

Imagining a different value set – What society would we build?	
Probable preferred Australian national values. The focus is towards ...	**Values in reverse. The focus would be towards ...**
	• Loss of control by the people over their future. • Driving people to despair and either self-destruction or aggression (or both).

Choices between value sets

In the 2020s Australians still have complete freedom in their choice of values. However, they have not yet been offered a decent, accessible discussion framework to help them organise their choices and form a coherent values statement. The above framework – which requires them to imagine the future that will be delivered if they choose to adopt a value that is, shall we say, unsupported by the evidence of our responses in surveys and commentary about our preferred values over recent decades – is quite easy to use. It also has the advantage of displaying that our choice of a coherent value set is really only governed by one thing: our preferred future. It is not governed by what governments may prefer (at least not yet).

Nevertheless there is one practical limitation on our choices that we should be aware of – and that is that this is an all-or-none choice. In explanation of that I will start with an observation about the probability of Australians' choosing to support the values on the left hand side of the above table versus those on the right hand side.

Were Australians to be offered a choice between the values on the left and right in the above table, it would be a surprise (indeed a big surprise given the results of the studies I have cited) if a majority of Australians were to choose the values on the right. Doubtless aspects of the values on the right would be preferred by:

- extreme nationalists,
- racists,
- multinational corporations,

- despotic and secretive regimes or individuals obsessed with control and/or neoliberal economic hegemony,
- empire builders,
- policy makers preferring war to diplomacy or aggression rather than respect for the sovereignty of other nations, and
- other intensely power hungry people fearful of other humans or nations.

Certainly anyone favouring *all* the values on the right side ought to be considered unfit for public office, inasmuch as that sort of intense, uncompromising focus is fully antipathetic to civil society and humanity per se. Save for a few characteristic values which post-date Nazi Germany (such as planetary exposure to climate change), the right hand side of the table approximates the character of Hitler.

Moreover, if we consider these two very different profiles it becomes obvious that we can't cherry pick from each side to compose a character for the nation that might reconcile different preferences. This is because each value on the left hand side depends for its effectiveness on all the other values on the left hand side. Take one out and replace it with its opposite on the right hand side and suddenly the national character will lose its cohesion and stability. The nation will take on a split personality disorder and will start operating at cross purposes to itself. It would never be safe to assume, for instance, that we could replace a value of peace with a value of war and still assume that our open democracy, freedoms and desired ethics in a truthful government would be assured. Truth is the first casualty of war, followed immediately by the loss of free speech rights and a general conscription of the public and the media to secrecy. In another example, adoption of a value favouring clampdowns on free speech would endanger expansion of our minds and our human capacity. Cherry picking from both sides of the table is clearly impracticable.

The two sides of this table are therefore mutually exclusive both in their individually aligned components and in their entirety. The choice set out in the table is an all-or-none choice. This should make the design of a new Australian values statement easier rather than harder but the fact that it is an all-or-none choice will certainly be annoying for some. It will be very annoying for those preferring values on the right hand side. Still, it is probably a choice that modern nations, pushed as they have been so close to potential extinction, will need to make – and soon. It encapsulates the choice nations must make as we attempt to ensure continuation of life on the planet. Noam Chomsky has spoken of this as an urgent choice arising from our having developed nuclear technology and technological approaches to industry to a level that is lethal for our species. He asserts that:

> A dread gap [now] obtains between our technical capacity to destroy [ourselves] and our moral capacity to control this impulse.[145]

And he further asserts that this gap can only be closed by finding a way to "use our capacities for thought in an arena of *rational discourse*". [Emphasis added.] Chomsky suggests that it might be an inherent feature of higher intelligence that the tendency towards self-annihilation through technology will triumph over a species' "moral capacity to prevent it":

> In the last few years a new concern has been added, the deterioration of the arena of rational discourse, which is all too apparent. Unless we can use our capacities for thought in an arena of rational discourse there is no hope of closing the dread gap in time to save ourselves.[146]

But in 2022 rational discourse is still an available option, as is the capacity to understand which choices are rational and which are not. A rational, life-affirming discourse is readily apparent on the left hand side of the above table. The right hand side represents the self-destructive impulse and is therefore irrational. The choice is neither complicated nor too subtle for straightforward interpretation. It is stark. In that regard the moral capacity to prevent our own

---

[145] Noam Chomsky, Speech to the American Solar Energy Society 51st annual conference, University of New Mexico, June 21, 2022, https://www.youtube.com/watch?v=ZkjJfTsXffY

[146] Noam Chomsky, Ibid.

destruction is fully accessible and in choosing the socially oriented values that they have favoured in the above-mentioned surveys and vast amounts of other commentary, Australians are demonstrating that they are actively using that moral capacity. Our apparent gravitation to human-centric values is shaping a morality that can drive us towards self-preservation rather than self-destruction.

Of course, given the noise created by those who lean towards the values on the right hand side of the table – the warmongers, climate change deniers, the corporately irresponsible, the politically craven, those who reject equality, the power-mad – it is evident that Australians in the main (especially if they are in an older generation) do not currently think that the value set they prefer as individuals is the same as the set they assume is preferred by the majority. As I have already indicated, they have a perception that the national value set has changed for the worse – or into something they personally admire less – and that they are a minority in their own land when it comes to values they wish to be able to share with other Australians in the future. They have a *perception* that

> we're becoming more selfish, less communally-minded, and fundamentally changed as a country,[147]

and in the "overwhelming majority", regardless of age differences, they feel negative about that. Where the older and younger generations differ is in determining the cause of the change. Based on the findings of the Havas Labs study, older generations, it would seem, tend to attribute the (perceived) increase in selfishness to migrants. Some older people seem to harbour a sense that they are not getting the "fair go" *because* of migrants and that disorder is on the land because the rule of law is not observed by newcomers (migrants and the young). By contrast, younger generations and newcomers (as you'd expect) do not see themselves as the problem. They see themselves as posing no challenge to the rule of law and orderly society and are instead simply choosing to solve the problems

---

[147] Havas Labs Australia and YouGov, "Australian National Values in 2022", page 8, Op. Cit.

of the future by intelligence (especially in climate science), creativity, hard work, and access to social justice.

Looking deep into the results in the above studies reveals that the pervasive *perception* that Australians have become more selfish and less communally minded has little if any basis in reality. It is simply a perception that is the inevitable product of a discourse that has been designed since 2001 to drive wedges into the society for political gain – a discourse which propagates fear of the other, a discourse which is very easy to promote when the world itself has so obviously become a much more dangerous place, a discourse which encourages us to blame each other rather than those we elect. To some extent, with older generations it has been convincing. But the evidence is that it is not finding a mark beyond that. While the majority of Australians might assume that the nation subscribes (for better or worse) to the traditional Aussie value set based more on nationalism, mateship and celebration of war heroism (and death), the evidence according to Havas Labs is that this value set is "facing potential extinction" and that:

> In a few short years, Australia could be seeing nationalism, tradition and mateship receding in favour of a more intellectual, sustainable, progressive mindset which favours arts and culture.[148]

If Havas Labs is right and Australians really do lament the rise of a value set that is "more selfish and less communally-minded" and that they are "looking forward to a future caring for the environment and our fellow Aussies … dialling up the 'fair go'"[149] – and this time for all, not just for some – then it is quite likely that Australians will converge towards the values on the left side of the table. It is highly likely they will speak and act rationally, consistent with a desire to survive and flourish, but only if they are given efficient mechanisms and processes they can use to ensure that a rational discourse – a

---

[148] Havas Labs Australia and YouGov, "Australian National Values in 2022", page 8, Ibid.

[149] Havas Labs Australia and YouGov, "Australian National Values in 2022", page 43, Ibid.

coherent, life-oriented voice – prevails over the irrational, divisive noise. Unless the Australian people are armed with this access to a rational discourse it will not be possible for a human-centred morality to emerge as their new prevailing value set – one in which the values of the nation and individuals are once more aligned, as they will absolutely need to be if we are to survive. A people's constitution needs to be designed to enshrine those mechanisms and processes. This is the only efficient means by which we can establish a well-functioning democracy.

In the final section of this chapter and in Chapter 7, I will discuss the practical means of enshrining those mechanisms and processes in Australia's Constitution. But before that, it is necessary to consider whether Australians will need to affirm values which may be essential to the future but which have not yet fully emerged into common discourse – in other words we have not been asked about them in surveys or they have not yet begun to occupy much space in news and social media. If we are to build a constitution that has sufficient capacity to help us chart a preferred course to the future and to be nationally resilient – that is, better prepared for crises and the unforeseen than we are now – then some anticipation of values that may need to be developed and included (because they are essential to ongoing resilience) is advisable.

There is no crystal ball on what these values might be but if we start with the values in the left hand side of the table we can interrogate these to see where there might be gaps we can fill in an ongoing discourse that will enable us to concur on what we value and keep the national value set in alignment with the values of people. Getting an alignment between the national and personal values is an important ingredient for resilience.

I am, of course, discarding the right hand side of the table because it is extremely unlikely that it could approximate what Australians value in the majority, either for the nation or personally. It is fundamentally irrational because it is destructive of life quality and life itself. On the left of the side, though, there are really only a few values which are not all that prominent in our rational discourse to date. They are:

- meaningful and fulfilling work;
- the contributions and dignity of everyone (regardless of employment status, disability and working life stage);
- universal human rights;
- independence in national sovereignty; and
- self-determination through a voice in our own governance.

We don't talk about these much yet in mainstream media, although acknowledgement of the need to value the contributions and dignity of everyone has been increasing due to the rise in discussion about gender equality.[150] Clampdowns on and breaches of human rights have also raised the topic of rights in the consciousness of Australians, leading to increasing discussions on the need for a bill or charter of rights – this is a topic I will explore in detail in Chapter 6. Overall though, only two of these values are likely to be central to survival and indeed to the possible realisation of all the others. Those values are:

- independence in national sovereignty; and
- self-determination through a voice in our own governance.

The next sections therefore set out the need for inclusion of those values in a rational discourse.

Values to future-proof Australia

Independence in national sovereignty

Chomsky's dire warning about the dread gap between our technical capacity to destroy ourselves and our moral capacity to control this impulse is likely to resonate with Australians in a way that will influence the shape of future values – values which may not be front and centre in our rational discourse yet, but which we will soon

---

[150] For instance, see Australia reMADE, "Creating the Best Version of Us", 2019, promotes a vision for the Australia of our dreams with nine pillars. Pillar Four is "a society where all contributions count and every job has dignity". FINAL+VISION+-+A5+-+28_6_2019+-+web.pdf (squarespace.com) Australia Remade last accessed 27 August 2022.

discover are essential if we are to navigate our way to a safe future. In particular, there is already some evidence of Australians' having begun to sense the need for independence in sovereignty and two associated values of self-sufficiency and resilience. These three values are closely related and they underpin our ability to stand on our own two feet, both in defending ourselves in case of foreign attack and in withstanding lengthy crises affecting the supply of essentials. This has been dialled up somewhat due to the coincidence of two events.

The first was the onset of the Covid-19 pandemic, an event which highlighted our current inability to sustain ourselves with sufficient essentials (like fuel, medical supplies, PPE, properly equipped hospital beds, doctors, nurses, aged care workers and vaccines), and the precariousness of our current economic structure which is reliant on the foreign owned/controlled maritime trade system for 98% of our imports and exports.[151] The Next25 "Navigator" survey of 3,000 Australians launched in the first year of the pandemic (2020) laid bare the fact that Australians had absorbed a new understanding of our exposure and vulnerability to these risks. In that survey 76% responded that it was important for Australia to be "self-sufficient and able to stand on its own two feet as a country."[152] This initial surge in a desire for self-sufficiency and an ability to "stand on our own two feet" may not have lasted long, as evidenced by the fact that in the Havas Labs study in 2022 only 42% of Australians rated resilience as an important value for the nation (albeit that this importance rating still placed resilience in the top ten national values

---

[151] Institute for Integrated Economic Research – Australia, "The Implications of the COVID-19 pandemic for Australia's Foreign Affairs, Defence and Trade" (submission to the Parliamentary Inquiry into the implications of the COVID-19 pandemic for Australia's foreign affairs, defence and trade) 2020, page 1. Department of Infrastructure, Regional Development and Cities, Submission to Senate Inquiry on the Policy, Regulatory, Taxation, Administrative and Funding Priorities for Australian Shipping, Submission No. 13, March 2019, page 5. https://www.aph.gov.au/Parliamentary_Business/Committees/Joint/Foreign_Affairs_Defence_and_Trade/FADTandglobalpandemic/Submissions

[152] Next25, Next 25 Navigator Social Research Report 2021, page 14. Next25_Navigator_2021_Report_Version1.1.pdf

in that study).[153] However, the lower importance score may simply reflect a realisation of the impracticability of cutting ourselves off from the world in terms of trade, rather than a reversal of the desire to stand on our own two feet.

On the other hand it may indicate a reversion to the complacency of trust in the American alliance, a trust and dependence which is perhaps perceived as an easier option than standing on our own two feet and which increased markedly between 2020 and 2022 as evidenced by the 2022 Lowy Institute poll. That poll registered a sudden jump in agreement that it is "likely" that "China will become a military threat to Australia in the next 20 years". Between 2009 and 2018 an average of 43% of Australians had thought it might be likely that China would become a military threat (16% thought it very likely and 27% somewhat likely).[154] But by 2022 – after some aggressive beating of the drums of war by a vocal Australian bureaucrat Mike Pezzullo, the Minister for Defence Peter Dutton,[155] and the Australian Strategic Policy Institute (which has been partly funded by US and other foreign arms dealers) – the perception that "China will become a military threat to Australia in the next 20 years" almost doubled to 75% (32% thought it very likely and 43% somewhat likely).[156] That bespeaks some very effective fearmongering about China and that has in turn obviously played a substantial part in transforming views about the necessity of our dependence on the American alliance. This may have been boosted further by the commencement of Russia's invasion of Ukraine.[157]

In the five years to 2021, an average of 75% of Australians had thought the US alliance was important for Australia's security and the importance of the alliance in the eyes of Australians had been

---

[153] Havas Labs Australia and YouGov, "Australian National Values in 2022", page 9, Op. Cit.

[154] Natasha Kassam, Lowy Institute Poll 2022, page 39. lowyinsitutepoll-2022.pdf (lowyinstitute.org)

[155] Paul Daley, "Dutton and Pezzullo talk up the beating drums of war – but it is not them who will have to fight", The Guardian, 29 April 2021.

[156] Natasha Kassam, Lowy Institute Poll 2022, page 18. Op. Cit.

[157] The Lowy Institute Poll 2022 was conducted just as Russia invaded Ukraine.

trending to decline over the decade. But in 2022 its perceived importance suddenly jumped to 87%,[158] indicating a preference for flight to the protection of the US even though the same survey showed that Australians had clearly comprehended that such a flight would be more likely to expose Australia to involvement in a war that is not in our interests:

> 77% agreed that Australia's alliance with the United States makes it more likely Australia will be drawn into a war in Asia that would not be in Australia's interests.[159]

Obviously, Australians do not find it hard to discern that a war with China – their biggest trading partner and one which happens to have nuclear capability – is highly unlikely to work out well, and that this likely adverse result will probably be made worse, not better, by siding with America. Most reason that it is better to remain neutral and do nothing to start such a war – or at least they did reason thus before persuasion was applied to convince more of them that their sovereignty and democracy will be at risk unless they are prepared to put the state on a constant war footing, fomenting the very conflict we should prefer to avoid. Perhaps Australians, in thinking through their options, have then reasoned that an increase in our subscription to the US alliance (an alliance that is intent on containment of China by organised, precipitate military brinksmanship or aggression) is the lesser of two evils. But if Australians agree that the war they are being drawn into is not in their interests, it is incumbent on governments to ask them just how far they are prepared to go with the American alliance. After all, if it involves ceding sovereignty entirely (to America), and ceding it to enter a war that we do not think is in our interest, then what is the point? Haven't we lost what we value most – sovereignty over our continent, democracy and destinies – even before a war with China starts?

What we may be witnessing here is a slow unfolding of the iterations in a debate full of such questions, questions about how Australia relates to the world while still safely navigating its way to a

[158] Natasha Kassam, Lowy Institute Poll 2022, page 19, Op. Cit.
[159] Natasha Kassam, Lowy Institute Poll 2022, page 19, Ibid.

destination of security, questions about whether we can continue to be the only nation in the world with unified sovereignty over an entire continent. I would suggest that this is exactly what we are witnessing: a nation struggling with a realisation about the continuance of our luck and a dim but discernible intimation of the fragility of our tenure over the continent, brought on first by the pandemic and then by a second alarming event in 2021.

That second event was the announcement of the AUKUS trilateral security pact which foreshadowed the possibility that Australia might (at very great expense) irretrievably lock itself into another nation's defence programs, those of course being the programs of the United States[160] to contain China – and to contain it by means not just of competition in trade or conventional military skirmishes in distant lands and seas, but by means of deployment of nuclear armaments.

AUKUS was developed in secret and foisted on the Australian people without even a gesture towards their consent. It resulted in a rush of quite justifiable fears (at least in progressive quarters) that Australia was surrendering its independence and sovereignty.[161] As one of Australia's most preeminent defence and intelligence analysts,

---

[160] It is arguable that Australia has been locked into the American alliance to some extent, ever since the establishment of Pine Gap and other joint defence facilities. In 2022, however, the lock-in was precipitously escalated with the establishment of the QUAD (Quadrilateral Security Dialogue – Australia, India, Japan and United states) and commencement of Australian involvement in offensive military programs in the South China Sea, including participation in aerial intelligence, surveillance and reconnaissance missions and operations off the coast of China dropping sonobuoys to detect Chinese submarines. These activities were promoted as part of a campaign to maintain free commercial navigation but they were essentially probing and targeting the defences of China. They were preparatory to war in a manner that would not be tolerated if China did the same thing in Australia's coastal waters. They constitute reckless provocation. See Mark J. Valencia, "Why is Australia conducting provocative intelligence flights and activities off the China coast in support of the US?", John Menadue's Pearls and Irritations, 18 August 2022.

[161] For example, Mike Scrafton "Ausmin and Aukus: It's even worse than you think. Australia is now openly a cog in America's war plans", John Menadue's Pearls and Irritations, 21 September 2021 and 10 August 2022.

Emeritus Professor Hugh White, observed at the time of the "bombshell announcement":

> Now AUKUS implies a much closer merging – if not a complete identification – of our interests with Washington's in dealing with China.[162]

Progressive campaigners for peace, such as the International Campaign to Abolish Nuclear Weapons (ICAN Australia) were not alone in condemnation of this "closer merging" or "complete identification" of interests, commenting in early 2022 that:

> The recently announced AUKUS security pact between Australia, the United Kingdom and the United States, which pledges a nuclear powered submarine fleet for Australia, is vastly out of step with a strong sense of Pacific regionalism and the long-standing commitment to a Nuclear Free Pacific. The pact also promises 'further trilateral collaboration under AUKUS to enhance joint capabilities and interoperability', including 'cyber capabilities, artificial intelligence, quantum technologies and additional undersea capabilities'. This decision results from escalating rivalry between the United States and China, in which Australia has been portrayed as the 'Deputy Sheriff' or otherwise, the '51st state of the United States of America.'[163]

AUKUS, being announced as it was without Australians being given the chance to confirm that it is in their interests, clearly signalled that a significant surrender of statehood had been negotiated – enough to rob Australians of a capacity to reject entry into another nation's wars and nationalistic campaigns.

This might explain the results of the Havas Labs study which so distinctly relegated nationalism towards the bottom of the importance scale on our personal values. It would seem Australians

---

[162] Hugh White, "Sleepwalk to War: Australia's Unthinking alliance with America", Quarterly Essay, Issue No. 86, 2022, Black Inc. Books, page 18.

[163] ICAN Australia, "Troubled Waters: Nuclear Submarines, AUKUS and the NPT", January and July 2022, page 17. Troubled-Waters-nuclear-submarines-AUKUS-NPT-July-2022-final.pdf (icanw.org.au)

reject nationalism when it morphs into jingoism and into a ceding of command over our own defence forces and decisions, especially when we are simultaneously capable of absorbing the plain truth that a US alliance of the type envisaged in AUKUS – essentially a pact for nuclear offensives – "makes it more likely Australia will be drawn into a war in Asia that would not be in Australia's interests".

In the wake of the pandemic, climate disasters and AUKUS, the Havas Labs study may indicate that Australians could be verging, albeit haltingly, towards development of a value set that they feel will be the most likely to secure the future of a nation situated geographically and economically a long way from the production centres of many of its vital supplies and yet well within the firing line in the event of a designed or accidental nuclear escalation. This is a subject for more research but available evidence suggests that Australians are instinctively and quite cleverly attempting in that context to develop what I might call an armoury of resilience or a practical capacity for independence. The Havas Labs study hints strongly at what this armoury might contain. It contains priority values which have nothing to do with relying on alliances or nationalism and everything to do with relying on each other. The results show the values we want "to dial up for the future". They are:

- equal opportunity for all,
- honesty,
- freedom,
- sustainability, and
- compassion.[164]

These have not been articulated as a call for independence per se, partly because none of the studies have asked whether we value our sovereign independence. But there is little doubt that Australia as a nation has arrived at a point where we are attempting to decide just how independent we wish to be and just how much of our independence and self-governance we might be willing to sacrifice for the protection we might get from trading it away. It is extremely

---

[164] Havas Labs Australia and YouGov, "Australian National Values in 2022", page 43, Op. Cit.

important to develop an understanding of this and refine our nation's (as opposed to the government's) position on it, particularly if, as has been foreshadowed, Australians will be asked once again whether they wish to become a republic (if the Australian Labor Party is awarded a second term of office in 2025), and particularly if they are to be asked to commit hundreds of billions of dollars to the armoury of a foreign nation. This is what AUKUS entails – a consignment of our defence capability and therefore independent command of our military forces and decisions on military campaigns to the United States.

Governments – both Labor and Liberal/National – might be ready to cede sovereignty on our behalf. Indeed, Australia's new defence minister Richard Marles indicated an intention on a visit to Washington in July 2022 to merge American and Australian interests at least in terms of defence. As Sydney University historian Professor James Curran reported, Marles:

> ushered in a new concept. Australian and US military forces would not only be interoperable but 'interchangeable'. Spelling it out, he said the two forces could then 'operate seamlessly together, at speed'. Marles is still sending the message, albeit differently from Peter Dutton, that Australia is readying for war.[165]

Curran remarked that in "rapturous if not sweaty rhetoric", Marles:

> spoke of the alliance in terms much like his predecessors did in London at the height of Empire. The relationship was not bound only by the ANZUS treaty, he said. It was a 'network of people' committed to a 'shared project' [global dominance].[166]

In this speech Marles followed through on an ethos promoted in 2016 by a former Labor Party defence minister Kim Beazley (jocularly known among the powerful as "Bomber Beazley" and at one time a board member of American weapons manufacturer Lockheed

---

[165] James Curran, "Marles' alliance rapture discards Australia's self-reliance", Financial Review, 24 July 2022.

[166] James Curran, Ibid.

Martin), suggesting that Australia was indeed "not bound only by the ANZUS treaty" but was, furthermore, interested in acting beyond its confines. As Curran noted:

> Speaking of the challenges facing the US armed forces, Beazley said that 'in the next five years the Americans are going to talk about integration'. Australia, he noted, was 'vastly more deeply engaged' with the US military than it had been during the Cold War, and the Americans would in the future want 'states prepared to do things … a show of hands of those prepared not to act necessarily in accordance with the strict terms of triggers in alliance relationships'.

This would imply that the Australia-US "alliance relationship" now defines no limits on the extent to which it may be co-opted or entirely redefined at the will of a belligerent America. We can be pressured into wars at the will of the US. Since World War II, we may have come to accept this participation in America's wars as a relatively benign state of affairs because the wars we rushed into were not in our region or were not likely to attract nuclear retaliation. However, that safe isolation from the theatre of the wars we might rush to in future at the behest of the US may no longer apply.

In considering this, James Curran opined that "the defence minister's rhetoric of 'interchangeability' with US forces goes to the heart of the debate that ought to be had in this country about policy flexibility and autonomy in the age of AUKUS." But we are not yet set up to have that debate. Space needs to be made – urgently – for it because Australians have given no indication that ceding sovereignty and independence is in their interests. The only thing they have indicated in this regard is that they have a preference to remain neutral in the event of a military conflict between China and the United States – or at least 57% indicated as such in the 2021 Lowy poll while only 41% thought we should support the United States. In the 2022 Lowy poll (after the invasion of Ukraine) only 51% indicated a preference to remain neutral and 46% thought we should support the US.[167] However, in both polls there was a generational difference on this question:

> More than half the population aged over 45 (55%) say Australia should support the United States, while only 36% of Australians aged 18–44 agree with that approach. Younger Australians are more likely to say Australia should remain neutral, with six in ten Australians aged 18–44 (60%) choosing this position. Only 43% of Australians aged 45 and over prefer neutrality.

Doubtless the preference of the over-45s for war is because they do not imagine they will be sent to fight, or that their children and grandchildren will be conscripted for the purpose, or that China will actually fight back by a nuclear strike on Australia. Or perhaps they are working on the logic that nuclear arms escalation will act as a deterrent and it will not come to war. If so, it is a doubtful bet because arms escalation will have at least as much propensity to cause a war as not. But regardless of what is behind the logic (or folly) of an increased appetite for war, the fact that it poses yet another existential threat to Australia (as if climate change wasn't enough) implies an imperative for development of resilience and for maximisation of the capacity for deciding which wars are worth fighting and which are not. If we are to determine that, we will need a conversation involving all Australians to identify our strategic interests, particularly in our region of the world. Only then can we devise a well-integrated foreign policy and defence strategy capable of protecting what is truly necessary to protect in order to maintain the standard of wellbeing we need. That absolutely necessary conversation can only be sustained if Australia maintains its independence in national sovereignty.

As yet, independence in national sovereignty is not a value enshrined in our consciousness. It's not like mateship or the fair go. It is not yet embedded in our discourse probably because we are still only dimly aware that our grip on sovereignty over this continent might be at risk, or might even be already lost in some measure to

---

[167] Natasha Kassam, Lowy Institute Poll 2022, page 20, Op. Cit.

America. But the value of independence in sovereignty is essential to a rational discourse for any people wishing to define and prepare themselves for a new era of self-determined nationhood. As such it is highly advisable to build it into a people's constitution. It underpins our capacity to realise every other value on the left hand side of the table.

Self-determination through a voice in our own governance

In the 2020s it should be self-evident that self-determination is valued not just as the rightful power of Australian citizens but as the key to a future in which we can maintain an acceptable level of wellbeing, security and cohesion as a nation. It should be evident that a voice in our own democracy means the difference between being able to build the future we want and being dragged to a future we do not. But in general discourse I would have to say that it is not evident that a noticeable majority of Australians give much thought to the need for a voice of their own in their polity – one that will enable them to determine their future themselves, either as individuals or as a nation. Australians speak about what they want for the future all the time but they also defer to a political system which assumes leaders will simply deliver it (or something like it), even though they have not coherently articulated their preferences for the sort of life they wish to be able to live. It is as though there is a step missing in the middle of our cyclical process of democratic elections – a step where we express our preferred national agenda before we take another step to choose who might be best qualified to deliver it.

The omission should be glaring. But apparently it is not. It should be obvious that if we wish to travel to a particular future we must describe that destination and build a map of the safe routes towards it. But apparently it is not. Australians engage in haphazard calls for progress but they do not call for collaborative development of well-integrated plans for progress. They do not call for establishment of a process by which they can think ahead in a collegiate, orderly framework. Despite the fact that lack of a national plan makes

Australians fully vulnerable to loss of their preferred future, they do not clamour for a change in the process of democracy that would enable them to reduce that vulnerability. They do not clamour for self-determination, as such.

This quietude might be explained by the fact that it is difficult to define what self-determination is and even more difficult to imagine how it might be achieved. How can so many diverse individuals and cultures cohere in their determination about the sort of nation they want to build and still determine their own personal future? How can they still preserve their diversity? Granted, it is a confusing notion. And this may explain, at least in part, why self-determination has not come to the fore as a value for Australians since it was first articulated in the Universal Declaration of Human Rights in 1948 as an absolutely essential right if human beings are to enjoy freedom from fear and want.[168] The failure may also have arisen from the fact that the majority of Australians have not suffered fear and want over recent decades and so have not felt the need to exercise the right of self-determination.

However, it is apparent that the majority of Australians are not feeling as secure in their wellbeing as they came to feel in the second half of the 20th century. And Indigenous Australians have *never* felt secure, which is why their voices have grown louder on the need for self-determination. In that rising chorus we might see that self-determination is not an indefinable and irrelevant abstraction for anyone living in a democracy. It can be defined simply as a voice

---

[168] The Preamble to the International Covenant on Civil and Political Rights states that: "The States Parties to the present Covenant, ... recognizing that, in accordance with the Universal Declaration of Human Rights, the ideal of free human beings enjoying civil and political freedom and freedom from fear and want can only be achieved if conditions are created whereby everyone may enjoy his civil and political rights, as well as his economic, social and cultural rights, ... agree upon the following articles: PART I Article 1 1. All peoples have the right of self-determination. By virtue of that right they freely determine their political status and freely pursue their economic, social and cultural development." International Covenant on Civil and Political Rights [1980] ATS 23 (austlii.edu.au)

within democracy, a voice to which we are all entitled and without which we will expose ourselves to a future we do not prefer.

As First Nations steam ahead on their course to a future where their children will flourish, they are trail-blazing for other Australians a course towards the sort of reformed and strengthened democracy that will be essential if we are to ensure that *all* our children will flourish. In the wisdom born of their heart-rending loss, they have concluded that the essentials for their future are Voice, Treaty and Truth[169] and this is wisdom they have offered to Australians without the slightest intimation of threat to our security or the stability of the post-colonial nation that was built at the expense of First Nations. On the contrary, as Indigenous lawyer Noel Pearson said in his Boyer Lectures for the ABC in 2022,

> The cause of [Indigenous] recognition is not a separatist cause. Far from it. It is a cause for peace and unity. It represents the desire for reconciliation and what the country's 21st prime minister, Gough Whitlam, called our people's rightful place in the nation. Let me combine Whitlam and Howard's words and suggest that recognition is about the rightful but not separate place of indigenous Australians in the Commonwealth of Australia. Indigenous Australians want *in* to the Australian Constitution. That is the point. Despite the history of discrimination and exclusion, despite everything, we want *in*, we want to be part of Australia formally and permanently.[170] [Emphasis in the original.]

In practical terms Australia's First Nations know that the first step on their path *in* to the Constitution is their Voice and that if they do not succeed in this step they will not secure their children's future. I would like to suggest that it is the same for non-Indigenous Australians. They likewise need a path *in* to the Constitution. We *all*

---

[169] Reconciliation NSW, Voice Treaty Truth, https://reconciliationnsw.org.au/voice_treaty_truth/

[170] Noel Pearson, "A Rightful But Not Separate Place", Boyer Lectures #2, ABC Australia, 11 November 2022. https://www.abc.net.au/radionational/programs/boyerlectures/a-rightful-but-not-separate-place/14099472

need a Voice in it. Furthermore, if the Indigenous Voice is to be a successful path to a better future for the children of Aborigines and Torres Strait Islanders, it will need to be enshrined in a Constitution which offers a process by which all Australians can express their will for the future. We will need a process by which we can express what a decent future means for us in all our diversity. I will explain this in more detail in the next few chapters but in short it means that the wisdom shown by First Nations in their call for a Voice, Treaty and Truth will need to be reciprocated and constitutionally supported by a synchronous call from all Australians for Values, Rights and a Voice in the Constitution. A people's constitution can offer a framework whereby *everyone who wants in* can move in and build a future where our children will flourish. That necessarily supportive mechanism starts with a statement of Australian values and I will now turn to the issue of how that may be enshrined.

Enshrining a Statement of Australian Values in The People's Constitution

A new statement of Australian values set out in a new preamble to the Constitution is not the only mechanism needed to ensure we can build a democracy that is strong enough to close Chomsky's dread gap. Nor is it all we need in constitutional reform to help us build the nation and future we want. Other essential reforms will need to be constitutionally enshrined to ensure that a coherent, life-oriented voice of the people expressed in a new values statement is not just an abstract piece of tokenism that can be forgotten as soon as it is written. Other mechanisms and processes are needed to ensure that it can function as a justiciable part of the Constitution. Justiciability of a values statement is essential, otherwise laws made under the Constitution can simply become unlinked again from the sovereign will of the people. But it must be acknowledged that it would be very difficult for the High Court to judge whether a law is consistent with that will if all they have to work with is a statement of Australian values. Some more specific things will be required to provide guidance on that will. One of those specifics is a statement of our human rights. Another is a process for deeper, more detailed expression of the national voice and for its regular revision.

Australia's First Nations have spent years designing an institution that can function as their Voice to Parliament. This is an essential reform for purposes of closing the gap in Indigenous disadvantage. But it is not a model for charting the future of the entire Australian nation. For that, we – Indigenes and non-Indigenes alike – need a constitutionally enshrined right to participate in a long term integrated planning process, a process which is accessible and useable by any Australian and enables them to come together to:

- assemble an agreed vision of the nation they want to become and the future they wish to establish for themselves and the next generations; and to
- select the paths or directions they prefer to take to make that desired future a reality.

Only rightful access to that sort of process can enable Australians to organise themselves efficiently to develop the details of their voice – their sovereign will – and provide sufficient guidance to their elected parliaments and governments as to policies and laws that may be made in accordance with that will. And only that sort of process can produce the specificity that the High Court, and the people for that matter, will need if they are to be able to ascertain whether laws made under the Constitution do not fundamentally conflict with and thereby disable the declared public interest and preferred national direction.

Until all that is enshrined in a people's constitution, until we have enshrined a process by which we may deliberate on and express our will for now and the future, Australia will not have a fully functional, strong democracy where sovereignty is clearly located in the people's will. In fact we will not have a democracy at all.

A mechanism for creating a place for the voice of the electors in the Constitution – a right of the people to express the sovereign will for now and the future that can be exercised by diverse citizens in an orderly and efficient manner – is essential to the full, proper and stable functioning of democracy and national sovereignty. It is essential to genuine self-government. It also offers the distinct advantage that the people cannot be divided against themselves as they so easily can be now. As such it is essential to peaceful progress towards a preferred and sustainable future.

Fortunately, as I have already indicated, it is relatively easy in a procedural sense to re-shape the Constitution to make space for orderly accession of the people's will to the place of sovereignty and I will elaborate on this in detail in the following chapters. However, at this point we can make a start on the draft terms of a statement of Australian values as they might be put to the Australian people in a constitutional convention or other citizens' deliberative process. Hopefully this first draft may serve as a useful point of departure or inspiration for a final form of the new preamble that many Australians – learned, political and otherwise thoughtful – have assumed we need since the last Constitutional Convention in 1998.

A draft new preamble for a people's constitution – a Statement of Australian Values

Readers should note that the following suggested starting version of a new preamble is drafted on the assumption that it is the Australian people who will, in effect, *enact* the legislation rather than the parliament. This may initially shock the elected, particularly those used to feeling entitled to the full exercise of power in a manner of their choosing and without the need to be accountable for observance of particular standards or outcomes (because none are specified in the current Constitution). At present, once elected, they are accustomed to exercising power without specified limits (other than "the law" that they can change anyway) and without particular obligations to the people. Rather than obliging governments to exhibit "responsible government" (a benefit we might assume obtains in the Westminster system of government as it is frequently described), the current Constitution enables those we elect to minimise responsibility and avoid accountability. Therefore, if a new preamble is inserted which, by setting out the values of the nation, sets a basis for what may be deemed the legitimate purpose of any government chosen to lead that nation, then executive power will be more tightly constrained and parliaments too will be more carefully guided and more easily held to account. Indeed, that is the point of a values statement in a constitution (unless its inclusion is restricted to mere tokenism and non-justiciability). The chief benefit of a preamble which functions as a genuinely respected statement of national values is to increase the capacity of the people to explain what national values executive governments must swear allegiance to and uphold, and what we must all understand as the legitimate purpose of the parliament according to the people that elect its members.

The specificity of the statement of values is crucial. It enables the people to convert the Constitution from being a tokenistic (and fundamentally insincere) statement that "parliaments derive their authority from the people" into a serious enshrined statement of *what* is being authorised in the exercise of power – and by extension what would be likely to be inconsistent with that authorisation. A specific values statement authorised by the people changes the parameters of power for the elected. It sets out the key terms of trust between electors and the elected. Once these terms are in place, the electors are entitled to expect that laws will accord with their values, not undermine them.

This is a whole new way of authorising power, one which places the public interests and purpose of the nation at the heart of the Constitution. No longer will the Constitution focus solely on the process for *who* might be elected; it will also describe *what* they are elected for – the overarching purpose of the nation, the reason why we wish in the 21st century to persist with the agreement we made 120 years earlier to "unite in one indissoluble Federal Commonwealth".

Doubtless there will be lawyers who will object and argue that the people cannot enact their own Constitution (even though anything can be done in lawmaking if the will is there). Images might be conjured up by cartoonists of the entire Australian voting population squeezed into the House of Representatives chamber or the Great Hall – the mother of all joint sittings, although this will look no sillier than the image of the populace squeezed into the body of the sovereign in the frontispiece of *Leviathan*. Should such new arrangements for establishing a legitimate people's sovereignty be subject to caricature, this will constitute nothing more and nothing less than a snide put-down of Australians and an attempt to displace them yet again from exercising a voice in their own governance. It implies that democracy's natural space is confined within the walls of Parliament House and must be controlled exclusively by those elected to a seat in the House.

But in the internet age the democratic space is now fully accessible. We operate in virtual open spaces every day and there is no reason why a process for enacting the most important piece of legislation in the land cannot be designed so that the people legitimise their new birth (or rebirth) as a nation by enacting that particular law themselves. In effect this is what the referendum mechanism in the current Constitution contemplates anyway. It stipulates that only the people can change it; therefore only the people can make it entirely anew. It is their will that counts in constitutional matters, although the present reality is that institutional arrangements provided for under the Constitution permit parliaments to deny that will by inserting themselves into the permission chain for constitutional amendments. In theory, and in law, the people are the only ones who can make a new constitution in Australia; but in reality they can't, unless the sovereign (parliament) says they can. This refusal of permission will need to be removed. Otherwise there can be no possibility of a place for the people in their own democratic state and the likelihood is that if referendums are permitted at all they will simply be locking in constitutional arrangements that leave the people in the same position of powerlessness. That is not a people's constitution.

If we take a logical approach to the establishment of a people's constitution, one which changes the location of the sovereign will from the current sovereign (that is, parliament and the executive in council with the governor-general in our case) to the people, this will require an acknowledgement by all elected federal parliamentarians and senators, now and into the future, that they derive their permission to exercise their powers from the people themselves and that those powers may only be exercised in accordance with the acknowledged will of the people (rather than the essentially arbitrary and unconstrained rule of some other unitary sovereign). No longer will Australians who have voted in a referendum need the permission of a governor-general (as they do now) to admit whatever amendments they have thereby approved into the Constitution.[171] Additionally, in the new arrangement a parliament will no longer be able to authorise its own sovereignty and those who are elected to parliament must instead swear an oath of allegiance to the new source of that sovereign will – which for the first time in Australia will be We the People. Unless we the people are acknowledged as the enactors of this legislation, we are not the source of power. And any oath or affirmation that the elected might swear, such as the one suggested by the Australian Republican Movement that,

> I will be loyal to the Commonwealth of Australia and the Australian people whose Constitution and laws I shall uphold,[172]

will be as false as the oath they take now to "bear true allegiance to Her Majesty Queen Victoria, Her heirs and successors according to law.[173] Australians will have no greater capacity to guide parliaments as to their will and hold them accountable than they do now. In other words they will have no power – again.

This problem is solved if we the people are acknowledged as the source of the sovereign will by their own (not the parliament's) enactment of the Constitution as law. In short, the referendum itself should constitute the enactment. Moreover, once that is acknowledged by the elected (when they make their oaths or affirmations) then a whole range of other benefits in governance open up for the electors and the elected alike. Significant benefits

---

[171] Section 128 of the Australian Constitution currently provides the Governor-General with the discretion to refuse assent to a proposed constitutional change endorsed by the Australian people at a referendum.

[172] Australian Republican Movement, The Australian Choice Model: Proposed Amendments to the Australian Constitution165, January 2022, page iii, Op. Cit.

[173] Commonwealth of Australia Constitution Act, 9th July 1900, section 42. The Australian Constitution – Parliament of Australia (aph.gov.au)

come from the fact that this newly acknowledged sovereign will is one that will be *specified*, so that it can no longer be arbitrarily reframed or departed from without the express permission of the people (as it has so easily been under the current Constitution). This establishes what I might call a new-world democracy – a real one instead of a masquerade, one fit for a nation wishing to start again and to do so with values that favour full inclusion and equality in life, liberty and the pursuit of happiness. Such a constitution has the capacity to usher in unprecedented stability in our democracy. I will expand on this in Chapter 7.

It is likely that the first opportunity Australians may have to establish this new-world democracy would arise if they choose to become a republic. This is not to say that if Australia becomes a republic this will automatically give power to the people. It won't if all that we do upon declaring ourselves a republic is to take the crown off the queen's or king's head and put it on the parliament, thereby saddling ourselves with the same exclusive, tin-eared, arbitrary power structure we have now – a structure deaf to our voice. But if we establish a constitutional convention or similar deliberative process to enact a people's constitution (something I will discuss more in Chapter 9), and if we ensure that this convention is not restricted in its terms of reference and can conduct fully open community engagement – perhaps building on the experience and success of the engagement undertaken in the Referendum Council, which resulted in a high degree of involvement and concurrence on the Uluru Statement from the Heart – then there is no reason why we cannot replace the current suboptimal power arrangements with a much more effective power-sharing system. To that end, this following starting draft of a statement of Australian values for insertion as a justiciable preamble in a people's constitution is offered as a contribution to deliberations. The starting draft is based on the voices of Australians as they have expressed their preferences for and against various values in surveys and commentary in the 21st century. Should readers determine that I have misread these preferences or neglected something that is important, they should clamour for the opportunity of a constitutional convention to correct the picture painted here, or endorse it if they choose.

Starting draft preamble

Australian People's Constitution – Preamble (draft for use in community engagement)

We the People of Australia,

- in enacting this Constitution as Sovereign in our own land, and
- in affirming that self-determination and self-governance are our inalienable rights as citizens of the democratic, independent sovereign nation hereby constituted with a federal system of government and henceforth to be known as the Commonwealth of Australia,

place our trust in the parliaments and governments we elect on the following terms:

That laws may only be enacted and upheld which:

- demonstrably support the public interest as a whole, the interests of future generations and the sustainability of the lands, seas, species and natural resources of Australia as determined from time to time in accordance with processes and requirements of law set out here and elsewhere in this Constitution; and which
- ensure the maintenance of the human rights of current and future generations as established here and elsewhere in this Constitution; and which
- are consistent with our values as a nation, these values for the present being specified in the following Statement of Australian Values:

Statement of Australian Values

We the people of Australia are at one in this our Sovereign Will to chart a course to a future where peace prevails and the common wellbeing is secured for all in a manner consistent with the preeminent value we place on:

- the safety of all members of the nation and the stability, security and cohesion of society as a whole;
- honesty, integrity and ethics in all relationships, in governance and in corporate responsibility;
- creation and maintenance of a fully inclusive, participatory democracy which exhibits openness, transparency and respect for the voices of all Australians in matters of policy and governance;
- universal human rights;
- social harmony and appreciation of diversity;
- Australia's First Nations particularly in relation to:
    - our recognition of their rightful and essential place at the Heart of the nation's past, present and future,
    - truth-telling on the history of colonisation and the violence and injustice of their dispossession,
    - Makarrata, reconciliation with and just treaty between First Nations and non-Indigenous Australians,
    - celebration of the culture and heritage of Aboriginal and Torres Strait Islander peoples,
    - our acknowledgement of their ancestral tie to the land and the sovereignty that arises from that as coexistent with the

sovereignty of all Australians, and, consequent on that acknowledgement,
    - the equal right of First Nations alongside all Australians to their own Voice in the Constitution;
- equality and egalitarianism – in ensuring wellbeing and in respect for all regardless of gender, sexual orientation, age, disability, race, national or ethnic origin, cultural heritage, religious persuasion or secularity, or wealth;
- benevolence and compassion for those close to us, for distant communities and for refugees;
- equal opportunity for all;
- social justice – meaning fair outcomes for all, fair sharing of national wealth, fair sharing of the burden and benefit of taxation, fair access to services, and equality before the law;
- life-long health, including physical, mental and societal health and happiness;
- life-long accessibility of education;
- life-long opportunity for expansion of the mind and human creative capacity;
- scientific intelligence and research capacity;
- unobstructed access to public information and protection of privacy and personal information;
- information markets that are properly regulated for the purpose of promotion of truth;
- national resilience, preparedness for crises and capacity to avert preventable crises;
- protection of the natural environment and conservation of natural resources;
- the planet, its ecosystems and species diversity;
- future generations and intergenerational equity;
- freedom of speech, expression, information, peaceful assembly and association, protest, choice in life path and partner, travel, belief,

religion, secularity and atheism, political communication, freedom of the press, and freedom from discrimination, unlawful or arbitrary detention, political persecution, fear and want;

- the contributions and dignity of everyone, regardless of employment status, disability and working life stage;
- the formation and ongoing support of a human-centred economy capable of providing continuous full employment and opportunities for meaningful work and life satisfaction;
- the formation and ongoing support of an environmentally sustainable economy capable of ensuring proper conservation of scarce natural resources;
- fairness and ethics in foreign and domestic trade and finance;
- decency, humanity, cooperation and integrity in our international citizenry;
- independence in national sovereignty; and
- self-determination through a voice in our own governance.

We affirm that these values stand as the shared values of the People and are indicative of the purpose of the nation and national character We seek to build. Therefore We also affirm that:

- these values shall stand as guidance to law and policy makers and to authorised justices of the courts as to whether laws and policies are in accordance with our Sovereign Will; and that
- laws and policies which are demonstrably inconsistent with these values are inconsistent with

> the Australian People's Sovereign Will and shall not stand.

> These values shall be reviewed every ten years from the date of this enactment by establishment of fully open constitutional conventions whose considerations shall not be constrained by the parliaments or laws of the Commonwealth or the states or other entities, which from time to time may comprise the Federation or may be otherwise empowered by this Constitution in accordance with our Sovereign Will.

Indigenous recognition in a new preamble

Readers will note that the above suggested starting draft of a statement of Australian values in a preamble to a people's constitution contains a statement that Australians value First Nations and in particular that value is placed on their recognition, their rightful place at the Heart of the nation, their culture and heritage, truth-telling, Makarrata, reconciliation, just treaty, the coexistence of sovereignties, and the equal right of Aborigines and Torres Strait Islanders alongside all other Australians to their own people's Voice in the Constitution.

Inclusion of these values in the starting draft preamble is intended to ensure that Indigenous people can visibly take their rightful place together with all Australians at the centre of our Constitution and the Commonwealth it creates. Such a prominent space in the preamble is necessary for full constitutional recognition of peoples and nations indigenous to Australia. This fuller form of words in recognition of First Nations peoples is necessary partly because the first draft of wording proposed in 2022 by the Albanese government for an amendment to the Constitution enshrining an Indigenous Voice was quite suitable for the purpose of establishing a good constitutional basis for an Indigenous Voice, but it was in all probability too scant to constitute recognition itself. The proposed wording on the principle of the Indigenous Voice in the Constitution was:

- There shall be a body, to be called the Aboriginal and Torres Strait Islander Voice.
- The Aboriginal and Torres Strait Islander Voice may make representations to parliament and the executive government on matters relating to Aboriginal and Torres Strait Islander peoples.
- The parliament shall, subject to this constitution, have power to make laws with respect to the composition, functions, powers and procedures of the Aboriginal and Torres Strait Islander Voice.[174]

This form of wording for the Indigenous Voice referendum also did not offer Australians the option to affirm that they value reconciliation and the Indigenous call for "a fair and truthful relationship with the people of Australia and a better future for our children based on justice and self-determination."[175] The opportunity to make that broader sort of affirmation should at some point in the future become the core statement by which Australians formally accept in full the invitation in the Uluru Statement from the Heart and at last assure First Nations of their rightful place in the Commonwealth of Australia as people entitled on an equal basis with all Australians to political, civil, economic, social and cultural rights. Additionally, if it states that reconciliation is the constitutionally affirmed intention, it should also create the basis for a truly just treaty with First Nations, a truthful relationship, and a stable coexistence of sovereignties. All these things have been called for in the Uluru

[174] Proposed wording for constitutional amendments to enshrine an Aboriginal and Torres Strait Islander Voice, announced at the Garma Festival by Prime Minister Anthony Albanese, July 2022. Lorena Allam, "Anthony Albanese reveals 'simple and clear' wording of referendum question on Indigenous voice", The Guardian, 30 July 2022.

[175] Uluru Statement from the Heart. See Appendix 1.

Statement and on its election in 2022 the Albanese government committed to implementing this "in full".[176]

Notwithstanding this commitment, Australia's Constitution currently provides no basis for a treaty or truth-telling. A preambular statement providing a constitutional basis for these is therefore essential but a number of other changes in terms of enshrined human rights and removal of clauses permitting racism will also be required if the invitation from Uluru is to be implemented in full. Chapters 6, 7 and 8 set out how:

- a people's constitution can be structured to provide the clear terms for the validity of an Indigenous Voice on a permanent basis;
- an enduring just treaty can be established with First Nations; and
- a coexistence of sovereignties can be made a reality in such a way as to enable all Australians to take rightful and empowering roles in building a better future together.

Evolution of Australian values

The above starting draft of an Australian values statement has been derived by reviews of research on public opinion and by comparing and contrasting the values expressed by Australians in that research with entirely different value sets – that is, by imagining the type of society we might build if we reversed these apparently preferred values. Throughout the 21st century it would seem that the values of everyday Australians have not changed all that much in terms of our preference for living in a democratic, free, open, multicultural, caring society and in a peaceful world. But they have changed in some key respects. Notable changes include that we value religion less and the natural environment more, the planet and

---

[176] Prime Minister of Australia, Anthony Albanese, ABC News, "Read incoming prime minister Anthony Albanese's full speech after Labor wins federal election", 21 May 2022: "On behalf of the Australian Labor Party, I commit to the Uluru Statement from the heart in full." Read incoming prime minister Anthony Albanese's full speech after Labor wins federal election - ABC News

species diversity more, Indigenous wellbeing and rights more, human rights more, women and gender-diverse people more, and nationalism less.

These perceptible changes have all been brought to bear on the development of the suggested starting draft of a statement of Australian values and this has produced a statement that in its initial form is quite different to the last preamble we were asked to consider – the one finalised by John Howard for the 1999 referendum on the republic:

The John Howard Preamble – 1999

With hope in God, the Commonwealth of Australia is constituted as a democracy with a federal system of government to serve the common good. We the Australian people commit ourselves to this Constitution:

- proud that our national unity has been forged by Australians from many ancestries;
- never forgetting the sacrifices of all who defended our country and our liberty in time of war;
- upholding freedom, tolerance, individual dignity and the rule of law;
- honouring Aborigines and Torres Strait Islanders, the nation's first people, for their deep kinship with their lands and for their ancient and continuing cultures which enrich the life of our country;
- recognising the nation building contribution of generations of immigrants;
- mindful of our responsibility to protect our unique natural environment;
- supportive of achievement as well as equality of opportunity for all;

- and valuing independence as dearly as the national spirit which binds us together in both adversity and success.[177]

This preamble was distinctly narrower in its range and in the character we might aspire to as a modern nation. The possibility of that wider character was not on offer in the Howard preamble. Instead it was:

- more insular and less outward looking than would be necessary for any nation attempting to build resilience sufficient to prevent or soften the impacts of externally generated crises;
- more tied up with values of mateship in war rather than prevention of war and most noticeably silent on promotion of peace;
- more focussed on social conformity achieved through tolerance and conformance to the rule of law (no matter how unjust, racist or discriminatory) rather than a multicultural harmony, appreciation of diversity and expansion of the mind;
- completely silent on the right of the people to participate in the design of laws;
- somewhat respectful of Aboriginal and Torres Strait Islander history and culture but silent on, and therefore dismissive of, anything more in terms of the wrongs done to them and silent on recognition of their prior possession of the continent, let alone the sovereignty that that implies;
- clear (some would say, patronising) in recognising the necessity of “generations of immigrants” to “nation building” but silent on the value of diversity itself;
- more focussed on individual rather than collective achievement;

---

[177] Wikipedia, 1999 Australian Republic referendum webpage, includes the wording of the preamble as put to the Australian republic. Last accessed 22 August 2022.

- silent on the benevolence and compassion that modern Australians are likely to prefer;
- silent on the value of ethics in governance;
- shallow in reference to environmental protection;
- silent on any value conducive to prevention of climate change;
- more assertive of a central place for "God" in our governance than is likely to be preferred by a nation used to humanistic frameworks for decision-making and rejecting theocratic models of governance; and
- most notably silent on the place of the Australian people in their own governance as the rightful authority on the sovereign will.

These are just a few of the glaring differences between the Howard preamble and the suite of values that Australians might choose from in the 2020s. But it will be useful for Australians to consider these differences as they move towards development of a new statement of Australian values.

Engaging Australians to confirm their values

In the intervening years since the Howard preamble was rejected by Australians, the Department of Home Affairs has moved in and attempted to fill the vacuum created by that rejection. In the attempt, it created an even narrower version of Australian values than the Howard preamble – a version which clearly does not reflect what Australians say they value. This is the inevitable result of allowing governments to determine what the people value, instead of the people themselves.

In Australia, governments are essentially political parties and therefore their values are designed based purely on their ideological preferences, which they then foist on everyone if they can. These preferences are essentially narrow and designedly divisive of populations. More to the point, governments have displayed a very poor track record of designing value statements that actually reflect what Australians value. In the case of the Home Affairs statement, the governments that may purport to endorse it are simply out of step with the broadly based values of 21st century Australians, especially the younger ones who will be required to do the vast amount of heavy lifting necessary to build a nation which supports the wellbeing and security of all generations.

The fact is that the true will of the people cannot be handed down by a government from above. A sovereign people's will cannot be narrowed down to the will a government is prepared to let them have. It has to be the other way around. A sovereign people's will, expressed in their statement of what they value, has to be the one that the people are prepared to let governments swear allegiance to and swear it in accordance with the terms of trust on which the people hand over power. Those terms of trust are inherent in the statement of Australian values (howsoever it may be worded); but they are also necessarily qualified throughout the Constitution, as and when the people see fit.

In short, if the people are sovereign then the will of the nation must be theirs to determine in its entirety – unobstructed by politics and ideology. In recognition of that, any constitutional convention that may happen to be established for the purpose of developing a new statement of Australian values should ideally be people-driven – no politicians. This is, after all, The People's Constitution; so the people need to be given space to lead the development of their own statement of values without having to start from or be infected by an ideological base. And ultimately the decision on the final composition of values should be exclusively theirs, not the parliament's and certainly not the executive government's.

This implies the need for a type of citizens' assembly and decision process that has not been attempted in Australia before – a special (but probably not permanent) national assembly whose inception does not require the permission of the parliament and whose recommendations, about national values at least, do not require the imprimatur of the parliament in order to be put to the people in a referendum. In this sense, parliaments must acknowledge that for the purposes of constituting a *people's* sovereign nation they must vacate their current position of power, temporarily, before they can get it back again – otherwise power cannot be newly enshrined in a form consistent with the people's will as sovereign. Unless the parliament can stand aside to allow the people to freely deliberate on their preferred constitution, we would be likely to end up with a situation where power would be merely re-installed in its current form (just as John Howard sought to do) – a form where the unitary parliament is still inordinately and exclusively powerful. It would be likely to reinstall the Hobbesian state with all the exclusions and powerlessness it implies for the subjects of that sovereign state. In that event, self-government and self-determination would once again be absent.

In effect, a people's constitution requires a genuinely humble parliament that from the outset acknowledges that the people are best placed to decide what is truly in their interests and that they must be taken at their word. Humility is, of course, not something to which politicians are accustomed, even though some may profess that they are the servants of the people. So if such a citizens' assembly or a constitutional convention on Australian values is enabled at all, it is likely to be infected at some point or other by "the flawed and grimy world of day-to-day partisan politics" (as Mark McKenna described it[178]). Nevertheless, if politicians (grimy or not) are involved somehow in the process (through permission of the people or without it), it is imperative that their ideologically driven conflicts of interest and partiality are safely contained by procedure, by insistence on complete disclosure and openness, and by selection of a steering committee and presiding convenor from outside the numbers of the elected.

Notably, there is nothing in the current Constitution that prevents the spontaneous formation of either a citizens' assembly or constitutional convention by the people. We can do this with or without the parliament's permission. The parliament can of course then refuse to accept the recommendations of the assembly or

---

[178] Professor Mark McKenna, "First Words: A Brief History of Public Debate on a New Preamble to the Australian Constitution 1991-99", Parliament of Australia, Research Paper 16, 1999-2000. Last accessed 30 August 2022. The requested content has been archived – Parliament of Australia (aph.gov.au)

convention but if it is popular – both in its establishment and its outcomes – it would be a brave parliament that would refuse its recommendations. If an assembly or convention is to be deemed popular, the selection process for delegates might best be designed as an open registration of interest process and then selection by sortition. Additionally, multiple forums of whatever vehicle is chosen (be it called a citizens' assembly or convention – call it what you will, they are basically the same thing) should be held in all states and territories and in this regard there are excellent community engagement models already in existence for large scale national citizens' assemblies of this kind. The process completed by Aboriginal and Torres Strait Islander communities for development of the Uluru Statement from the Heart stands as a world-class benchmark in the sort of community engagement needed here. Another example of a successful model was the engagement program undertaken for the introduction of the Victorian Charter of Human Rights and Responsibilities Act 2006.[179] Features of these best practice approaches could be combined to embed the process of collaborative formation of a people's constitution, and the resultant constitution itself, in the Australian people's hearts.

This does not mean that all aspects of this entirely new constitution need to be made by the people in this popular assembly. As a beginning, the focus of the popular assembly could be on designing the statement of Australian values. This in turn could be used as a basis by constitutional experts for guidance in design of other parts of the new constitution. Everything in the broader constitution should be designed to give effect to the people's will as expressed in the statement of Australian values they have designed. Inherently this means the values must be comprehensively expressed in terms that are useful for justiciable purposes but without legalistic language. Humanistic language evocative of heartfelt aspiration is required to ensure Australians connect with the values. A second round and/or successive rounds of popular assemblies could then be

---

[179] George Williams and Daniel Reynolds, *A Charter of Rights in Australia,* UNSW Press, NewSouth Publishing, Sydney, 2017, Op. Cit., Chapter 6 – Charters of Rights in the States and Territories.

conducted to check whether Australians concur that the entire constitution reflects their will and has the maximum capacity to help them build the future they genuinely wish to share. I will elaborate further on options for this in Chapter 9.

Regardless of how community engagement for development of a people's constitution might be organised, the essential thing in the process at the very beginning is to ensure the values in the preamble encapsulate the sovereign will of the nation. If Australians can assemble those values freely and without ideological precepts or restrictions, it is highly likely that a values statement will emerge that speaks truth to power and clarifies the purpose of power. Sitting alongside two other essential additions to the Constitution that I will discuss in Chapters 6 and 7, the statement of values forms the core of the terms of trust on which power can be safely handed over to the elected. It thereby creates a basis for the enduring stability of the nation – because it enables the elected thereafter to assess whether their ideologies and policies accord with the will of the people (as they should if they are seeking election to represent that will).

As it is currently structured, Australia's Constitution is designed exclusively to override the will of the people, whatever it may be. Their voice is deliberately excluded. But this can be easily overcome. And once this statement of values is established, other essential elements of a people's constitution will fall into place. Those other essential elements are the subject of the next chapters.

Chapter 6 – Essential No. 2: Enshrinement of human rights and obligations in an Australian people's constitution

Australia is the only democratic country in the world without a national charter of human rights.[180] This is an astounding lapse in lawmaking for a country claiming to be democratic. It is doubly astounding given that Australia was in fact one of only eight nations involved in drafting the Universal Declaration of Human Rights in 1948[181] – a Declaration that stands to this day as the basis for a range of international covenants (treaties) Australia has freely signed and which have even been ratified by our parliaments. These treaties include seven core international covenants and conventions:

- the International Covenant on Civil and Political Rights (ICCPR),[182]
- the International Covenant on Economic, Social and Cultural Rights (ICESCR),[183]
- the International Convention on the Elimination of All Forms of Racial Discrimination (CERD),[184]

---

[180] George Williams and Daniel Reynolds, *A Charter of Rights in Australia,* UNSW Press, NewSouth Publishing, Sydney, 2017, Chapter 1 – An absence of human rights, Op. Cit., page 21.

[181] The Universal Declaration of Human Rights, accessible at https://www.un.org/en/about-us/universal-declaration-of-human-rights

[182] International Covenant on Civil and Political Rights- external site

[183] International Covenant on Economic, Social and Cultural Rights- external site

[184] International Convention on the Elimination of All Forms of Racial Discrimination- external site

- the Convention on the Elimination of All Forms of Discrimination Against Women (CEDAW),[185]
- the Convention Against Torture and Other Cruel, Inhuman or Degrading Treatment or Punishment (CAT),[186]
- the Convention on the Rights of the Child (CRC),[187] and
- the Convention on the Rights of Persons with Disabilities (CRPD).[188]

Various other treaties and "optional protocols" have also been adopted, although reservations apply in several cases. For example, Australia has ratified one of the most important human rights treaties – the International Covenant on Civil and Political Rights (ICCPR) – but has nevertheless reserved (withheld) its commitment to some elements of that treaty, including Articles 10, 14 and 20 which require:

- the segregation of children from adults in prison and accused detainees from convicted detainees;
- compensation for miscarriages of justice; and
- the prohibition of both war propaganda and advocacy of national, racial or religious hatred.[189]

The Universal Declaration of Human Rights, which overarches all these treaties and is considered by Australian governments in official policy to have "great moral authority",[190] is not binding in law. However, the treaties made under the Declaration do constitute international law as far as human rights are concerned and in acceding to them (with or without reservations) a state that is party

---

[185] Convention on the Elimination of All Forms of Discrimination against Women- external site

[186] Convention against Torture and Other Cruel, Inhuman or Degrading Treatment or Punishment- external site

[187] Convention on the Rights of the Child- external site

[188] Convention on the Rights of Persons with Disabilities- external site

[189] Australian Human Rights Commission, "Scope of International Obligations – Australia's 3rd UPR", 2021. PowerPoint Presentation (humanrights.gov.au)

[190] Department of Foreign Affairs and Trade, "Australian and Human Rights: An Overview, 4th edition", December 2017, page 32. human-rights-manual-fourth-edition.pdf (dfat.gov.au)

(a "State Party") to any of these treaties is, at least in principle, signalling that it is consenting in good faith to be bound by those laws.

States Parties have different arrangements for signing, ratifying or acceding to these treaties and they have different arrangements for giving effect to them in domestic law. For some, a signature (known as a "definitive signature"[191]) is sufficient to signal that the treaty is binding under their domestic law. For others (like Australia), ratification may be required; it depends on their constitutional and other legal arrangements. Even so, where ratification may be the preferred procedure for signalling a State Party's "consent to be bound" by the treaty, this does not mean that a ratified treaty automatically applies as domestic law; again, it depends on each country's constitutional and legal arrangements.

Certainly in Australia's case – because of our current constitutional arrangements – ratification does not mean that the international laws set down in these treaties apply as domestic law. On a few occasions, such as with the passage of the Racial Discrimination Act 1975 and the Sex Discrimination Act 1984, Australia has codified some aspects of the international treaties on human rights into domestic law. But in the main it has displayed only a sporadic willingness to extend human rights to Australians in our laws and to be held accountable for abuses of those rights. This applies despite the fact that in official domestic policy, Australia accepts that human rights – and this means the rights transferred from the Universal Declaration into the covenants and conventions that we have then signed – are "universal and indivisible".

Official policy from the Department of Foreign Affairs and Trade (DFAT) states that:

- "Australia considers all human rights to be universal"[192] – meaning that despite differing cultural and religious beliefs,

---

[191] Department of Foreign Affairs and Trade, "Australian and Human Rights: An Overview, 4th edition", December 2017, page 21, Ibid.

[192] Department of Foreign Affairs and Trade, "Australian and Human Rights: An Overview, 4th edition", December 2017, page 15, Ibid.

rights in the treaties are the inherent, inalienable, inviolable, common entitlement of all humans; and

- "Australia also considers human rights to be interrelated, interdependent and indivisible" – meaning that "there is no hierarchy or priority of the rights enshrined in the UDHR [Universal Declaration of Human Rights], nor are there pre-conditions imposed on the enjoyment of some of these rights".[193]

It is noteworthy that the official Australian policy position is that there are no pre-conditions imposed on enjoyment of "some" of the rights, the implication being that the Australian government holds a view that pre-conditions do apply to some rights, despite their being unquestionably "interrelated, interdependent and indivisible". This suggests that while the only "pre-condition" for enjoyment by any Australian of an acknowledged universal human right should be that the said Australian is *a human*, the Australian government would nevertheless prefer to impose pre-conditions at will. And in practice, that is exactly what it does.

When it comes to human rights, the Australian government has retained full power to giveth and to taketh away – leaving us with little to say but "blessed be the name of the government". In Australia's current legal arrangements it is the government (not the parliament) that retains godlike power in terms of determining the "great moral authority" in relation to human rights for Australians, irrespective of the acknowledged universality and indivisibility of human rights. And it retains this power by virtue of the way the Australian Constitution is structured. It retains this power because there is nothing in the Constitution that stops governments from making executive decisions to act inconsistently with their commitments and obligations under the treaties, even if the treaty has been ratified by the parliament – that is, even if the parliament has given its consent to be bound by the treaty.

---

[193] Department of Foreign Affairs and Trade, "Australian and Human Rights: An Overview, 4th edition", December 2017, page 15, Ibid.

This executive power to disregard human rights has been confirmed by the High Court. As the Department of Foreign Affairs and Trade has noted, the High Court ruled in the 1995 case of Minister for Immigration and Ethnic Affairs v Ah Hin Teoh that:

> Ratification of a treaty by the Australian executive gave rise to a legitimate expectation that decision makers would act consistently with the provisions of the treaty and take them into account in making administrative decisions, even if those provisions had not been incorporated into domestic law. [But] it also held that such a legitimate expectation could be set aside by an executive or legislative indication to the contrary.[194]

And on 25 February 1997, the Howard government did indeed set aside the legitimate expectations of Australians when, as DFAT further notes,

> the Attorney-General and the Minister for Foreign Affairs issued an Executive Statement to the effect that the act of entering into a treaty does not give rise to legitimate expectations that could form the basis for challenging an administrative decision.[195]

This is a breathtaking Executive Statement of faithlessness in commitments to and observance of the "rule of law" that the Australian government otherwise claims to revere. What it means is that the whole principle of "responsible government" – in which the executive government is supposed to be accountable to the parliament, and through that to the people – has been discarded, and with the permission of the High Court, no less. This permission doubtless arises from High Court interpretations of what the Constitution allows, or else it arises from the fallibility of the Court. Either way, what it means is that the executive government can do the opposite of what the parliament has ratified in international

---

[194] Department of Foreign Affairs and Trade, "Australian and Human Rights: An Overview, 4th edition", December 2017, page 26, Ibid.

[195] Department of Foreign Affairs and Trade, "Australian and Human Rights: An Overview, 4th edition", December 2017, page 26, Ibid.

treaties – and without so much as a by-your-leave from the parliament, the High Court, or the people (by a referendum).

It also means the Australian government can be entirely two-faced. It can present one face to the world which purports to support human rights and another face at home that says they have no intention of allowing a consideration of human rights to affect executive power and particularly their ability as governments to make decisions that contravene their commitments under treaties. In other words – at home, our commitments under the treaties and human rights themselves mean nothing. We have no guarantee of any rights, given that the rights in the covenants can be withheld under administrative decisions at home – and that there is no limit to which they may be withheld (unless specific legislation prescribes a limit, which in some cases it does but in other cases does not[196]). In other words, for the most part, the government doesn't necessarily need a reason to deny a human right. It may need a reason in politics but not necessarily in law. The corollary is that, according to government policy, Australia can enter international agreements in bad faith – that is, with no intention of observing them unless it might suit. In that vein, national sovereignty means nothing more and nothing less than an installed autocracy fully capable of denying all rights that are otherwise conferred on humans in international law.

The United Nations Charter is based on the idea that member states do not surrender their national sovereignty when they become members. As I noted in Chapter 1, nothing in the UN Charter authorises the UN to intervene in matters which are essentially within the jurisdiction of a member state.[197] Indeed we would expect no less from a Charter that is based on the fundamental "principle of equal

---

[196] For instance, the government can suspend elements of the Racial Discrimination Act, denying rights conferred under the Act. Such a suspension occurred in 2007 to enable the Howard Government to mount the Northern Territory Intervention and send troops and public servants into remote First Nations communities without consultation. See Chapter 1.

[197] "Charter of the United Nations and Statute of the International Court of Justice", San Francisco, 1945, Article 2. uncharter.pdf

rights and self-determination of peoples".[198] But this does not mean that international law should be flouted at the will of a member nation and it does not mean that a sovereign nation can expect to flout international laws without consequence. A mindset within a government that says otherwise is a very dangerous thing. It implies that Australia has walked away from its "determination" in 1945, when it became a member of the United Nations to:

- "re-affirm faith in fundamental human rights and the worth of the human person"; and
- "establish conditions under which justice and respect for the obligations arising from treaties and other sources of international law can be maintained".[199]

As the decades have passed, however, Australia appears to have licensed itself to evade international law and almost all its obligations under human rights treaties. In addition to pernicious "executive statements" like that described above, Australia has chosen to evade or cover up its abuses of the rights of other nations, foreign individuals and Australians themselves, sometimes by means of withdrawing from the jurisdiction of international courts, sometimes by breaching legal privileges and immunities (famously in the case of the trial of whistleblower Witness K and his lawyer Bernard Collaery it did both[200]), and sometimes by laws which are introduced with insufficient scrutiny as to their effect on human rights. It would appear that Australia has a Constitution that enables all this because it prevents none of it. In the 2020s it is now possible to perceive the impact of this autocratic mindset founded on arbitrary denial of human rights. The following section provides some examples.

---

[198] "Charter of the United Nations and Statute of the International Court of Justice", San Francisco, 1945, Article 1, Ibid.
[199] Preamble to the "Charter of the United Nations and Statute of the International Court of Justice", San Francisco, 1945, Op. Cit.
[200] Human Rights Law Centre, "Explainer: The unjust prosecution of Bernard Collaery" website, last accessed 7 September 2022. Explainer: The unjust prosecution of Bernard Collaery | Human Rights Law Centre (hrlc.org.au)

Australia's record of abuse of human rights

Since the above mentioned Executive Statement was made in 1997, Australia has proceeded to make several of the fundamental rights and freedoms Australians used to enjoy illegal or inaccessible. As I noted in Chapter 1, between 2002 and 2021 Australian governments enacted more than 80 pieces of legislation limiting freedom of expression, freedom of assembly and protest, freedom of information, freedom of the press, whistleblower protections, rights to open trial, rights to not be detained without charge, rights to privacy, and the public's right to know of possible misconduct and illegal conduct by elected parliamentarians and government officials.[201] Citing "national security" as a justification, this legislative program was a full-on assault on powerless Australians and therefore on democracy itself – since a democracy isn't a democracy if citizens have no civil and political powers or rights. The program reduced almost every right that had until then been assumed as a given by Australians under the International Covenant on Civil and Political Rights.

This situation has prevailed since the late 1990s because there is nothing in the Constitution preventing the executive government from arbitrarily acting inconsistently with a commitment it has given on human rights. The Constitution allows executive governments to set aside obligations in international law and prevent challenges to its administrative decisions regardless of the degree to which they infringe universal human rights. We have authorised ourselves to violate the international laws we have otherwise bound ourselves to. Some of those violations display an appalling inhumanity. An example I cited in Chapter 1 referred to changes to the migration laws which allowed indefinite detention of adults and children. As the then

---

[201] For summaries of many of the assumed rights that were attacked in this legislative program see Bronwyn Kelly, *By 2050: Planning a better future for our children in 21st century democratic Australia*, March 2020, Chapter 8 – Subsection: Checking for Threats to Democracy. By 2050: Planning a better future for our children in 21st century democratic Australia eBook : Kelly, Bronwyn: Amazon.com.au: Kindle Store

president of the Human Rights and Equal Opportunity Commission John von Doussa, QC noted at the time:

> In the case of Al-Kateb v Godwin in 2004[202], the High Court determined that amendments to the Migration Act did lawfully allow indefinite detention, and that the Act was not unconstitutional. This ruling pertained "even though the detention was recognised as arbitrary, [and] contrary to Article 9 of the International Covenant on Civil and Political Rights. ... The Court held Parliament had sufficiently expressed its intention that children could be detained, notwithstanding that their detention ran foul of human rights principles."[203]

It is hard to think that we or at least our parliaments could sink lower than this, but migration is not the only area where Australia has refused to confer and observe universal human rights. In addition to the reservations mentioned above in relation to Articles 10, 14 and 20 under the International Covenant on Civil and Political Rights, Australia employs a wide range of administrative, policy and legislative mechanisms in denial of human rights. As such Australia has received repeated adverse reports on its performance in human rights both from the United Nations Human Rights Committee and the United Nations Human Rights Council under the process known as the Universal Periodic Review (UPR). The general tenor of the findings in these processes is that Australia consistently ignores the recommendations of the Reviews and has persisted in denial of rights for decades.

In the most recent periodic review report from Human Rights Committee[204] in relation to Australia's observance of rights and

---

[202] Al-Kateb v Godwin [2004] HCA 37, (2004) 219 CLR 562, High Court (Australia).

[203] John von Doussa QC, President, Human Rights and Equal Opportunity Commission, "Why We Need An Australian Bill of Rights – a joint forum", University of South Australia, 7 December 2005 accessible at https://www.humanrights.gov.au/about/news/speeches/why-we-need-australian-bill-rights-joint-forum

[204] United Nations, Human Rights Committee, CCPR/C/AUS/CO/6, International Covenant on Civil and Political Rights, Concluding observations on the sixth

obligations as a State Party to the International Covenant on Civil and Political Rights, the Committee made observations on the following "principal matters of concern":

- the fact that there is no "comprehensive incorporating legislation", enshrining the rights in domestic law;[205]
- Australia's repeated failure to implement procedures which would guarantee the rights of victims of human rights abuses to an effective remedy when there has been a violation of the Covenant;[206]
- the fact that despite the introduction of the Human Rights (Parliamentary Scrutiny) Act 2011 (which requires all new legislation to be accompanied by a statement of compatibility with human rights) and a Joint Parliamentary Committee on Human Rights (to scrutinize bills for incompatibility with human rights), bills are still passed into law without the required reviews or with poor quality compatibility statements;[207]
- political attempts to discredit the work of the Australian Human Rights Commission in ways that might threaten its independence and the high public esteem in which it is held[208] –
    - Note: this political interference resulted in April 2022 in Australia's failure to achieve reaccreditation for our Human Rights Commission as an A-status national human rights institution. Its reaccreditation was deferred, due in the main to the fact that feedback from the Committee over a 10-year period about Australia's processes for appointments to the Commission had not been heeded, with three

---

periodic report of Australia, 1 December 2017 Treaty bodies Download (ohchr.org)

[205] United Nations, Human Rights Committee, CCPR/C/AUS/CO/6, Ibid., page 2.

[206] United Nations, Human Rights Committee, CCPR/C/AUS/CO/6, Ibid., page 2.

[207] United Nations, Human Rights Committee, CCPR/C/AUS/CO/6, Ibid., pages 2-3.

[208] United Nations, Human Rights Committee, CCPR/C/AUS/CO/6, Ibid., page 3.

appointments in this timeframe that did not meet the accreditation requirements;[209]

- the haste with which some counter-terrorism measures have been adopted which unnecessarily restrict human rights in a manner disproportionate to the risk of terrorism –
    - Note: excessive counter-terrorism powers included "control orders, stop, search and seizure powers, questioning and detention warrants, preventive and post-sentence detention order regimes, 'declared areas' offences and revocation of citizenship";[210]
- the failure to review the compliance of counter-terrorism measures with the Covenant to check that any limitations of human rights for national security purposes serve legitimate government aims, are necessary and proportionate to those legitimate aims and are subject to appropriate safeguards;[211]
- reports of discrimination on the basis of ethnic, racial, cultural or religious background and a failure to prevent discrimination, incitement to racial violence and hate speech in accordance with Articles 19 and 20 of the Covenant;[212]
- the persistence of violence against women and its disproportionate effects on Indigenous women and women with disabilities;[213]
- the (then still applicable) explicit ban on same sex marriage due to a Howard era amendment of the Marriage Act 1961 to restrict equity of access for same sex couples to the benefits and protections of the institution of marriage and the unacceptability of a plebiscite as a decision-making process on this issue;[214]

---

[209] Australian Human Rights Commission, "Statement on international accreditation of the Australian Human Rights Commission", 7 April 2022.
[210] United Nations, Human Rights Committee, CCPR/C/AUS/CO/6, Op. Cit., page 3.
[211] United Nations, Human Rights Committee, CCPR/C/AUS/CO/6, Ibid., page 3.
[212] United Nations, Human Rights Committee, CCPR/C/AUS/CO/6, Ibid., page 4.
[213] United Nations, Human Rights Committee, CCPR/C/AUS/CO/6, Ibid., page 4.
[214] United Nations, Human Rights Committee, CCPR/C/AUS/CO/6, Ibid., page 5.

- instances of the excessive use of force by police in denial of a wide range of human rights – a failure evident in the disproportionate incidence of Aboriginal deaths in custody and in the increasing evidence of strip searching and other mistreatment of minors:[215]
    - Note: evidence of abuses of minors from the age of 10, particularly in prisons in Tasmania (for example, the Ashley Youth Detention Centre), Western Australia (for example, the Banksia Hill Detention Centre) and the Northern Territory (for example, the Don Dale Detention Centre), continues to emerge as an ongoing violation by Australia of human rights – abuses include violence such as sexual assault by guards, isolation, strip searching and other brutal punishments;[216]
- prison over-crowding and failure to extend mental health care to prisoners, including by excessive use of solitary confinement and strip searching;[217]
- the significant over-representation of Indigenous Australians in prison and the need to implement recommendations of Royal Commissions which have not been implemented, despite the passage of decades;[218]
- the extreme difficulties in obtaining native title and in obtaining compensation where native title has been extinguished or where Indigenous children have been stolen;[219]
- the fact that the domestic legal framework governing extradition, transfer or removal of non-citizens, including

---

[215] United Nations, Human Rights Committee, CCPR/C/AUS/CO/6, Ibid., page 6.
[216] Greg Barns SC, National Criminal Justice Spokesman for the Australian Lawyers Alliance, "Children and the justice system", John Menadue's Pearls and Irritations, 31 August 2022.
[217] United Nations, Human Rights Committee, CCPR/C/AUS/CO/6, Op. Cit., page 8.
[218] United Nations, Human Rights Committee, CCPR/C/AUS/CO/6, Ibid., page 8.
[219] United Nations, Human Rights Committee, CCPR/C/AUS/CO/6, Ibid., page 10.

asylum seekers and refugees, does not afford full protection against refoulement[220] –

  - Note: the experience of the Murugappan family from Biloela, whom the Morrison government attempted to deport despite clear evidence of the danger they would face if returned to Sri Lanka,[221] testifies to the failure of the Australian government to attend to its human rights obligations;

- the unjustifiable claim by the Australian government that it does not have control over or legal responsibility for refugees arriving by sea when they are taken to offshore processing facilities funded by Australia (such as Nauru); and
- the need to shut down offshore processing and protect the rights of all asylum seekers.[222]

The above list does not represent the full list of Australian government failures in observance of obligations we have freely accepted to protect human rights under the International Covenant on Civil and Political Rights. And it does not touch on the litany of our failures to observe obligations under the other covenants.

Australian governments have submitted various distracting arguments to human rights committees at the UN and in other documentation in support of their case to deny human rights, but these have often been supported by plainly false statements. For instance, in official policy the Department of Foreign Affairs and

---

[220] United Nations, Human Rights Committee, CCPR/C/AUS/CO/6, Ibid., page 6.

[221] For evidence of the illegality of this attempted refoulement, see Bruce Haigh, "The Rajapaksas – rotten to the core", John Menadue's Pearls and Irritations, 8 August 2022, reporting on the findings of the Second Session of the Peoples Tribunal on Sri Lanka sitting in Bremen from 7-10 December 2013: "A tribunal of eleven eminent judges from around the world unanimously found the Sri Lankan Government guilty of the crime of genocide against ethnic Tamil people. It found the crime of genocide had been and was being committed against the Eelam Tamils as a national group. It is estimated that 140,000 Tamils were killed as soldiers or murdered as civilians since 1983." The Murugappan family were Tamil refugees with a clear case for asylum. https://johnmenadue.com/the-rajapaksas-rotten-to-the-core/

[222] United Nations, Human Rights Committee, CCPR/C/AUS/CO/6, Op. Cit., page 7.

Trade attempts to extenuate the fact that Australia has no "comprehensive incorporating legislation" (that is, we have no charter enshrining human rights in our domestic law) by making the following entirely misleading policy statement:

> Although the Australian Constitution does not contain a bill of rights, it does contain five *express guarantees* [DFAT's emphasis] of rights and immunities. These are:
>
> - the right to vote (section 41);
> - protection against the acquisition of property on unjust terms (section 51 (xxxi));
> - the right to trial by jury (section 80);
> - freedom of religion (section 116); and
> - prohibition of discrimination on the basis of state of residency (section 117).[223]

This statement may be reasonably accurate with respect to the right to freedom of religion. That right is probably our best protected human right under the current Constitution. But otherwise this statement is culpably misleading in relation to the purported "express guarantees" because:

- the right to vote is not "guaranteed" at all:
  - the very wording of section 41[224] makes it apparent that the right to vote can be discontinued, as it is for prisoners and as it can be on the grounds of race (under section 25) and as it probably can be when several other sections are invoked;

[223] Department of Foreign Affairs and Trade, "Australian and Human Rights: An Overview, 4th edition", December 2017, page 96, Op. Cit.

[224] *Australia's Constitution with Overview and Notes by the Australian Government Solicitor*, page v. foi-2021-017.pdf (pmc.gov.au), Section 41: "No adult person who has or acquires a right to vote at elections for the more numerous House of the Parliament of a State shall, *while the right continues*, be prevented by any law of the Commonwealth from voting at elections for either House of the Parliament of the Commonwealth" [Emphasis added.]

  - the section only operates where a state law already allows a person to vote;[225]
  - High Court decisions and other reviews such as the 1988 Constitutional Commission have made it clear that "the Constitution does not guarantee a right to vote";[226] and
  - the Constitution does not guarantee voting consistent with the fundamentals of democratic suffrage – that is, that it be universal, equal and secret;[227]
- protection against the acquisition of property on unjust terms is not "guaranteed":
  - section 51(xxxi) provides that any acquisition of property by the Commonwealth from a state or person must be made on "just terms" but this does not apply for the territories – the High Court having ruled that it does not apply when the Commonwealth is making rules pursuant to section 122, which grants "plenary authority" (complete and absolute power) to the Commonwealth to make laws for any territory;[228] and
  - notably, because much of the land subject to native title claim is in the Northern Territory, governments are likely to continue resisting extension of this right of just terms compensation to Northern Territorians;
- trial by jury is not "guaranteed":
  - the wording of section 80 offers this guarantee only for indictable offences against Commonwealth law – a

---

[225] George Williams and Daniel Reynolds, *A Charter of Rights in Australia,* UNSW Press, NewSouth Publishing, Sydney, 2017, Chapter 3 – Our rights under the law, page 45.

[226] George Williams and Daniel Reynolds, *A Charter of Rights in Australia,* UNSW Press, NewSouth Publishing, Sydney, 2017, Chapter 3 – Our rights under the law, page 46.

[227] John McMillan, Gareth Evans and Haddon Storey, *Australia's Constitution: Time for Change?*, Law Foundation of New South Wales, Allen and Unwin Australia, 1983, page 246.

[228] John McMillan, Gareth Evans and Haddon Storey, *Australia's Constitution: Time for Change?*, Law Foundation of New South Wales, Allen and Unwin Australia, 1983, Ibid., page 155.

guarantee that can be easily evaded by a declaration that an offence is not indictable;
    - High Court rulings have held that section 80 is "'integral to the structure of government and to the distribution of judicial power' rather than being 'a right or privilege personal to the accused'";[229] and
    - section 80 is another of those "guarantees" that do not apply for territorians; and
- prohibition of discrimination on the basis of state of residency is not "guaranteed":
    - the wording of section 117 prohibits a state from discriminating against someone from another state but does not oblige a state to refrain from discriminating against a resident of a territory.

In fact in all four of these cases it is apparent that citizens of territories in Australia have fewer rights than citizens of states. This discrimination against territorians is most obvious in the case of referendum votes, inasmuch as the vote of a citizen registered on the electoral roll in a state counts twice towards the result, whereas the vote of a citizen registered on the electoral roll in a territory counts only once. This inequality arises from the fact that section 128 of the Constitution requires that alterations to the constitution can only be made if a "double majority" is achieved in favour of the change in a referendum – that is, the change must be approved by a majority of people voting nationwide *and* a majority of people in a majority of States. In other words, for a referendum to succeed, at least four of the six states must vote Yes. Because the territories are not states under the Constitution, their citizens' votes are counted in the nationwide tally but are disregarded when it comes to determining whether a majority of "states" has been achieved. This relegates territorians to second class citizens in terms of the impact of their vote – a circumstance which is likely to reduce the chances of successful passage of a referendum on an Indigenous Voice to

---

[229] George Williams and Daniel Reynolds, *A Charter of Rights in Australia,* UNSW Press, NewSouth Publishing, Sydney, 2017, Chapter 3 – Our rights under the law, page 47.

parliament. In the case of referendum questions relating to increasing Indigenous rights, it might be expected that the majority of Australians nationwide could vote Yes but the referendums could still fail because the votes of territorians do not count towards the second required majority – the majority of states. In this regard, and in several other ways, the principle of "one vote one value" does not apply in Australia. Instead, inequality is inherent in our political system and it is reinforced in the Constitution.

Given the looseness of the Constitution in terms of its capacity to prevent arbitrary abuses of human rights by governments, it should not be surprising that non-government organisations (NGOs) have identified ongoing failures to protect and affirm human rights in Australia. In 2020, 202 NGOs across Australia joined together to engage in coordinated development of a submission to the third Universal Periodic Review being conducted by the United Nations Human Rights Council. This is not to be confused with the Human Rights Committee review mentioned above, although the abuses and failures uncovered in both processes are not at odds with each other. Both processes uncover alarming failures which have been ongoing for years to decades. The NGO report in 2020 – called "Australia's Human Rights Score Card"[230] – identified a number of failures including the following:

- "The Constitution does not support self-determination" and enables the parliament to enact race-based legislation which is having particularly harmful effects on Indigenous Australians, non-whites, women, children, gender diverse and disabled people, and non-Christians.
- "Australia continues to fail to fully incorporate international human rights obligations into domestic law."
- Australia has not compensated the members of Stolen Generations in some jurisdictions.

---

[230] Australian NGO, Coalition, Human Rights Law Centre, Kingsford Legal Centre, Caxton Legal Centre, "Australia's Human Rights Score Card", April 2020. Australia's Human Rights Scorecard: Australia's 2020 United Nations UPR NGO Coalition Report | Human Rights Law Centre (hrlc.org.au)

- Australia has failed to ratify key international human rights instruments, including conventions covering migrant workers and enforced disappearances.
- Australia has not withdrawn reservations to existing ratifications, and has not implemented a number of previous UPR and UN recommendations.
- Australia has not adequately funded social and community services to underpin the realisation of human rights.
- Mechanisms such as the Cashless Welfare (or Debit) Card and the "Community Development Program" discriminate significantly against Indigenous people, for instance in making them work for welfare payments and imposing a disproportionate number of penalties for non-compliance.
- Legal arrangements for water rights and mineral rights severely impact the health, wellbeing, cultural cohesion and sustainability of Indigenous communities.
- "The Native Title Act 1993 is fundamentally flawed, favours mining interests, and is inconsistent with the principle of 'equality before the law'."
- "Australia remains the only former British colony without a treaty [with its First Nations]."
- "Asylum seekers, including children and stateless persons, remain subject to mandatory, indefinite and nonreviewable detention. Some people have been held in immigration detention for over ten years. Since 2015, detention facilities have become more prison-like; use of force has become commonplace."
- "Debate about population, national security and crime has seen a sharp rise in anti-immigration sentiment."
- "Australia has not fulfilled its 2016 UPR commitment to use existing human rights mechanisms to report on and protect the rights of older persons, nor to include an older people section in their UN reports. Australia is largely disengaged from the Open-Ended Working Group on Ageing (OEWGA)."
- A range of democratic freedoms have been withdrawn or reduced such as rights to free speech and protest.

- Legal assistance is wholly inadequate and the legal aid sector is underfunded.
- A whole range of other abuses are noted relating to health, the prison system, policing poverty, housing and homelessness, and conditions for workers.
- "Australia is failing to prevent human rights harms caused by climate change. Australia's emissions are increasing, its 2030 emissions reduction target is inadequate, and it spends more money supporting fossil fuels than climate action."
- "Australia is failing to implement appropriate measures to ensure all persons have the capacity to adapt to climate change and provide a just transition for workers and communities."
- "Australia is failing to ensure equity in climate action and ensure meaningful participation in decision making."
- "Australia is failing to assist developing countries to mitigate and adapt to climate change."[231]

All up, Australia's record on human rights marks it out as a serial abuser of rights, not a supporter. But this can be reversed if we examine the causes. In the next section I will set out some of the key factors that are causing the trend towards abuse of human rights by and in Australia.

Causal factors in Australia's abuse of human rights

If Australia is to have a chance of reversing its record as an abuser of human rights, we will need to examine elements of our cultural attitudes and viewpoints and assess the extent to which these are causal factors in the abuse.

The most serious abuses of human rights in Australia arise from three main causes which might be described as "destructive mindsets" in our governance:

---

[231] Australian NGO, Coalition, Human Rights Law Centre, Kingsford Legal Centre, Caxton Legal Centre, "Australia's Human Rights Score Card", April 2020, Ibid.

- One is Australia's desire to protect itself from terrorism – a natural and understandable mindset but one that has become more intense since 2001 and has been used to license increasing restrictions and breaches of human rights to a degree that is disproportionate to the threat of terrorism.
- The second is the desire of successive Australian governments to retain possession of title to certain lands (where native title hasn't been extinguished) and resources, particularly mineral resources but also water rights, and to maintain possession of those titles and rights (or the right to dispose of them) without providing compensation to the original Indigenous possessors – a mindset which has been constant since colonisation.
- The third is the desire of Australian governments from time to time to build support for entry into wars – a mindset constant since colonisation but which has been deeply embedded since World War I with great loss of life and at the expense of human rights.

Each of these destructive mindsets is fuelled by domestic political considerations and each is enabled by the inadequacies of the Constitution. Analysis of these mindsets can show how pervasive they are and how difficult it will be to shed them. But shed them we must if we are to secure human rights for Australians.

Destructive mindset No. 1 – The perceived need to counter threats of terrorism

In the first of these causal factors – the perceived need to counter threats of terrorism – Australia probably behaves neither better nor worse than several other powerful countries in allowing human rights abuses to occur within its area of control, ostensibly for the sake of protecting us from terrorism, although the scale on which we might commit such crimes, or allow them to be committed, may be somewhat smaller due to our remoteness from the theatre of many of the world's conflicts and the fact that we share no borders with other countries. Because of this remoteness we have also, for the most part, been conveniently able to shield ourselves from too close a view of any of our own crimes by the creation of offshore processing and detention facilities and by the sheer remoteness of communities on the continent where these crimes and abuses may abound – that is, in Indigenous communities.

In relation to non-citizens, we have directly or indirectly perpetrated these abuses on immigrants and refugees who in large part have committed no crime themselves but have nevertheless been transferred to vile places outside our view, where they have been detained in appalling conditions, subjected to what is defined as torture under the Convention Against Torture and Other Cruel, Inhuman or Degrading Treatment or Punishment, and subjected to other denials of their rights under a number of treaties to which Australia is a party.

As I have said, Australia's treatment of refugees and other people suspected of contemplating terrorism may be no worse than several other countries, although if a character like Donald Trump (a US president who took pride in separating refugee children from their parents) can see fit to shower our prime minister (Malcolm Turnbull) with praise for our offshore detention in terms as blackly comedic as "You are worse than I am,"[232] then it is surely time for a reappraisal. Such "compliments" indicate that we have entered a race to the bottom in showcasing who can be the cruellest. This is certainly the view of large numbers of other countries, 47 of which raised serious concerns about the Australian government's refugee, asylum and immigration detention policies when Australia's human rights record came up for its third five-yearly Universal Periodic Review (UPR) in 2021. As the Refugee Council of Australia reported:

> Of the 122 UN member states participating in Australia's UPR hearing before the UN Human Rights Council on 20 January 2021, 45 states made comments or recommendations on refugee and detention policies and another two states raised

---

[232] Luke Henriques-Gomes, "Donald Trump says 'much can be learned' from Australia's hardline asylum seeker policies", The Guardian, 27 June 2019.

> formal questions prior to the session. Critical to the 50 formal recommendations were the issues of offshore processing of people seeking asylum, indefinite immigration detention, lack of legislation to prohibit detention of children, refoulement, and lack of compliance of Australia's asylum and border management policies with international law.[233]

Australia has clearly sunk to a point where we showcase human rights abuses as a deterrent to asylum seekers. And we do this by design. It is deliberate. In the view of organisations such as Amnesty International and Human Rights Watch, Australia displays a level of deliberate cruelty that surpasses most other countries:

> Few other countries go to such lengths to deliberately inflict suffering on people seeking safety and freedom. Australian authorities are well aware of the abuses on Nauru. The Australian Human Rights Commission (AHRC), the Office of the United Nations High Commissioner for Refugees (UNHCR), a Senate Select Committee, and a government-appointed independent expert have each highlighted many of these practices, and called on the government to change them. The Australian government's persistent failure to address abuses committed under its authority on Nauru strongly suggests that they are adopted or condoned as a matter of policy.[234]

Nevertheless, this policy of performative cruelty is known to be a risk to our international reputation. Therefore for purposes of protecting ourselves against a charge of criminality in this deliberate

---

[233] Refugee Council of Australia, "UN Member States Challenge Australia's Refugee and Asylum Policies", 22 January 2021. UN member states challenge Australia's refugee and asylum policies (refugeecouncil.org.au)

[234] Human Rights Watch, "Australia: Appalling Abuse, Neglect of Refugees on Nauru", 2 August 2016. Australia: Appalling Abuse, Neglect of Refugees on Nauru | Human Rights Watch (hrw.org) Refugee Council of Australia, "Australia's man-made crisis on Nauru", 4 October 2020: "The Australian Human Rights Commission (AHRC), the Office of the United Nations High Commissioner for Refugees (UNHCR), a Senate Select Committee, and a government-appointed independent expert have each highlighted many of these practices, and called on the government to change them."

design, Australia has steadfastly refused over recent decades to revoke its reservations regarding Articles 10, 14 and 20 of the International Covenant on Civil and Political Rights. By maintaining these reservations we have attempted to persuade ourselves and the world that we can derogate from our duties under the Covenant – in a way that we would condemn for other nations – and that we can, among other things:

- freely expose women and children to harm; and/or
- shield ourselves from compensation claims for:
    - abuses and crimes committed in Australian jails and detention centres within Australian territory or offshore; and for
    - breaches of the principle that all people are equal before the law.

We may persuade ourselves that we need to commit these abuses for national security purposes, but that does not make them any less a crime. To the extent that the mindset (of using the need to avert terrorism as an excuse for depriving people of their rights) may lead to horrific crimes, if it hasn't already, it must be considered that a review of the necessity of this particular mindset is overdue and that there would surely be benefits in reappraising the extent to which terrorism is really a threat in Australia, relative to the damage we do to other things we value – such as our reputation, integrity and fundamental humanity – by too great a focus on national security at the expense of human rights.

Destructive mindset No. 2 – The desire to thwart native title claims

In the case of the second causal factor – the desire to thwart native title claims – Australia probably behaves worse than any other nation in the current century. As the Australian NGO Coalition has noted:

> Australia remains the only former British colony without a treaty [with its First Nations].[235]

Without a treaty and an Indigenous Voice to parliament enshrined in the Constitution, Australia will find it impossible to address the current extraordinary social and economic disparity and political marginalisation of Aboriginal communities. In some respects, such as the incarceration rate for Australia's Indigenes, that disparity is the worst in the developed world. It will only get worse if there is no constitutional recognition for Australia's First Nations. And as the economic disparity worsens and the disparity in the political influence of First Nations compared to mining and fossil fuel interests widens, so the nation's contribution and vulnerability to climate change will spiral towards catastrophe. So this mindset, too, is long overdue for reappraisal.

Destructive mindset No. 3 – The desire of Australian governments to build support for war

In the case of the third causal factor – the desire of Australian governments to build support for wars – this is probably the most destructive mindset of all within our governance system. We tolerate it at our direct peril, inasmuch as it increases Australia's exposure to retaliatory attack on military and/or economic fronts. And we tolerate it at the immediate expense of our freedoms, inasmuch as the mindset schools Australians to accept a loss of freedoms for the sake of national security, even though the threat to our national security is one of our own making when we seek to be an aggressor.

Australia is often an aggressor – injecting itself into conflicts in territories that have not posed a direct threat to us. Our history is as a nation that seeks to fight the wars of other countries – particularly Britain and the US. Australia is a subaltern to these powers. And to ensure it stays that way, Australian governments have worked hard to build war and readiness for war into the national psyche ever since Gallipoli, where we submitted our sons as canon fodder in a country

---

[235] Australian NGO, Coalition, Human Rights Law Centre, Kingsford Legal Centre, Caxton Legal Centre, "Australia's Human Rights Score Card", April 2020, Op. Cit.

on the other side of the world that had not attacked us. We have been schooled to assume that war and war heroism are essential parts of our identity, so much so that the topic of government obligations to Australians to secure *peace* hardly features in our national discourse. In any sane governance system (even in the modern Hobbesian state), citizens should be able to expect that their governments will consider it their *primary* duty to protect them from war. In particular, Australians should expect their governments not to provoke or start one – ever. But the default stance is that war readiness must be maintained and for that purpose Australians should be denied their rights and even the right of protection from war itself.

The world is a place of constant global conflict but the right to protection from war would be available to Australians to the fullest extent possible in such a world if the government exercised responsible compliance with its obligations under Article 20 of the International Covenant on Civil and Political Rights. And yet successive Australian governments have refused to do that. Article 20 states that:

1. Any propaganda for war shall be prohibited by law.
2. Any advocacy of national, racial or religious hatred that constitutes incitement to discrimination, hostility or violence *shall be prohibited by law*.[236] [Emphasis added.]

In an attempt to comply with at least some of the spirit of this Article, Australia enacted the Racial Discrimination Act in 1975. This legislation was amended in 1995 by the Racial Hatred Act and it prohibits acts designed to offend, insult, humiliate, intimidate or discriminate against persons on the basis of race, colour, national or ethnic origin.[237] Several states (but not the Northern Territory) have also legislated against racial vilification and incitement to racial hatred. In general though, war propaganda is not unlawful in Australia and we might reasonably assume that any such propaganda

[236] International Covenant on Civil and Political Rights, Article 20, International Covenant on Civil and Political Rights- external site

[237] See in particular sections 18B, 18C and 18D of the Racial Discrimination Act 1975, http://www8.austlii.edu.au/cgi-bin/viewdb/au/legis/cth/consol_act/rda1975202/

in the form of a national policy or executive statement by the federal government itself could lawfully include racially discriminatory postures and policies.

These policies could manifest in the domestic setting, for instance, through segregation or internment preparatory to or during war, particularly of citizens with Asiatic or Muslim heritage. In reality they already *do* manifest in the domestic setting in the form of illegal detention of genuine refugees and denial of their rights under international law. But they are also apparent in their deep intrusion into the lives of all citizens in metadata laws enacted in 2015.[238]

The metadata laws made under the Telecommunications (Interception and Access) Amendment (Data Retention) Act 2015 require phone and internet providers to store metadata of all subscribers. But they are by no means a benign instrument. They are quite specifically designed to provide a platform on which abuses of power by intelligence agencies can be more easily mounted, including selective (mis)use of metadata to form a "reasonable suspicion" that a person has committed an offence (even though the actual contents of calls, emails and internet browsing are not being stored). Based on said reasonable suspicion (formed with no evidence other than a log of a call, email or internet search) a person can be raided, detained without charge, provided with no information of the nature of any offence, and is unable to complain because it is a criminal offence to disclose information relating to a "special intelligence operation".

These metadata laws are just one part of a wider framework of anti-terrorism laws which significantly erode the rights of Australians without sufficient accountability and safeguards[239] being in place to

---

[238] Telecommunications (Interception and Access) Amendment (Data Retention) Act 2015. TELECOMMUNICATIONS (INTERCEPTION AND ACCESS) AMENDMENT (DATA RETENTION) ACT 2015 (NO. 39, 2015) - SCHEDULE 1 Data retention (austlii.edu.au)

[239] See Commonwealth of Australia, "Council of Australian Governments Review of Counter-Terrorism Legislation", 2013, pages xiii, 45 and 54: This review recommended the need for additional safeguards against abuse by government. Recommendations were also made by a Senate committee in 2005 to increase safeguards but not all of these were accepted by the government. Accessible at

prevent abuse of the extra powers granted under these laws. They include over 80 pieces of legislation[240] since 2002, several of which introduce or increase:

- powers of police to hold people in police custody without charge,
- powers of surveillance and interrogation of non-suspects,
- powers of monitoring non-suspects' computers,
- powers of coercion in testimony,
- secret warrants and secret evidence,
- warrantless search powers for persons and homes,
- immunity from civil and criminal prosecution for ASIO officers in covert "special intelligence operations" (except in cases of torture, murder, and rape), and
- powers to jail journalists who inadvertently reveal ASIO "special intelligence operations".

In short, these policies that are ostensibly designed to keep us safe from the threat of terrorism and wars – wars we are told by defence hawks are necessary to protect what on ANZAC Day in 2021 the Secretary of Home Affairs Mike Pezzullo called "our precious liberty"[241] – are already seriously impacting the precious liberty of citizens.

In the international setting these racially discriminatory postures and policies are fully manifest in the obvious antagonism of

---

https://www.ag.gov.au/Consultations/Documents/COAGCTReview/Final%20Report.PDF

[240] Tony Walker, Vice Chancellor's Fellow at La Trobe University, "Press freedom must be enshrined in a charter of rights", Sydney Morning Herald, 3 November 2019, Op. Cit. See also Nick Evershed and Michael Safi, "All of Australia's national security changes since 9/11 in a timeline", The Guardian, 19 October 2015, accessible at https://www.theguardian.com/australia-news/ng-interactive/2015/oct/19/all-of-australias-national-security-changes-since-911-in-a-timeline

[241] Mike Pezzullo, Secretary of Department of Home Affairs, "The Longing for Peace, the Curse of War", ANZAC Day Speech 25 April 2021. "By our resolve and our strength, by our preparedness of arms, and by our statecraft, let us get about reducing the likelihood of war – but not at the cost of our precious liberty." ANZAC Day message (homeaffairs.gov.au)

Australian defence hawks towards China and Russia. This antagonism – reliant as it is on vague and (hitherto) unsubstantiated assertions of threats to our liberty being posed by authoritarian regimes – is the equivalent of the sort of advocacy of national hatred that is prohibited under Article 20. This sort of advocacy, particularly when it is used in relation to China, is only poorly disguised racism. It is very effective in inciting many Australians into supporting hostility and possibly violence – meaning war – with China.[242] As the Director of the Australia Institute's International and Security Affairs program and former senior Foreign Affairs, Attorney General's and Defence official, Allan Behm, observed after nation-wide research polling Australian and Taiwanese attitudes to China in August 2022:

> The more that the anti-China lobby beats the drums of war, the more afraid of China Australians become. This research indicates that the rhetoric on China and the fearmongering around the risk of war has had an impact on public opinion. It is astonishing that Australians are more afraid of an attack from China than the Taiwanese are.
>
> The results show popular opinion is detached from geopolitical and geostrategic reality. The results support the case for a reset in the Australia-China relationship and the manner in which we hold this important national conversation. Such a reset should be based on facts and the national interest rather than the fear peddling we saw in the recent Australian federal election by some for domestic, partisan interests.[243]

---

[242] The 2022 Lowy Institute poll mentioned in Chapter 5 shows how effective propaganda about China can be in building support for war. In 2021, 57% of respondents to the Lowy poll indicated that they have a preference to remain neutral in the event of a military conflict between China and the United States, while only 41% thought we should support the United States. In the 2022 Lowy poll (after the invasion of Ukraine) only 51% indicated a preference to remain neutral and 46% thought we should support the US. Natasha Kassam, Lowy Institute Poll 2022, page 20, Op. Cit.

[243] The Australia Institute, Media Release, 22 August 2022, "Research Shows Impact of Fearmongering: Australians more Frightened of China than Taiwanese".

The effectiveness of this anti-China propaganda as an incitement to war has been increased (unfortunately) by the fact that over the four years to 2022 large sections of Australian news media businesses weighed in on the discourse by adopting words such as "aggressive" in relation to China, and did so without actually providing tangible evidence of aggression towards Australia from that source, certainly not military aggression. For instance, China was not reported to have conducted in Australian waters the sort of forward military activities by which Australia aggressively probes and targets the defences of China in the South China Sea. At the time of writing, China does not appear to have reacted to that aggression with tit-for-tat intrusion into Australian waters. Nevertheless Australian governments have licensed themselves to do in Chinese waters and its nearby international waters what they would surely not tolerate in their own. Australian governments do not stop to ask themselves how they would feel if Chinese intelligence, surveillance and reconnaissance planes were operating off our coast, probing our defences and even dropping sonobuoys to detect our submarines (as Australia has done in the South China Sea).[244] The fact is that neither Russia nor China has adopted an "aggressive" stance towards Australia. And although sections of the media and even the prime minister in 2022, Anthony Albanese, might have preferred to portray China's complaints (about Australia's treatment of trade relationships with China) and its suggestions (on how those relationships could be improved) as "demands", there is no evidence that China has made "demands" of Australia at all, let alone unreasonable demands which threaten our sovereignty. Nor could it be said that China's agreements with some Pacific nations on various economic and civil assistance programs constitute a threat to Australia or a restrictive intrusion into our region.

More thoughtful commentators have struggled to provide some balance to this portrayal of China as aggressive towards Australia.

---

[244] Mark J. Valencia, "Why is Australia conducting provocative intelligence flights and activities off the China coast in support of the US?", John Menadue's Pearls and Irritations, 18 August 2022.

Experienced diplomats such as Geoff Raby, a former ambassador to China, have stated that:

> Exercising military power to create the new [world] order is not part of China's grand strategy. Military strength is for China's own security, not regional or global hegemony.[245]

But such views and the substantial evidence these more thoughtful analysts[246] provide in support of their assessments of China have had little effect in calming the situation and the fears of Australians. Instead (at least until the time of writing) the tension and fear has escalated, prompted by a "drums of war" discourse so irresponsibly brandished by Canberra hawks. The implication of this hawkishness is that Australia could win a war with China when the odds are plainly that we would not. At the very best we would have to expect that we could not emerge unscathed. Experienced analysts who should be listened to have shown that even with America's help, Australia could not succeed in a war with China and that America itself is unlikely to succeed in such a war, despite its military might.[247]

Ironically, what this might suggest is that, for all the bluster of its China hawks, Australia is unlikely to hazard a real war with China. Hawks might be irresponsible but they're not likely to be that stupid. It is much more likely that the point of the bluster and the senseless proposal for spending on nuclear submarines under AUKUS lies elsewhere. It lies probably in the competition between the defence establishment and the rest of the public sector for funding and in the desire of the American military and arms industry for more buyers. But it also lies in the value it offers (at least to the most conservative and secretive in our polity) in creation of an illusion that the rights of Australians need to be curtailed and more than that, need to be

---

[245] Geoff Raby, *China's Grand Strategy and Australia's Future in the New Global Order*, Melbourne University Press, 2020, Kindle edition, Loc 562 of 4894.

[246] Among these more thoughtful analysts, we can count Allan Behm of the Australia Institute and former senior diplomats and public servants such as Bruce Haigh, Mike Scrafton, John Menadue, Mike Gilligan, Richard Tanter and Hugh White.

[247] See Hugh White, "Sleepwalk to War: Australia's unthinking alliance with America", Quarterly Essay, Black Inc. June 2022.

considered as a threat in and of themselves to the very national security we crave, rather than as the legitimate, primary object of the citizens who choose to live their lives in a democratic country precisely because they think these rights will be available. The bluster serves the purpose of quelling calls for these rights.

It is difficult to understand why Australian politicians are unique among democratic countries in the developed world in not prioritising human rights. But the fact is the vast majority have shown no sign of paying any more than lip service to the codification of rights in law, at least not at the federal level. Some progressive politicians such as Gareth Evans, Gough Whitlam and Susan Ryan, have prominently championed constitutional reform for human rights purposes, or more specifically to provide protections for individuals against the misuse of government power. As Gareth Evans and others observed in 1983:

> A frequent complaint ... is that the framers of the Constitution were so interested in preserving State rights that they forgot about the fundamental rights and liberties of the citizens. That complaint has been expressed by many civil liberties councils, constitutional reform groups and others who have argued that, since the cornerstone of liberal democracy is the individual, our constitution should contain a Bill of Rights. As the former New South Wales Attorney General, Mr Walker put it, 'there are things so fundamental that they should not be left to the whim or arrogance of the government of the day'. More narrowly, it has been argued that a 'Makarrata' or compact, between white and black Australians, might appropriately be given a constitutional foundation, the object being to right a wrong, and 'to establish a firm foundation for the future relationships of Aborigines and other inhabitants'.[248]

---

[248] John McMillan, Gareth Evans and Haddon Storey, *Australia's Constitution: Time for Change?*, Law Foundation of New South Wales, Allen and Unwin Australia, 1983, page 19.

These remarks were made in 1983, when of course many politically active Australians would still have been reeling from the spectacular example of "misuse of power" that brought about the dismissal of a prime minister by a governor-general in 1975 – the nearest we have ever come to a constitutional crisis. But more than 40 years later, Australia has still made no progress towards embedding "the fundamental rights and liberties of the citizens" in law. And the foreshadowed need for a Makarrata with a constitutional foundation is also still in doubt, although there is some movement on that particular front. Any detached assessment would have to conclude that progress at the federal level for any Australian – black, white, or otherwise – is non-existent when it comes to human rights. If anything, we have gone backwards and an increase in racism – in both political and general discourse, but especially in discourse surrounding defence policy – is the result.

Fundamentally, Australia's defence and intelligence establishment (but notably, not the diplomatic corps) has, at least between 2016 and 2022, persisted with a strong undertone of racism in defence postures. This is a discourse which runs contrary to the spirit, if not the terms, of international law under Article 20. And yet it is not illegal in Australia. On the contrary it is enabled here because the Constitution is structured to allow the federal government to make laws "for the people of any race" (section 51 (xxvi)) and confers unlimited external powers on the Commonwealth (section 51 (xxix)). Notwithstanding the Racial Discrimination Act 1975, there is no effective limit on the extent to which an Australian government may permit itself to be discriminatory on the basis of race and to use that discriminatory power to incite war.

To summarise, the inadequacies of Australia's Constitution render it antithetical to peace. It acts instead as a blanket permission for incitement to war. In the 21st century Australian defence hawks take full advantage of that permission, very often in a manner that is contrary to the best interests of Australians and fully at odds with preservation of their liberties – their rights and freedoms (not to mention peace itself). Since 2002, Australian governments have persisted in enabling themselves to obviate human rights considerations in their policies on war, defence, military and weapons build-up, strategic alliances, intelligence, secrecy, privacy and any other national security consideration (legitimate or illegitimate). Legally, rights can be trashed on the basis of race and so can races themselves if it helps build an appetite for war. As I have already said, this is fully contrary to the purpose of Article 20, and in refusing to withdraw our reservation on the Article, Australia is doing nothing less than licensing itself to behave as a fascist, pugnacious, warmongering state. This is the inevitable result of the entrenched practice of successive Australian governments to prioritise war over peace in policy and in general discourse on the national identity.

In an attempt to justify its refusal to make war propaganda illegal, Australia has stated that in relation to the International Covenant on Civil and Political Rights:

> Australia interprets the rights provided for by articles 19, 21 and 22 as consistent with article 20; accordingly, the Commonwealth and the constituent States, having legislated with respect to the subject matter of the article in matters of practical concern in the interest of public order (*ordre public*), the right is reserved not to introduce any further legislative provision on these matters.[249]

In this entirely specious argument Australia is asserting that it may rest on legislation it has created that supports the right of Australians to freedom of expression (Article 19), assembly (Article 21) and association (Article 22). But these rights have not been codified in legislation at the federal level and it is fully misleading to imply that they have. On the contrary, since 2001 these rights have been reduced by federal legislation. Nevertheless, in misleading submissions to Universal Periodic Reviews the Australian government has brazenly persisted with assertions that its credentials in protection of human rights are demonstrated thus:

> The Australian Government is focussed on protecting civil and political rights for all persons within Australia. The High Court

---

[249] Department of Foreign Affairs and Trade, "Australian and Human Rights: An Overview, 4th edition", December 2017, page 35, Op. Cit.

> has interpreted Australia's Constitution to include a fundamental protection for the freedom of political communication. Other fundamental rights and freedoms, such as freedom of expression more generally, are protected by the general common law presumption that in the absence of clear and unambiguous legislation to the contrary (which would be subject to the human rights scrutiny processes described above), parliaments do not intend to interfere with fundamental rights and freedoms. All Australians are free to express their views within the framework of Australian law, including controversial and challenging ideas and opinions.[250]

This attempted assertion of the Australian government's credentials as a supporter of political rights (such as the right to free speech) is false. For a start, the High Court has not "interpreted Australia's Constitution to include a fundamental protection for the freedom of political communication". The Court has found that "freedom of political communication" is "implied" by the Constitution but it is not a personal right of individuals and only applies in certain circumstances. For instance, the Court ruled that the right to freedom of political communication could not be relied on by federal public servant, Michaela Banerji, who in 2018 appealed unsuccessfully against the termination of her employment by Comcare for her anonymous social media posts criticising Australian government immigration policy.[251] The ruling against Michaela

---

[250] Australian Government, Attorney-General's Department, "National report submitted in accordance with paragraph 5 of the annex to Human Rights Council resolution 16/21, Australia", Submission to the Universal Periodic Review 2020, paragraph 18. https://www.ag.gov.au/rights-and-protections/publications/universal-periodic-review-national-report-australia-2020

[251] High Court of Australia, Comcare vs Banerji at https://jade.io/article/657141?at.hl=Banerji: "It [the implied right to political communication] is a restriction on legislative power which arises as a necessary implication from ss 7, 24, 64 and 128 and related sections of the *Constitution* and, as such, extends only so far as is necessary to preserve and protect the system of representative and responsible government mandated by the *Constitution*[44]. Accordingly, although the effect of a law on an individual's or a group's ability to participate in political communication is relevant to the assessment of the law's effect on the implied freedom, the question of whether

Banerji demonstrated that not only is freedom of political communication not a right conferred on individual Australians, it may also not be relied on by public servants in general. By virtue of the Banerji ruling, public servants would be wise to assume that they should not seek to exercise a right to free expression lest they lose their job. The ruling emboldened the government to increase its suppression of free speech by public servants by tightening Australian Public Service Guidelines so that they restricted public comment by public servants, even to the point of prohibiting a "Like" on a politically charged Facebook comment. Something is on the verge of being seriously out of joint in terms of equal human rights in Australia, especially when someone contemplating joining the public service must simultaneously contemplate giving up the right to participate in civic debate. And no other conclusion can be drawn than that it is an outright lie for the Australian federal government to testify to the Universal Periodic Review that "All Australians are free to express their views within the framework of Australian law, including controversial and challenging ideas and opinions."

Beyond the sobering example in the Banerji case of systematic denial of a fundamental human right, it is also plainly specious for the government to assert (as it did in the quote I have just cited) that freedom of expression in Australia is protected by "the general common law presumption that in the absence of clear and unambiguous legislation to the contrary ... parliaments do not intend to interfere with fundamental rights and freedoms".[252] This is nothing more than a statement that the right to free expression will only be tolerated by the government for as long as it doesn't make a law

---

the law imposes an unjustified burden on the implied freedom of political communication is a question of the law's effect on political communication *as a whole*[45]. More specifically, even if a law significantly restricts the ability of an individual or a group of persons to engage in political communication, the law will not infringe the implied freedom of political communication unless it has a material unjustified effect on political communication as a whole."

[252] Australian Government, Attorney-General's Department, "National report submitted in accordance with paragraph 5 of the annex to Human Rights Council resolution 16/21, Australia", Submission to the Universal Periodic Review 2020, paragraph 18, Op. Cit.

against it. And since Australian governments in the 21st century have frequently made laws against it, laws which they seek to defend on the grounds of national security (or any other ground they can find), the statement is entirely disingenuous. Some of these laws are truly frightening. They include laws which:

- treat journalism and peaceful protest as "espionage";
- impose extensive prison sentences (25 years to life) merely for reporting or "dealing with" "information or an article" which "concerns Australia's national security";[253]
- place the onus of proof on the defendants (the government does not have to prove you did it, you have to prove you didn't – in effect this removes the presumption of innocence for defendants);
- enable the Commonwealth to refuse access by a defendant to evidence necessary for their defence;
- rob defendants, particularly whistleblowers making genuine public interest disclosures (including of government misconduct in national security matters), of the right to plead public interest as a defence;[254] and

---

[253] Australian Government, "National Security Legislation Amendment (Espionage and Foreign Interference) Act 2018", Section 91.1: "A person commits an offence if: (a) the person deals with information or an article; and (b) the information or article: (i) has a security classification; or (ii) concerns Australia's national security; and (c) the person intends that the person's conduct will: (i) prejudice Australia's national security; or (ii) advantage the national security of a foreign country; and (d) the conduct results or will result in the information or article being communicated or made available to a foreign principal or a person acting on behalf of a foreign principal."

[254] Bronwyn Kelly, *By 2050: Planning a better future for our children in 21st century democratic Australia*, March 2020, Op. Cit., Chapter 8 – Subsection: Checking for Threats to Democracy: Australian law in 2022 significantly limits the rights of whistleblowers who make public interest disclosures of classified information on immigration or border enforcement matters – legislation which deems any and all such disclosures "reckless", before the fact, merely because the information being disclosed has a security classification. In these disclosures, no onus exists on the government to prove that the disclosure was reckless and contrary to the public interest, and a defendant cannot plead public interest as a defence. This legislation effectively makes it impossible for any public interest disclosure at all in

- trigger wide-ranging suppression of any outside scrutiny or media reporting.[255]

These laws can consign any Australian – no matter how responsible, innocent and peaceful – to a nightmare of repression, torture and ruin. None of this escapes the attention of either the United Nations or its member states. In their eyes, Australia will not be seen as a state where "parliaments do not intend to interfere with fundamental rights and freedoms". On the contrary, successive Australian parliaments have displayed an escalating tendency to do the opposite.

The apparent stubbornness with which Australia resists removing its reservation about Article 20, and continues to legislate against human rights (particularly the rights to free speech), is testimony to the stubbornness of its commitment to building support for war whenever a government may wish. In the main, this wish to build support for war will be politically motivated for domestic electioneering purposes (as it was in the lead-up to the 2022 federal election) rather than having anything to do with the actual need to defend Australia from aggression and external threats. Both major

---

the area of immigration and the operation of the Australian Border Force established in 2015 and there is now no mechanism by which Australians can be advised when the government is secretly acting contrary to the public interest in these areas. By 2050: Planning a better future for our children in 21st century democratic Australia eBook : Kelly, Bronwyn: Amazon.com.au: Kindle Store

[255] See Nicola Paris, "Suppression of the Right to Protest" in "Green Agenda", 29 April 2019. In this legislation the right and left ends of the Australian political spectrum are in agreement in their concern about restrictions on the right of free speech: "25 years jail for peaceful protest. That is the potential outcome from the *Espionage and Foreign Interference Bill* (EFI) that was introduced by the Liberals and rubber stamped by Labor in 2018. It was slammed through with such speed that the cross-benches had one hour to examine what was described as the most serious overhaul to national security in 40 years. Introduced alongside the *Electoral Funding and Disclosure Reform Bill* (EFDR) and the *Foreign Influence Transparency Scheme Bill* (FITS) it even troubled the Institute of Public Affairs, which called for the withdrawal of the legislation, stating 'The IPA is inherently concerned about any proposal that seeks to 'manage' political debate by limiting freedom of speech.'" Accessible at https://greenagenda.org.au/2019/04/right-to-protest/

parties – Labor and Liberal/National – seek to rely on election tactics that engender fear about terrorism and war. That is, they rely on war propaganda or discourses which attempt to legitimise war. They both heavily prioritise discourse favouring war over any discourse on peace. This is evident in the policy platforms of the two major parties for the 2022 election – platforms which almost identically prioritised arms escalation over diplomacy and human rights.[256] These two party platforms – in their unambiguous preference for war over peace and human rights – are fully antithetical to the Charter of the United Nations. As the Charter says:

> WE THE PEOPLES OF THE UNITED NATIONS DETERMINED
>
> to save succeeding generations from the scourge of war, which twice in our lifetime has brought untold sorrow to mankind, and
>
> to reaffirm faith in fundamental human rights, in the dignity and worth of the human person, in the equal rights of men and women and of nations large and small, and
>
> to establish conditions under which justice and respect for the obligations arising from treaties and other sources of international law can be maintained, and
>
> to promote social progress and better standards of life in larger freedom,
>
> AND FOR THESE ENDS
>
> to practice tolerance and live together in peace with one another as good neighbors, and
>
> to unite our strength to maintain international peace and security, and

[256] For a detailed breakdown of the policies of the major parties – Liberal/National, Labor and the Greens – see Bronwyn Kelly, Australian Community Futures Planning, "Election 2022 – Australian Federal Parliament: Assessment of Major Party Policies", May 2022, pages 33 and 51. https://www.austcfp.com.au/better-futures-commitment-index

> to ensure, by the acceptance of principles and the institution of methods, that armed force shall not be used, save in the common interest, and
>
> to employ international machinery for the promotion of the economic and social advancement of all peoples,
>
> HAVE RESOLVED TO COMBINE OUR EFFORTS TO ACCOMPLISH THESE AIMS.[257]

On at least three of these determinations and aims, Australia has failed in the 21st century to live up to the full measure of its "resolve". In refusing to withdraw reservations about Articles 10, 14 and 20 in the International Covenant on Civil and Political Rights and by virtue of promotion of aggressive defence policies (not to mention breaches of the "rule of law" in several international matters) it has largely:

- failed to "establish conditions under which justice and respect for the obligations arising from treaties and other sources of international law can be maintained";
- failed to "unite our strength to maintain international peace and security"; and
- failed to "ensure, by the acceptance of principles and the institution of methods, that armed force shall not be used, save in the common interest".

Other nations have of course failed in these matters too; but Australia cannot exonerate itself. Despite being one of the first signatories on this Charter, Australia – apart from a brief period between the late 1970s and the end of the Cold War[258] – has

---

[257] Preamble to the "Charter of the United Nations and Statute of the International Court of Justice", San Francisco, 1945, Op. Cit.

[258] From the late 1970s until the end of the Cold War Australia shifted from a "Forward Defence" policy to a "Defence of Australia" policy. Hugh White, *How to Defend Australia*, La Trobe University Press, Black Inc., 2019, page 65: "The Defence of Australia policy, unlike the Forward Defence policy it replaced, was absolutely clear that Australia's forces would not be designed for alliance operations, but solely for the defence of Australia. Without ever ruling it out, the policy downplayed Australian military support to America, and made it clear that any support would be provided by the capabilities designed for the defence of the

persistently pursued war at the expense of human rights (our own and others'). We live with a Constitution which enables the fabrication of policies to help Australia start a war (like Iraq) or enter one that is offensive rather than defensive (like Vietnam). It is well suited to starting wars and entirely ill-suited to avoiding or ending them. And it is well suited to denying rights rather than preserving them. The Constitution likewise facilitates suppression of dissenting voices on climate change, treatment of refugees and Indigenous exclusion and it will continue to deny Australians those rights for as long as it contains no charter of human rights.

The impact of destructive mindsets on human rights and the prospects for peace

The above three examples of pervasive destructive mindsets show that Australian governments have distinctly preferred a Constitution in which human rights can be set aside whenever – and preferably *before* – everyday Australians (perhaps in a mood for self-determination) might choose to exercise those rights in a manner that would interfere with any government agendas that have the objective of goading the populace into war, frightening them into silence, or suppressing support for the claims of Indigenous communities for shares in returns from Australia's vast mineral and resource assets.

While these mindsets persist, the nation itself as well as the governments we elect will tacitly or openly support the subjugation of human rights so that they will be a secondary or even irrelevant consideration in policy development. This is likely to apply despite the fact that subjugation of human rights is fully perverse – a self-destructive self-denial – by which I mean that Australians have tended to perversely deny themselves rights in a manner that propels them to war rather than protects them from it.

---

continent. That inevitably set rather low limits on what our contribution would be worth militarily."

The fact that a large proportion of Australians have been well-schooled – or, shall we say, tamed – to accept limitations of their human rights in exchange for "national security" shows just how effective the mindset for war and counterterrorism is. As the results of the 2020 Lowy Institute poll suggested, a substantial majority of Australians (59%) in 2019 agreed that "the Australian government has got the balance right between the need for press freedom and the need to enforce the law and protect national security". The same proportion (59%) thought "Australia's intelligence agencies have got the balance right between protecting national security and also being appropriately open and transparent with the Australian people about their activities". And an overwhelming proportion of Australians (80%) thought "Australia's intelligence agencies are effective at protecting Australia's national security".[259] In short, Australians, at least in 2019, readily accepted that despite a massive legislative program removing their rights and despite a clear decline in transparency and ethics in governance,[260] national security concerns had not unacceptably overridden their rights and the need for transparency in governance.

These results might reasonably be taken to indicate that, culturally, most Australians are generally comfortable with secrecy and a lack of transparency and suppression of free speech by governments – as though loss of rights is the price we must pay (and are quite willing to pay) for safety from war and terrorism. But if this is actually the cultural preference of Australians it is nevertheless a high risk preference, particularly in circumstances where governments are untrustworthy and trust in them is proportionately low (as it is in Australia). It is also a highly perverse preference insofar as the loss of rights of free speech, assembly and association is likely to expose Australians to the risk of wars they don't actually want. The mindset that suggests that:

---

[259] Natasha Kassam, Lowy Institute Poll 2020, page 38. lowyinsitutepoll-2020.pdf (lowyinstitute.org)

[260] In 2019, Australia's score in Transparency International's annual Corruption Perceptions Index declined by more than any other developed country. 2019_CPI_Report_EN.pdf (transparency.org)

1. war is inevitable, particularly by implying that an external, authoritarian style power (in Australia's case in the 21st century this power is represented as China) is intent on invasion, world domination, destruction of democracy and negation of all human rights; and that
2. the only way to protect ourselves from this is to create a secret state and exclude ourselves from any say in whether the war should be provoked or entered; and that
3. we therefore should give up rights and freedoms to be safe from that ostensibly aggressive external power,

is essentially and fatally perverse, not simply because it wildly misrepresents China as more a threat than an opportunity – and actually creates the threat where none existed beforehand – but also because it encourages Australians to think that giving up their human rights is in their best interests when in fact *their primary interest is their human rights*. The mindset encourages us to presuppose that to be safe from those who would ostensibly take away our rights, we must give up our rights even before the supposed war has started. More than that, we should lock ourselves down into the same sort of secret and autocratic state we revile in our newly simulated enemy. We must accept that war propaganda – which in the 1960s we agreed at the United Nations should be prohibited by law – is vital to our security and freedom when in fact it is more capable of bringing on a war and represents an instant loss of freedom.

Bearing in mind that this entirely perverse mindset is so ingrained in Australian culture, we might not have much reason to be too optimistic about our prospects for escaping it to the safer place of peaceful collaboration we longed for at the United Nations in 1945. But as I showed in Chapter 5 there is evidence of a will to peace among Australians. And we also have the *means* of reversing both the mindset for war and the other two destructive mindsets. In the next sections I will begin to outline how we can do that.

The reversibility of destructive mindsets

That the Australian government has refused since 1966 to make war propaganda illegal marks out Australia as a nation whose governments are hungry for enemies – because that is how populations are made passive and control is exercised by entirely unimaginative and plainly incompetent governments in both peace time and in war. Defence policy analysts will assert that this posture of simulating enemies well before they emerge as real military adversaries or even palpable military threats is simply healthy vigilance and is essential for strategic defence planning. They will perhaps claim that "eternal vigilance is the price of liberty". This might be reasonable if strategic defence planning were matched by strategic peace planning and if eternal vigilance were matched by support of liberty and freedoms. But as I have already said, the topic of government obligations to Australians to secure *peace* hardly features in our national discourse and in any case eternal vigilance is not the price of liberty. In a free society it should be evident that the opposite is true: that is, the price of eternal vigilance is liberty – liberty lost.

The form in which this propaganda is foisted on Australians may look like mere readiness for war and healthy vigilance, but it is in no way so benign and harmless. It is self-harm, destroying instantly the very thing it purports to save – human rights. The lost liberty of Australians in the first two decades of the 21st century arises mostly from government sponsored war propaganda (sometimes veiled, sometimes not) rather than from any genuine emergency such as the Covid-19 pandemic, when restrictions were invoked on a temporary basis to stop a loss of life on a massive scale. But unlike the temporary lost liberties of the pandemic, the restrictions on freedom that were legislated by federal governments ostensibly in the interest of "national security" after 2001 are likely to be permanent (unless we choose to reverse them) and are likely to expose Australians to loss of life on a scale more massive than the pandemic, especially if they nullify those voices calling on governments to stem the risks arising from climate change. And yet, as the Lowy poll showed, the majority of Australians have been tamed to quietly accept these restrictions. As Hugh White might put it, we sleepwalk to war.[261] I would add that we have shown a distinct preference to sleepwalk to climate disaster too.

That said, Australians can still choose to reverse this. In the early 2020s they are showing distinct signs of reversing their sleepwalk to climate disaster. At the same time they can choose to secure the human rights and freedoms which have been fast disappearing. And in placing those rights squarely on policy agendas as essential to the *primary* purpose of government – which is *peace* – they can use them to release Australians from the expense and the likelihood of destruction from war and climate change. If we put human rights and peace first and relegate readiness for war from its current disproportionate priority and dangerous pedestal to its proper place – that is, to a place we work to avoid – we are far more likely to preserve the lifestyle, freedoms and democracy we value. To do this we will need to remake the Constitution to insert our first claim of universal human rights. In a parallel set of amendments we will also need to consign the racist clauses in the Constitution to the dustbin of history. Unless we do that, we will find that citizens are dragged back again into the politics of warmongering and its attendant curtailing of the very rights such belligerence would claim to protect.

Despite poll results showing that Australians are willing to accept limitations of their human rights in exchange for national security, other evidence is emerging that strongly suggests Australians are likely to be ready for a transition in national identity and cultural orientation in favour of human rights. In 2021 the Human Rights Law Centre commissioned a poll of over 1,000 Australians on support for a charter of human rights. Results showed that support for a charter had risen sharply since the onset of Covid-19:

- 83 percent of people believe there should be a document that sets out in clear language the rights and responsibilities

[261] Hugh White, "Sleepwalk to War: Australia's unthinking alliance with America", Quarterly Essay, Black Inc. June 2022.

that everyone has here in Australia, an increase from 66 percent in 2019.

- 74 percent agreed that a charter of human rights would help people and communities to make sure the government does the right thing, compared to 56 percent two years earlier.
- There was a similar surge in support for the idea of a charter of human rights, with 46 percent supporting a charter and only 10 percent opposed, compared with 33 percent support and 10 percent opposition in 2019. The increased support came from the category of people who were not sure, which dropped 14 percent across the two years.
- The biggest increases in support were from younger people.[262]

These results suggest that the experience of Covid-19 may have woken Australians from the above-mentioned sleepwalk, at least as far as they may perceive a need to codify their human rights in law before they are extinguished entirely and perhaps forever by an intrusive state. However, the Constitution itself presents Australians with significant challenges to any program of reform, let alone one as fundamental as constitutional enshrinement of a charter of human rights. These challenges can be overcome if the will is there. In fact they are far easier to overcome than challenges posed by climate change and somewhat easier to overcome than the challenges posed by tensions between global superpowers. Unlike laws about war and climate change, enshrinement of human rights in the Constitution is an issue that can be dealt with without the need to defer to the priorities of other nations. It is within our domestic control, and other than for the mindsets I have discussed above, there is no major cultural barrier to conferring equal rights on all citizens. Ask any Australian whether she or he thinks she or he should have equal and universal human rights. It would be extremely difficult in any statistically valid polling to come up with a majority who would say

---

[262] Human Rights Law Centre, "COVID-19 sees huge increase in support for a Charter of Human Rights: poll", Media Release, 9 September 2021. COVID-19 sees huge increase in support for a Charter of Human Rights: poll | Human Rights Law Centre (hrlc.org.au)

No. Results of the surveys I have quoted in Chapter 5 about the high value placed by Australians on equality, egalitarianism, social justice, freedom and democracy, would suggest that such a result would be impossible. These results all imply strong support for access to universal human rights on an equal basis. Nevertheless there are likely to be political barriers – politicians who will come up with crazy campaigns against a charter of rights without providing a single, defensible reason as to why a charter of rights is not in the public interest.

The probability of such political resistance and the challenges presented by the Constitution itself – inasmuch as politicians control our ability to amend the Constitution – are the two biggest process hurdles to a charter of human rights for Australians. As such, the chances of success in such a reform will be increased if we can isolate a simple process for enshrining our rights. In the following sections I will examine the most effective constitutional barriers to a human rights charter and pose an option for the simplest way to overcome the problem.

The Constitution as a barrier to human rights

Australia's Constitution almost entirely undermines the possibility of its citizens' access to political, civil, economic, social and cultural rights. This is a serious failure that often gets lost in lawyerly debate on constitutional details. But if we step back and look at the Constitution from the point of view of equitable access to rights, it is apparent that it locks Australians into a position where human rights are the fiat of their governments and may be arbitrarily withheld at any time either for the whole population or subsets of it. This arrangement runs absolutely counter to the assertion that rights are universal and inalienable – the self-evidently inherent property of humans (collectively and individually) which cannot be denied by governments. Nevertheless, Australian governments have purported to hold these two utterly contradictory ideas at the one time. Australia's policy documents on human rights start with an acknowledgement that:

> These rights are considered to be inherent, inalienable and universal: *inherent* as the birthright of all human beings, enjoyed by all simply by reason of their humanity rather than granted or bestowed; *inalienable* in the sense that they cannot be given up or taken away; and *universal* as they apply to all regardless of race, colour, gender, sexual orientation, gender identity, language, political or other opinion, national or social origin, property, birth, age or disability.[263]

But Australia's Constitution comprehends no such thing. On the contrary, every mechanism within it, even the referendum mechanism, is geared towards denial of rights, not confirmation of them and certainly not remedy for abuses by federal governments. Insofar as the Constitution is either silent on human rights or may contain built-in mechanisms to deny them, Australians are living entirely without protection of their rights in law. They are told that their rights are protected by convention dating back to Magna Carta, or by the operation of the principle of "responsible government", or by common law, or by the now much vaunted but never defined (and frequently not adhered to) "rule of law". But the reality is that in relation to their rights the "rule of law" is non-existent in several states in Australia (because only two states and the Australian Capital Territory have some human rights legislation) and unstable on a nation-wide basis (because a federal law can override state law). Rights can be and are being extinguished and abused everywhere in Australia because there is nothing in the Constitution that says they can't be extinguished and abused. The human rights treaties our governments have signed and ratified are not enforceable here.

This is a situation that is now dire. In the space of about 40 years Australia has moved from being a society that could reasonably take rights for granted – because it was assumed leaders would act in good faith in the public's best interests in accordance with convention and the common law – to one where it must be acknowledged that the

[263] Department of Foreign Affairs and Trade, "Australian and Human Rights: An Overview, 4th edition", December 2017, page 10, Op. Cit.

law can no longer protect Australians from human rights abuses by the government. As John von Doussa observed in 2005:

> When I went through the Law School, more than forty years ago, human rights law was not a subject on the curriculum. Lectures we received about the English common law system and the unwritten British constitution, led us to believe that the protection of fundamental rights and freedoms would always be the cornerstone of our legal system, and that there was no need to reduce those rights to a statutory form. ... However, things have changed. I well remember an occasion in 1992 when one of my colleagues was about to hear an application by asylum-seekers who had arrived in Darwin by boat. At that time, judges of the Federal Court were granting bail to asylum-seekers who arrived unlawfully whilst their claims were processed. On the night before the case was to be heard, the mandatory detention provisions were rushed through Parliament. The protection against detention without trial was removed in one strike. Many other amendments followed to limit the power of the court to do justice according to common law principles.[264]

So in 1992, the capacity of parliaments to override human rights – by introducing laws that facilitate the exercise of arbitrary power – was already being exhibited by Australia's parliaments. From this point the human rights record of Australia began to plummet, as shown in some of the examples of abuses provided above. This trend of increasing abuse then grew unabated because of our entirely inadequate Constitution and in parallel with an argument run by politicians that it should stay that way – that is, silent on our rights. This argument speciously posited that if a charter of rights were to be enshrined in the Constitution (rather than in a mere act of parliament) it would transfer sovereignty from the elected parliaments to the unelected courts. With sophistry rather than

---

[264] John von Doussa QC, President, Human Rights and Equal Opportunity Commission, "Why We Need An Australian Bill of Rights – a joint forum", University of South Australia, 7 December 2005, or Why we need an Australian Bill of Rights - a Joint Forum | Australian Human Rights Commission

evidence, it implied that enshrining rights in the Constitution would transfer key decision-making powers to the judiciary and that it was therefore safer to run with a system which gave the last word on legislation to the elected parliaments, who after all were responsible to the people. The troubles with this are manifold. For a start, parliaments have hardly behaved responsibly on human rights issues. But more than that, the whole argument that it is right for either the parliament or the courts to have "the last word" on human rights is a nonsense in a democracy. In a democracy it is the *people* and only the people who should have *both* the *first and last* word on human rights and therefore:

- unless they have a constitution which states what their first and last words are (until they say otherwise); and
- unless the people can say what line shall not be crossed – particularly in relation to their rights – by the elected when they exercise power; and
- unless the people can say what would constitute abuse and what would constitute dereliction of duty by the elected,

then they are at risk of full exposure to arbitrary power and abuse. They do not have the benefits of a democracy at all.

Notwithstanding the completely illogical thinking behind the idea that the abusive potential of parliaments should not be restrained by the Constitution, the Australian judicial establishment was beaten into submission by this tactic over an extended period. Common law protected nothing, and by 2004 the courts signalled complete capitulation when Justice McHugh of the High Court in the case of Al-Kateb v Godwin resignedly stated that

> the justice or wisdom of the course taken by the Parliament is not examinable in this or any other domestic court. It is not for courts, exercising federal jurisdiction, to determine whether the course taken by Parliament is unjust or contrary to basic human rights. The function of the courts in this context is simply to determine whether the law of the Parliament is within the powers conferred on it by the Constitution. The doctrine of separation of powers does

> more than prohibit the Parliament and the Executive from exercising the judicial power of the Commonwealth. It prohibits the Ch III courts from amending the Constitution under the guise of interpretation.[265]

This is one of those landmark moments in the judicial history of Australia. It is a moment that should have taken the breath of Australians away, insofar as it implies that they will be left defenceless against abuses of power by unscrupulous and unaccountable parliaments or executive governments (the type that make executive statements to the effect that "entering into a treaty does not give rise to legitimate expectations that could form the basis for challenging an administrative decision" [266]) and that both the Constitution and the judges who are responsible for interpreting it can offer them no protection. In effect, Justice McHugh exposed the truth that Australia has a Constitution that gives parliaments and governments free rein to be unjust.

Of course, the judgment did not create much of a ripple outside the small sections of the community that were championing human rights in 2004 but in the 2020s it stands as a salutary lesson from which it is not too late to learn. As Justice McHugh states, the High Court may be prohibited under Chapter III of the Constitution from amending it "under the guise of interpretation", but this is an argument *in favour* of enshrining a charter of rights in the Constitution. It is not an argument for listing human rights in legislation rather than in the Constitution.

Since the Al-Kateb judgement, Australians have effectively lost the help and protections that the judiciary could provide them if the doctrine of the separation of powers were properly invoked so that the separation allows *both* the parliament and the judiciary to exercise their properly balanced share of power in the public interest. This can't happen if the Constitution is silent on the obligations of parliaments and governments to uphold and adhere to the treaties

---

[265] Al-Kateb v Godwin [2004] HCA 37, (2004) 219 CLR 562, High Court (Australia).

[266] Department of Foreign Affairs and Trade, "Australian and Human Rights: An Overview, 4th edition", December 2017, Op. Cit., page 26.

they sign and ratify. It can't happen while the power sharing between the parliament and the judiciary is so out of balance as to make the separation of powers useless for its fundamental purpose – protection of the electors from parliamentary or government abuse. Certainly the courts should not be able to amend the Constitution under the guise of interpretation; but if they can be given a Constitution that actually says what must be upheld in law, then they should be fully able to interpret whether laws made by parliaments are consistent with the Constitution that the parliamentarians should (but currently don't) swear to uphold.

The current Constitution of Australia states that

> In all matters: (i) arising under any treaty; ... the High Court shall have original jurisdiction.[267]

In a sensible, human-centred world this ought to imply that because the parliament has already ratified human rights treaties, the High Court should at least be able to assume it has jurisdiction not merely to "determine whether the law of the Parliament is within the powers conferred on it by the Constitution" (a function Justice McHugh asserted was valid for federal courts) but also to "determine whether the course taken by Parliament is unjust or contrary to basic human rights" (a function Justice McHugh did not think was valid for a federal court under the current Constitution, at least in the context of the Al-Kateb case). After all, the human rights treaties to which Australia is a signatory are used as the basis of some of the laws Australia has made to protect rights. For instance:

- the International Convention on the Elimination of All Forms of Racial Discrimination underpins and is a schedule to the Racial Discrimination Act 1975;[268] and

---

[267] *Australia's Constitution with Overview and Notes by the Australian Government Solicitor*, Chapter III< The Judicature, section 75, page 21. foi-2021-017.pdf (pmc.gov.au).

[268] Racial Discrimination Act 1975. RACIAL DISCRIMINATION ACT 1975 (austlii.edu.au)

- the Convention on the Elimination of all Forms of Discrimination Against Women underpins and is a schedule to the Sex Discrimination Act 1984.[269]

As such, lawmakers and judges alike are well used to interpreting whether parliaments are behaving justly in relation to human rights treaties. And yet judges have felt the need for specific incorporation of treaties into domestic law – or rather, into the actual Constitution – before they will exercise the full measure of their judicial power in relation to rights under these treaties. In the Al-Kateb case, Justice McHugh shed some light on why:

> Eminent lawyers who have studied the question firmly believe that the Australian Constitution should contain a Bill of Rights which substantially adopts the rules found in the most important of the international human rights instruments. It is an enduring – and many would say a just – criticism of Australia that it is now one of the few countries in the Western world that does not have a Bill of Rights. But, desirable as a Bill of Rights may be, it is not to be inserted into our Constitution by judicial decisions drawing on international instruments that are not even part of the law of this country. It would be absurd to suggest that the meaning of a grant of power in s 51 of the Constitution can be elucidated by the enactments of the Parliament. Yet those who propose that the Constitution should be read so as to conform with the rules of international law are forced to argue that rules contained in treaties made by the executive government are relevant in interpreting the Constitution. It is hard to accept, for example, that the meaning of the trade and commerce power can be affected by the Australian government entering into multilateral trade agreements. It is even more difficult to accept that the Constitution's meaning is affected by rules created by the agreements and practices of other countries. If that were the case, judges would have to have a "loose-leaf" copy of the Constitution. If Australia is to have a Bill of Rights,

[269] Sex Discrimination Act 1984. SEX DISCRIMINATION ACT 1984 (austlii.edu.au)

> it must be done in the constitutional way – hard though its achievement may be – by persuading the people to amend the Constitution by inserting such a Bill.[270]

This is a logical or at least understandable reason for the reluctance of judges to determine "whether the course taken by Parliament is unjust or contrary to basic human rights" when there is no specific rendering of any human rights treaties in the Constitution itself. And it is a plea from the judiciary to the people to take the chains off the courts that prevent them from protecting people against abuses of power and rights by governments. It is also a clear statement to the effect that mere legislation is not sufficient to protect human rights. It must be done in the Constitution. Otherwise there is no balance of power that can be achieved. No balance of power is possible if one of the powers (in this case the High Court) has no power at all under the only instrument that can give it power – the Constitution. The Court's lesson is that only the people can solve this problem, via a long overdue referendum to insert human rights into the Constitution.

Over the 40 years to the 2020s, every referendum put to Australians to amend the Constitution failed. This record of defeat acted to dispirit human rights advocates from doing what Justice McHugh suggested is essential. Leading lights in the area such as George Williams and Daniel Reynolds have opted to fly the white flag and forsake the idea of enshrining rights in the Constitution in favour of something that is "sound and achievable". In 2017 they stated that:

> We should jettison the US model and any idea of a constitutional bill of rights. If that is ever to occur it is at least a generation away. The more modest and flexible legislative approach takes into account the strong concern held by many Australians that a US-style bill of rights would give judges the final say in too many areas, and would entrench rights in the

[270] Al-Kateb v Godwin [2004] HCA 37, (2004) 219 CLR 562, High Court (Australia).

Constitution that the community might not support in the future.[271]

But this pragmatic capitulation is likely to leave the Australian public without the rights and constitutional protections it needs. For instance:

1. As Justice McHugh has shown, the lack of a charter or bill of rights means that Australian judges have *no* say at all. They cannot protect us from injustice by a government that might be intent on abusing rights, even if legislation like the Racial Discrimination Act is enacted that grants pieces of those rights.

2. Nor is it the case that enshrining rights in the Constitution that are already supported in treaties would give judges "the final say in too many areas". There is no inherent need to enshrine treaty rights in a way that would inordinately increase the power of judges over the parliament. If that is an issue (which is unlikely) then it is simply the job of constitutional lawyers and parliamentary counsel to devise amendments that will eliminate the risk of an imbalance between the necessarily separated powers of the parliament and the judicature. In devising such amendments though, counsel should consider abandoning all presumptions that parliament should have the last word on human rights legislation. As I have already suggested, it is the people who should have the first and last word on what rights they want and what obligations they will insist their governments observe. That requires nothing more and nothing less than an enshrinement of human rights in a people's constitution.

3. Finally – since this whole debate about human rights has been dragging on for over thirty years with the result that rights have been eroded down to near zero – it is also time

---

[271] George Williams and Daniel Reynolds, *A Charter of Rights in Australia,* UNSW Press, NewSouth Publishing, Sydney, 2017, Chapter 7 – An Australian charter of human rights and responsibilities, page 140.

to abandon the prejudice that enshrining rights in the Constitution will lock Australians into rights "the community might not support in future". This seems to imply that Australians are somehow flaky about rights that governments have otherwise stated are universal, indivisible, interrelated, interdependent, inalienable, inherent, inviolable and the common entitlement of all humans.[272] Since Australia adopted the Universal Declaration of Human Rights and progressively signed onto treaties made under the Declaration, neither the people of Australia nor their governments have suggested that the treaties need be abandoned and the rights in them are not universal and indivisible. Of course governments have resisted enshrining them in law, but that is merely a measure of the desire of successive governments not to give up power. It is not an indication that Australians think these rights should not be available to them. If anything, the evidence is that Australians want surety about their rights – a guarantee that they will be permanent. 83% want "a document that sets out in clear language the rights and responsibilities that everyone has here in Australia" and 74% agree that "a charter of human rights would help people and communities to make sure the government does the right thing."[273]

In summary it is clear that Australians would be better off than they are now if human rights were legislated but they would not be as secure from abuse of power as they would be if the rights were enshrined in the Constitution. As John von Doussa observed in 2005:

> What happened with the Migration laws is being mirrored across the executive branch of government. More and more discretionary power is given to the executive, and less and less detail of conditions governing the rights and duties of individuals is stated in legally enforceable statutory

---

[272] Department of Foreign Affairs and Trade, "Australian and Human Rights: An Overview, 4th edition", December 2017, pages 10 and 15, Op. Cit.

[273] Human Rights Law Centre, "COVID-19 sees huge increase in support for a Charter of Human Rights: poll", Media Release, 9 September 2021, Op. Cit.

> provisions. It is all very well for government to say we are all protected by the rule of law and the respect that Australia accords to that core principle. However, if the regulation of our lives is not stated expressly in the law, but is a matter of discretion, what protection does the rule of non-existent law give? To give real substance to the principle, enforceable and certain rights need to be express – and this could be achieved in a charter of rights.[274]

The insightful von Doussa also made one other very important observation which is highly relevant in the 2020s to the issue of a treaty with First Nations:

> One important purpose of a human rights charter will be to protect the rights of people in minority groups. One minority group in Australia that is particularly in need of enforceable fundamental rights is the Indigenous community. Aboriginal people have advocated for a treaty, but their advocacy has fallen on deaf ears. ... Without debating the merits of that proposition, if there were a universal charter to protect the rights of everyone, the basic rights recognised in it would go a long way to giving protection to one community which plainly needs it.[275]

What this indicates is that as Australia moves towards Makarrata and a treaty with Indigenous nations, it is likely that the treaty itself will need to be enshrined in the Constitution alongside enshrined human rights, otherwise the treaty itself is likely to be unstable. And because of the specific circumstance of the need for a treaty with First Nations, those rights will need to include not just the rights in human rights treaties that parliament has already ratified but the rights in another treaty it has signed but not ratified – the United Nations

---

[274] John von Doussa QC, President, Human Rights and Equal Opportunity Commission, "Why We Need An Australian Bill of Rights – a joint forum", University of South Australia, 7 December 2005, Op. Cit.

[275] John von Doussa QC, President, Human Rights and Equal Opportunity Commission, "Why We Need An Australian Bill of Rights – a joint forum", University of South Australia, 7 December 2005, Ibid.

Declaration on the Rights of Indigenous Peoples (UNDRIP).[276] Unless *all* these rights are incorporated into the Constitution, any treaty with First Nations is likely to be as unenforceable as all the other treaties on human rights that we have signed but not enshrined in the Constitution. First Nations treaty rights will be as unprotected as all our other human rights and the obligations of government to Australians in compliance with those treaties will be too easily escapable.

To ensure that all the rights that have been withheld from Australians since World War II and all the rights that have been so cruelly and unjustly withheld from Indigenous Australians are finally enforceable by the courts, Australians need a well-made people's constitution which codifies those rights. They also need a well-made constitution which codifies the obligations of governments to all Australians in the benefit and protection of those rights. This may seem like an insurmountably complex challenge, especially to those who have been understandably dispirited about the possibility of success in a referendum. As more than one constitutional expert has observed,

> Not only is the Australian constitutional system old in world terms, but it has resisted change. As far back as 1967 Australia was described by Geoffrey Sawer as 'constitutionally speaking ... the frozen continent'. It is an understatement to say that changing the Constitution is difficult. Former prime minister Robert Menzies went so far as to say in 1951, after his own proposal to ban communism had been narrowly rejected by the people: 'The truth of the matter is that to get an affirmative vote from the Australian people on a referendum proposal is one of the labours of Hercules.'[277]

Menzies, however, was a patrician from a time gone by. And while it was certainly true that Australians in the 1950s were not

---

[276] United Nations Declaration on the Rights of Indigenous Peoples, 2007. DRIPS_en.pdf (un.org)

[277] George Williams and Daniel Reynolds, *A Charter of Rights in Australia,* UNSW Press, NewSouth Publishing, Sydney, 2017, Chapter 4 – Why doesn't Australia have a charter of rights?, page 73.

easily persuaded of the wisdom of proposals (like banning communism) which were effectively designed to deny civil and political rights and increase centralised political power, it does not follow that Australians in the 2020s would react in the negative to proposals designed to *affirm* their rights. On the contrary, as long as the proposal is simply designed such that Australians can perceive a benefit to them, and that the affirmation is their free choice, there is no reason to assume at the outset that Australians would reject it. And the benefit of such an affirmation would be enormous. It would consist in:

- confirmation of their rights at last in Australian law,
- protection from abuse of their rights by an unjust or arbitrary power, and
- enunciation of the parliament's and the executive government's obligations to them.

The real barrier to acceptance of human rights in the Constitution would not come from the people. It would come from politicians who under the current Constitution have their foot firmly stamped on the neck of the people's rights and freedoms inasmuch as they can stop a referendum from ever getting started. I will discuss ways around this in Chapter 9. For the moment I would like to concentrate on how the success of a referendum on human rights might be achieved. As I said above, the chances of success in such a reform will be increased if we can isolate a simple process for enshrining our rights. In the next section I will pose an option for the simplest way to overcome the problem.

Enshrining human rights and obligations in a people's constitution

In 2004 the government of the Australian Capital Territory passed the ACT Human Rights Act[278] and the government of Victoria followed suit in 2006 with the Victorian Charter of Human Rights and

[278] Australian Capital Territory Human Rights Act 2004.

Responsibilities Act.[279] The latter legislation was achieved through a well-run consultation process which resulted in a charter which now protects twenty main rights considered to be "the most important to an open and free democracy". These rights were:

- recognition and equality before the law,
- the right to life,
- protection from torture and cruel, inhuman or degrading treatment,
- freedom from forced work,
- freedom of movement,
- privacy and reputation,
- freedom of thought, conscience, religion and belief,
- freedom of expression,
- peaceful assembly and freedom of association,
- protection of families and children,
- taking part in public life,
- cultural rights,
- property rights,
- rights to liberty and security of person,
- humane treatment when deprived of liberty,
- rights of children in the criminal process,
- fair hearing,
- rights in criminal proceedings,
- the right not to be tried or punished more than once, and
- retrospective criminal laws.[280]

In the main these rights were adapted from the International Covenant on Civil and Political Rights but at the time, one key right under that Covenant was qualified in the Act and another was omitted because it was deemed in the consultation process that these two rights did not "match" the contemporary views of the Victorian people. The qualified right was the right to life. It was

---

[279] Victorian Charter of Human Rights and Responsibilities Act 2006.

[280] George Williams and Daniel Reynolds, *A Charter of Rights in Australia,* UNSW Press, NewSouth Publishing, Sydney, 2017, Chapter 6 – Charters of rights in the states and territories, page 118.

modified by means of a savings provision to accommodate differences of beliefs held at the time by Victorians about abortion. The provision has since worked successfully to ensure that rights to abortion can be legislated, as they have been in Victoria.

The omitted right in the Victorian Act was the central right under the Covenant – the right to self-determination. This was omitted because, like the issue of abortion, it "attracted strong views both for and against"[281] in the consultation process.

The committee that oversaw the consultation process in Victoria did not recommend that the suite of rights in the other main human rights treaty – the International Covenant on Economic, Social and Cultural Rights – should be included in the new Charter at that time, even though the committee found that "the distinction between these civil and political freedoms can be arbitrary and even non-existent".[282] In the main this was because:

> overall 41% of submissions argued for the inclusion of some or all of [the economic, social and cultural] rights while 95% argued for the inclusion of civil and political rights.[283]

Accordingly, the Victorian Act did not extend rights relating to matters such as food, education, housing and health to Victorians and it did not extend more specific rights for women, children, persons with disabilities, and Indigenous people.

It might be reasonably assumed that with the passage of time since 2006, a higher proportion of Australians would be supportive of the inclusion of economic, social and cultural rights in a charter, especially after the experience of privation during the Covid-19 pandemic and also after the experience of neoliberalism which has

---

[281] George Williams and Daniel Reynolds, *A Charter of Rights in Australia,* UNSW Press, NewSouth Publishing, Sydney, 2017, Chapter 6 – Charters of rights in the states and territories, page 119.

[282] George Williams and Daniel Reynolds, *A Charter of Rights in Australia,* UNSW Press, NewSouth Publishing, Sydney, 2017, Chapter 6 – Charters of rights in the states and territories, page 119.

[283] George Williams and Daniel Reynolds, *A Charter of Rights in Australia,* UNSW Press, NewSouth Publishing, Sydney, 2017, Chapter 6 – Charters of rights in the states and territories, page 119.

resulted in significant growth in economic inequality in Australia as well as:

- growth in hunger, poverty and homelessness;
- falls in educational standards;
- long periods of unnecessarily high unemployment and underemployment; and
- a decline in the accessibility of health care.

In the 2020s Australians are less likely to take economic, social and cultural rights for granted than they were in 2006. Many are also likely to be more aware of the contractionary effects that neoliberal austerity projects have on the economy and the devastating effects on the environment that arise from diversion of government funds away from public services towards private businesses that act inconsistently with the public interest (such as fossil fuel businesses and banks[284]). This is very likely to have had an impact on the consciousness of Australians such as to suggest that they have an even more immediate need of economic, social and cultural rights than they do of political rights.

Some Australians may hesitate about economic rights if they labour under the assumption that the nation cannot afford them – in short, if they labour under the assumption that a sovereign monetary nation like Australia, with probably more resource wealth per capita than can be dreamed of by most nations, cannot afford a high standard of living, education and health care for everyone. But for a country like Australia, the economic reality is that the sky is the limit. As a sovereign monetary power fully capable of:

- creating our own money supply;
- organising resources (human and natural) and consumption into a fully sustainable regenerative economy; and

[284] The Banking Royal Commission chronicled the history of the banking industry's illegal behaviour particularly in money laundering. Final Report | Royal Commissions. Also Market Forces has reported on how the fossil fuel and banking industries have colluded in exploitation of public resources contrary to the interests of the Australian public. Home - Market Forces

- achieving ongoing full productive employment at stable prices,

wealth is not the limiting factor for our quality of life. The limiting factor is simply a political one. In Australia, until such time as climate change drastically affects our productive capacity, especially in food production, it is not the case that “we can only do it if we can afford it”. Instead, the Keynesian view of the economic, social and cultural capacity of advanced wealthy nations is far more likely to apply. As the renowned economist John Maynard Keynes put it in 1942:

> Let us not submit to the vile doctrine of the nineteenth century that every enterprise must justify itself in pounds, shillings and pence of cash income ... Why should we not add in every substantial city the dignity of an ancient university or a European capital ... an ample theater, a concert hall, a dance hall, a gallery, cafes, and so forth. Assuredly we can afford this and so much more. Anything we can actually do, we can afford. ... We are immeasurably richer than our predecessors. Is it not evident that some sophistry, some fallacy, governs our collective action if we are forced to be so much meaner than they in the embellishments of life?[285]

And in the 2020s, after the pandemic and neoliberalism, it is fully evident that Australian governments have the financial capacity to fund whatever is essential in services and investments for our wellbeing and security, although politically it still suits some to propound the sophistry and fallacy that they don’t. The pandemic has taught many Australians, such as those calling for more fiscal stimulus and government involvement in the economy, that this financial capacity is fully available to the nation and morally it is right to use it. As the eminent economic and political historian Adam Tooze stated in September 2021:

> The double-edged lesson that 2020 taught us [is] about our capacities for collective action: We have huge capacities for crisis-fighting. We spent trillions on giant fiscal programs to

[285] John Maynard Keynes, Address to the BBC, 1942. Anything We Can Do, We Can Afford – J. W. Mason (jwmason.org)

put our economies on life support. We backed them up with huge central bank activism. Financial markets were stabilized. Crash programs of vaccine development produced a suite of vaccines that as of this week have allowed 5.29 billion doses to be distributed worldwide, providing 39 percent of the world's population with at least one dose. Vaccines that many considered to be impossible as recently as the spring of 2020. We can, as one of my favorite quotes from Keynes says, pay for 'this and much more. Anything we can actually do we can afford'. But the question is in the doing. Think of everything we have not done. The opportunities gone begging. The discovery of our financial freedom robs us of excuses. This is the hard political edge of the related schools of post-Keynesianism, functional finance and modern monetary theory. If we fail to do something, we should not blame lack of money.[286]

The upshot of this is that Australians will only have themselves to blame if they continue to let governments off the hook in their obligations to us. These obligations are the fundamental means by which governments must deliver and protect our fundamental rights. Australian governments have attempted to deny the rights of Australians and their obligations to us for decades but it is now apparent that this plainly abstemious mindset – a mindset which may be even more destructive than the three I cited above (if only because it deeply embeds inequality) – need not be the mindset for the future. In fact, the mindset that we can't afford a decent life for everyone can be shuffled off fairly easily if Australians can become attuned to the fact that universal human rights treaties, to which we are a signatory, have already spelled out all the rights we need, and all the obligations governments need to observe in order to ensure our rights.

---

[286] Adam Tooze, "Chartbook on Shutdown: Keynes and why we can afford anything we can do", Chartbook, 2 September 2021. Chartbook on Shutdown: Keynes and why we can afford anything we can do. (substack.com)

In the early part of the 2000s decade, it seemed likely, based on the consultation for the Victorian Charter of Rights and Responsibilities Act, that a majority of Australians might not have felt the need for economic, social and cultural rights. But times have changed and it is much more likely in the 2020s that Australians would question why they should not be given – or indeed give themselves – full access to every right in the covenants our parliaments have signed and/or ratified. It should be an easy offer to make and take, especially since we have seen that wealth and affordability is not a barrier. As such, why should we deny ourselves rights that other nations have? This opens up the possibility of a relatively simple option for enshrining the full array of human rights available under international law in an Australian people's constitution.

An option for enshrining human rights and obligations in an Australian people's constitution

The full array of human rights that are available already in international treaties can be enshrined in the Australian Constitution in a single stroke. There are no legal barriers to this. We can simply choose to incorporate any international human rights covenant, convention, declaration, protocol or treaty into the Constitution – either into the core of the document or as a schedule, or in both places if necessary. That parliaments have not yet done this, even though they have ratified most of the core human rights treaties, is indicative of a mindset which says human rights are the fiat of governments rather than an inalienable, natural, universal entitlement. But if we consider a proposition that it is not politicians but we the people who are truly entitled to confer rights on ourselves and equally on all members of the human family in our country – and to take them away from ourselves (again equally) if need be – then everything changes in the way we are able to organise our right to life, liberty and the pursuit of happiness. Suddenly, we the people are the sovereign deciders on rights and parliaments must desist from withholding them as they have done for so many decades. They must also desist from their refusal to comply with their obligations to the Australian people under those treaties.

This option of a straightforward transference of all the rights, responsibilities and government obligations in each signed human rights treaty (and other human rights instruments if desired) directly into the Constitution would reverse the way the current permission system works in our society and political/legal arrangements to grant freedoms and take them away when it is demonstrably in the public interest to do so. The reversal would work simply as follows. We would replace one prospect with another:

Prospect 1:

> This is the current prospect for attaining human rights in which Australians must wait for the permission of parliaments to enshrine their rights either in the Constitution or just in legislation, probably in a piecemeal approach where we are likely at best to be granted rights selectively and the government is likely to be exonerated from obligations.

would be replaced with

Prospect 2:

> This reverses the current prospect. In the reversal, the human rights conferred in any treaty or instrument signed by Australia are automatically incorporated into the Constitution (even before ratification by the parliament) and the government must argue for permission from the people to remove a human right in law and/or be exonerated from obligations under the treaties. Such permission must be sought by a referendum.

If the first prospect is retained, the government will be able (as it is now) to withhold and even delete rights and obligations at its will, possibly even to the point of denying and abusing all rights and obligations in the treaties. It will be able to enlarge on all the denials of rights that have been legislated since 2001. But in the second prospect it is the people and only the people who will be able to delete or add rights and obligations in law at *their* will. The first prospect starts with a blank slate and lets the elected decide what might be allowed into law. The second prospect starts with the full menu of possible rights and obligations, taking them as a given (because they are inherent), and then lets the electors delete what they truly don't want or need – on the proviso that if they delete a right they must delete it for everyone and if they delete an obligation, the deletion will not adversely impact any particular group compared to others. In effect, invocation of Prospect 2 would transfer ratification powers on human rights away from parliaments and to the people. It would give the people the first and last word on their rights.

Prospect 2 is a process that is entirely consistent with the concept that rights are universal and indivisible – the natural entitlement of all humans from birth – and it has the added advantage of allowing Australians to sign off on which rights and obligations may be deleted (if any) in the public interest and in line with whatever national values they may have adopted. And by this reversal of process, we can far more efficiently assure ourselves that rights will at last be conferred on all Australians in line with their cultural preferences and values. After the passage of more than 70 years since Australia signed the Universal Declaration of Human Rights, Australians might actually get the rights that successive federal governments have thus far refused to allow them. And we might get to keep them, because in Prospect 2 we can also efficiently safeguard ourselves from the denial of or assaults on our liberty that Australian governments have so successfully prosecuted since 2001 – through:

- their amendments of legislation that have enabled human rights abuses;
- their refusal to legislate human rights per se;
- their refusal to withdraw reservations on human rights treaties; and

- their refusal to enter agreements on terms consistent with their obligations to Australians in these treaties (for example, their refusal to commit to the Paris Agreement on terms which would be consistent with rights and obligations to protect the health and wellbeing of Australians).

Prospect 2 is a practicable solution to the problem of human rights abuses that have arisen from political manipulation and denial of the need for human rights in Australia. It is the option for constitutional enshrinement of human rights that should fall naturally into the hands of any nation in which the sovereign will is located in the people themselves (not in the government or parliament or a monarch) and which has also resolved, in accordance with that will, to stipulate its values. It is the option fitted for any nation ready and willing to exercise the fundamental right that underpins all the human rights treaties and declarations – the right to self-determination.

Of course, governments are frightened of conferring rights to self-determination on their populations, even though they have agreed in the covenants that self-determination – the right of all people to freely determine their political status and freely pursue their economic, social and cultural development – is essential to any process for conferring universal rights. Both autocratic and democratic governments are frightened of any such transfer of power. Therefore in all likelihood it will be protested that there are logistical and legal hurdles in the current Constitution that Australians will face in invoking this option for the first time. These might be expected to arise from the fact that the current Constitution does not allow referendums unless the parliament approves the wording of the question that is to be put to the people. This, however, is not a logistical or legal hurdle; it is simply a political one. And specifically, it is a political hurdle that, in accordance with the International Covenant on Civil and Political Rights, the parliaments of Australia are not legally entitled to (at least under international law). The constitutional barrier that allows parliaments to stand between Australians and their human rights – by refusing to allow the people to control the process that triggers their own referendums and designs the questions that may be put – is fully at odds with the International Covenant on Civil and Political Rights.

This, of course, presents Australians with a conundrum – how to bring on a referendum that they are entitled to in all good governance but are likely to be prevented from having by their parliaments. How do we bring on a referendum to approve the wording of the amendment necessary to enable insertion of the human rights treaties directly into the Constitution, as per the intention in Prospect 2? To even begin to think about it we need to shuffle off the "mind-forg'd manacles"[287] that ban the people from having a say in their own governance and determining their sovereign will. Fortunately, while the Constitution does make that difficult in legal process, it doesn't make it impossible to introduce the option of a citizens-initiated referendum. If anything, in this particular case of enshrining human rights, it will be considerably easier with Prospect 2 to surmount both political and logistical hurdles than it would be to attempt to enshrine human rights in the Constitution or in legislation on a piecemeal basis, bearing in mind the complexity of explanation that would be required in that prospect (Prospect 1) about which rights and obligations should be included or excluded. The proof of this is that Australia has been living with Prospect 1 since 1945 and we still have no human rights in Commonwealth law. It might be expected that this situation could pertain forever if we opt to stay stuck within it. Still, this is a tragedy we can easily avoid.

Once we shift our mindset away from the notion that only elected parliaments can bestow rights on Australians – dripping them into (and out of) legislation one by one, *a la* Prospect 1 – and toward a prospect that puts Australians fully in charge of an efficient process to bestow rights on themselves and others *equally*, enshrining them in the Constitution until such time as we the people say otherwise, it should become obvious that Prospect 2 is entirely consistent not just with democracy but with the spirit of the current Constitution itself.

---

[287] William Blake, "London", first published in 1794. Stanza 2: "In every cry of every Man, In every Infants cry of fear, In every voice: in every ban, The mind-forg'd manacles I hear."

The spirit of the Constitution is that it can only be amended and altered by the people. If that is so – and it *is* so – then Prospect 2 is as straightforward as it is overdue.

Prospect 1 on the other hand is nothing more and nothing less than what tyrannical governments will attempt to maintain for as long as possible. But it is likely that its moment is over in Australia. Seventy years of denial of rights by Australian governments and their refusal to accept their obligations to the people are enough. As the results of polling show, Covid-19 has put paid to the patience of Australians in relation to denial of rights and it has unmasked the entirely unnecessary and destructive capacity of neoliberal austerity in which governments refuse to observe their obligations to provide all Australians with the full measure of those rights and the quality of life that would come from them. This makes the 2020s the moment for seizure of human rights for Australians by Australians. Preparatory to that, the early 2020s is the moment to open discussion of the risks and benefits of invoking a constitutional reform which will enable Australians to confer human rights equally on each other, to safeguard those rights for all, and to bind governments to their obligations in relation to these rights. In support of that discussion the following section outlines how there is little if any risk in such a reform and how the benefits far outweigh any risk.

Assessing the risk of enshrining human rights and obligations in the Constitution

Were Australians to invoke Prospect 2 and access all the rights in human rights treaties, and were governments to observe their obligations under those treaties, Australia would be a much better place to live than it is. More importantly, we would have a far better chance of addressing existential threats such as climate change and war in ways that do not increase inequality. In the 2020s there is every reason to reverse the current permission system for human rights and no reason not to. There are no downsides to the reversal, except perhaps for multinational corporations and for the worst sort of politicians who measure the success of their lives in terms of the amount of power they have corralled to themselves and denied to all others. Nevertheless, despite the obvious advantages of a switch to Prospect 2, it is likely to be necessary to convince Australians that full assumption of their rights in our national laws is an option that can be accessed without serious risk for the electors.

On this point I would have to concede that, obviously, nothing in life is risk free. But assumption of human rights on an equal basis is about as risk free as it gets. In fact, a people's assumption of rights on an equal basis *reduces* risks that arise from every human activity. It reduces the risk that human endeavours in progress will adversely impact on one group more than another. As such it should be relatively straightforward to convince a majority of Australians that full assumption of rights and full imposition of attendant obligations on governments – in a single, efficient stroke as per Prospect 2 – is in their interests and that any government that refuses to accept these obligations is acting contrary to the public interest.

This is evident if we contemplate the fact that the human rights and obligations in the treaties to which we are a party come closer than any other statement in law to describing what the public interest actually is. It is inarguable that the primary right of all humans

> to self-determination, by virtue of which they freely determine their political status and freely pursue their economic, social and cultural development,[288]

is a central tenet of the public interest. At least, no argument has been posed by any Australian government against this point. The strategy of successive governments has been simply to avoid the argument entirely and doggedly deny in the domestic forum what they have plainly accepted for over seven decades in international forums – namely, that free people are entitled to self-determination (because without it they are not free) and they are entitled to every benefit that may legitimately flow from that. But even were an Australian government of the 2020s able to mount a rational argument that it is not in the public interest to confer all rights on Australians and impose all attendant obligations on governments,

[288] Article 1, International Covenant on Civil and Political Rights- external site

there is still no real risk that would arise for electors and any other beneficiaries of human rights from invoking Prospect 2. On the contrary, risk in this single-stroke approach is entirely in the control of the Australian public.

Because the straightforward approach in Prospect 2 is simply that all human rights are transferred into the Constitution as the indivisible whole that our governments have insisted they are, the Prospect opens out the full array of choices to Australians as their starting menu. From there Australians can choose to:

- subtract or moderate rights – one at a time if they so choose – should circumstances arise that force them to conclude that any of these rights may be risky in some crucial way or contrary to their best interests overall;
- add rights if they are deemed to be required in a specified form (the right to abortion on demand may be a case in point here, or perhaps the right to free pre-school education); and
- let the government off the hook (or not) for any particular obligations – again, one at a time if they so choose.

Alteration of rights on a permanent basis in this process (particularly subtraction of rights and government obligations) would be subject to limits and these limits are posed by the two main treaties themselves. In Article 5 they both state that:

> 1. Nothing in the present Covenant may be interpreted as implying for any State, group or person any right to engage in any activity or to perform any act aimed at the destruction of any of the rights or freedoms recognized herein, or at their limitation to a greater extent than is provided for in the present Covenant.[289]

---

[289] Article 5, International Covenant on Civil and Political Rights- external site and Article 5, International Covenant on Economic, Social and Cultural Rights- external site

However, this limitation is not designed to protect people from some risk that might arise from a right. It is designed to protect them from the risk of *reduction* of their universal human rights, for instance:

- by a government acting in contravention of the covenants without the consent of the people and against their will or interests; or
- by a group which may amass enough power to reduce rights on an unequal basis or in a manner inconsistent with "the general welfare of a democratic society";[290] or
- by a group which may not wish to observe the same level of responsibility to another group in the free exercise of their rights on an equal basis.

Accordingly, this limitation is likely to make referendums for subtraction of rights or reduction of the full extent of a right a very infrequent occurrence. Addition of rights is more likely. This is only to be expected since subtraction of rights that are acknowledged as universal would make a country less democratic and free and the whole point of the covenants is to ensure that universal rights, once enshrined in national laws, are not then diminished. The limitation is soundly designed to minimise the risk that a political, autocratic or even democratic process can be misused so as to limit rights that would otherwise be available under the treaties consistent with their intention to foster "the general welfare of a democratic society". This is the particular type of welfare that all the human rights instruments are designed to promote. They are designed to ensure that the rights of the less powerful within a democratic society are maintained on an equal basis with the more powerful. Because of this protection for

[290] This is consistent with Article 29 under The Universal Declaration of Human Rights: "1. Everyone has duties to the community in which alone the free and full development of his personality is possible. 2. In the exercise of his rights and freedoms, everyone shall be subject only to such limitations as are determined by law solely for the purpose of securing due recognition and respect for the rights and freedoms of others and of meeting the just requirements of morality, public order and the general welfare in a democratic society. 3. These rights and freedoms may in no case be exercised contrary to the purposes and principles of the United Nations." Universal Declaration of Human Rights | United Nations

the less powerful and the powerless, no net detriment can arise from invoking Prospect 2 that would be larger than (or indeed anywhere near as large as) the outright detriment Australians have suffered and will suffer even more if governments continue to deny Australians, especially the least powerful, their universal human rights in domestic law.

In the decision process that would pertain in Prospect 2, there is also little or no risk to the public due to the way the rights and obligations have been listed in the treaties themselves. Every human right listed in these originating treaties entails the need for acceptance by signatory states of particular obligations to use the machinery of government to ensure each right is conferred in full. But the form of the obligations as a whole is such as to ensure that:

- no government or sovereign authority will expose itself or its people to risk by virtue of observing an obligation when it is contrary to the interests of a nation to do so; and
- no individual or group will expose another individual or group to risks in public safety, public order, the protection of public health or morals or the protection of the rights and freedoms of others (meaning, rights may only be legitimately exercised when they do not cause these risks).

In both of the core treaties – the International Covenant on Civil and Political Rights and the International Covenant on Economic, Social and Cultural Rights – there are clauses that safeguard nations, groups and individuals against such exposures. The most comprehensive safeguard is provided in the first of these covenants, which states in Article 4 that:

> In time of public emergency which threatens the life of the nation and the existence of which is officially proclaimed, the States Parties to the present Covenant may take measures derogating from their obligations under the present Covenant to the extent strictly required by the exigencies of the situation, provided that such measures are not inconsistent with their other obligations under international law and do

not involve discrimination solely on the ground of race, colour, sex, language, religion or social origin.[291]

In general this means that governments may derogate from the International Covenant on Civil and Political Rights (or most of it) if there is a national emergency, as long as they do not derogate on an unlawful or discriminatory basis and only to the extent required by the emergency. This is an ample safeguard in national emergencies or security crises, inasmuch as there are only a small number of rights in the Covenant where derogation may *not* be exercised by a government in such circumstances. No derogation by a government is permitted at any time under:

- Article 6 on the right to life;
- Article 7 on the right not to be subjected to torture or to cruel, inhuman or degrading treatment or punishment;
- Article 8 (paragraphs 1 and 2) on the right not to be held in slavery or servitude;
- Article 11 on the right not to be imprisoned merely on the ground of inability to fulfil a contractual obligation;
- Article 15 on the right not to be held guilty for an offence which was not a crime when the offence was committed or have a penalty imposed beyond that applicable at the time of the offence;
- Article 16 on the right to recognition everywhere as a person before the law; and
- Article 18 on the right to freedom of thought, conscience and religion and to manifest one's religion and beliefs.

In other words, rights and obligations conferred under these seven Articles may not be denied in any circumstance. All the other rights and obligations, however, may be derogated from in a genuine emergency which threatens the life of the nation and as such nations are protected from putting themselves at risk by being unable to limit human rights, freedoms and obligations when it is clearly necessary. Because of this structure of specified responsibilities and limits in the Covenant in relation to both rights and obligations, there is little if

---

[291] Article 4, International Covenant on Civil and Political Rights- external site

any risk in simply transferring the whole Covenant into the Constitution, as is. This is an approach that has been considered reasonable and feasible since the Covenant first came into force. In 1983, for instance, eminent policy analysts and experts in constitutional law, responding to perceived problems in drafting piecemeal legislation to recognise civil and political rights for Australians, noted that:

> One possible way of avoiding at least some of these drafting difficulties is to adopt without alteration one of the existing declarations of rights, such as the UN Covenant on Civil and Political Rights, or the European Convention on Human Rights. Although those documents define the rights to be protected in a very heavily qualified form (the outcome of intergovernmental compromise), the documents may at least provide an agreed starting point to which further specific changes could be later made as circumstances warrant.[292]

Accordingly, it is obvious from a legal perspective that there are neither legal barriers nor major national risks that would inherently arise from vesting this or any other human rights instrument in full in Australian law (either in the Constitution or in legislation), particularly bearing in mind that civil and political rights have been defined in a "very heavily qualified form" that has been acknowledged as a satisfactory "intergovernmental compromise". Indeed, risks multiply when we take the opposite approach and start to pick the eyes out of international laws to which we have already agreed in full. Risks multiply when we start to treat civil and political rights as though they are not universal and indivisible.

It should be noted, however, that, in contrast with the structure of permissible derogations under the International Covenant on Civil and Political Rights, it is quite a lot harder for governments to lawfully derogate from rights and obligations under the International Covenant on Economic, Social and Cultural Rights. Obviously in

---

[292] John McMillan, Gareth Evans and Haddon Storey, *Australia's Constitution: Time for Change?*, Law Foundation of New South Wales, Allen and Unwin Australia, 1983, page 328.

relation to this Covenant and the other main treaties, States Parties found "intergovernmental compromise" was more easily reached, probably because the rights conferred under these other covenants do not pose the same level of risk – or shall we say, challenge – to the power of governments per se. As John von Doussa has noted:

> The civil and political rights are regarded as "first generation rights". They have the feature that they are negative rights in the sense that the state is required to refrain from certain actions against individuals so that the individual can enjoy a freedom to be left alone to pursue, within acceptable limits, happiness and prosperity.

In short, these civil and political rights could threaten the power of governments (in any country) and so they have been curbed by governments wherever they can in the originating treaties. By contrast, though:

> Economic, social and cultural rights on the other hand are often described as "positive" or "distributive" rights, since they require an activist response by the state to ensure the provision of the money and services necessary for the realisation and enjoyment of the rights. These rights are often defined as "second generation" rights. It will be apparent from the nature of these rights that their enjoyment is dependent upon the policies and philosophy of the government of the day. In this sense there is a political element in their enjoyment.[293]

Because governments have sensed there is a political element that may be quite easily used to disallow our enjoyment of these rights, they have probably assumed that they can ignore them and their obligations to realise those rights in full. Indeed since the 1970s, when neoliberalism began to take hold, each "government of the day" in Australia has complacently assumed that there is no legal obligation to assure economic, social and cultural rights and that all

---

[293] John von Doussa QC, President, Human Rights and Equal Opportunity Commission, "Why We Need An Australian Bill of Rights – a joint forum", University of South Australia, 7 December 2005, Op. Cit.

they need to do to be released from an obligation to ensure their enjoyment is to plead a lack of money. They have assumed this breach of international law will be politically tolerable because the neoliberal myth that Australians can't afford to enjoy their own rights in wellbeing has been persuasive. In 2009, the myth was quite persuasive for those who drafted a Human Rights Bill as part of a submission to the National Human Rights Consultation chaired by Father Frank Brennan, who was Chair of the Commonwealth Government's National Human Rights Consultation at the time. This draft bill included a get-out clause for governments on economic, social and cultural rights by stating that

> it is acknowledged that these human rights are subject to progressive realisation and that their realisation may be limited by the financial resources available to government. Accordingly, in any proceeding under this Act that raises the application and operation of these human rights, a court must consider all the relevant circumstances of the particular case including –
>
> - the nature of the benefit or detriment likely to accrue or be suffered by any person concerned; and
> - the financial circumstances and estimated amount of expenditure required to be made by a public authority to act in a manner compatible with human rights
>
> before determining that the provisions of any law or that the acts or conduct of a public authority are incompatible with the Act.[294]

But in contrast with the assumption here that the financial circumstances of a government will lawfully limit their obligation to people, the international covenants conferring these "positive rights" do not give governments a free pass to be so dismissive. Under Article 4 of the International Covenant on Economic, Social and Cultural Rights, the human rights and obligations conferred thereby:

---

[294] John Menadue, "A Human Rights Bill 2009", John Menadue's Pearls and Irritations, 7 January 2018.

> may be subject only to such limitations as are determined by law only in so far as this may be compatible with the nature of these rights and solely for the purpose of promoting the general welfare in a democratic society.[295]

There is nothing in the Covenant that says lack of finance can be used as an excuse to withhold economic, social and cultural rights. And while in Article 2 the Covenant does state that:

> Each State Party to the present Covenant undertakes to take steps, individually and through international assistance and co-operation, especially economic and technical, to the maximum of its available resources, with a view to achieving progressively the full realization of the rights recognized in the present Covenant by all appropriate means, including particularly the adoption of legislative measures,[296]

this does not create a basis on which governments – especially monetary sovereign governments like Australia that can create their own currency without limit – may plead limited *financial* resources as an excuse for denying economic, social and cultural rights. And should they attempt to plead as such, it is likely that they would be easily defeated by arguments that any risk to national finances is more likely to arise from *not* observing all obligations to provide health, education and welfare for all.

Overall, the wording of the International Covenant on Economic, Social and Cultural Rights does not supply a get-out for governments on financial grounds. Limitations by democratic governments on economic, social and cultural rights would only be lawful (at least under international law) if it could be lawfully argued that the rights did not promote their general welfare. Bearing in mind that these economic, social and cultural rights have been enshrined in this Covenant precisely because they *will* promote the general welfare, it would be exceedingly difficult for a government to argue that they do

---

[295] Article 4, International Covenant on Economic, Social and Cultural Rights-external site

[296] Article 2, International Covenant on Economic, Social and Cultural Rights-external site

not, and just as difficult to argue that limitation of them will promote the general welfare. For instance, quite contorted reasoning would be required to argue that limitation of the right to primary schooling would promote the general welfare.

In theory therefore, a nation could lawfully derogate under this treaty from all economic, social and cultural rights and obligations but only to a certain extent – and that extent is likely to be near zero for a nation like Australia that is not short of wealth. In this sense, the Covenant works to protect people from the risk of losing their economic, social and cultural rights when there is no need and where it would be contrary to their interests. It maximises their chances of realising the full benefit of the treaty and in Australia that can be done without risk to monetary sovereignty and national financial sustainability. Australia is simply too wealthy to even need a get-out clause, and should it choose in some folly to argue before a court that a financial limitation prevented it from realising an economic, social or cultural right, it is doubtful of success because its choices for management of finances are simply too wide to be convincingly portrayed as a reasonable justification for withholding the right.

Of course, in contemplating the pressure that may be placed on them to realise rights to health, food, education, welfare, housing and all other economic, social and cultural rights, some governments may argue that enshrinement of these rights in the Constitution will open the floodgates to litigation. But it will only open those floodgates if governments are so incompetent as to refuse to "promote the general welfare in a democratic society" consistent with the Covenant, and so at odds with their people as to refuse to demonstrate they have comprehensive plans in place for

> achieving progressively the full realization of the rights recognized in the Covenant by all appropriate means, including particularly the adoption of legislative measures.[297]

All that each government will need to do construct a decent defence against litigation is to adopt long term financial plans which show how

---

[297] Article 2, International Covenant on Economic, Social and Cultural Rights-external site

and by when that “full realization” can be achieved and that their genuine intent is to achieve it consistent with the Covenant. Again, this is not something that is limited by lack of funds. It is simply limited by human incapacity or governmental incompetence and by a lack of will in some politicians to promote equality and wellbeing for all. Any decent government could reasonably defend itself and prevent litigation simply by developing reasonable agreements with its peoples which demonstrate how it intends to overcome this incapacity progressively to achieve the goals to which most developed nations, including Australia, have long since committed themselves. These goals are the United Nations Sustainable Development Goals. They contemplate a world that by 2030 will be free from hunger, poverty and homelessness, and well organised enough to provide good health, education, gender equality, clean water and energy, decent work, environmental sustainability, biodiversity protection, responsible consumption and production, climate action, peace, justice, strong institutions and reduced inequality. Processes to assist governments in this regard are discussed in Chapter 7.

If there are any other foreseeable risks that may arise from enshrining human rights in Australia’s Constitution via the process suggested in Prospect 2, these will doubtless be raised by interested parties. In consultation processes conducted for enactment of human rights legislation in Australia it is not evident that there are serious risks beyond those I have considered above, except perhaps the risk that rights which have not yet been specifically extended under the international instruments – such as the right to abortion or euthanasia on demand – might be considered inaccessible if Australian governments refuse to become a party to a treaty by a definitive signature or refuse to otherwise support a particular human rights instrument in international agreement-making processes. This is a reasonable risk because Prospect 2 assumes that the process for including human rights in the Constitution begins with a government’s consenting to become a signatory to or supporter of the relevant originating convention, treaty, declaration, protocol or other instrument of international human rights law. This should not be an issue in relation to human rights treaties and declarations to which Australia is already a party at the time they might be first enshrined in our Constitution. But, depending on how the process of Prospect 2 is elaborated in the Constitution, it could be an issue for rights that may be required in the future if, say, a government chooses to refuse to supply a definitive signature as a State Party to the relevant human rights treaty or declaration. This risk, however, can be minimised by specifying in the Constitution that it is the people's intention that the process described in Prospect 2 will not limit their access to rights and will not prevent enactment of legislation granting rights which are not yet contemplated in international law or are bound up in treaties to which the Australian government has refused to become a signatory. That sort of specification would be consistent with Article 5 of the International Covenant on Civil and Political Rights, the intention of which is clearly to stop governments from destroying, limiting or denying access to human rights.[298]

In other words, it should be clear that the treaties enshrined in the Constitution describe the *minimum* rights; they do not limit rights and do not prevent Australians from seeking to enshrine rights which have not yet found their way into an international human rights instrument or rights in conventions to which the Australian government might refuse to become a signatory. In that regard the wording of the Constitution should ensure that a definitive signature by Australia on an international human rights instrument is not the sole trigger for enshrinement of a right in the Constitution. Commonwealth and state legislation may also trigger a referendum to enshrine a new right and there should be no barriers to referendum processes for inclusion of additional rights if community engagement suggests there is a legitimate demand. If there is evidence that it is the people's sovereign will to acquire a new right, they should not be barred from that by a parliament or executive government.

---

[298] Article 5, International Covenant on Civil and Political Rights- external site and Article 5, International Covenant on Economic, Social and Cultural Rights- external site

In summary, given the safeguards inherent in the structure of rights and obligations in the treaties, and given other measures that can be taken to eliminate risk, it is apparent that the risk of not giving the people of Australia the first and last word on their rights is far greater than the risk of giving them every single one of these rights in full (and more if they wish). That being so, all arguments for more delays in enshrinement of all human rights treaties in Australia's Constitution are null. They are just so much subterfuge for the purpose of continuing to deny people the power to freely determine their political status and freely pursue their economic, social and cultural development. These are, after all, powers that successive Australian governments have acknowledged in international instruments and in official domestic policy to be the rightful entitlement of all peoples in other nations. Why then should they continue to deny them to Australians?

Appendix 3 contains, in summary form, a list of 305 of the rights conferred by the seven main human rights treaties to which Australia is a signatory and 351 of the obligations imposed on governments by the treaties. The list also includes another 52 rights and 41 obligations in the United Nations Declaration on the Rights of Indigenous Peoples. The lists do not cover all the rights and obligations in those instruments but perusal of the lists will allow readers to assess for themselves the risk of enshrining the rights and obligations in the Constitution. They can use the lists to ask themselves if they want these rights on an equal basis with all other Australians.

More importantly, readers can use the lists to ask themselves what life will be like without some or all of these rights. Although Australian governments have not specifically enshrined these rights in Commonwealth law, it is obvious that as a democratic society we have organised the nation's governance systems in a manner that has allowed most Australians to enjoy most of the benefits intended under the treaties at least to some extent. But not all Australians enjoy these benefits equally. And no Australian can take it for granted that everyone will be able to enjoy these benefits in the future. Until the 21st century, it was probably a reasonably safe proposition for Australians to take these rights, freedoms and protections for granted, even though they weren't enshrined in domestic law. But that sort of complacency is not a safe strategy for 21st century Australians, especially with the rise of political movements that are anything but democratic, for example:

- far-right political parties and extremist (politically organised) religious groups which absolutely reject power sharing arrangements that distribute human rights equally (or at all);
- autocratic governments that purport to be democratic but make laws that establish a secret state geared towards denial of civil and political rights;
- aggressive forms of international relations which rely on and encourage military escalation and new types of colonialism that deny the rights of Indigenous Peoples; and
- international economic and banking institutions that impose austerity on vulnerable nations in exchange for loans and also shift finance to multinational corporations that exploit non-renewable natural resources contrary to the interests of both the environment and humankind.

It will be difficult enough in the 21st century for any nation to escape the effects of this world-wide shift of power to cruel, exploitative political and corporate regimes. But unless people in democratic nations like Australia do whatever they can to assume and assert their rights in law in full – so that they cannot be arbitrarily or unlawfully extinguished – there is probably no hope at all of organising power so that it can counterbalance the destructive impulses of these ultimately anti-human political movements. In particular, if we wish to mitigate climate change, assertion of the full array of human rights is essential. Technical solutions alone will be ineffective against climate change. To be successful at all, they must be underpinned by a human-centric political order where nations determine what is and isn't in the public interest.

A human rights charter in the Constitution can give Australians this capacity. Without it ... well, I will leave that to readers to imagine for themselves. They will not have to look too far because in Australia the consequences of deprivation of rights are already apparent. It is clear in news items every month that abuses of human rights by Australia and in Australia have reached the depths of inhumanity. Australia clearly breaches some of the most basic rights such as freedom from torture (for instance in the extreme brutality that has occurred in the Australian prison system[299]) and some of the most important protections from exposure to war (for instance in the illegal and as yet unatoned for propaganda that was peddled by the Australian government to justify Australia's participation in the Iraq war). Our systems of government also provide the basis for crimes against future generations. And they provide the basis for perpetuation of the three main destructive mindsets for war, disproportionate fear of terrorism and theft of Indigenous property rights that I have already discussed – mindsets which can predispose governments to commit crimes against humanity on a massive scale. Indeed it could be said that Australia's mindset about Indigenous property rights has already caused it to attempt a crime against humanity – Indigenous genocide.

Despite the grip of these destructive mindsets, it is still possible to convert these governance systems so that they work to provide positive benefits rather than abuse. But it will only be possible to achieve this if Australians act quickly to secure their rights before even more are extinguished.

Australian governments have displayed a distinct and persistent tendency to remove rights from Australians and in the light of this evidence we should not take it for granted that they will not attempt again to remove more rights, particularly civil and political rights such as the right to vote. Some conservative politicians have attempted to introduce "voter-ID" laws,[300] which had they been successful would have had the effect of disenfranchising some Australians, particularly the most vulnerable such as homeless people and Aboriginal Australians who live in remote areas. There have also been occasional

---

[299] George Newhouse and Duncan Fine, "What kind of country are we that treats children in prison with such cruelty and brutality?", The Guardian, 21 September 2022.

[300] Paul Karp, "Proposed voter ID laws 'real threat' to rights of Indigenous Australians and people without homes", The Guardian, 27 October 2021.

attempts to abolish compulsory voting and the preferential voting systems in Australia, which would have had the effect of making the Australia's voting system much less "universal and equal" than it currently is.

Voting rights are tenuous in Australia because there is no constitutional confirmation of most civil and political rights, and governments cannot be trusted not to manipulate the voting system for political purposes. But voting rights are not the only civil and political rights at risk. Appendix 4 provides an indication that out of approximately 62 rights listed in the International Covenant on Civil and Political Rights:

- only 9 are likely to be available to natural persons in Australia with some reliability because they have some legislative basis underpinned by the Constitution;
- approximately 53 are not likely to be reliably available to natural persons in Australia because they are not fully provided for in the Australian Constitution; and
- approximately 36 are quite likely to be at risk in their availability to natural persons based on evidence of abuse of these rights by Australian authorities, reservations held in regard to those rights by the Australian government, or legislative action by the parliament which has had the effect of reducing these rights. Some of these rights at risk include:
    - the right of any state, group or person not to have a right or freedom (that is recognised in the Covenant) destroyed by any state, group or person or limited to a greater extent than is provided for in the Covenant,
    - the right not to be subjected to torture or cruel, inhuman or degrading treatment or medical or scientific experimentation,
    - the right of accused persons to be segregated from convicted persons,
    - the right of accused and convicted juvenile persons to be separated from adults in the detention system,
    - the right to speedy justice for juveniles,
    - the right to freedom of movement,

- the right to leave a country,
- the right of citizens to enter their own country,
- the right of presumption of innocence until proved guilty,
- the right to be informed fully and promptly of the detail of charges,
- the right to adequate time to prepare a defence and communicate with counsel of choice,
- the right to be tried without undue delay,
- the right of defendants to be present at their trial and to defend themselves or through their chosen counsel,
- the right to legal aid and interpreter services,
- the right to examine witnesses,
- the right to compensation for wrongful conviction,
- the right to privacy,
- the right to reputation and to protection from attacks on privacy and reputation,
- the right to hold opinions without interference,
- the right to freedom of expression,
- the right to seek, receive and impart information and ideas of all kinds,
- the implied right to peace,
- the right to protection from and prevention of racial hatred, hostility and violence,
- the right to peaceful assembly,
- the right to freedom of association with others,
- the right of every child to protection of the state,
- the right of every citizen to take part in the conduct of public affairs directly or through freely chosen representatives,
- the right of every citizen to vote and be elected in elections of universal and equal suffrage and with secret ballot,
- the right of every citizen to access, on general terms of equality, to public service,

- the right to be equal before the law,
- the right to equal protection of the law, and
- the right of minorities to use their own language.

As I have already said, Australians may wish to imagine for themselves what life would be like if the above listed rights were removed in full. Conversely, they may imagine the better life that would be available were these rights to be made available in full to everyone, along with the benefits that can arise from economic, social and cultural rights. There is a vast difference between the two types of Australian state that may be imagined. A nation with these rights is a truly liberal democracy. A nation without them risks becoming a hell of insecurity where there are no reliable defences against a merciless autocratic state.

If Prospect 2 were to be invoked, a range of crucial political rights that are at risk would be secured. Enshrinement of the full International Covenant on Civil and Political Rights into Australia's Constitution would secure the right to vote for all Australians and ensure that the voting system itself is one where elections are based on universal and equal suffrage with secret ballot. These and all the other benefits of international human rights instruments can be efficiently accessed if Australians enter into an agreement with each other on human rights and obligations – but only if they formulate that agreement themselves in their constitution as the expression of their sovereign will. In the following section I will elaborate on two of the most significant benefits that could be secured by free entry into such an agreement by the means described in Prospect 2. This Prospect gives Australians:

1. a feasible means of exercising rights of self-determination, both as a collective and as individuals; and
2. a feasible means of achieving a peaceful coexistence of sovereignties.

These two benefits are closely related in that it is unlikely either one can be realised without the other. Both are essential to establishment of a sound governance system suitable for a fully democratic modern state – one that is capable of supporting all its different peoples, cultures and individuals to live in peace without sacrificing their essential cultures, diversity and political agency.

Enabling orderly coexistence of sovereignties by agreement on human rights and obligations

In the early 2020s Australia has arrived at a pivotal point in its history – a point where we could move towards securing wellbeing and sustainable prosperity for the future, or away from it. Similarly we are at a point where we could move towards our own destruction as a species or away from it. There is a growing awareness among Australians about the precariousness of their future in the hitherto "lucky country" and particularly a concern that future generations will have less access than the current generation to a peaceful life with civil, political, economic, social and cultural rights and benefits. As such it might be expected that Australians would be open to Prospect 2. And in contemplation of the gloomy outlook for their children, many might well reason that if governments won't proactively give them rights that are essential for their protection, then the only option left is to simply take them before it is too late. Otherwise the current generation of Australians will be complicit in crimes against their own children and other crimes that have, until now, been committed by governments and corporations without the permission of Australians (for instance climate crimes,[301] crimes of entry into illegal wars, theft of public resources, and ecological extinctions). Once any human nation knows about these crimes – and in the internet age we can hardly avoid knowing – and once we know that there is something that could be done to stop these crimes, there is no excuse for delay, especially if the solution is readily available.

To the extent that Australia's current governance system is the cause of these crimes, the solution is readily available. As such, it is time to propose a starting draft of a new section in Australia's

---

[301] For examples, see The Guardian Climate Crimes series, 2022, https://www.theguardian.com/environment/series/climate-crimes

Constitution enshrining human rights and obligations. However, it will be important to design this in such a way as to ensure that:

- rights can be realised to the fullest extent possible by *everyone*, not just by some; and
- obligations to protect those rights and the benefits that can come from them cannot be unlawfully escaped by governments.

Full realisation of all human rights and obligations has not yet been attempted in any draft of a charter or bill of rights considered in Australia. But full realisation by all – on an equal basis – is essential. It is what Australians need if they are to break free of the mindsets locking us into wars, disproportionate fear of terrorism, theft of Indigenous property and other illegitimate state actions (such as those which impose the subsidisation by the public of private fossil fuel businesses). Half measures and frameworks which allow governments to continue to limit or withhold rights when it is contrary to the public interest to do so will be insufficient for the purpose of shedding these destructive mindsets. And anything less than the full measure of the primary human right – self-determination – will defeat the purpose entirely. This is because self-determination is central to the realisation of all the other rights. Unless each of us is able to freely determine our political status and freely pursue our economic, social and cultural development, none of the other rights can be assured to any of us.

No bill or charter that has been drafted in Australia has yet included a grant of self-determination as a right. As I have suggested above, this is probably because governments are frightened of the loss of centralised and exclusive power that would be implied. But it may also be because it is difficult to imagine how power might be exercised simultaneously by more than one sovereign entity. It is hard to imagine how multiple sovereignties may coexist – accustomed as we are to being governed by a *unitary* power outside all of us and to which we willingly conform in the (often misplaced) hope that order will prevail. It is hard to imagine how each of us might exercise self-determination without chaos and a clash of wills. It has been hard to imagine this for many hundreds of years and this is why nations –

both autocratic and democratic – have always fallen back on the notion that it is necessary to have a unitary sovereign will – one authority located above us all with a unique right to freely determine what shall and shall not be permitted in the rights and freedoms of all others and particularly to determine when the nation shall go to war.

And yet the times call on us to imagine how full rights of self-determination for all might be achieved, not just because Australia like the rest of the world is on the brink of life threatening chaos, but also because the Australian nation has been served in the Uluru Statement from the Heart with the most plangent and entirely legitimate call for a coexistence of sovereignties. There is a major piece of unfinished business in our nation's founding and until it is amicably solved Australia will be unable to lay claim to being a truly democratic and free country.

Australians in the 21st century have slowly come to recognise that First Nations' sovereignty has never been ceded and that therefore it is necessary, both in law and in conscience, to find a way to organise a new political and governance system so that these two sovereignties can coexist peacefully. Some may assume this can be achieved through a treaty, which without doubt is necessary. But depending on how it is framed and how it is connected with (or disconnected from) the Constitution, a treaty might not necessarily deliver the full measure of change in governance necessary to secure ongoing justice. It might declare peace between First Nations and the Australian government of the day. But if negotiated outside a more inclusive framework – such as a people's constitution – it would not necessarily set up the systems by which:

- just rules of law may therefrom be made; and
- peace might be secured and managed on an ongoing basis by a collegiate Australian nation as a whole – a nation in which all members make a mutual commitment to henceforth respect and protect each other's rights.

In the absence of such a mutual commitment, a treaty would lack a solid foundation and would accordingly be tenuous. Two sovereignties of the Crown and First Nations might be temporarily reconciled, but a lasting reconciliation, where ongoing justice can be relied upon, will require a holistic pact that encompasses a mutual commitment between First Nations people and non-Indigenous people – a pact acknowledged in a constitution which also accepts that human rights are the equal entitlement of all and that unless and until everyone is confident that that they each have all human rights in full on an equal basis, justice simply cannot have been done.

Any treaty negotiated in the absence of an agreement on rights for all would mean that Australia could not really make good on the request from Uluru for "a fair and truthful relationship with the people of Australia and a better future for our children based on justice and self-determination".[302] As such we will need to make the Constitution fit for the purpose of installing and sustaining a treaty with First Nations and we will need to do this by enshrining equal human rights for all in full.

Providentially, help is available to both First Nations and the Australian parliament for this purpose in the United Nations Declaration on the Rights of Indigenous Peoples (UNDRIP).[303] This Declaration has been "supported" by the Australian government, albeit only "as a non-legally binding document".[304] As I noted in Chapter 1, Australia was one of only four nations to vote against the UNDRIP when it was first adopted in 2007. 144 other nations voted in favour and 11 abstained. In 2009, Australia reversed its rejection but regrettably its commitment to the Declaration remains muted and there is still a sense in which Australian governments have not got past their fear that it will "disrupt their territorial integrity" and

---

[302] Uluru Statement from the Heart. See Appendix 1.

[303] United Nations Declaration on the Rights of Indigenous Peoples, 2007. DRIPS_en.pdf (un.org)

[304] Australian Government, Attorney-General's Department, "International Human Rights System" webpage, last accessed 28 September 2022. International human rights system | Attorney-General's Department (ag.gov.au)

perhaps "enhance the rights of Indigenous citizens vis-à-vis all others".[305]

However, there is nothing in the UNDRIP that enhances the rights of one group over any other. Instead, the Declaration makes it clear that the rights established in it – and for that matter, the things Indigenous people are calling for in the Uluru Statement from the Heart – are nothing more and nothing less than the natural and equal entitlement of *all* humans. It confers nothing more on the world's Indigenous peoples than the rights that non-Indigenous peoples would want and would assume they are entitled to, particularly in relation to property and security of title on land. In particular it does not allow Indigenous peoples to do to non-Indigenous people what was done to Australia's Aborigines and Torres Strait Islanders by the British colonial power. It does not allow Indigenous people to illegally dispossess others of property to which they hold valid title. And it does not allow an Indigenous group or culture to assert authority over others. It simply provides a foundation on which Indigenous nations and non-Indigenes may determine how they shall coexist with compatible rights of self-determination as equal citizens.

The United Nations Declaration on the Rights of Indigenous Peoples is an aspirational document rather than an instrument of customary international law. But this should not diminish its status or eligibility for inclusion in our list of international instruments establishing universal human rights in our Constitution via the use of Prospect 2. The UNDRIP's nominal status as a "declaration", rather than as a document accorded status as an international law, makes the human rights included in it no less real and valid, especially insofar as the UNDRIP negates no other right listed in the instruments that *are* accepted as law. Given that the basis of all the other human rights instruments is to insist that rights are equal for all, and given that official policy in Australia is that

---

[305] Dominic O'Sullivan, *We are All Here To Stay: Citizenship, Sovereignty and the Universal Declaration of Human Rights*, Australian National University Press, 2020, page 10. 'We Are All Here to Stay' (anu.edu.au)

> there is no hierarchy or priority of the rights enshrined in the UDHR [Universal Declaration of Human Rights], nor are there pre-conditions imposed on the enjoyment of some of these rights",[306]

an insistence by churlish Australian lawyers or policy makers that the Declaration has some sort of lesser status is really nothing more than a lawmaker's feint attempting – yet again – to subjugate the rights of Indigenes to non-Indigenes. It is nothing more than the usual ploy of the dispossessors – a totally artificial and arbitrary distinction founded on a conception of morality that seeks to justify theft. To insist that the Declaration be excluded from instalment in domestic law merely because it has not (yet) been accorded the same customary status in international law as other human rights agreements would be to break faith with those other instruments. Indeed, excluding the Declaration from designation as law should be seen as a breach of the other treaties. And for as long as the Australian government continues to maintain the stance that the UNDRIP may be supported, but as no more than a "non-legally binding document", that stance should simply be seen for what it is – a government intent on continuing to breach its agreements on human rights. To deny Indigenous rights is to deny that all humans are equal in their rights. And until we can trust the federal government to honour in full the spirit and letter of the UNDRIP we can in no way trust them to honour any part of any other human rights treaty.

With a people's constitution, however, Australians need not be restrained by the ploys of the dispossessors, especially when they have the immoral purpose of creating a hierarchy of people who are entitled to rights, with Indigenes at the bottom and non-Indigenes at the top. That would be a world of re-installed injustice. In a people's constitution rights must be the equal property of all. We should be able to work on the understanding that we are free to make our laws as we see fit, in accordance with our values, and can bind our

---

[306] Department of Foreign Affairs and Trade, "Australian and Human Rights: An Overview, 4th edition", December 2017, page 15, Op. Cit.

governments legitimately to compliance with those laws precisely because they have been made in accordance with values specified in the Constitution. Accordingly, if the values we share are that everyone should have equal rights, there should be no barrier to including rights established in the UNDRIP in the Australian Constitution. Moreover, if they are not included, we are less likely to be able to settle a stable treaty with First Nations – one that is stable because it has been made freely by equals in terms comprehensive enough to achieve a permanent resolution of the conflict occasioned by dispossession.

The United Nations Declaration on the Rights of Indigenous Peoples includes, among other things, a wide array of rights about lands and in particular the government's obligations to:

- give legal recognition and protection to these lands, territories and resources;
- establish and implement, in conjunction with Indigenous peoples concerned, a fair, independent, impartial, open and transparent process, giving due recognition to Indigenous peoples' laws, traditions, customs and land tenure systems;
- recognize and adjudicate the rights of Indigenous peoples pertaining to their lands, territories and resources, including those which were traditionally owned or otherwise occupied or used;
- provide, unless otherwise freely agreed upon by the peoples concerned, compensation in the form of lands, territories and resources equal in quality, size and legal status or of monetary compensation or other appropriate redress;
- consult and cooperate in good faith with the Indigenous peoples concerned through their own representative institutions in order to obtain their free and informed consent prior to the approval of any project affecting their lands or territories and other resources, particularly in connection with the development, utilization or exploitation of mineral, water or other resources;
- ensure Indigenous lands are not used for military purposes or disposal of hazardous materials; and to

- provide redress, by means that can include restitution or, when this is not possible, just, fair and equitable compensation, for the lands, territories and resources which they have traditionally owned or otherwise occupied or used, and which have been confiscated, taken, occupied, used or damaged without their free, prior and informed consent.

In Australia's case, adherence to these obligations will be a tall order for governments, bearing in mind that almost the entire continent was illegally possessed or alienated in some form by British colonisation without the free prior and informed consent of Indigenous nations. But again, this is only likely to be a tall order because of politics and patrician attitudes to power. It is not difficult at all from a legal or financial point of view. Indeed, adoption of Prospect 2 would function as the means by which Australians could confer rights of self-determination and security of property on themselves and each other without causing chaos at all. It is probably the only way to achieve this because enshrinement of *all* human rights in a constitution – as the equal property of all people – is the only known and rational way (in the Australian democratic federation at least) to set down in law a basis for stable governance that tolerates everyone's equal right to freely determine their political status and freely pursue their economic, social and cultural development. It is the only way such a nation can avail itself of the capacity to establish a legitimate people's sovereign will that can accommodate diversity and the peaceable balancing of competing interests. In the same way that it is not practicable to cherry pick national values and still expect to retain order within the state, it is not possible to cherry pick human rights that are otherwise acknowledged to be universal and indivisible and still expect that peace can be guaranteed. Full inscription of *all* human rights, including those under the UNDRIP, is likely to be the only way a treaty with First Nations can be cast in reliable terms. It is therefore also the only way to establish a coexistence of sovereignties in which an inclusive order can be safely and fairly maintained.

Prospect 2 offers all this because it is built on acceptance of the propositions on which the Universal Declaration of Human Rights was founded – propositions which simply accept that order and wellbeing themselves can only obtain if human rights are conferred in full and equally on all members of the human family. The international treaties and declarations on human rights are founded on the agreed principle that:

> the equal and inalienable rights of all members of the human family is the foundation of freedom, justice and peace in the world,

and more, that

> the ideal of free human beings enjoying civil and political freedom and freedom from fear and want can *only* be achieved if conditions are created whereby everyone may enjoy his [sic.] civil and political rights, as well as his [sic.] economic, social and cultural rights.[307] [Emphasis added.]

It is that simple. We cannot thrive at all without rights and we certainly cannot coexist happily, especially after more than 200 years of colonial disruption and injustice which in Australia is as yet entirely unresolved. If there is another way to make multiple sovereignties coexist happily, it would seem humankind has not yet discovered it. Nor, failing some unanticipated enlightenment, are we likely to – mere mortals that we are. This makes it morally incumbent on parliaments to release Australians from subjection to a life where they have no guarantee of their rights and no power to determine their rights consistent with their aspirations to be a fully democratic nation and with the value they place on social harmony, diversity, inclusion, equality, egalitarianism, equal opportunity, social justice and wellbeing for all. With a people's constitution, especially one that enshrines a statement of Australian values, perhaps along the lines suggested in Chapter 5, Australians could establish a new framework for a coexistence of multiple sovereignties based on justice and self-determination – just as First Nations have contemplated in the Uluru Statement from the Heart.

---

[307] Preamble to the International Covenant on Civil and Political Rights.

The Uluru Statement contains the same enlightened insight as the Universal Declaration of Human Rights into what it is that is essential to the continued existence of the human family. Both statements display a profound understanding of what makes a tolerable existence, and ongoing existence itself, possible – the universal right of self-determination and the freedom that can only inhere in that right. This might not be surprising since both statements were born directly from an existential crisis. Both were born out of events which threatened the continuance of a human civilisation. Both were born from a desire to escape the scourge of war. And both were born from an acute consciousness of how

> disregard and contempt for human rights have resulted in barbarous acts which have outraged the conscience of mankind.[308]

In Australia, as the decades of the 21st century are passing, more and more non-Indigenous Australians are encountering a crisis of conscience about the heinous faults of the nation's founding and the injustice suffered by the Nations that possessed the country before colonisation. And in the 2020s, as the world faces unprecedented existential threats of climate change and nuclear war, these sorts of statements – statements which affirm that human rights are essential to human existence – are probably the only things we have which can supply us with a path to a secure future for all that is not inherently chaotic and destructive and, as a consequence, will not result in the sort of mutually assured destruction that is the inevitable outcome of a war of all against all or a war of all against nature and the planet. For Australians in their lucky country, these statements are all the enlightenment that we need. They light a path to avoidance of a war we cannot win – a war against ourselves. As such they light the path to a secure peace.

A decision to claim those rights, and secure them safely in the Constitution in the manner offered under Prospect 2, has the capacity to pull the nation back from the brink of its destruction and set it on

---

[308] Preamble to The Universal Declaration of Human Rights. Universal Declaration of Human Rights | United Nations

a path to peaceful coexistence of multiple sovereignties within Australia's democracy. Simply by replacing a process which will lead to mutually assured destruction with a process of mutually assured rights, Australia can transform its prospects for security and wellbeing. Prospect 2 has the necessary capacity for this purpose because it is founded on the principle that human rights are not the gift of governments; they are what we freely give to each other. They are what all member nations of the United Nations since World War II have freely acknowledged as the universal and indivisible entitlement of every single human being and unless we give them freely and equally to each other – and assure each other that they will not be taken away – we are not capable of securing a lasting peace. Assured equal human rights are the primordial treaty that underpins and is a prerequisite for all other treaties between nations and particularly between governments established by colonial dispossession and the Indigenous nations that have been dispossessed.

If a human rights framework is to deliver self-determination and a peaceful coexistence of sovereignties, this can only arise if Australians freely agree to confer all these rights on themselves and each other – equally. Accordingly, in a fully democratic people's constitution, any human rights that are enshrined in it must be the product of a free agreement between all the people. The referendum process in Prospect 2 can enable this free agreement but the exact nature of the agreement itself must be clear. Everyone must be able to understand the terms of the agreement, the fundamental values on which the terms are based, and to confirm that those terms are a mutual commitment that they are prepared to make and be bound by. Here it should be borne in mind that, if in an Australian People's Constitution the people have already adopted a Statement of Australian Values, they will have a yardstick that they can then use to determine for themselves that the rights they are agreeing to grant to each other on an equal basis are consistent with what they freely value for themselves as individuals and as a nation.

Put simply, this means that values should ideally be agreed before rights can be agreed. Unless individuals can be reasonably comfortable that the "others" who will benefit from the rights hold the same values as they do, it is unlikely that they will have sufficient confidence to trust others with those rights. This in turn suggests that a referendum on human rights would need to be preceded by a referendum on national values. I will talk more about the order in which various issues like this may be solved by community engagement and referendums in Chapter 9. For the moment it is simply necessary to observe that in the same way that the stated values of Australians should provide the starting point for all laws made in Australia, they should provide the context in which universal human rights are legitimised in Australian law as the indivisible whole that they are.

At this point it might be noted that I have shifted from the concept of a *charter* of rights to an *agreement* on rights. This is consistent with a shift from a constitution made at the will of a unitary head of state to a constitution made at the plural will of the people of that state. A "charter" is the instrument of a unitary, monarchic, exclusive and therefore essentially undemocratic power. It is

> a written grant by the sovereign or legislative power of a country, by which a body such as a city, company, or university is founded or its rights and privileges defined.[309]

But in a people's constitution, the sovereign will that creates the rights and privileges is located in the people, not in the crown or the legislative power as we have known it. Should Australians choose to rely on a notion that rights may only be conferred by the fiat of governments – in other words, should they choose to stick with Prospect 1 – then "charter" is probably the right term for a group of rights in the Constitution. But if a grant of rights is left to a legislative power then, based on experience to date, Australians might expect to wait a long time for such a gift. As I have already suggested it is more likely that if Australians really want their rights, they will have to grant them to themselves and this will entail a shift in lawmaking in which they will have to go around their obstructive governments

---

309 "Charter" meaning in Google Definitions from Oxford Languages.

in order to make an open agreement with each other on these rights and, at the same time, impose obligations on the recalcitrant governments that have become more and more inclined towards denial of rights and abuse of power.

Prospect 2 gives the Australian people the means to go around obstructive governments before it is too late. By enshrining an agreement that we freely make with each other, it gives us all the means to ensure that governments will finally act consistent with what is, after all, their current official policy position – that human rights are "*inherent* as the birthright of all human beings" and are therefore to be "enjoyed by all simply by reason of their humanity rather than granted or bestowed."[310] They are also "*inalienable* in the sense that they cannot be given up or taken away."[311] And they are *indivisible* – meaning they cannot be split up with some people enjoying more than others. So if we are to take current official Australian government policy at its word, we should conclude that human rights cannot be conferred or denied by a government by means such as a charter. They can only be secured by an agreement freely entered into by the people themselves.

Of course, not everyone will agree with all the values and all the human rights that may from time to time be enshrined in any constitution. But if we establish a process of constitutional reform to enact an Australian people's constitution, and if we ensure that this process is not restricted in its terms of reference and can conduct fully open community engagement – perhaps building on the experience and success of the engagement undertaken in the Referendum Council, which resulted in a high degree of involvement and concurrence on the Uluru Statement from the Heart – then there is no reason why we should not expect that Australians in a significant majority will be able to commit to a national agreement on human rights and obligations. To assume otherwise would be to assume that no advanced nation, acting on the basis of an agreed set of values,

---

[310] Department of Foreign Affairs and Trade, "Australian and Human Rights: An Overview, 4th edition", December 2017, page 10, Op. Cit.

[311] Department of Foreign Affairs and Trade, "Australian and Human Rights: An Overview, 4th edition", December 2017, page 10, Ibid.

could cohere on something as fundamental as the right of all humans to freely determine their political status and freely pursue their economic, social and cultural development. Were we to assume that they could not cohere on this as a majority, we would in logic have to give up on the entire enterprise of human freedom and accept that we are stuck irreversibly on the path to chaos and self-destruction.

For those who are not ready to confine themselves to that destructive path, the following starting draft of a National Agreement on Human Rights and Obligations is offered as a contribution to deliberations. Readers will note that the starting draft creates a constitutional framework for development, democratic passage, enshrinement and maintenance of the agreement, because from a constitutional and public interest perspective, the capacity to conduct a fully democratic decision process for enshrining a national agreement on human rights and obligations in the Constitution is as important as the agreement itself. This democratic decision framework is consistent with Prospect 2.

It is also very important to note that this proposal for a process to enshrine a national agreement on human rights and obligations is predicated on an assumption that Australians will have already established a statement of Australian values in their Constitution that is comprehensive enough to enable them to determine that the rights they are thereby granting to themselves and each other are consistent with their national values. It is also assumed that, as a matter of democratic process, Australians may have participated in one or more plebiscites (non-binding referendums) to get to the point at which an obstructive parliament may approve that a binding referendum question be put to the people of Australia along the lines I have described below and which I have called "an inception referendum". There may be other ways to break the vice-like grip parliaments have on what questions may and may not be put to Australians in referendums. If so, we might anticipate that Australians who are eager to bring this new form of protection of their rights into being at last will make suggestions on other ways around the "brick wall" of "that anachronism of contemporary Australia, the federal Constitution".[312]

Starting draft of a National Agreement on Human Rights and Obligations and a democratic process for its constitutional enshrinement

Part 1: Australian People's Constitution – Inception of a National Agreement on Human Rights and Obligations (draft for use in community engagement)

1) Pursuant to our approval in an Inception Referendum, it is the Sovereign Will of We the People of Australia that We shall make an inaugural agreement to be known as *The National Agreement on Human Rights and Obligations* and that this *Agreemen*t shall:

    a) be enshrined and upheld in this Constitution in accordance with the principles and democratic processes described here and elsewhere in this Constitution and shall thereby be taken to stand as the freely expressed will and agreement of the People of Australia to:
        - confer human rights that are acknowledged to be universal and indivisible in full and equally on all natural persons; and
        - impose on each other and on elected parliaments and governments full obligations to:
            - uphold and observe these rights as the just and equal entitlement of all, and
            - build a society and democratic governance system capable of progressively realising these rights for all on an equal basis, up to the fullest extent

[312] Manning Clark, Essay on "The People and the Constitution" in Sol Encel, Donald Horne and Elaine Thompson (eds.), *Change the Rules: Towards a democratic constitution*, Penguin, Ringwood Victoria, 1977, pages 19-20.

possible, and in a manner that is demonstrably in the public interest;

b) pursuant to and consistent with 1(a) above, have the effect of incorporating into Australian law the full set of human rights and obligations that are established in international instruments to which Australia is (or becomes) a signatory, or of which it is (or becomes) a supporter, as the equal entitlements and obligations of all natural persons, such international instruments to include those listed in Part 2, clause 2(b) below as the Minimum Instruments necessary for fulfilment of the People's intention in regard to the rights they shall enjoy under *The Agreement*; and

c) be binding in law on all persons, parliaments and executive governments of the Commonwealth, States and Territories of Australia as well as their agents and subsidiaries and be maintained as Australian law unless and until such time as Australian enfranchised electors seek in a duly constituted referendum to vary *The Agreement*.

[**Note:** It is assumed here that a referendum will be called in the first instance to establish that this is in fact the People's Sovereign Will. This referendum may be known as the Inception Referendum for the inaugural *National Agreement on Human Rights and Obligations*. An option for a straightforward question for the Inception Referendum may be as follows:

> Do you support an alteration to the Constitution that will allow the people of Australia to make a *National Agreement on Human Rights and Obligations* wherein the full set of human rights and obligations that are established in international instruments to which Australia is a signatory, or of which it is a supporter, will form the basis of *The Agreement* and will be maintained as the minimum of human rights and

obligations under Australian law until such time as Australian enfranchised electors seek in a duly constituted referendum to vary *The Agreement*?

It is further assumed that because this is an agreement that the people of Australia freely make among themselves, the referendum for inception of the inaugural *Agreement* shall not be obstructed by the parliament or executive government in the manner permitted under the current wording of section 128 of the current Constitution but shall be called (in this instance, and only in this instance) by the governor-general (or other nominal head of state, should such an office be created), with or without the agreement of parliament.

In the current Constitution it is unlikely that the governor-general has the power to call a referendum in this way – that is, without a parliamentary vote in favour of calling a referendum. As such, if the parliament behaves obstructively (including by seeking to reduce the rights and obligations that may be enshrined in this process) and no lawful way around the obstruction can be found, community pressure will need to be brought to bear to ensure that human rights can at last be assumed as the property of Australians consistent with the international human rights instruments to which Australia is a signatory.]

Part 2: Democratic process for enshrining and upholding *The National Agreement on Human Rights and Obligations* (draft for use in community engagement)

2) Pursuant to the passage of the Inception Referendum in Part 1, and consistent with the declaration in clause 1 above that it is the sovereign will of the People of Australia to enter into *The National Agreement on Human Rights and Obligations*, the parliament shall within one month take all steps necessary to:

   a) ensure that the inaugural *National Agreement on Human Rights and Obligations* is incorporated into this Constitution in a form and wording that is consistent with the Sovereign Will of the People as expressed in the Inception Referendum; and

b) ensure in particular, in accordance with Part 1, clause 1(b) above, that the following international instruments shall be incorporated in full into the inaugural *Agreement* and be acknowledged therein as the Minimum Instruments necessary for fulfilment of the People's intention in regard to the human rights they shall enjoy and the obligations that shall be accepted under *The Agreement*:

    i. the International Covenant on Civil and Political Rights (ICCPR),
    ii. the International Covenant on Economic, Social and Cultural Rights (ICESCR),
    iii. the International Convention on the Elimination of All Forms of Racial Discrimination (CERD),
    iv. the Convention on the Elimination of All Forms of Discrimination against Women (CEDAW),
    v. the Convention Against Torture and Other Cruel, Inhuman or Degrading Treatment or Punishment (CAT),
    vi. the Convention on the Rights of the Child (CRC),
    vii. the Convention on the Rights of Persons with Disabilities (CRPD),
    viii. the United Nations Declaration on the Rights of Indigenous Peoples (UNDRIP),
    ix. the Optional Protocol to the International Covenant on Civil and Political Rights (ICCPR-OP1),
    x. the Second Optional Protocol to the International Covenant on Civil and Political Rights (ICCPR-OP2),

xi. the Optional Protocol to the Convention on the Rights of the Child on the Involvement of Children in Armed Conflict (OP-CRC-AC),

xii. the Optional Protocol to the Convention on the Rights of the Child on the Sale of Children, Child Prostitution and Child Pornography (OP-CRC-SC),

xiii. the Optional Protocol to the Convention on the Elimination of All Forms of Discrimination Against Women (OP-CEDAW),

xiv. the Optional Protocol to the Convention on the Rights of Persons with Disabilities (OP-CRPD),

xv. the Optional Protocol to the Convention against Torture and Other Cruel, Inhuman or Degrading Treatment or Punishment (OP-CAT);

c) ensure that all other steps that may be required in order to fulfil the purposes of this Part, as set out in clauses 3 and 4 below, are taken in full and in a manner faithful to those purposes; and

d) make any and all laws necessary to establish and maintain a fully democratic process by which We the People of Australia may, in accordance with our Sovereign Will as expressed here and elsewhere in our Constitution, and by means of duly constituted referendums, seek to vary the duly enshrined *National Agreement on Human Rights and Obligations*, if such variation has been deemed necessary in, or due to, processes for community engagement and review of *The Agreement* as provided for here or elsewhere in this Constitution.

3) The primary purposes of this section (including Parts 1, 2, and 3), and of any laws that may be made under this Constitution in relation *The National Agreement on Human Rights and Obligations*, must be to ensure that:

a) human rights that are established in international instruments to which Australia is a signatory, or of which it is a supporter, will be established automatically, and in any case without unreasonable delay or obstruction, in Australian law as the minimum of human rights available in Australia; and that
b) unless and until We the People of Australia in a duly constituted referendum deem otherwise:
    i. the rights so established shall not be reduced or withheld from any natural person; and
    ii. no obligation that is specified or implied in the instruments cited in clause 2(b) above as an obligation which "shall" be observed by a State Party to or supporter of these instruments, may be obviated, evaded, escaped or derogated from by the parliament in lawmaking or by the executive government in policy, action or administrative practice, except as provided for by these instruments and except as may be demonstrably consistent with the national interest and the values of the nation as expressed in the *Statement of Australian Values* in this Constitution.

4) Other essential purposes of this section are to ensure that:

    a) no parliament or executive government may unreasonably deny or delay extending any human right to a natural person if that right is deemed to be lawful under international law and is demonstrably consistent with the values of the nation as expressed in the *Statement of Australian Values* in this Constitution;
    b) parliament may make laws which confer human rights on natural persons which are additional to the human rights conferred under the above instruments, but no parliament or executive government may take any action

in law, policy, administration or executive statement to reduce or restrict these duly conferred human rights, except insofar as the instruments themselves allow and only to the extent allowed under international law;

c) no parliament or executive government may refuse to comply with a State Party obligation set down in the above instruments except to the extent that may be permitted by international law;
d) no parliament or executive government may take action to dismiss, deny or derogate from a State Party obligation set down in the above instruments except to the extent that may be permitted by international law;
e) parliaments shall ensure the full protection of all natural persons from abuse of their human rights by ensuring that any provisions in this and all other laws and subordinate legislation made by the parliaments of the Commonwealth, the States and the Territories, which are in part or in whole demonstrably inconsistent with the terms of *The National Agreement on Human Rights and Obligations*, are deleted or amended in a manner that ensures this Constitution and laws made under it are brought into accord with the public interest as expressed in *The Agreement*;
f) no human rights may be accorded to corporations or to any entity that is not a natural person;
g) parliaments will take action to ensure that referendums for the purpose of amending or altering *The Agreement* are duly constituted in accordance with referendum processes permitted for amendment or alteration of this Constitution;
h) community engagement preparatory to any referendum is fully open to and accessible by all Australians and is not constrained or delayed by inadequate funding, or funding which is distributed on a discriminatory basis or in a manner likely to result in discrimination against a particular group; and

i) parliaments and executive governments will take any and all other necessary action to ensure that all Australian peoples, including First Nations, have the right of self-determination and that by virtue of that right they freely determine their political status and freely pursue their economic, social and cultural development.

Part 3: *The National Agreement on Human Rights and Obligations* (draft for use in community engagement)

[**Note:** The following is an indicative draft of a *National Agreement of Human Rights and Obligations*. It is provided to illustrate the sort of *Agreement* that is likely to arise from Prospect 2 if it is invoked and enshrined in a manner that accords with the processes described in the draft of Parts 1 and 2 above. This is a starting draft of a possible *Agreement* to assist in community engagement for the making of an Australian People's Constitution.]

We the People of Australia, being satisfied that the processes as specified in Parts 1 and 2 of this section for inception and enshrinement of *The National Agreement on Human Rights and Obligations* has been conducted lawfully, in full consideration of the public interest as expressed in the *Statement of Australian Values* in this Constitution, and in complete accordance with our Sovereign Will as expressed here and elsewhere in this Constitution, do hereby affirm and declare that we freely agree to:

1) confer all universal human rights in full and equally on all natural persons in accordance with and to the extent specified in the following international human rights instruments:

    i. the International Covenant on Civil and Political Rights (ICCPR),
    ii. the International Covenant on Economic, Social and Cultural Rights (ICESCR),

iii. the International Convention on the Elimination of All Forms of Racial Discrimination (CERD),
iv. the Convention on the Elimination of All Forms of Discrimination against Women (CEDAW),
v. the Convention Against Torture and Other Cruel, Inhuman or Degrading Treatment or Punishment (CAT),
vi. the Convention on the Rights of the Child (CRC),
vii. the Convention on the Rights of Persons with Disabilities (CRPD),
viii. the United Nations Declaration on the Rights of Indigenous Peoples (UNDRIP),
ix. the Optional Protocol to the International Covenant on Civil and Political Rights (ICCPR-OP1),
x. the Second Optional Protocol to the International Covenant on Civil and Political Rights (ICCPR-OP2),
xi. the Optional Protocol to the Convention on the Rights of the Child on the Involvement of Children in Armed Conflict (OP-CRC-AC),
xii. the Optional Protocol to the Convention on the Rights of the Child on the Sale of Children, Child Prostitution and Child Pornography (OP-CRC-SC),
xiii. the Optional Protocol to the Convention on the Elimination of All Forms of Discrimination Against Women (OP-CEDAW),
xiv. the Optional Protocol to the Convention on the Rights of Persons with Disabilities (OP-CRPD),
xv. the Optional Protocol to the Convention against Torture and Other Cruel, Inhuman or Degrading Treatment or Punishment (OP-CAT); and

2) impose on each other as responsible persons and communities, and on all parliaments and executive governments of the Commonwealth, as well as all State and Territory governments, lawfully elected from time to

time under this Constitution or State Constitutions, full obligations to:

a) uphold and observe the rights conferred in (1) on all natural persons as their just and equal entitlement, and
b) build a society and democratic governance system capable of realising these rights for all on an equal basis and in a manner that is demonstrably in the public interest and is consistent with the underlying principles and legal requirements of the instruments listed in (1).

We further affirm and declare that:

a) No obligation that is specified or implied in the instruments listed in (1) as an obligation which "shall" be observed by a State Party to or supporter of these instruments may be obviated, evaded, escaped or derogated from by a parliament in lawmaking or by an executive government in policy, action, administrative practice or executive statement, except as provided for by the listed instruments and except as may be demonstrably consistent with the national interest and the values of the nation as expressed in the *Statement of Australian Values* in this Constitution.

b) The rights conferred and the obligations imposed consistent with the instruments listed in (1) are law in Australia unless and until We the People say otherwise in a referendum held in accordance with the referendum processes permitted in this Constitution for its amendment or alteration.

c) Parliaments may make laws which confer human rights on natural persons which are additional to the human rights conferred under the above instruments, but no parliament or executive government, either of the Commonwealth or a State or Territory, may take any action in law, policy, administration or executive statement to reduce or restrict these duly conferred human rights, except insofar as the instruments themselves allow.

d) No parliament or executive government may take action to dismiss, deny or derogate from a State Party obligation set down in the above instruments except to the extent that may be permitted by international law or to the extent permitted by any processes that are or may be established for this purpose elsewhere in the Constitution in accordance with our Sovereign Will.

e) No parliament or executive government may frustrate, delay or reduce access to the benefits of any right or obligation in the listed instruments by unreasonably applying a reservation to or withholding support for any aspect of the listed instruments.

f) No parliament or executive government may seek to frustrate, delay or deny the inclusion of human rights and obligations in Australian law by unreasonably refusing to become a State Party to or supporter of human rights declarations or treaties in international law and no barrier shall be imposed by parliaments or executive governments to referendum processes for inclusion of new human rights in Australian law when rights conferred in instruments of international law or declarations are demonstrably consistent with the values of Australians as expressed in the *Statement of Australian Values*.

g) Parliaments shall ensure the full protection of all natural persons from abuse of their human rights by ensuring that any provisions in this and all other laws and subordinate legislation made by the parliaments of the Commonwealth, the States and the Territories, which are in part or in whole demonstrably inconsistent with the terms of *The National Agreement on Human Rights and Obligations*, are deleted or amended in a manner that ensures this Constitution and all other laws are brought into accord with the public interest as expressed in *The Agreement*.

h) No human rights may be accorded to corporations or to any entity that is not a natural person.

i) Parliaments and executive governments shall take any and all other necessary action to ensure that all Australian peoples, including First Nations, have the right of self-determination and that by virtue of that right they freely determine their political status and freely pursue their economic, social and cultural development.

We also declare and affirm that the human rights and obligations encompassed in the instruments listed in (1) in this *Agreement* stand as the rights and obligations that are indicative of the public interest and are necessary for its protection, and that it will be contrary to the public interest to make laws which withhold these rights, either in whole or in part, from any or all natural persons. Therefore we also affirm that unless and until We the People agree otherwise in a duly constituted referendum conducted pursuant to and in accordance with Part 2 of this section:

- *The Agreement* here made shall stand as guidance to law and policy makers and to authorised justices of the courts as to whether laws and policies are in accordance with our Sovereign Will; and that
- laws and policies which are demonstrably inconsistent with *The Agreement* are inconsistent with the Australian People's Sovereign Will and shall not stand.

[**Note:** The human rights instruments listed in 1 above are not the only international instruments in which human rights have been proclaimed. But they are the ones that have been supported by Australia either by signature or ratification and as such they offer a good starting list of instruments that should reasonably be included in *The National Agreement on Human Rights and Obligations*. It would, after all, be fully unreasonable for any government to refuse inclusion of these instruments, given that Australia has already supported them in international agreement processes and has therefore agreed that these rights should be the universal and indivisible entitlement of all peoples. This is not to say that governments will not behave perversely, especially if they think their power is being limited. But at the very least they will have a tougher time justifying such perversity and mounting arguments as to why the instruments listed in (1) should not form the core of the first *National Agreement on Human Rights and Obligations*.

Having established this core of human rights instruments, Australians may nevertheless deem it necessary at some time in the future to include other international human rights instruments that exist in the 2020s but have not been signed by Australia. At the time of writing these included:

- the International Convention on the Protection of the Rights of All Migrant Workers and Members of Their Families (ICMW),

- the International Convention for the Protection of All Persons from Enforced Disappearance (CPED),
- the Optional Protocol to the Covenant on Economic, Social and Cultural Rights (ICESCR-OP), and
- the Optional Protocol to the Convention on the Rights of the Child on a communications procedure (OP-CRC-IC).[313]

There is nothing in Prospect 2 or in the above starting draft of *The Agreement* and the process for enshrining it that would prevent Australians from adding these to the list of core human rights instruments at some time in the future, should that be affirmed by them as their Sovereign Will.]

Likely impacts on democracy from a process establishing a national agreement on human rights and obligations

A distinctive feature of the above proposed *National Agreement on Human Rights and Obligations* is that it is structured as an agreement to be made between the people of Australia, not as an agreement between the people of Australia and their parliament. Nor, as I have already noted, is it a grant of rights in the form of a "charter" graciously conferred on Australians by parliamentary or government fiat. Notably, elected parliaments and governments are not to be parties in or to this *Agreement* and their involvement (in inception, passage or approval) is not required to legitimise it. Instead, the agreement process is structured so that *The Agreement* itself (however it turns out) will stem directly from the nation's people who, by their organised and collective expression of their sovereign will, have empowered themselves to establish a fully democratic process from which they shall derive the particular agreement they wish to enshrine in the Constitution on their rights and obligations as members of that democracy.

---

[313] A full list of the Core International Human Rights Instruments can be found at https://www.ohchr.org/en/core-international-human-rights-instruments-and-their-monitoring-bodies

This is a new arrangement of power in democracy. It is an arrangement that acknowledges the nation's people as the source of power. But new as it might be it is not irrational and it ought not to be surprising. This is, after all, a *people's* constitution in the making. As such it is entirely appropriate that elected parliaments and governments should be relocated to a new place of defined and properly limited legislative and administrative power and the people should take a new place as the ultimate sovereign decider of what shall and shall not be lawful *constitutionally*. To put this more clearly, this new arrangement of power would openly accord the people the power to write their constitution, leaving parliament, executive governments, the states and the judicature to exercise their current powers, but in accordance with that new constitution. This will require individual enfranchised Australians, in the first instance, to become accustomed to acknowledging each other as equal partners in a state where they are the sole source of power as a collective, not just for purposes of conferring human rights but for the purpose of making or remaking all the other parts of the Constitution that set the parameters within which laws may be properly made by elected parliaments and actions taken by executive governments on behalf of the people. This does not substantially deplete the powers of parliaments or governments. It simply clarifies what is legitimate in the exercise of those powers.

It will take some time for Australians to become accustomed to this new distribution of rightful powers. But invocation of Prospect 2, for purposes of reaching agreement on the human rights that shall be available equally to all, can help Australians shift to this new understanding of sovereignty – a people's sovereignty. And because it involves the use of a fuller version of democracy than the limited version currently available under the system where the parliament or a monarch is sovereign, it can also help Australian electors to participate more fully in their own governance in an orderly and efficient fashion. Prospect 2 invokes mechanisms of participatory democracy that can help equalise the shares of power for electors and the elected, or at least reduce the current massive inequality in the distribution of power in Australia. By using community engagement, plebiscites and referendums to collaborate on the making of a constitution that will

- set clear terms of trust on which electors hand over governing power to the elected; and
- set clear rules within which laws may be made,

it can function as an exercise in more equitable power sharing without being disorderly. In effect, processes like that described in Prospect 2 – and similar processes empowering people to freely determine their national values and aspirations – reduce the possibility of chaos and inequality because they offer the most efficient way of:

1. separating the different types of power to be distributed or shared among the electors, the elected and any other unelected parties empowered under the Constitution (such as the judicature); and
2. equalising power across all the electors.

In the first case, the role of the parliament and executive government is qualified but not so as to create disorder or unreasonable restraint on their exercise of their rightful powers. The parliament still retains the power to legislate and the government still retains its executive functions. But they both shift their energies to a role that requires them to use those powers to maintain order, public safety and wellbeing in manner consistent with the stated national values and human rights. It might be said they shift their energies to a less adversarial arrangement of politics.

In the second case, processes like that outlined in Prospect 2 come closer to building democracies where one vote has one value. As such they come closer to making elections truly democratic. Instead of confining the electors to the pathway of selecting who will have the sole right arbitrarily to decide on policy, they offer electors a pathway into setting the substance or at least the overarching principles of policy mandates themselves.

True democracy cannot exist without this sort of equitable and efficient participation by electors on matters of substance and principle in policy. A constitution that enables electors to set the preferred values for the nation, to claim their human rights, to set the government's obligations to them, and to prescribe all other essential terms of trust on which power is handed over to parliaments and executive governments is essential for any true democracy. A people's constitution can offer all this. But for purposes of promoting order and efficiency, a people's constitution is more likely to provide a successful transition from parliamentary or monarchical sovereignty to a people's sovereignty if it includes another extremely important enabling factor – a process for expression of the people's voice. In the next Chapter I will outline how this process can be enshrined so that it boosts the power of the Australian people and the capacity of those they elect to act as proper custodians of their plans for the future.

Chapter 7 – Essential No. 3: A process for expression of the Australian people's national voice

If Australians take up the opportunity to enshrine human rights and obligations in their Constitution in the manner suggested in Chapter 6, they will at last have safely secured their right to vote. But as I have said, a vote is not a voice. In our current arrangement of democracy, where we hand over power in elections without instructions, we lose our voice as soon as we have voted. Some of us continue to speak, protest and even scream about what we want and need but the combined voices, by their disarray, create so much noisy dissonance and babble that politicians find it quite easy to pick and choose which demands they will listen to and which ones they will simply ignore (no matter how legitimate they might be). In that process democracy is reduced to a process of divide and conquer. Nothing secures the power of a government as much as our disorganised babble.

Conservative governments are particularly adept at taking advantage of this disorganisation. But it is a matter of convenience for *both* progressive and conservative governments that the constant adversarial discourse that arises daily from the babble acts as a very effective means by which they can attain and keep power. All political "parties of government" – those that with all their might work to ensure that the arrangement of parliamentary democracy is confined to a two-party system of government versus opposition – rely and thrive on this adversarial arrangement of parliamentary government. They are aided and abetted in this divisiveness by unethical news media and by the consequent complete disarray of the general populace.

The two-party system and the adversarialism it thrives on both work to exclude minor political parties and independents from a reasonably proportional power share. We might think that because the Australian election system involves proportional representation in the Senate and preferential voting in the House of Representatives that the election system will guard us against disproportionate exertions of power in the parliament. And sometimes it does to some extent – if the votes happen to fall in a lucky way that favours the more ethical, socially inclusive candidates. But generally, once the votes are cast the whole process of the parliament is captured by the two major political parties, and even if they are required to make compromises with minor parties and independents, these compromises tend to support powerful sectional interests more than the national interest and certainly more than the interests of powerless minorities.

This mode of democracy is essentially an arrangement where the agendas of the already powerful are the only ones that are served. Every other reform that would serve the legitimate interests of the less powerful is pushed off the table or takes decades longer than it should. And if the prevailing agendas of the powerful do not happen to align with the national interest, then the result is predictably disastrous. In that case, peaceful progress for the majority grinds to a halt or is slowed so much that advances are overwhelmed by regressive forces. Nowhere has this been displayed more graphically than in relation to climate change, where for the period between 2006 and 2022 a majority of Australians (averaging 52%) in the Lowy Institute Poll clearly stated that "global warming is a serious and pressing problem and we should begin taking steps now even if this involves significant costs" and another 35% on average thought that "the problem of global warming should be addressed, but its effects will be gradual so we can deal with the problem gradually by taking steps that are low in cost". And yet, government policies throughout that period catered overwhelmingly to the views of the 12% who thought that "until we are sure that global warming is really a problem, we should not take any steps that would have economic cost."[314] The result has been that Australia has contributed significantly to the problem of global heating and in 2022 is really no closer to meeting a target of net zero emissions than it was at the start of the century. At the rate Australia's greenhouse gas emissions are dropping we will be lucky to reach net zero by the end of the century, let alone before the world locks in planetary heating of more than 1.5 degrees Celsius (which at present rates of global emissions is likely to by around 2025[315]). Nor have we realised the economic opportunities that could have come our way if we had accelerated our progress towards 100% renewable energy.

This utter inefficiency in the systems that should support national progress happens because the electoral system of our parliamentary democracy is designed to ensure that once the people have voted, their voices count for nothing. As soon as seats have been taken in the arena created by this system, the arena itself locks the doors on the powerless, and becomes a space in which the short term agendas of powerful sectional interests will be the only things considered. This is inevitable because it is the essential nature of a political party that it shall ensure its survival by doing nothing more and nothing less than what is necessary to get elected next time and everything necessary to squeeze out agendas extraneous to that purpose. The survival of the political party becomes the primary purpose of the democracy and if this survival requires legitimate minority interest and even the national interest to be sidelined, so be it.

Minority political parties and independents inevitably get swept up into this same cycle of doing what is necessary to survive. They find themselves making concessions and compromises on their agendas in order to achieve at least some small degree of progress. In this process they hope to prevent being sidelined even further at the next election. The result is that everyone's agendas are compromised. This compromise is what politics is about, of course; but there are far too many occasions when the compromises amount

---

[314] Natasha Kassam, Lowy Institute Poll 2022, page 27, Op. Cit.

[315] Climate Council of Australia, "Aim High, Go Fast: Why emissions need to plummet this decade", 2021, pages 26-27. Aim High, Go Fast: Why Emissions Need to Plummet this Decade | Climate Council

to outright perversion of legitimate agendas – full sacrifice of the national interest and subordination of it to sectional interests.

Having worked closely with all manner of politicians for thirty years, I can vouchsafe that there are times in the career of a politician – at least the decent ones – where these concessions and compromises will cause them pangs or even deep crises of conscience. In a system which is built on exclusive rather than shared power, all who hold it and wish to keep it will at some time find themselves corrupting their own moral precepts or community commitments. As former prime minister Gough Whitlam once said, "Only the impotent are pure." The pragmatism that is required in politics means that any politician with the capacity for ethics and self-insight will at some point in their occupation of a seat in parliament find themselves in a deep quandary as a result of the horse-trading that goes on in debates on bills. Such horse-trading will frequently require them to sell out one part of their agenda to obtain another part, and very often they will gain less for their constituency than they give up. Over a long career many politicians will sacrifice more than they gain. In that process at the federal level, the most frequent casualty is the national interest.

The national interest is easily subordinated in any parliamentary system that is organised to give priority to the short term re-election agendas of its members. It is easily subordinated because there is no agenda which stipulates what the national interest actually is. Australians themselves are never asked about their preferred agenda by politicians. Yet logically they are the only ones who can define it and define it they must if they are to stop its incessant subordination to sectional interest.

No space has been created by our political leaders at the national level where the people of the nation can work together to define that interest. In part this may be because the whole enterprise of defining the national interest seems too complex. And certainly it will appear that way to politicians who, mired as they are in the day-to-day demands of those with competing interests, must always be reacting to immediate problems and demands by pasting short-term fixes piecemeal onto the issues that pop up, like an insane game of whacka-mole from which they can never escape. This piecemeal reactive approach consigns everyone to inefficient paths to progress. Everyone's eye is taken off what they might prefer to achieve over the longer term for the nation as a whole, and everyone is repeatedly dragged back into confining their gaze to the short term.

In the sweep of history, because living standards have improved since the industrial revolution and more people have been lifted out of poverty than ever before, it will appear that this system – the system of electing people to a national parliament without instructions and without specifying the ultimate purpose of their election – is not too much of a problem. But further consideration would suggest that if living standards have improved for Australians, that is more likely to be due to luck and the hard work of Australians. It is unlikely to be due in the main to their political arrangements. And in any case, there is ample evidence available in the 2020s that attests to a distinct decline in living standards in Australia in the 21st century. In 2022, Australian Community Futures Planning released its second report on the state of Australia to coincide with the end of the term of office of the 46th parliament of Australia.[316] *The State of Australia 2022* examined over 260 indicators of the health of Australia's society, environment, economy and democracy and found that policies promoted by federal parliaments and governments since 2000 had not resulted in an improved quality of life. On the contrary, the evidence abounds that:

- our economy had been adversely impacted by government pursuit of neoliberal policies;
- inequality, particularly wealth inequality, had steadily increased;
- millions of Australians had been consigned to deep poverty and unnecessarily extended periods of unemployment and underemployment;
- inaction on gender inequality had stopped women and LGBTQI+ people from participating in their economy as fully

[316] Australian Community Futures Planning, https://www.austcfp.com.au/state-of-australia

as they might and has confined many to situations of domestic abuse;

- there were large scale attacks on our public education system which set the country onto a path of decline for the economy and in productivity;
- corruption in government had exploded and the state was subject to capture by corporations;
- foreign policy had turned pugnacious and we were ill-prepared in defence of the nation;
- a secret state had been entrenched which had seriously reduced the freedoms and rights of Australians;
- the natural environment and biodiversity had been decimated; and
- climate change was seriously impacting the lives and livelihoods of Australians.[317]

This is just a sample of the ways in which the decline of Australia had been manifest between 2000 and 2022. In some respects Australians may hope that the decline will be arrested by their election of a Labor government in 2022 – for example, in some aspects of corruption in the federal government. But in general, the trends of decline are likely to persist inasmuch as the new government did not seek election on a policy platform that would confidently address problems in social cohesion, poverty, the economy, the natural environment, the secret state, corporate capture, and most of all climate change. This suggests that, at least as far as the capacity of political system goes, Australia's long run of luck has turned and there is no guarantee that either the political system or our putative luck will prove as useful to future generations as they might have in the past. There is certainly no guarantee that mere luck will be enough to overcome the obvious deficiencies in a political system which gives its people no voice and takes no notice of their concerns for the longer term. That being so, it is at the very least

---

[317] Bronwyn and Sean Kelly, Australian Community Futures Planning, *The State of Australia 2022: End of Term Report, 46th Parliament of Australia*, Overview – Are we progressing towards a better Australia, pages 10-31. March 2022. 2b062e_e1d65bf9e9b94d798a2ff40726994d32.pdf (austcfp.com.au)

advisable to develop new political systems and a process which can enable Australians to ensure they can express with a coherent voice their aspirations for their wellbeing and security in the future.

It may be expected that the proposed Indigenous Voice may serve as a possible model for a wider reform of Australia's political system that will help all Australians speak with a coherent voice to their parliaments and governments. But while models for the Indigenous Voice that have been developed through co-design to date[318] are likely to improve the prospects for Indigenous wellbeing and security, they are not likely to be as effective if applied on the scale necessary to achieve a fully inclusive Australian society capable of more active and efficient participation in democracy. Something needs to be added to the type of institutional reform that might arise from the Indigenous Voice. That something is a *process* reform rather than an institutional reform, and it is this process reform that needs to be enshrined in Australia's Constitution if We the People are to be able to issue the instructions our parliaments and governments need if Australia is to track towards a future of wellbeing and security for all. In the next section I will begin to outline this process reform.

What is a national people's voice?

In Chapter 2 I spoke of the need to design a new democratic public square – an open space in which the people of Australia can organise their voice – the voice of the whole nation. This voice will be an enabling instrument by which we can express not just what we value and stand for now but what we aspire to for the future, and what we want to become as a nation on the way to that particular future. It is a voice we can use to describe everything we might aspire to for the type of society, environment, economy and democracy we want to live in and belong to. In this sort of voice we are continually defining our national project – the comprehensive, integrated project for our wellbeing and security across generations. We are expressing our sovereign people's will as to our future. We are describing the

---

[318] "Indigenous Voice Co-design Process: Final Report to the Australian Government", July 2021, Op. Cit.

purpose of our coming together – and staying together – as the people of a new Commonwealth of Australia.

This type of voice is an essential component of a people's constitution for that new Commonwealth. In fact we will gain relatively little from a people's constitution if it does not include a capacity for us to assemble this voice. If we go to the trouble of building a people's constitution at all, we will want to be able to use it for all it is worth. The type of voice that I am proposing can enable that; it can enable Australians to *efficiently* play a fully meaningful and effective role in their democracy. It is also the positive part of the "double power" I spoke of in Chapters 1 and 4, the part by which the people can empower themselves to set the agenda for their future. It is the part that can enable them to establish the specifics of their will as to the future wellbeing and security they intend to create.

I am going to call this voice a national voice or a national people's voice. But to prevent confusion I need to distinguish this at the outset from a national Indigenous Voice. For brevity's sake, I will simply say here that when I speak of a national people's voice I am speaking of a *process* for assembling that voice. It is not intended that this process would exclude or in any way act against the institution of a national Indigenous Voice or the interests of First Nations as they may express them through that institution. On the contrary, I am working on the assumption that First Nations must be given full rights to design both the institution of the national Indigenous Voice and any processes they feel are appropriate to assemble their national Voice, particularly taking into account cultural preferences about how their member nations and communities within those nations engage with each other. I am taking it as a valid given that if they can't do that, then it is not their voice. In turn, I intend that this should logically imply that a national people's voice must not be designed to exclude the possibility for First Nations to achieve self-determination, including by being able to design the national Indigenous Voice in whatever form they deem fit. Thus at the outset it should be understood that my intention here is to ensure that these two voices should not be designed so that they are mutually exclusive. On the contrary, the two need to be designed to coexist and ideally the

Constitution should create the most stable platform for that coexistence. Otherwise we cannot ensure that First Nations and the entire nation can coexist harmoniously, each with full rights of self-determination – a right we might hope *all* Australians will have if we succeed in the constitutional reform proposed in Chapter 6 of a national agreement on human rights and obligations. I will enlarge on the importance of achieving a coexistence of these two voices later in this chapter. Obviously, it is central to the question of how to achieve and recognise a coexistence of sovereignties.

Returning to the topic of a national people's voice, though, I need to set out what I mean by the term. A national people's voice is not something that the people of Australia have organised themselves to produce before, and they have not settled on what it will look like in form or content once it is assembled. The form that it might take is likely to be as mysterious to them as the form an Indigenous Voice might take. But if the whole project of creating a people's constitution is to be worthwhile at all, this is a voice we must learn to assemble, probably from school-age. If we assemble it well, by an inclusive process, we can make the task of building national prosperity so much easier, particularly for the politicians that we charge with responsibility for delivery of that project.

So what sort of national voice am I talking about? As I have said in Chapter 2, the voice we are trying to make space for in this new people's constitution is

> *essentially pluralist and yet integrated – the many in the one.*

It is the voice that must be introduced when we shift away from a Hobbesian model of state sovereignty – where the one presides over the many – and take up a more powerful, well organised, expressive position in the body politic. It is polyphonic not monotonal, harmonic not unison. It assumes that we don't all need to – and indeed we will not – sing exactly the same tune and we certainly don't need to wait until the whole nation sings the same tune on an issue before we take action to deal with a new challenge, such as climate change. Instead it assumes that we the people simply need to *integrate* our voices so that, despite their being different, they harmonise and enhance each other. The objective is to ensure that those of us who may wish governments to start doing something about, say, climate change can increase the chance of speeding up necessary reforms. We can get started earlier on reforms that appear on the horizon as a necessity for future security, or we can make up for lost time and reduce the burden of climate change on future generations. But we can do this in a framework that does not eclipse the concerns of those who will be negatively impacted by the reforms.

If we can assemble this polyphonic voice, and if we can set that in place alongside:

- an agreed statement of our values as Australians,
- an agreement on our human rights and obligations, and
- a national Indigenous Voice,

this will enable Australians to establish essential and quite comprehensive instructions about the national project for those they elect to power. Inasmuch as it will define the long term national interest, it will establish clear terms of trust on which power is being handed over in an election. It will outline what power is for and provide guidance on what the elected may not do with it. It will enable the people of Australia to inject themselves into their own Constitution so that they strengthen their democracy and add hitherto unimagined value to their ongoing national project.

As I have observed, this should be a liberation for politicians. With an assembled national voice politicians will acquire something they do not have now – an understanding of the preferred destination of the nation – the destination preferred by its peoples. They will also have something solid that they can fall back on and refer to when they need help to resist the sectional interest claims from lobbyists and corporations. But probably the most significant benefit of a national people's voice is that it can enable all Australians, politicians included, to rise above politics and set the agenda for the nation's future collaboratively and in such a way as to provide assurance to everyone that there will be a place for them in that future. It is essentially to build a nation to which everyone, no matter how different, can feel they belong.

This is a voice arcing towards the highest level of inclusion possible and in that it is establishing a full democracy. In that vein it is very unlikely to be favoured by those who prefer exclusive power arrangements and the adversarial models of politics which operate daily to perpetuate disagreement, especially about whether we should favour the short-term policies of the conservatives or the short-term policies of the progressives. However, a high level of inclusion in democracy is not at all impossible. On the contrary, research has shown that, despite the divisive successes of the adversarial models of exclusionists, there is still one place of policy advocacy where we are not easily driven to disagreement and where, by contrast, we exhibit a capacity for a very high level of agreement. Despite our apparent diversity we all agree on what we want for our kids, or for our nieces, nephews, grandchildren and anyone we love who has been born or will live on after us. We all want the same things for their future – the same things for their wellbeing and security.[319] In imagining that place – the future – and imagining it as we would prefer it to be for ourselves and future generations, we exhibit an extraordinary capacity to discard disagreements about what we should do in the short term in favour of what makes sense to all of us for the longer term. As the community-based research collective Australia reMADE observed when in 2017 they conducted major community engagement through a project group called A24[320] which asked Australians to imagine "the Australia of their dreams":

---

[319] We know this from studies such as the University of Western Australia's Values Project, examined in Chapter 5, a research project which singled out "benevolence – expressed as the welfare of people who are close to us" as the highest value of Australians.

[320] See Australia reMADE website, accessible at https://www.australiaremade.org/who-we-are: "In June 2017, the A24 Engagement Project began. The project sought to hear from ordinary Australians about the future they want for Australia. ... People were asked to dream out loud about the Australia they want and to think with us about how such a transformation could happen. Their ideas and dreams have come to give life to a vision for Australia, Australia reMADE, adding depth, breadth, spirit and hope to previous draft vision statements developed in 2016 by many others who attended a series of A24 Gatherings and considered the same questions."

> Listening to hundreds of people, from many walks of life, we came away understanding that the hopes and dreams we share for our future are staggeringly similar.[321]

Australians are seldom asked about what we want for the long term but when we are given space to consider it, disagreement about what we want fades and divergent desires begin to converge into a vision for the future that is comparatively calm, demonstrably rational and remarkably uniform. It is life-affirming. And because this future is the only thing we agree on, the national voice must be framed in the form of a plan for that future. A long term integrated plan is the only useful way of organising that national voice and if we can efficiently establish it, we can achieve a social contract with those whose future we wish to secure (even if they have not yet been born) and with the politicians we elect to help us usher in that future.

In short, a national people's voice is the process by which Australians can collaborate to build an integrated plan to secure the future of their society, environment, economy and democracy – or to put it less bureaucratically, it is a process by which Australians can build a plan to secure the future of those they each love. As Havas Labs found in its study of "Australian National Values in 2022",

> We're lovers, not fighters.[322]

As surely as humans start to think about those they love, they will stop fighting about the short term worries and start to think of the future; and this will provide an impetus to build plans for their safety, security and wellbeing. We do it every day as families. But as yet we do not build those plans as nations, and to the extent that we fail in that national level of planning we will strip away the chances that those we love will thrive. In that sense, a national people's voice is nothing more than a planning process that builds on the natural inclination of humans to love someone else and to increase the chance of bequeathing to them a decent and sustainable future.

---

[321] Australia reMADE, "Creating the Best Version of Us", 2019, Op. Cit.

[322] Havas Labs Australia and YouGov, "Australian National Values in 2022", page 13, Op. Cit.

The plan which arises from that process of exercising our voices in the cause of those we love will constitute the national project. Alongside the Statement of Australian Values proposed in Chapter 5, it will form an important part of the instructions that can be issued to governments on the primary purpose of the nation. The two together can form clear and understandable terms of trust on which power is handed over to parliaments and governments. The Statement of Australian Values will provide those we elect with a clear expression of the values that, in the here and now, underpin our preferred national character, and the plan will add another dimension to that – a picture of our aspirations for the future. In the plan, the terms of trust are articulated in a form whereby we express our vision for our preferred destination as a nation and specify what we want our nation to become along the way.

Australians have never developed this sort of plan, at least not at the national level. But the Constitution can be altered to make an open public space for them to do that. In the next section I will set out how this can be done. There are models available for it which have been working well in local governance for more than a decade.

Creating a public square for a national people's voice

The public square in which this polyphonic voice can be developed is a single open space on the internet but this space will need to be organised, equipped and skilfully supported so that it can safely function as a transparent and freely accessible mechanism that allows democracy to thrive on a much wider scale than has been possible to date – a fully inclusive scale where the diversity of the Australian community is not just protected, but is appreciated and capitalised on. In that regard we will need a process for assembling the voice that reduces the possibility of exclusion as much as possible. Otherwise, we cannot be confident that the voice reflects the diversity of the people. We will also need to maintain the independence of the voice, by which I mean it will need to be administratively supported in a manner that ensures it is actually the people's voice and has not been captured by political parties or corporations. This means we will need to create a new type of democratic process for the purpose of composing the voice, recognising that this particular type of voice will be *an integration of diverse voices*. That process needs to be something all Australians can use to express their aspirations for the future, understand the aspirations of others, and build an optimised strategic road map towards realisation of all these diverse aspirations.

Many Australians may not realise it but that type of process is already operating in some states in Australia at the level of local governance. It is called Integrated Planning and Reporting or IP&R,[323] a title which sounds more drily esoteric than it actually is. Integrated Planning and Reporting at the local government area level is simply a way of assisting everyday Australians to engage in public debate and policy development for the purpose of building a plan for the best future they can imagine for their particular community. It is a system whereby local councils are required under the law in certain states[324] to engage with and support their communities to help them build their own distinct long term plan for the future they want and to hold their elected councils accountable for their particular parts of that plan. Communities are also enabled in this legislation to work with their councils to figure out how best to fund their plan. A distinctive feature of this system is that it is the communities that own their plan (not the elected councils), and the plan forms a type of social contract between the electors and the elected in the local government area.

Originating legislation for Integrated Planning and Reporting was established in New South Wales in 2009 and was eventually mirrored to varying degrees in most other states of Australia. In New South

---

[323] Visit the NSW state government's Integrated Planning and Reporting website for local governments in NSW at https://www.olg.nsw.gov.au/councils/integrated-planning-and-reporting/

[324] New South Wales has the most detailed legislation for Integrated Planning & Reporting. For more information on the history and practice of IP&R in Australia see Bronwyn Kelly, "Local governments can show national governments how to plan better: integrated planning and reporting reforms in Australia", Commonwealth Journal of Local Governance, Issue 27, 2022: https://epress.lib.uts.edu.au/journals/index.php/cjlg/issue/view/510

Wales the legislation included quite specific Guidelines[325] for the structure of the new, long term plans that each community could build. These Guidelines also set minimum standards for compliance with the Integrated Planning and Reporting process itself and for community engagement on the plans.

During the first decade of the operation of the New South Wales laws the standard of performance and compliance with the legislation varied from year to year and across different councils, and the standards set in the New South Wales Guidelines have themselves been varied since the introduction of the framework. But throughout the decade the overarching intention of the legislation was faithfully maintained. The community remained the centre of the planning process and electors were given more power to influence the agenda for their council areas. In 2022, consistent with this overarching intention, the NSW Office of Local Government's Integrated Planning and Reporting webpage stated that:

> In essence the IP&R Framework *begins with the community's, not councils', aspirations* for a period of at least 10 years. It includes a suite of integrated plans that set out a vision and goals and strategic actions to achieve them. It involves a reporting structure to communicate progress to council and the community as well as a structured timeline for review to ensure the goals and actions are still relevant.[326] [Emphasis added.]

Since its inception, local IP&R has proved on the whole to be a very successful reform in terms of its original objectives. Despite the

---

[325] Guidelines made under the NSW legislation for Integrated Planning and Reporting have been amended over the decade since proclamation in 2009. Although they are called "Guidelines" they have the effect of a regulatory requirement under the NSW Local Government Act 1993. The latest Guidelines are generally accessible at Integrated Planning and Reporting - Office of Local Government NSW: IPR-Guidelines-2021.pdf (nsw.gov.au) and Integrated Planning & Reporting Handbook for Local Councils in NSW

[326] NSW Government, Office of Local Government, Integrated Planning and Reporting webpage. Last accessed 25 May 2022 at: Integrated Planning and Reporting - Office of Local Government NSW

fact that the quality of implementation has not been uniform across all the states, wherever it has been implemented it has:

- drawn local community members into a more active and deliberative role in their own governance and in designing what wellbeing really means for them;
- helped them increase their influence on how public funding is raised and spent;
- established a means of sustainable long term financial and public asset planning; and has
- provided communities with a means of monitoring whether councils are delivering whatever the residents have said they want over the long term.

That last benefit – arising from the fact that the process concentrates as much on *Reporting* as it does on *Integrated Planning* – provides communities with a means of holding elected councillors accountable to a degree and level of transparency that had not been possible until the reforms. With IP&R, an extra strength was added into the process of local democracy. Accountability was and is still available at the ballot box in local government elections; but in addition to that it is now possible for electors to access verifiable data about the performance of a council in relation to the community's preferred agenda and send stronger, transparent messages and instructions about what the elected councillors are actually accountable *for*. That degree of specificity had always been absent in Australia's governance and its cycle of democratic elections. With the advent of IP&R it need be absent no longer, at least at the local governance level.

Additionally, because the IP&R process includes an element of long term financial planning *integrated with* plans which describe the social, environmental and governance objectives of a given local community, it actually offers those communities a better chance than they have ever had not just to build the sort of future they really want but to build it at the lowest long run cost. It offers this chance by virtue of the fact that it adjusts the power arrangements that have pertained in the Australian system of representative democracy –

switching it from top-down governance to bottom-driven planning and partnership. Power is shared more evenly because the IP&R process changes – indeed creates – the terms of trust on which power is granted or renewed through elections. No longer does power come without any indication of restrictions or instructions, but rather for specified purposes. Long-term community plans roll over two or three terms of a council: they must be reviewed after each election, but their specified purposes can only be amended through a further rigorous process of community engagement. This requires a dialogue between councils and communities, which runs generally as follows:

1. Councillors ask their communities what they would ideally like to achieve as a community and for their local amenity and life quality over a minimum of ten years (not just one term of office).
2. Electors state their aspirations for the type of society, environment, lifestyle quality and governance they want.
3. Councillors then tell them how much that will cost over the decade (in terms of service provision and asset management) and whether there is a shortfall in the council's financial resources for that purpose.
4. If there is a shortfall, a dialogue commences about options for either reducing aspirations or raising funds to meet them.
5. Electors state their final preferences for the future and the degree to which they are prepared to fund that future – as well as the method of funding (be it more by taxes or increases in other forms of revenue generation or a combination of both).

This sequence of dialogue – specifically designed as it is to enable orderly collaboration in development of a viable (financially sustainable) long term plan – is a fundamental shift in the roles played by electors and the elected in democracy. Not only does it give communities a role for the first time, it also gives them a highly influential and productive role because they are not limited at the outset in what they can and can't choose to want and do. This is not a process by which councillors tell communities what they can and can't have. Instead the dialogue that occurs under local IP&R starts in an entirely different place. It starts with communities telling councillors what they do and don't want. From that starting point, the dialogue leads the parties (the electors and the elected) into a further agreement designed to give confidence to all that:

- safe paths and strategies to achieve the expected future have been chosen through meaningful and respectful consultation;
- a relevant measurement framework will be available to assess changes in wellbeing under the plans; and
- expected long run costs to achieve targets are not only as low and sustainable as they can be but that the cost burden itself will be shared in an optimal, efficient and fair manner across all sectors of the community and between existing and future generations.

In short, the dialogue broadens and deepens the terms on which trust is being vested in elected councils. It also fundamentally changes the relationship between the electors and the elected – for the better. It replaces top-down, short term, purely political agenda setting with a process of agenda setting through a collaboration of mutually respectful partners. It also qualitatively changes the terms in which the agendas themselves are framed and delivered, adding in explicit instructions about:

- what is being bought,
- what is being willingly foregone,
- how the final mix is to be financed,
- who shall bear the burdens and various obligations,[327] and
- how benefit is to be distributed or shared.

IP&R introduces a new deal between electors and local governments and this new contractual format is built on terms which transparently

[327] Integrated plans developed under local IP&R are effectively partnership agreements made between councils, residents, community groups, other local stakeholders such as commercial businesses, and the state government. Responsibilities are allocated across the stakeholders. Councils are therefore only held to account for their allocated responsibilities.

link – or *integrate* – the social with the fiscal. By this integration they establish a social contract that is quite specific in its terms.

Of course, governments have offered "new deals" or "social contracts" or "agreements" or "accords" in the past. The difference with IP&R is that communities can to a large extent craft the terms of the "deal" and have a tighter method of holding those they elect to account for delivery of what they have agreed to fund (and to fund in a particular way). In this arrangement tax revenue is in the electors' gift and control; it is not the property of a government. That shift in control over the purse-strings is a remarkable microeconomic reform offering previously unavailable opportunities for efficiency and effectiveness in policy development and distribution of resources (financial and non-financial). It also offers new opportunities for efficiency and effectiveness in the operation of democracy itself.

Obviously, the shifts in roles, powers and control described above only pertain if (and for as long as) the parties honour the "deal" in good faith – which some with vested interests are unlikely to do if the public interest as represented by the deal specified in the community-built integrated plan does not favour them as much as they would wish. Nevertheless the intent of IP&R is to draw electors and the elected together in such a way as to enable the community to assemble their preferred agenda and the council to assemble and finance the provision of its services in support of that agenda. In effect, IP&R offers councils and communities a way to relate to and respect each other that is more likely to result in a financially sustainable pathway to the community's preferred level of wellbeing over the longer term, not just for a short period of time. Services necessary for the preferred level of wellbeing are reliably and affordably secured.

IP&R also improves efficiency in decision-making simply by setting out the purposes of power: it clarifies the public interest and the preferred direction of the community, and ensures that everyone knows what they are accountable for. The agreements reached through IP&R, especially in aligning the social with the fiscal, create quite new types of partnerships, which are likely to be more productive because they are based on a clear sense of the benefit every partner will obtain if they honour their part of the deal.

Overall, it is evident that in its first decade of operation IP&R in NSW has functioned well as an experiment in a new arrangement of power and transparent accountability, building on the good faith presupposed by the legislation that elected councils will both duly implement the legal requirements for community engagement and honour the outcomes from that engagement as expressed in the community's plan. This flows to a large extent from the reporting component of the IP&R process, which ensures either that councils *do* honour the deal, or that electors will be able to see the extent to which they have *not* honoured it and hold them to account at the ballot box.

On the whole, IP&R has emerged as a very healthy aid to local decision-making and one which is highly efficient. Because involvement in the integrated planning part of the IP&R process is neither seriously time-consuming nor elitist for anyone wishing to increase their influence in decisions about their community's future – in other words, because it facilitates inclusion of the time-poor in a practical and orderly cycle of community futures planning – IP&R speeds up a community's progress toward their preferred future. In Australia, this efficiency is fortunately coincident with a rise in appreciation of the value of localism – meaning, a rise in appreciation of the benefit of making decisions on what is best for a community at the level of that community. A localist approach differs markedly from the paternalistic or insensitive interventions in local affairs often favoured by various federal and state governments, for instance, in regional and Indigenous communities in Australia.

Over the decade to 2022 Australians witnessed an array of heavy-handed and even cruel and discriminatory interventions[328] from distant authoritative levels of government (i.e., state and federal governments) – authorities that are essentially disconnected from local concerns and expertise and have far less skill than local councils

[328] For example, the Northern Territory Intervention and the Cashless Welfare Card, which are referred to in Chapters 1 and 6.

and community groups in organising solutions that actually suit a local culture and circumstance. The evidence is that these federal and state interventions are inclined to fail. Federal interventionist approaches to Indigenous disadvantage in Australia, for instance, have failed to "close the gap" between Indigenous and non-indigenous Australians in almost every measure.[329] By contrast, locally organised community-driven initiatives which capitalise on local expertise (particularly Indigenous expertise) have been credited with success and these self-guided collaborations now set the benchmark for effective and more lasting problem solving and service design in regional and remote areas of Australia.[330]

The rise of IP&R, just at the time when support for localism is growing, offers the possibility of a boost to the effectiveness of localism inasmuch as IP&R provides an orderly and very efficient process by which local communities can organise self-governance and affordable delivery of their preferred future. If anything can be reliably concluded from the local IP&R experiment in Australia it is

---

329 For a comprehensive report up to date at March 2022 on Australia's failure to close the gap on Indigenous disadvantage see Dr Bronwyn Kelly and Sean Kelly, Australian Community Futures Planning, *The State of Australia 2022; End of Term Report on the 46th Parliament of Australia*, March 2022, specifically Chapter 3: Society 2 – Indigenous Heart, pp. 51-53, and Chapter 7: Society 2 – Indigenous Heart, pp. 120-136, accessible at The State of Australia 2022 and at https://www.austcfp.com.au/state-of-australia.

330 For a pace-setting example of localism at work, see the success of the Maranguka experience in the community of Bourke NSW in remarkable rates of reduction in domestic violence and juvenile crime. Eg.: Australian Government, Australian Institute of Health and Welfare, "Family, domestic and sexual violence in Australia: continuing the national story 2019", page 107: In November 2018, KPMG's impact assessment of the Maranguka Justice Reinvestment Project between 2015 and 2017 reported that there had been improvements in: [1] family strength: a 23% reduction in the number of family violence incidents and a 19% reduction in family violence reoffending incidents reported to police; [2] youth development: a 31% increase in Year 12 student retention rates and a 38% reduction in charges across the top 5 juvenile offence categories; and [3] adult empowerment: a 14% reduction in bail breaches and a 42% reduction in days spent in custody. Accessible at https://www.aihw.gov.au/getmedia/b0037b2d-a651-4abf-9f7b-00a85e3de528/aihw-fdv3-FDSV-in-Australia-2019.pdf.aspx?inline=true.

that the more local communities learn how to use the opportunity of IP&R, the more likely they are to move sustainably towards their preferred future rather than away from it.

That said, it is also likely that even if local communities master the art of beneficent social contracts through IP&R, any advances arising from those plans are still likely to be lost or reversed if the art of good faith social contracts and plans is not mastered at the national level. Almost every aspect of a well-made local plan can be undone by bad faith and incompetence at the national level, especially in economic management, in suboptimal distribution of national wealth and in unethical behaviour on the national and international stage. That being so, and bearing in mind the success of local IP&R, a new and irresistible question now arises:

> Can the concepts and processes of integrated planning and reporting be adapted and applied effectively at a national level to avoid the risk of federal government actions undermining local achievements, and also to improve the quality of federal engagement with and accountability to the Australian community?

New research and experimental programs applying the lessons from a decade of operation of IP&R strongly suggest that the answer to this question is Yes. IP&R serves as a model by which we may create a well-functioning national public square. In fact the experiment of IP&R has already been adapted by experienced IP&R practitioners to become national IP&R and, in this adapted form, is being tested to assess whether a scaled up process of IP&R can work efficiently to open up participation for all Australians in their democracy at the national level. Pilot testing of this adapted system of Integrated Planning and Reporting for use at the national level was commenced by Australian Community Futures Planning (ACFP) in 2020.[331] In the

---

[331] Australian Community Futures Planning (ACFP) is a non-aligned centre of excellence in national community futures planning and is necessarily community-based. It was established in March 2020 for purposes of trialling and supporting forms of National Integrated Planning & Reporting driven by the community. Its Founder, Dr Bronwyn Kelly, is the author of this book and of *By 2050: Planning a better future for our children in 21st century democratic Australia*. Dr Kelly is an

following section I will outline how IP&R has been adapted for that purpose and is working well in these trials to provide a model for the process we may enshrine in the Constitution for a national people's voice. It is working well to enable orderly and efficient participation in an open public square to develop a long term integrated plan for the nation. It is working well to position Australians so that they can do something with their democracy that has hitherto proved impossible – creating a full scale democracy that need no longer exclude the voices of its electors.

Equipping the public square for efficient operation of the national voice

Two specific adaptations of local IP&R were required to produce a process of national IP&R that would be workable in the Australian context. These were required to ensure that the process could deal with two things it had not been required to deal with at the local level:

1. the extraordinary cultural and socioeconomic diversity that now prevails within the Australian nation (a diversity which characterises many local communities but usually to a narrower degree); and
2. the national economy.

In regard to the first of these, practitioners of local IP&R knew that it operated efficiently and effectively as a means of integrated planning for social, environmental and governance matters. They also knew the process dealt well with conflicts that might arise from diversity within a given community, not least because IP&R was an essentially *inclusive* planning process. But while IP&R had apparently worked well at a local scale to deal with and protect diversity and multilateral interests, there was no guarantee that the sort of community engagement relied on in standard IP&R Guidelines – most of which was face-to-face interaction supplemented by local surveys – would

---

experienced practitioner of IP&R in Australia and has lectured at and consulted on behalf of the University of Technology Sydney in this field of expertise. For full information on all activities of Australian Community Futures Planning visit https://www.austcfp.com.au/

scale up well to be successful at a national level and still retain the efficiency features inherent in local IP&R.

Questions about the feasibility of using IP&R to protect diversity and inclusivity on a national scale therefore became important questions to resolve before it might be expected that IP&R could work well at the national level in a country like Australia – a federation of quite different states governing more than 500 local government areas spread out across a continent. This issue was resolved eventually by development of the IP&R process so that it could make use of the internet to maintain efficiency for those wishing to become involved in integrated planning. The rise of the internet made it possible to establish the potential for a continuous increase in the range of participation (geographically and in terms of topic) and a more inclusive range of participants. But this natural potential of the internet needed to be optimised by the development of mechanisms for efficient use of this new open public square. These included the design of feedback forms and other interaction processes but in particular they involved the design of a special structure for the integrated plan itself – one which offered the possibility of a high degree of independence from politics in the formulation of a national vision and the selection of targets and strategies. In other words it offered Australians the ability to populate their plan by selecting longer term targets and strategies in a non-politically charged context and without the need to argue on ideological grounds, especially about short-term party political policies. The structure of the plan, which for purposes of pilot testing was given the name of *Australia Together*,[332] achieved this by being structured as a map through time, complete with:

- a clear idea of a preferred destination for the nation by 2050 – a draft vision statement describing the best destination we can imagine in the 2020s (this was based on the responses of Australians in a multiplicity of surveys, research programs and visionary planning exercises since 2010 in which they

[332] For information about the testing of *Australia Together* visit https://www.austcfp.com.au/.

were asked about or voluntarily described their preferred ideal future);[333]

- a signpost system articulating which routes towards the destination so described are likely to be the safest and which are best avoided (because they drag us away from that particular preferred destination or disable other important and safer strategies); and
- a major new data base setting out data on our wellbeing and security at the start of the planning period and targets for the level of wellbeing and security that should be acceptable at the end of the period, at the latest by 2050.

This sort of structure for the plan offered significant advantages in that it left space for as many targets and strategies as may be deemed necessary by electors and the elected acting collegiately through time, and it functioned as a means of reconciling conflict about the worthiness of strategies by providing everyone with a simple yardstick by which to assess their potential to help the nation realise its preferred aspirations. That yardstick was the vision and the signpost system. In short it offered an automatic quarrel settling mechanism.

Of course, this mechanism could not guarantee the infallibility of any plan that may result, but there is no doubt that if used properly it will reduce the policy errors we make as a nation because we do not currently employ any sort of yardstick by which to judge the probable capacity of a policy to propel the nation to its preferred destination. It also helps people explain to themselves why one policy is a better bet than another. This alone is worth billions of dollars in savings and avoided costs.

In regard to the second necessary adaptation of IP&R, practitioners knew that the experiment of IP&R had provided no insight into whether a long term integrated plan could be developed for a local economy, let alone a whole national economy. IP&R at the

---

[333] For information on how the draft Vision for the draft integrated plan was extracted visit https://www.austcfp.com.au/vision-and-directions-of-australia-together.

local level hardly touched on issues economic, except insofar as communities could design plans to stimulate local business development. Because local government in Australia has little if any influence in economic development beyond the local government area boundaries – and because long term integrated economic plans (as opposed to financial plans) simply haven't been developed in Australia by any level of government – researchers found that they were at the very beginning of exploratory research on whether IP&R could be adapted to inject the diverse Australian community into a role in development of national macro- and microeconomic reforms and plans, including for:

- fiscal and monetary policy,
- market regulation and competition policy,
- economic structure (eg. the composition of industries and incentives to influence that composition),
- employment planning (particularly during economic transitions),
- income and wealth inequality,
- taxation and national wealth distribution,
- scientific and technological development,
- urban and regional development, and
- international trade and rules.

These economic issues have not been traditionally viewed as ones that can be dealt with well by everyday Australians, even though they are the people most affected by any incompetence, lack of foresight and conflict of interest that might be displayed at the national level – negative impacts which arise frequently because of a refusal by national governments to develop long term economic plans.

But there is no reason why the Australians of today need be excluded from the process of planning for a stronger national economy and there is an argument that their accession to that role is simply the next, quite logical step in a long history of the evolution of democracy. The history of democracy is in fact the history of gradually enlarging the share of citizenry playing a role in national decision-making. Beginning with landowners only (male, white, and holding property above a certain level), it graduated in the post enlightenment world to a much wider composition of influential citizenry, as the populace itself became more educated, as information circulated more freely, and as the rights of those originally excluded came to be recognised (including women, indigenous peoples, younger people and non-whites). Citizen involvement in economic planning is therefore not a disruptive or radical undermining of democratic order. It need not be baulked at or resisted by anyone seeking social justice and equity. In Australia, given that we have one of the most educated populations in the world, it is simply something that we can take part in as a natural progression in history itself.

Indeed, unless we take part in it, we will not be able to develop a viable national economic plan for the simple reason that such a plan must start with something that can only come from the people – a statement of our agreed purpose for the economy. Fortunately, the Australian population is quite capable as an educated and legitimately interested community in articulating what they want their economy to be *for*. But at present they do not have an engagement and planning process by which to make their view of the purpose of their economy clear to federal and state governments. As such they lack any means of injecting themselves into an orderly decision process on the overarching purpose of their own economy. And, by extension, parliaments lack the knowledge of the very thing on which a fair and viable economic plan should be based – namely, a specific agreement about the type of nation the people want to build, the country they want to protect, the resources they wish to share and sustain, the level of wellbeing and security they wish to attain, and the place they aspire to in international citizenry.

Recognising that within the framework of national IP&R a national economy was not an end in itself but merely a means of building a preferred society, environment and democracy in which every diverse individual and group could find a place of wellbeing and security, it became apparent that the mechanics of a national long term economic plan were in fact quite straightforward and that the process of building a national economic plan was likely to be quite an accessible one for Australians wishing to build a better future *for everyone* – one in which everyone acknowledged that the full diversity of talents among Australians would need to be utilised to ensure economic success sufficient to sustain diverse aspirations.

Taking all this into account, it emerged that only small adjustments were required in local IP&R to make it fit for use in a public square at the national level. It was only a small step to develop a workable draft structure for a long term national plan, integrating social, environmental, economic and governance objectives and strategies capable of supporting and indeed capitalising on diverse aspirations. And it was only a small step to develop an efficient engagement process capable of drawing diverse Australians into the centre of strategic decision-making and planning for their future. In effect all that was required was to make these two adjustments and thereby insert a simple extra step into the existing cycle of democratic elections – that step being inclusive, integrated planning and reporting.

Of course, it was expected that this rendition of national IP&R was likely to be more complicated in delivery than it was in concept – complicated, that is, for the facilitators of engagement and participation in planning, not for the users within the community itself. Significant upskilling will be required for those who may be charged with ensuring that community engagement for development of a national integrated long term plan (and for reporting on it) is run in a fully open and inclusive but orderly and efficient framework. And these facilitators of this new public long term planning space will themselves need to be fully supported by parliaments – parliaments that understand that in a country where the people wish to express their sovereign will and their purpose in coming together, they must be enabled to do so in an orderly and inclusive manner as independent, self-determining people. This means there should be no obstruction by parliaments or executive governments of that process for expression. By extension that means that the national voice or, more accurately, *the process by which it may be legitimately expressed* should be enshrined in the Constitution as a right of the people – a right which is as important as any other civil and political right – and that when elected members of parliaments swear to uphold the Constitution they cannot be mistaken about the full import of their oath and the nature of their obligations under it. If this right of the people to expression of their national voice is enshrined in the people's own constitution it will resolve the problem I spoke of in Chapters 3 and 5 about the failure of the Australian people to specify what they want their parliaments to be loyal to. It should remove much if not all of any ambiguity that may still exist about the nature of the sovereign will of the Australian people and clarify at last what parliamentarians are actually swearing to be loyal to when they take an oath similar to that suggested by the Australian Republican Movement that

> I will be loyal to the Commonwealth of Australia and the Australian people whose Constitution and laws I shall uphold.[334]

If this right to a national voice is present and if it results in a well-constructed specification of the nation's will for the future, those who are privileged by elections cannot be mistaken about what they are swearing to uphold.

Politicians are always talking about the need for national conversations, particularly on issues like taxation, the Indigenous Voice and the republic. But they never give themselves or us a form or process in which to have those conversations. Nor do they give up their jealous guard on some other issues which affect our national interests and security. There are some topics, such as war powers and strategic defence posture, which desperately need community conversation but which in the rise of the secret state have been withdrawn completely from the purview of those who stand to lose the most in situations of executive eagerness for war.

But were parliaments to countenance the idea that the people are the only legitimate source of power and that their primary responsibility is to do the people's will, then an amazing set of new benefits would open up for everyone, the elected included. Everyone

---

[334] Australian Republican Movement, The Australian Choice Model: Proposed Amendments to the Australian Constitution327, January 2022, page iii, Op. Cit.

would have a far greater prospect of being able to secure a better future.

It will be neither difficult nor expensive to equip this new public square so that it can operate inclusively and efficiently to secure the interests of such a diverse nation. What is required is a constitutional specification of the people's national voice as a right, a process for expression of the voice and a suitably independent institution for facilitation of the engagement necessary to ensure that the people of Australia can:

- assemble their voice in an open, accessible, inclusive and well-resourced forum;
- monitor their nation's progress toward their preferred future; and
- hold themselves and their parliaments to account for making that future a reality.

But before I suggest the possible wording of a starting draft of a constitutionally enshrined process for expression of the people's national voice, I would like to set out two major benefits that Australia can reap from the establishment of that process. One of those is that such a voice would position non-Indigenous Australians to achieve a lasting reconciliation with Indigenous Australians and for the Australian state to achieve a truly just reconciliation with First Nations as coexistent sovereignties. The second is that a national people's voice would enable Australia to fairly finance a sustainable future in the age of climate change.

The importance of an Australian people's national voice for a just reconciliation with First Nations

In the Uluru Statement from the Heart First Nations have irrefutably asserted that the ancestral tie between the land, or "mother nature", and the Aboriginal and Torres Strait Islander peoples is the basis of their sovereignty in that land, and further, that this sovereignty has never been ceded or extinguished. It coexists with the sovereignty of the Crown.

The extent to which "the Crown" may consider that this is irrefutable is unknown, given that the said Crown has never countenanced open discussion of the matter. However, irrespective of the Crown's silence, it is impossible to conclude that the sovereignty of the Crown has been established and confirmed as though it is "just". A dispossession as brutal as that which was perpetrated on Australia's First Nations – one in which no treaty was struck in accordance with the laws of either party so as to legitimise the theft of an entire continent from its original owners – cannot be considered just.

But despite the scale of this injustice, Australia's surviving First Nations have called for a Makarrata – a coming together after a struggle – to supervise a process of agreement-making between governments and First Nations and truth-telling about this history. They are saying to non-Indigenous Australians:

> Let's establish a fair and truthful relationship, and if we do we can walk together to a better future for our children based on justice and self-determination.

It is a straightforward but at the same time deeply thoughtful proposal to make peace with a state which has prosecuted wars and committed crimes against humanity. Australia has been constituted as a nation by means of the most grievous crimes, crimes from which the descendants of the perpetrators still benefit and the descendants of the survivors still suffer. But for those non-Indigenous Australians who may be ready to accept that there is a need to come together after this 230-year struggle and strike a just and fair reconciliation, there is a problem. The problem is that the state itself – which, for the purposes of agreement-making or, shall we say, a just treaty, would need to come to terms with a form of sovereignty that is very different to its own Hobbesian form – is not trustworthy. It can certainly not be considered honourable as a potential treaty negotiator or signatory, given:

- its track record of refusal to enshrine human rights treaties in Australian law, particularly rights of self-determination;

- its refusal to give anything other than provisional support to the Declaration on the Rights of Indigenous Peoples; and
- its conduct in relation to the few laws it has made to provide some sort of restitution to First Nations on Native Title – conduct which is often obstructive and makes it as difficult as possible for Indigenous owners to prove title and claim benefits from land ownership or transactions.

Aboriginal people know that the state they must deal with if they are to establish a fair and truthful relationship and a mutually beneficial coexistence of sovereignties does not have a track record of good faith in its treaty negotiations. And in relation to justice with Indigenous peoples the state has exhibited a dishonourable interference and obstruction, even to the point of suspending its own laws to allow for racist interventions. As eminent Indigenous anthropologist, Professor Marcia Langton insightfully put it in the SBS series, "The Australian Wars", aired first in 2022:

> Aboriginal people are, I wouldn't say resentful, I would say burning with a desire for justice. And if you have been treated unjustly, if there is this great injustice that hangs over your own life and the lives of generations of people before you, you will naturally feel unwilling to grant the modern day state an honourable place. You simply won't want to while this great injustice underlies *all* relationships.[335] [Langton's emphasis.]

This implies an entirely logical and justifiable reluctance on the part of First Nations to rush into a treaty with the Australian state and it may shed some light on why the word "treaty" was not used in the Uluru Statement and why a Voice in the Constitution was considered to be the priority. It seems as though there was a sense at Uluru, within the assembled wisdom of those who had come from all points of the southern sky, that the Australian state itself was not yet ready for the sort of treaty that would guarantee the justice Indigenous peoples have been denied for so long, although many of the Australian people may well have been ready for it for decades.

---

[335] Professor Marcia Langton speaking in "The Australian Wars", SBS 3-part series, 2022.

Clearly, from the point of view of Indigenous peoples the injustices they have suffered have not yet ceased, and while they persist – while the truth of it all remains untold and unacknowledged – the state which we might otherwise expect to enter into an agreement-making process in good faith is likely to be seen as none-too-well credentialled in good faith negotiation of treaties, let alone a treaty for coexistent sovereignties. It is quite unlikely that the Australian state could be classed as one ready to come to the negotiating table with creditable honour, especially since that modern state of which First Nations are so rightly suspicious operates on a legal system that is simply not structured to countenance a multiplicity of sovereignties and self-determination for its populace. Indeed I would argue that until we restructure our system of governance so that it may support a multiplicity of sovereignties and self-determination for all, a *just* treaty with First Nations is not likely to be viable.

The fact is that the Australian state is *not* yet trustworthy as a party to such a vital agreement. It is still too fond of its exclusive system of power and, as such, First Nations are right to be wary. After all, the agreement that may arise from any Makarrata could be likely to set arrangements for sovereignty in legal stone for decades or even hundreds of years to come. Neither party should want to get it wrong – that is, neither party, assuming they both aspire to be good faith negotiators, should want it to turn out unfairly. Neither party should want to reinstate injustice.

Doubtless, the Makarrata Commission to which the newly elected federal Labor government devoted funding in 2022 will begin, among other things, a process whereby both parties can learn to understand the differences between some very different systems of law – First Nations law, the law of a colonial state (which is what Australia's Constitution still is), and the system of lawful relationships contemplated in the United Nations Declaration on the Rights of Indigenous Peoples. A full understanding of these differences is likely to be necessary if agreement-makers are to find a way to make the two sovereignties coexist in a manner that each thinks fair and just. The fact that the Labor government moved quickly in 2022 towards establishing the Makarrata Commission was proof of its good faith intentions and was an encouraging turnaround. It implied that the Labor government aspired to create a treaty consistent with the full breadth of the aspirations of the Uluru Statement – namely, for coexistent sovereignties based on justice and self-determination. But it will be a big project, and moreover a project made more difficult by the structure of Australia as a modern state which does not yet admit self-determination as a right. It is a project that may be made impossible outright if neither Indigenous nor non-Indigenous people have a voice to parliament.

However, this whole task can be made easier if the modern state, as it operates in Australia, is itself open to change – if the modern state can be opened up to wider democratic inclusion, or in other words, if the modern state can become a people's state working on a model of the many in the one rather than the one over the many, the pluralist voice rather than the silence of the electors. This transformation is possible if all Australians are accorded a voice in the Constitution alongside all the human rights that should flow through to them from the International Covenants on Civil and Political Rights and Economic, Social and Cultural Rights. In fact, the transformation of the state necessary for a *just* treaty with First Nations is only possible if all Australians are enabled by the Constitution to express their commitment to a future of peaceful coexistence of sovereignties and to say that it is by our will that this shall be accorded the status of law. Putting that another way, a treaty which establishes coexistent sovereignties based on self-determination is not possible at all unless Australians expressly establish it as their sovereign will. To do that, a people's national voice must be enshrined as the political right of all Australians and it must coexist with an enshrined Indigenous Voice. If we can achieve that we should be able finally to realise a benefit for Australia that has been seen by many as essential for decades. In 1992, the International Year of the World's Indigenous Peoples, former prime minister Paul Keating spoke of this when he said that the point of the Year was

> to bring the dispossessed out of the shadows, to recognise that they are part of us, and that we cannot give indigenous Australians up without giving up many of our own most

deeply held values, much of our own identity and our own humanity. Nowhere in the world, I would venture, is the message more stark than it is in Australia. We simply cannot sweep injustice aside. Even if our own conscience allowed us to, I am sure that in due course the world and the people of our region would not. There should be no mistake about this – our success in resolving these issues will have a significant bearing on our standing in the world.[336]

At the time, Keating imagined we would have this problem of the nation's founding – its dispossession of the original possessors – fixed within the decade. He felt emboldened to rely on the fact that Australia had made a great success of multiculturalism:

> Isn't it reasonable to say that if we can build a prosperous and remarkably harmonious multicultural society in Australia, surely we can find just solutions to the problems which beset the first Australians, the people to whom the most injustice has been done.

He assumed Australians had an appetite for reversing this injustice because they had been "ever so gradually learning how to see Australia through Aboriginal eyes, beginning to recognise the wisdom contained in their epic story":

> I think we are beginning to see how much we owe the indigenous Australians and how much we have lost by living so apart.

And so with the optimism of the time Keating concluded:

> We cannot imagine that the descendants of people whose genius and resilience maintained a culture here through fifty thousand years or more, through cataclysmic changes to the climate and environment, and who then survived two centuries of dispossession and abuse, will be denied their

[336] P J Keating, Australian Launch of the International Year for the World's Indigenous People, otherwise known as The Redfern Speech, 10 December 1992. SPEECH BY THE HON PRIME MINISTER, P J KEATING MP AUSTRALIAN LAUNCH OF THE INTERNATIONAL YEAR FOR THE WORLD'S INDIGENOUS PEOPLE REDFERN, 10 DECEMBER 1992 (pmc.gov.au)

> place in the modern Australian nation. We cannot imagine that. We cannot imagine that we will fail. And with the spirit that is here today I am confident that we won't. I am confident that we will succeed in this decade.

Thirty years later, though, we are probably no closer to succeeding in the just solutions Mr Keating imagined. And as Professor Langton has said, a great injustice still underlies *all* our relationships.

For as long as this injustice remains unresolved it will continue to poison the well of trust we should be able to draw from to build a new, inclusive form of the modern state – one that can sustain a much stronger participatory democracy for all. If trust is to grow, we will need an open forum where all policy cards can be laid on the table and assessed as to whether they suit the people's sovereign will or not. We will need a space and process by which we can speak up about the nation we all want, a space where we can use the full diversity of our voice to create a new context in which a treaty with First Nations can finally be settled so that it guarantees self-determination for everyone and thereby ensures that justice rather than injustice underlies all relationships.

If Australians want to live in that "prosperous and remarkably harmonious multicultural society" that Paul Keating imagined, the reality in the 2020s is that they will need to usher in a form of statehood that sustains a multiplicity of sovereignties and self-determination for all its peoples. If they can achieve that it would surely be the best outcome imaginable. But to achieve it we will need a Constitution that can support a multiplicity of voices in the body politic. This should not be difficult if we instigate a process of national Integrated Planning and Reporting and if, within and alongside that process, we accord First Nations the constitutional right to their own Voice. The right of First Nations to participate in decision-making on matters which would affect them is already supported by Articles 18 and 19 of the United Nations Declaration on the Rights of Indigenous Peoples. Australia is a signatory to this Declaration and so parliaments and government should have no difficulty complying with the obligations they have already accepted under it to

> consult and cooperate in good faith with the Indigenous peoples concerned through their own representative institutions in order to obtain their free, prior and informed consent before adopting and implementing legislative or administrative measures that may affect them.[337]

In summary, governments which want to bring Australians together should have no difficulty allowing a multiplicity of voices and all the institutions and processes necessary for their harmonious articulation of the future they want to create. And should we succeed in that, the benefits we can enjoy will not be confined to a harmonious society. They will include a vastly increased capacity to deal with the existential threat we all face, regardless of our racial or ethnic origins – climate change. In the following section I will outline how we can access those benefits if we establish a national people's voice in the Constitution.

The importance of a national people's voice for a sustainable future in the age of climate change

According to the annual Lowy Institute Polls, in the 16 years between 2006 and 2022 the proportion of Australians who wanted the government to do something to prevent climate change never dropped below 80%.[338] As early as 2006, over 90% wanted the issue to be addressed, with approximately 70% of that group wanting something done immediately "even if this involves significant costs".[339] This indicates strongly that the vast majority of Australians wanted the country to get started early on heading off the problem.

---

[337] United Nations Declaration on the Rights of Indigenous Peoples, 2007, Articles 18 and 19. DRIPS_en.pdf (un.org)

[338] Natasha Kassam, Lowy Institute Poll 2022, page 27, Op. Cit. The tables on this page show that between 2006 and 2022, an average of 52% of Australians wanted immediate action on climate change even if it involved significant costs and another 35% on average wanted more gradual action at lower cost. Only 12% on average wanted no action.

[339] Natasha Kassam, Lowy Institute Poll 2022, page 27, Op Cit. The table indicates that in 2006, 92% of Australians wanted action on climate change including 68% who wanted immediate action "even if this involves significant costs".

And in the years since 2017, the same proportion – 90% on average – have responded that steps need to be taken to deal with the threat. So while the people of Australia at the start of the 21st century had the foresight to see that it would be in their interest to begin taking steps sooner rather than later "even if this involves significant costs", or at least consider taking steps "that are low in cost",[340] successive federal governments failed to establish a plan to prevent or mitigate climate change and conservative governments in particular used any argument they could, no matter how unfounded, to kill off every chance of the Australian people to rise to the challenge of climate change and protect their economic interests.

If lack of imagination and respect for the wishes of the Australian people were a crime, then this disregard of their interests would have to rank as the highest of crimes imaginable, only one step down from actual genocide. No other event in human history comes as close to wiping out the future of the planet, the species it sustains and the possibility of prosperity for future generations as does the world's inability to organise itself to prevent global heating. And the Australian government has, for most of the 21st century, played a leading role in that global disorganisation. By their constant bickering at home and their destabilisation of the international negotiation process under the Paris Agreement,[341] they have brought us to the brink of a catastrophe.

It makes it no easier to stomach this failure of political leadership by a very wealthy advanced country to observe that it all could have been avoided. Plainly, if we had taken up the challenge to reduce emissions when Australians first wanted to deal with the problem, probably from as early as 1990, we could have easily afforded a transition to a new Australian economy based on renewable energy, leaving us with room to help other nations get their carbon emissions

---

[340] Natasha Kassam, Lowy Institute Poll 2022, page 27, Op. Cit.

[341] For a summary of Australia's failure to comply with its commitment under the Paris Agreement to mitigate climate change, view The State of Australia in 2020, Episode 6 Part 2: Climate policy failure and how to fix it by global leadership, YouTube, Australian Community Futures Planning, 18 October 2020. The State of Australia in 2020 - Episode 6 Part 2 - YouTube

down. Australia could have showcased what developed countries should have been doing all along – global leadership on phasing out fossil fuels – and we could have significantly strengthened our economy in the process. As it is, all we have succeeded in doing is narrowing down the time we have deal with climate change from 25 or 30 years to about three. In 2022, that is how much time we have left before we and the rest of the world emit so much in tonnes of greenhouses gasses that we lock the planet irreversibly into heating above 1.5 degrees Celsius. That is how much time we have left before we reach a point where every dollar we spend on trying to reduce emissions is exceeded, probably several times over, by the cost of repairs we must make (if they are still possible) to ensure that our children can live safely on a heated planet. That is how much time we have left to ensure that our children can afford a decent standard of living.

Prevention would have been much cheaper than cure but we have missed our chance for that path. As a result, the standard of living that future generations of Australians may attain is not going to be as high as the standard of living enjoyed by the generations of the post-World War II era. That statement is, of course, open to dispute but this only goes to show that all efforts should be assembled to prove it wrong. Proving it wrong should surely be every caring citizen's aim. This implies that the most important questions for Australians today, having been left with this abject and very expensive failure of leadership by the Australian partisan political system, are:

> How do we assemble ourselves so that we can ensure future generations will be able to afford a decent standard of living?
> How do we reassemble our democracy so that this crime against all our futures never happens again?

It should be notable here that I have not suggested that the key question should be about how we might reassemble our *economy* so that future generations have a better chance of a decent standard of living. Of course, it is essential to restructure the economy for that purpose but this can only be achieved if we open a space for it to be restructured according to our specified will. That implies that before we can restructure the economy, we must give ourselves the chance to specify its purpose. What do we want our economy to be *for*? Is it to be for the benefit of the few and some corporations, or should it be established in a sustainable form that supports rewarding opportunities and continuous improvements in living standards for everyone? Should it be structured so that vital services are fully accessible and that scarce resources are conserved and fairly shared? And should it be structured so that national wealth is fairly raised and fairly shared? These are all fundamental questions that we have never had an open national conversation about. We have never coherently specified our will for the economy; but if we want to build a new one, this is conversation that is long overdue.

Until now, however, we have not had our democracy set up in a form that will allow us to have that conversation, let alone have it in a manner that is orderly and therefore likely to establish a clear vision for the economy we prefer to build for our future. So the question about how we should reassemble our democracy is a necessary precursor to our ability to restructure the economy. We need democratic arrangements which enable us to assemble our national voice. This is all the more urgent because if we are to head off the worst impacts of climate change it is not only the economy that needs restructuring. Our capacity as a society needs to be lifted to underpin our chances of building a sustainable economy, as does our approach to environmental management and consumption.

Social capacity, or what some would call social capital, is in decline in Australia. From the late 1990s it was hit hard by attacks from the Howard, Abbott, Turnbull and Morrison governments on Australia's education system[342] and from some state governments.[343]

---

[342] See Mike Seccombe, "Turnbull's war on universities", The Saturday Paper, 6-12 May 2017: "In the early days of his prime ministership, John Howard shared with some a private view about universities: don't spend money on them, the people there don't vote for us." Accessible at https://www.thesaturdaypaper.com.au/news/education/2017/05/06/turnbulls-war-universities/14939928004602

[343] For an example of state attacks on the school education system in New South Wales see Bronwyn Kelly, *By 2050: Planning a better future for our children in 21st*

The proof of this decline in social capacity is clear in the decline in PISA (Program for International Student Assessment) scores for Australian school students compared to other OECD nations.[344] Between 2000 and 2018, mean performance by Australian children on PISA scores declined steadily:

- in reading from a score of 528 points to 503;
- in mathematics from a score of 524 to 491 (which is below the OECD average); and
- in science from a score of 527 to 503.

In 2018, Australia ranked 30th out of 38 rich countries in scores for enrolment and educational attainment. We had a greater proportion of our children left at the bottom of the literacy scale than 29 other developed countries.[345] And the situation was made significantly worse under the Morrison government's attacks on higher education during the Covid-19 pandemic, attacks which resulted in the loss of 40,000 jobs (35,000 in universities and another 5,000 in the vocational training sector).[346] The failure to invest in tertiary education makes no sense at all from an economic perspective bearing in mind that economists at Deloitte have found that investment in higher education returns much more to an economy than it costs:

---

century democratic Australia, March 2020, Chapter 4 – Subsection: Problem No. 2 – A failure of reporting. By 2050: Planning a better future for our children in 21st century democratic Australia eBook : Kelly, Bronwyn: Amazon.com.au: Kindle Store

344 OECD, PISA (Program for International Student Assessment) Results 2018. Education GPS - Australia - Student performance (PISA 2018) (oecd.org). See also Dr Bronwyn Kelly and Sean Kelly, Australian Community Futures Planning, *The State of Australia 2022; End of Term Report on the 46th Parliament of Australia*, March 2022, pages 155-156, Op. Cit. https://www.austcfp.com.au/state-of-australia

345 UNICEF, "Innocenti Report Card 15, An Unfair Start, Inequality in Children's Education in Rich Countries", 2018, page 8. an-unfair-start-inequality-children-education_37049-RC15-EN-WEB.pdf (unicef-irc.org)

346 The Australia Institute, An Avoidable Catastrophe: Pandemic Job Losses in Higher Education and their Consequences, September 2021. An Avoidable Catastrophe - The Australia Institute

> Deloitte Access Economics reported [in 2015] on the contribution of tertiary education to Australia's prosperity and found 'the socioeconomic benefits accrue both to those directly engaging in university-led activities and to society at large. In some cases, and in research especially, it is broader society that is by far the greatest beneficiary'. Deloitte valued the contribution of tertiary education to Australia's productive capacity at $140 billion in 2014, of which $24 billion accrued to the tertiary educated themselves. The 'spillover effects', it found, meant that for every one percentage point increase in the number of workers with a university degree, the wages of those without tertiary qualifications rose 1.6 to 1.9 per cent.[347]

Aggravating this decline in social capacity is Australia's record in gender inequality. In 2021, although women in Australia were ranked at the number 1 spot for educational attainment in the World Economic Forum's Global Gender Gap Report, the Report showed that women have otherwise been prevented from contributing to the economy as much as they might. Their educational achievements have not translated to jobs and job pay at the same rate as they have for men. Between 2006 and 2021 all other rankings in the Report dropped for Australian women:

- In women's economic participation and opportunity – Australia ranked 12th in 2006 but 70th in 2021.
- In women's health and survival – Australia ranked 57th in 2006 but 99th in 2021.
- In women's political empowerment – Australia ranked 32nd in 2006 but 70th in 2021.[348]

If Australia is to be able to build an economy that will allow us all to maintain our quality of life and standard of living in the face of climate change, we will obviously need to maximise our social

---

[347] Mike Seccombe, "Turnbull's war on universities", The Saturday Paper, 6-12 May 2017, Op. Cit.

[348] World Economic Forum, "Global Gender Gap Report 2021". WEF_GGGR_2021.pdf (weforum.org)

capacity. In short, we will need to stop building inequality into our socioeconomic arrangements and stop systemic exclusions of significant portions of the potential workforce. A much broader conversation than one confined to the economy is required to achieve this. That conversation also needs to be orderly, if only because it is a much bigger conversation than we have ever attempted. In reality it will not be possible to have it at all if we do not create an orderly framework in which to assemble all our diverse voices and integrate the strategies most likely to push us towards a sustainable future before climate change overwhelms our current social, environmental and economic capacity. The most likely framework that can suit that purpose – in other words, one that is efficient enough to help us make up for lost time – is of course an integrated, long term planning framework – National IP&R.

National IP&R can turbo charge our remaining potential for preventing the worst effects of climate change. This is because IP&R can integrate preventative efforts so that the sum of those efforts will be greater than the individual parts. Because it can be equipped with independent data about our current wellbeing and security, it can help us take account of the multiple causes of our various breakdowns, and we can synchronise preventative efforts with curative efforts, the former making the latter cheaper and cheaper as time passes. Developed countries like Australia are very well placed to make a success of this because the technological solutions they will need are already well developed and they have enough total wealth at their disposal to pick up speed in reduction of greenhouse gas emissions. It is unlikely that any country will pick up enough speed to prevent heating above 1.5 degrees Celsius but there is still time to prevent further heating. Every 1% of a degree counts. Every 1% of a degree of heating that we avoid is a massive economic saving. Every 1% of a degree of heating avoided is a life saver.

Bearing in mind the scale of the benefits Australians may enjoy and the scale of the costs they may avoid if they choose to organise themselves to build a coherent voice on their preferred future, there is no reason to deny Australians the opportunity to step into a more influential space in their democracy – a space in which they can work together for that future and impress a coherent idea of it on those they elect. There is certainly nothing to be gained by passing up the opportunity of participation in an efficient process of agenda setting, especially one which benefits both electors and the elected in terms of what they can achieve for future generations. The chances of success in such a reform will be increased if, in addition to the process we might invoke for enshrining our human rights, we also enshrine one additional right – the right to a national people's voice. In the next section I will propose an option for this purpose.

Enshrining a national people's voice in a people's constitution

The question of how Australians might safely enshrine a national people's voice in their Constitution revolves essentially around the question of how relationships of trust may be established between the people and the parliaments they elect. In the transition from the current Constitution, which gives exclusive supremacy to the parliament as the maker of laws (with or without guidance from the people), to a new Constitution which locates sovereignty in the expressed will of the people, the practical capacity for development of terms of trust between the parliament and the people will be essential. There is probably no other way to encourage the parliament to grant an appropriate share of power to the people in their own Constitution. Indeed it is highly unlikely that any set of elected parliamentarians will consider it safe to create a role for the people in the Constitution at all unless and until they can be confident that satisfactory terms of trust have been agreed which accord the parliament a share of power sufficient to ensure the stability of the system of representative government – or to put it perhaps more accurately, the stability of their positions of power within that system of governance.

Australian parliaments, especially their conservative members, have always jealously guarded parliamentary supremacy; but to date, this has come at the expense of our human rights. As I noted in Chapter 6, there has been a general insistence that parliamentarians must be free to determine laws as they see fit and must be unobstructed in that process by any High Court judgement that, "under the guise of [constitutional] interpretation", may seek to amend the powers of the parliament conferred on it by the Constitution. In general terms this is an assertion by those elected to parliament that they shall not be constrained by any unelected persons (such as the people or a few High Court judges) and shall only be restrained by the strict letter of the Constitution itself. This seems reasonable on the surface but it is actually an assertion that parliaments or governments may move as close to exercise of arbitrary power as the Constitution allows them to. In that regard, Australia's Constitution should suit the parliamentary supremacists just fine, because it simply says what each legislative body empowered under it may make laws for but places no limits on that power. For instance, it places no limits on the extent to which human rights may not be abused in lawmaking, or the extent to which someone may be discriminated against on the grounds of race, or even the extent to which the national interest may not be undermined.

The modern state as it is manifest in Australia's Constitution conflates the power to determine the national interest, and to make laws for it, into one body. This is not to say that governments often define the national interest, much less express the national will. On the contrary, they either refrain wherever possible from defining the national interest or confine their articulation of it to ad hoc pronouncements of narrowly focussed reactive policies. But nor do they facilitate public opportunities for expression of the national interest or will. In that sense, the Australian modern state enabled by our Constitution is as far from democracy as any other system of governance that we are accustomed to characterising as "autocratic". This too suits the powerful just fine. Accustomed as they are to near unlimited power, it might therefore be expected that elected members of future parliaments will continue to work assiduously to ensure that the Constitution should include no terms which might enable the High Court to diminish that supremacy in power by determining its lawful limits or its obligations to the people. In particular they will be likely to argue that it should include no terms like a statement of Australian values and an agreement on human rights and obligations which might, as justiciable elements of the Constitution, have the potential to bind a parliament and a government in ways that vested interests do not wish them to be bound.

Contemplating that, it is apparent that there is a need to break the nexus between the power to express the national interest and the power to make laws in the national interest. In a people's constitution these two powers would be separated so that the national interest should be determined by the people but the parliament would still be free to exercise judgement whenever it is making laws and the executive government would be free to do the same in determining policy. In principle we would hope that the lawmaking and policy development powers would be exercised consistent with the national interest as expressed by the people and would be based on evidence and independent advice as to the best course of action. This advice need not exclude the advice of vested interest groups, but if we have devised a system by which we might articulate the overall national interest – and articulate it as the lively, dynamic thing that it is, something constantly evolving as world circumstances and prospects change, in other words, something that is future-focussed – then we can contextualise sectional interests in relation to the national interest and make it easier for lawmakers and policy setters to make far better, more balanced judgements. In particular we can ensure that parliaments and governments can take the interests of future generations into account. This is something they cannot do now, because they have no guidance about the will of the people for their future.

So as I said, enshrinement of the power of the people to express the national interest comes back to the need to develop terms of trust between the people and the parliaments they elect. These terms must be comprehensible to parliaments and therefore the people must be enabled to express the terms on which they are willing to share power in a coherent form. That is step No. 1 towards a true democracy. I will discuss this further in Chapter 10 but at this point it is necessary to at least scope the form those terms might take and to provide some indication of their potential to bind or at least bend parliaments and governments to an expressed will of the people. It is necessary to resolve this because any change to the Constitution that introduces a new level of specificity to the limits of power and the obligations of governments will have a major impact on the nature of the oath that a person elected to the federal parliament will be required to faithfully swear. At the moment, because there is no specificity at all as to the purposes of power in the Constitution, elected members can take the oath as lightly as they please. Indeed it binds them to nothing but a dead Queen and her foreign heirs and successors. But if we introduce terms of trust – if we say that in the best judgement of the people this is what power is legitimately *for* – then those who swear allegiance will, from that moment, need to think more deeply about what they may rightly do with power.

At the same time though, the people themselves will need to think reasonably about the limitations and obligations they might impose on the elected. It is likely that some parts of the terms of trust should be accepted as constants because they are less likely to change quickly and indeed constitute the fundamentals that hold our society together. Statements of national values and agreements on human rights would be likely to fall into that category because they describe a moral character for the nation and the public interest overall. As such they should not be problematic if they are justiciable. They should present no problem to any elected member when swearing allegiance (and if they do, we should be concerned as to whether we have elected a person whose moral commitments match those of the nation).

But in contrast to values and rights, a national people's voice is very unlikely to be constant through time. Nor would there be any utility in attempting to make time – or for that matter, our aspirations – stand still. And indeed, if the national voice is to be expressed in the form of a long term integrated plan for making our preferred future a reality (rather than as a moral precept or a minimum right), then it could be problematic both for those who must swear allegiance to the Constitution and for those courts that must issue legal judgements about whether a government or parliament has failed to comply with it. The logical solution to this issue is that, rather than make a national people's voice (as expressed in a dynamic, long term plan) justiciable – in other words, rather than try to bind a government to a people's voice about what they want for their future and the strategies for its realisation – it would be better to allow both the people and the parliament some latitude in their respective roles to exercise their best judgement consistent with the national interest.

The national interest itself can only be defined by the people. Its minimum may be expressed as values and human rights – in other words values and human rights must be enshrined in the Constitution as the bottom line of the people's tolerance of their consenting to be governed. Values and human rights provide the list of the powers of Australians that may *not* be abused by those they elect. And a key right among all those human rights is the right of the people to express their sovereign will. This is a right that is consonant with the right to self-determination but it has a collective dimension. It might be said that the sovereign will is the collective expression of a self-determining nation of equals. This right to express a sovereign will – to have a national people's voice – must be acknowledged in the Constitution if we are to ensure that our system of merely representative government matures into and actually functions as a system of *responsible* government (instead of an unaccountable autocracy). At the moment, Australia's system of representative governance cannot function responsibly because there is nothing in the Constitution which states what the elected are to be responsible *to*. Ministers are responsible *for* their portfolios but not responsible *to* the people. In other words they are not accountable to any will other than their own temporal appetites (and as legislators they can change the rules to suit such appetites whenever they can gather the numbers). It might be said that they are held accountable at the ballot box but if so, it is only to a very light extent. In fact, as far as their accountability to future generations goes, the ballot box provides none.

In effect this means we must make a distinction between the national people's voice and the right of the people to express it. It is the right to express the national voice that must be enshrined in the Constitution rather than any particular statement of aspirations for the future that may arise from the process of expression of that voice. The extent to which any such statements as they arise may be binding on a parliament or a government is a matter for each parliament and government. But once the statements have been made, the elected would be well advised to remember that the ballot box is just around the corner and there is an ultimate point of accountability for their judgements.

If, in this proposed arrangement, we take it that:

1. a statement of Australian values;
2. a national agreement on human rights and obligations; and
3. a people's right to expression of a national voice

will be justiciable, but that any statements (such as a long term integrated national plan) will not be justiciable but will function as guidance to governments and as a means of measuring how well a parliament or government behaved in relation to the people's will, then we may well have the makings of a system for setting terms of trust which do not unreasonably bind or hobble either the parliament or the people. In short, we may have found a way to avoid the trap of replacing one overweening power arrangement with another. We may have found a way to build our trust in governments and their trust in us, sufficient to install a power for people in the Constitution that will not undermine the system of representative government. Instead it should enhance the capacity for responsible behaviour in that system.

If the people have the power to express their sovereign will and the parliament retains the power to choose how it may observe that will, consistent with the interests of the nation and future generations, we will have finally installed a system by which government can be, and can be *seen* to be, responsible to the people. We will have a system where the parliament and government retain the power to decide how they shall work together to make the people's sovereign will for their future a reality. The powers of parliamentarians will be the same as they are now but the potential for its abuse of certain powers will be limited due to the transparency of the terms of trust on values and rights. The potential for abuse of the national voice will also be curtailed in the sense that if a choice is exercised to depart from the people's will, it will be clear that their preferences for the future have not been respected. To the extent that a government or parliament can explain the reasons for its departures, and show how the departures still positively contribute to the national project, then a government and parliament may be deemed responsible. To the extent that they cannot adequately explain those deviations, they should expect to pay the price at the ballot box. This is the arrangement that should result if we combine the strengths of a representative system of democracy with a participatory system of democracy.

It should be noted that this suggested form for the terms of trust – combining values, rights and voice – happens to line up well with proposals for an Indigenous Voice in the Constitution. That too is an amendment that would support a better relationship between people and the parliaments but without placing unreasonable constraints on the ability of elected members to freely exercise their judgement.

In the main, the form that the Indigenous Voice might take as an institution is yet to be detailed but it would be reasonable to assume that the independence of the Indigenous Voice would be a primary principle in its formation as an institution. We might imagine therefore that the Indigenous Voice would operate in parallel to a national people's voice. The potential is there, if both are enshrined, to achieve a coexistence of sovereignties.

However, the form of Indigenous Voice that has been contemplated under the Indigenous Voice Co-design Process[349]

---

[349] Australian Government, National Indigenous Australians Agency, "Indigenous Voice Co-design Process: Final Report to the Australian Government", July 2021, Op. Cit.

released in 2021, is not, shall we say, as capacious as the form of the national people's voice that I have described. The national people's voice – at least as I have envisaged it – would operate as an independent institution that has been constitutionally enabled to organise people to work together in a well-formed process to build a long term integrated plan, whereas we might expect that an Indigenous Voice at the national level may be somewhat more of a reactive than a proactive policy body. The proposed wording of constitutional amendments put forward for consultation by the newly elected Labor government in 2022 suggests that a planning function for the national Indigenous Voice was not front and centre in the minds of the government. In suggesting that

> there shall be a body, to be called the Aboriginal and Torres Strait Islander Voice [and that this Voice] may make representations to parliament and the executive government on matters relating to Aboriginal and Torres Strait Islander peoples,[350]

it wasn't readily apparent that a national Indigenous Voice would be supported to build long term plans. Rather the inference was that the Voice would react to government proposals simply on matters that affect Aboriginal and Torres Strait Islander peoples. However, this reactive model for an Indigenous Voice has arisen through consultation that has been conducted in the context of a structure for our democracy that assumes no role for the people and total parliamentary supremacy on both the determination of the sovereign will (ad hoc and probably narrowly focussed) and the power to make laws for it. In other words, it was a model conceived in a political framework that did not consider the opportunities offered by a people's constitution. Chief among those opportunities is co-sovereignty.

---

[350] Proposed wording for constitutional amendments to enshrine an Aboriginal and Torres Strait Islander Voice, announced at the Garma Festival by Prime Minister Anthony Albanese, July 2022. Lorena Allam, "Anthony Albanese reveals 'simple and clear' wording of referendum question on Indigenous voice", The Guardian, 30 July 2022.

This suggests that it might be worthwhile in the final design of the Indigenous Voice if room is left within it for Aborigines and Torres Strait Islanders to develop their own long term integrated planning capacity, learning from the experience of the Integrated Planning and Reporting reforms discussed above. If that could be achieved, we would have two national voices enabled in the Constitution that would be of equal capacity.

But regardless of whether Aboriginal and Torres Strait Islander peoples choose to establish an integrated planning capacity in their national Voice, Australians at large should not risk modelling their own national people's voice on the Indigenous Voice as it seems to have been designed – that is, as a reactive non-binding instrument instead of a proactive non-binding planning instrument. A national people's voice could not be successful if it were merely reactive because that would mean that we were simply reverting to a system where the government determines our will, sets the agenda, and confines it to the short term items that suit its political purposes. There would be little to be gained if that were all we attempted. For a truly visionary voice, we need more. We need a well-resourced, professional, independent centre of excellence in community engagement, social research and integrated planning. We should also expect that the level of expertise required for facilitation of such a wide-ranging process would be a major undertaking. It would require:

- significant centralisation of research materials and data that Australians will need if they are to participate efficiently in the planning process; and
- staff with facilitation skills which will maximise the possibility of open access and involvement by any Australian who may wish to contribute.

It will be no easy task to establish skills in community engagement which can make everyone feel welcome to participate should they so desire but the prospect of what could be achieved would be very attractive for both the public and the facilitators. There would be no shortage of people wanting to become involved but a good place to start would be to introduce skills training for Year 10, 11, and 12 students in policy development for national issues. At the same time it would be advisable to drop the voting age to 16. This would enable young people to become accustomed to more active involvement in their democracy.

Bearing in mind that the simple objective in enshrining a right to a national people's voice in the Constitution is to establish an open public square for collaborative development of an integrated long term plan for our society, environment, economy and democracy, so that we can track towards a future of wellbeing and security for all, the most appropriate institutional arrangement for such a voice is likely to be a well-resourced but entirely independent commission for community engagement in national integrated planning. In some ways this commission might resemble the national Indigenous Voice, at least insofar as, like the Indigenous Voice, it would not be able to bind governments and instead would rely on building relationships of mutual respect between Australian people and their parliaments, but recognising always that the expression of the sovereign will is primarily the people's right, not the parliament's. An independent commission built on this model should ideally have no power to override either the parliament or the Indigenous Voice. In fact no party in this new sort of body politic should be given power to interfere with another in their rightful exercise of power. They simply need to be given a means to increase and maintain their trust in each other.

Rather than a system where one part of the body politic – such as a parliament – is considered the superior or paramount power, it would be more useful to conceptualise a body politic where power is shared more widely and its separate components are rebalanced more sensibly between the parliament, the executive government, the states, the judiciary, First Nations and the Australian people. This sort of rebalanced system of power relations has the capacity to redefine the responsibilities of all parties to Australia's democracy. If those new responsibilities are defined well, they should help us limit the potential for abuses of power but also maximise the benefits of new, more equal power relationships.

At a time when the nation is being called on to secure its future via a model that supports a coexistence of sovereignties, this wider spread of power presents a particularly adroit option – one that offers the possibility not just of a voice for all but a coexistence of diverse voices. It also offers a form in which every Australian – Indigenous and non-Indigenous alike – can maximise their chances of exercising rights to self-determination. But perhaps most importantly, it offers Australians an enormous increase in their capacity to speed up their transition to a sustainable future and to do so without increasing political and economic inequality.

The vast majority of Australians know that we have lost a decade, perhaps two, that we shouldn't have lost in our progress towards a society, environment and economy that offers a sustainable and affordable future in the age of climate change. But although we have started late, we can still pick up a lot of speed if we integrate our strategies. For those who wish to pick up the necessary speed, the following starting draft of a National People's Voice is offered as a contribution to deliberations.

Starting draft of an enshrined constitutional process for expression of the national people's voice

Australian People's Constitution – The National People's Voice (draft for use in community engagement)

As the source of sovereignty, the People of Australia shall be enabled to exercise their right to express their Sovereign Will for the future of their society, environment, economy and democracy. Expression of this Sovereign Will for the future shall take the form of a collaboratively assembled and regularly monitored and reviewed, integrated plan for the wellbeing and security of all Australians over the longer term (up to 30 years). The process for expression of the Sovereign Will for the future and any emergent statements and plans from that process shall be known as The National People's Voice.

For purposes of assisting the People in the orderly composition of their National Voice, there shall be an Independent Commission for National Engagement and Integrated Planning.

The Commission shall have a charter of independence from the Parliament and Executive Government, shall be accountable by annual reports to the People of Australia, and shall be charged as a minimum with responsibility to the People of Australia for development and maintenance of fully open forums and accessible processes by which all Australians may be enabled to:

- accurately assess the state of their health, wellbeing and security as a nation;
- participate at will in planning processes to articulate a vision for their preferred future and their preferred safe paths to that future; and
- receive independent reports on the progress of the nation towards or away from that future.

The Commission shall be established and maintained with sufficient funding and resources to support Australians in the orderly composition, review and revision of their National Voice, including as a minimum:

- all research resources necessary to ensure that The National People's Voice can be formulated and monitored on the basis of credible and comprehensive data and information on all aspects of the performance of the Australian society, environment, economy and democracy; and
- all communications and facilitation resources necessary to enable best practice in inclusive community engagement and active citizen participation in building a cohesive nation.

The Commission shall also be entitled to access and rely on the financial and economic planning capacities of the Treasury and the Parliamentary Budget Office for any information necessary to conduct dialogues with Australians on options for sustainably financing their preferred future.

Statements and plans arising from the operation of the National People's Voice shall be understood to be non-binding on the

Executive Government and shall not constrain the Parliament in its power to make laws in accordance with this Constitution but shall constitute guidance to the Parliament as to the People's Sovereign Will for the future and shall therefore be accorded the status of a primary consideration in all parliamentary deliberations. In making laws (including laws pertaining to budgets and appropriations) and in reviewing the appropriateness of administrative decisions on and adherence to policy, Executive Governments shall accordingly be obligated to prepare and Parliaments shall be required to consider comprehensive Statements of Compatibility with the National People's Voice and to provide reasons for any incompatibility with its expression of the People's Sovereign Will.

Maximising the effectiveness of a new balance of power in democracy

If Australians seek to enhance the capacity of their democracy by the means I have suggested thus far, they will be likely to step into an era where democracy functions far more effectively than it has in the past to service the public good and protect the public interest. The three constitutional amendments I have suggested, enabling Australians to:

- build a statement of their values as a society;
- enshrine human rights and obligations in law along with a process for conferring and protecting those rights; and to
- enshrine a system or process which will lift the voice of Australians to a level of coherence at which their will can be understood and actively fulfilled by the elected,

all combine to significantly increase the chances that Australians of the future will have an acceptable degree of wellbeing and security. However, the benefit we might obtain from injecting Australians into the centre of their democracy by these mechanisms will be diminished if certain other features of the Constitution remain unamended. For example, if the racist clauses in the Constitution are retained, they will have the capacity to allow a government to undermine human rights. And if the governor-general retains more power than the king, as is the case at present, that would obviously be wholly incompatible with an arrangement which vests sovereignty in the people.

We are also likely to lose benefits if no action is taken to deal with some other matters on which the Constitution is silent. For instance, the Constitution currently contains no provisions to prevent corruption of election processes, particularly as it places no restrictions on the extent to which election campaigns may be funded and political donations may be made. It leaves the way open for voter suppression and capture of election processes by corporate powers. And notably, the current Constitution is silent on a key player in the arena of power – the prime minister – and his or her capacity to override the will of all others in relation to war. By virtue of its silence on this matter the Constitution enables a tyranny on the thing that matters most to Australians, their safety from immoral war and nuclear destruction.

As I mentioned in Chapter 3 there is a myriad of reforms that are necessary to bring Australia's Constitution into the 21st century. But if the primary objective here is to establish the Australian people as the source of the sovereign will and to distribute power so that for the first time in our country's history We the People actually have some, then the focus needs to be on amendments that are necessary to protect the gains we will make for our democracy and the power of the people within it by the three main changes I have suggested. Amendments which are extraneous to that purpose, such as those which alter the distribution of power between the states or between different levels of government, or those which might redefine the rules on free trade, can be dealt with at a later time. The priority here should be to develop a program of amendments to ensure that we can increase the clarity of the Constitution about how power is distributed fairly and properly between the entities empowered by it. In the following chapter I will make some suggestions as to the more pressing items in that program.

Chapter 8 – Essential No. 4: Priority constitutional amendments for an inclusive democracy

Australians don't talk much about the Constitution, but this doesn't mean they exhibit no interest in how power is exercised and shared. On the contrary suggestions abound about how reform of the political system in Australia may be achieved to prevent abuse of power. Usually though, these focus on mechanical alterations of the existing system and institutions of government. They tend to concentrate on electoral reform, reduction of the possibility of corruption, the establishment of fixed terms for parliaments, and transparency in government.[351] Some reformers question the usefulness of the federation. Others argue that local government should be recognised in the Constitution and that there should be a re-distribution of powers exercisable by the Commonwealth, the states, their parliaments and executive governments, the governor-general, the courts and the territories. And then there are those who argue that a focal point for constitutional reform should be the establishment of Australia as a republic.

These are all important areas for reform but it must be observed that they don't offer much in terms of the possibility of political inclusion. In the main they are just an attempt to make elected leaders do a better job, pushing all the responsibility back on to them. They rely on some sense or, shall I say, blind faith that there is

---

[351] Examples of programs of mechanical improvements include the #OurDemocracy, "The Framework - Our Democracy" and Citizens for Democratic Renewal, Mark Triffitt, "Australia's Democracy: A strategic roadmap for renewal". Australias-Democracy-—-A-Strategic-Roadmap-for-Renewal.pdf (democraticrenewal.org.au)

wisdom, capacity and generosity in those leaders who manage to climb to the top of what Mark McKenna called "the flawed and grimy world of day-to-day partisan politics" and that better leadership by politicians is itself the answer. They rely on a faith that if the system of power-sharing by the powerful elite could be tweaked, then the talent of the powerful would be unleashed and become a force for good. Most tellingly, they assume that politics is the sole arena for resolution of debates and for decisions on change. None of this promotes inclusion. It is simply a set of selective repairs to the mechanics of a failing system.

As I said in Chapter 2, it is evident that politics doesn't work – certainly not as a mechanism for inclusion. But I should add here that if *democracy* is reduced to mere politics, then democracy won't work either. In fact, democracy doesn't work well now, precisely because it is reduced to the antics of those best able to navigate the flawed and grimy world of politics. A healthy democracy requires people – electors and the elected alike – to rise above base politics and participate in a much wider, more open and respectfully conversational arena than our adversarial parliaments. We cannot rise above this if people do not offer support to politicians to enable them to do the better job we expect.

In the last decade, the world has watched while the number of democracies has declined. According to the Museum of Australian Democracy:

> Democracy is on the retreat globally. We have now entered what the Pew Research Centre has termed a global 'democratic recession' (Pew Research Centre, 2017). Satisfaction with democracy is tipping around the world — there are now more authoritarian regimes than full democracies (Kellogg, *Varieties of Democracy Project*, 2018).[352]

[352] "Democracy 2025" webpage at https://www.democracy2025.gov.au/.

And in 2022, researchers from Democracy – Our World in Data reported that the leading approaches to measuring democracy indicate that the world is becoming less democratic:

> Democracy is in decline, regardless of how we measure it — whether we look at big changes in the number of democracies and the people living in them; at small changes in the extent of democratic rights; or at medium-sized changes in the number of, and people living in, countries that are autocratizing.[353]

Some communities in Australia have already tried to circumvent this by establishing an array of mechanisms for strengthening democratic processes at the local level. These include citizens' juries and processes for the co-design of individual policies by citizens and politicians. These processes have excellent potential to re-empower those Australians fortunate enough to get the opportunity to participate. But those opportunities tend to arise ad hoc and because there is no overarching plan in which any piecemeal local democratic decisions can be assessed, there is only a limited potential for national benefit overall. As such, the support that federal politicians need most from the Australian people can best be organised by the inclusive reforms I have already suggested for the Constitution. But because there is no guarantee that these suggestions will readily find favour in politics – especially to a level where they are given constitutional status – and because we might expect that inclusive reforms are not likely to be appreciated by governments that thrive on division, there is a strong argument for prioritising some of the mechanical alterations of the existing system and institutions of government that I have just referred to. While they might not promote inclusion per se, some of these reforms can at least help prepare the ground for the wider inclusive reforms of the type suggested here for a new constitution for a people's sovereign state. And in the event that an appetite for a people's constitution emerges

---

[353] Bastian Herre, "The world has recently become less democratic", Democracy – Our World in Data, 6 September 2022. The world has recently become less democratic - Our World in Data

and Australia adopts such a law as a means of advancement to a fully inclusive democracy where the people can play a more significant role in shaping their future, then a few of the mechanical reforms to the process of politics would be essential. The more important of these mechanical reforms include:

- the need to prohibit corporate capture of governments and donations by sectional interest groups;
- the need to limit the powers of the governor-general;
- the need to specify the limits of power of the prime minister; and
- the need to eliminate the basis of racism in Australian law.

Each of these reforms needs a basis in the Constitution, by which I mean that if Australians are to be confident that these reforms will not be scaled back by a government that may seek to act contrary to the public interest, then a constitutional imperative should be provided to prevent lawmaking (or silence in law) that is inconsistent with the public interest. The following sections provide context for the necessity of constitutional amendments to secure reforms.

Essential No. 4a – Prohibition of corporate and other organisational donations to political entities

It is likely that those most accustomed to wielding power in Australia in a manner that is largely unrestrained by anything other than their own self-interest will be ranged against the entry of another party into the arena of power – that party being the people of Australia, replete with their own chapter in the Constitution. Any change in the arrangement of our democracy for the purpose of increasing the power of the Australian people will be fiercely resisted, even if it involves no diminution of the powers of the elected. Any change to empower the people will be especially resisted by the corporate powers that have captured those that have been elected and made them beholden for their continuance in parliament on the patronage of corporations.

Corporations hold Australia's democracy in chains, especially the Murdoch media and the fossil fuel industry.[354] But with a people's constitution we can begin to unleash both the people and those we elect from those chains. We can do that more surely, however, if we break the nexus between political parties and the public service on the one hand and corporate donors and lobbyists on the other. In fact, what is required is a complete abolition of donations from corporations but also from other powerful groups such as unions. This system of patronage needs to be replaced completely and until it is, Australia will not be able to claim that its democracy works on a system of equality, where one vote equals one value.

Most discussions about the failure of Australia's electoral systems to ensure adherence to a principle of one-vote one-value focus on "malapportionment" of registered voters between electorates or malapportionment of the permitted number of seats for each state and territory – a problem which tends to be exhibited in the senate. Doubtless these problems of malapportionment need to be addressed but a significant impact on whether one individual's vote has more value than another also arises from the distortion caused by inequities in the capacity to make donations. In a fair electoral code it should be evident that no elector should have more power than another to influence the outcome. In short, no-one should be able to buy an election. At present there is nothing prohibiting this. As a result, Australia has experienced some quite spectacular instances of electoral funding distortion.[355]

---

[354] For information on the effect of state capture in Australia see Australian Democracy Network, "Confronting State Capture", February 2022. State Capture — Australian Democracy Network

[355] In Australia electoral funding distortion is rampant. Lobby groups and rich individuals are allowed to buy elections. For example, mining magnate Clive Palmer paid $83 million in the 2019 election to sway preferences towards the Coalition and in 2016 Malcolm Turnbull paid almost $2 million in person to boost the Coalition's electoral campaign. Yet the Coalition government attempted to introduce legislation in 2018 which would restrict small donations by householders to activist groups like GetUp and charities like the Climate Council – in other words, all the legislative actions of Coalition governments in the decade to 2022 were aimed at capping the small donations of the many, not the massive

This would imply that donations by groups, such as corporations and unions or other entities that have the power to amass funds that can be donated to campaigns, should be prohibited and donations by individuals should be strictly limited in value and frequency – say, an upper limit of $5,000 from individuals (distributed among as many candidates as they wish) and no more than once in each parliamentary term. Ideally this would result in replacement of the current largely unregulated system of donations with a system in which elections, including the costs of candidate participation in the election process, are mainly funded by the state itself. Rules for free and fair access to those state funds would need to be devised, along with rules for disclosures by candidates that the money was spent in accordance with the rules, but this could be achieved through legislation as long as the Constitution itself included some guiding principles. Such principles would, as a minimum, emphasise that no laws shall be permitted which do not promote equal suffrage.

The practice of state funding of federal elections is already provided for in Australia under the Commonwealth Electoral Act 1918, Part XX of which provides that registered political parties, candidates and groups may be entitled to election funding. The election funding is payable in relation to any candidate who received at least 4% of the total formal first preference votes cast in the election.[356]

Abolition of corporate and other group donations would imply the need for the state to establish a significantly bigger budget for federal and state elections. But the necessary increase would be easily affordable and, in any case, if democracy is worth having it is worth paying for. It is certainly worth paying to keep corruption out of it. Having said that, the investment would only be worth it if it is

---

donations of the few. See Bronwyn Kelly, *By 2050: Planning a better future for our children in 21st century democratic Australia*, March 2020, Chapter 8 – Subsection: Checking for Threats to Democracy. By 2050: Planning a better future for our children in 21st century democratic Australia eBook : Kelly, Bronwyn: Amazon.com.au: Kindle Store

[356] Commonwealth Electoral Act 1918, Part XX, Section 286A.

fairly distributed. There would be no point to increased state funding of elections if the distribution systems undermined political equity.

Of course, the most effective way of ensuring political equity is not undermined would be to amend the Constitution to include a national voice for the people. A clear understanding of what candidates are elected to strive for as the primary purpose of the nation is likely to offer financial savings and economic gains which will significantly outweigh the extra cost for taxpayers in funding their elections. In fact, the more we move towards a firm articulation of the job we expect parliaments and governments to do, the less likely we are to have to worry about the effect of corruption in the election process. Even so, it would be a mercy to unchain those we elect from servitude to corporations and lobby groups by ensuring that they can no longer bribe the elected with donations or offers of jobs when they retire. Reforms which prohibit the revolving door between corporations and politics (when there is a conflict of interest in passage backwards and forwards through that door) are long overdue. And anyone who enters politics should expect no benefit other than the satisfaction of promoting nothing more and nothing less than the public interest as it may be articulated in a national people's voice.

Essential No. 4b – Limitation of the powers of the governor-general

In the 2020s Australians are likely to be called to a referendum on whether the nation should be re-constituted as a republic. Support for a republic in 2022, according to opinion polls, appeared to be uncertain and was negatively impacted by the death of Queen Elizabeth II.[357] As such, the probable outcome of a referendum on this issue is anybody's guess.

---

[357] In January 2022, Nine's Resolve News Monitor reported that: "Australians are willing to vote for a republic by a narrow majority of 54 per cent but are split over the best way to choose the head of state". David Crowe, "Support for republic is strong enough to win approval in bigger states: poll", Sydney Morning Herald, 24 January 2022. By September 2022 the Essential Poll reported that support for a

The result in such a referendum is likely to impact the way the Australian nation is viewed and views itself in the 21st century. A Yes result will signal a decision that the preferred character of Australia is as a mature, independent nation standing on its own two feet and with a distinct sense of sovereignty. A No result will signal that the preferred character is colonial – a dominion of a foreign power without a need to develop independence or establish distinct sovereignty.

Either way, it is apparent that from the point of view of culture the outcome of a referendum on a republic will be significant. But from the point of view of *good governance in a democracy* the outcome of such a referendum is less relevant. By this I mean that for purposes of good democratic governance it doesn't matter whether Australians elect to remain a dominion of a British monarchy and be subject to the British king or queen, or opt to become a republic and elect their own head of state. What matters, irrespective of whether Australia becomes a republic, is whether we continue to allow governors-general or any other nominal heads of state to exercise the inordinate power they can now under the Constitution.

As mentioned in Chapters 3 and 5, the Australian Republican Movement (ARM) acknowledged in January 2022 that more work needed to be done on the Constitution beyond installing a republic with an Australian head of state. Among other things, the ARM's Constitutional Advisory Body recommended a range of amendments to reduce the powers of the head of state in an Australian republic, compared to the current powers of governors-general. There is no reason why these reductions of power should not apply regardless of whether a republic is the chosen form of state for Australia. Specific

---

republic had dropped to 43% compared to March 2021 when it was 48%, whereas those who opposed a republic had risen from 37%, up from 28% over the same period. Those who were unsure tended to switch to being opposed to the republic, not supportive of it. Essential Research: Support for Australia becoming a republic, 19 September 2022. Support for Australia becoming a Republic - essentialreport.com.au

amendments suggested by ARM's Constitutional Advisory Body included:

- That all powers of the Head of State be exercised on the advice of the Prime Minister, ministers or the Federal Executive Council, except when:

    a. Appointing a Prime Minister whom they believe is likely to be able to form a Government which has the confidence of the House of Representatives;
    b. Terminating the appointment of a Prime Minister. The Head of State may not terminate the appointment of a Prime Minister who holds the confidence of the House of Representatives;
    c. A Prime Minister who does not hold the confidence of the House requests an election: the Head of State may not grant an election to a Prime Minister who does not hold the confidence of the House;
    d. Summoning the House of Representatives to determine the confidence of the House;
    e. Dissolving the House of Representatives (and the ability to issue writs for an election) if the confidence of the House of Representatives is indeterminate for a period of no less than seven consecutive days.

- That assent to proposed laws endorsed by voters now be granted automatically on the seventh day, unless the Head of State has been advised to grant assent earlier.

- That the Head of State no longer has the power to withhold assent to a bill. That the power to return a bill with amendments to Parliament be exercised on advice. That the (obsolete) provision granting the power to veto laws 12 months after they have received assent, or reserve assent for up to 24 months assent [sic.] be removed. That the Head of State no longer have the discretion to refuse assent to successful referenda.

- That a Head of State may be removed by a motion passed in both Houses of the Parliament calling for the Head of State's removal for proved misbehaviour or incapacity.[358]

Australians should be given the opportunity of a referendum to amend the powers of the governor-general, recognising that as the Constitution is currently worded, the governor-general has powers which exceed that of the British monarch in relation to control over the parliament. Australians have no need of a governor-general in that capacity. And if there are some who would argue that there is a need for control over the parliament, or perhaps some adjustment of the balance of power between the parliament and some other constitutionally empowered state player, then that player should be the people (using constitutionally lawful processes). If the people are enabled as the source of sovereignty by the constitutional amendments suggested in Chapters 5, 6 and 7, and if the High Court is given sufficient guidance by the Constitution to determine whether a head of state has lawfully exercised a power to call an election or dismiss a prime minister or parliament, then there is less need to worry that power might go to a governor-general's head, as many think it did in 1975.

Essential No. 4c – Limitation of the powers of the prime minister

Those Australians who remember Remembrance Day 1975 will have an understanding of what vice-regal overreach can do. It can go so far as to create a constitutional precedent whereby a person elected by no-one can dismiss a government elected by the Australian people.[359] It is difficult to conceive of something more offensive to the principles of representative democracy, particularly if we consider that electing a government is one of the few things Australians can do under the Constitution – and yet it can be undone

---

[358] Australian Republican Movement, The Australian Choice Model: Proposed Amendments to the Australian Constitution, January 2022, page ii, Op. Cit.

[359] Remembrance Day 1975, The Dismissal, YouTube, https://www.youtube.com/watch?v=8K6WSFMj0fk

by a single person who can entirely disregard the people's expressed will. Constitutional reform to moderate abuse of power by a head of state in Australia's form of democracy is long overdue.

However, the abuse of power that can be caused by a prime minister is probably far more dangerous. Because the Constitution places no limitations on their power, prime ministers can directly imperil the lives of Australians inasmuch as they need not consult parliament about either entry into war or sacrifice of independence in sovereignty to a foreign power. In practice the prime minister may consult the executive council (cabinet) but the Constitution does not make such consultation obligatory and the reality is that a prime minister need seek no advice before committing Australia to wars that under international law are illegal – in other words, they breach the "rules based order" to which we claim to adhere. This has resulted in needless loss of life by both Australians and those we have attacked in countries that had not attacked our country.

Prime ministerial overreach has also been more alarming in the 21st century in regard to the permission Australia has given to the stationing of foreign military personnel and weapons on Australian soil, deployments which are increasingly likely to commit Australia to nuclear war – both in other countries and on our own continent.[360] It is to be hoped that such arrangements may be reversed and that sanity may prevail but in 2022, as I mentioned in Chapter 5, it was evident that Australia, in seeking to achieve a military force and capability that is "interchangeable" with America's, in countenancing the prospect of basing nuclear capable B-52 bombers in the Northern Territory's Tindal Air Base,[361] and in negotiating to accommodate foreign troops and long-range weaponry on Australian lands,[362] the

---

[360] Mike Gilligan, "Why Labor can't be trusted with Australia's security. It started with US Marines in Darwin", John Menadue's Pearls and Irritations, 8 November 2022.

[361] ABC, Four Corners, "How could a war between China and Taiwan play out?", YouTube, 31 October 2022. How could a war between China and Taiwan play out? | Four Corners - YouTube

[362] Australian Government, Minister for Defence Richard Marles, "Tenth Japan-Australia 2+2 Foreign and Defence Ministerial Consultations Joint Statement", 10

Prime Minister Anthony Albanese and his Deputy Richard Marles (as Minister for Defence) were endorsing the participation of Australia in America's nuclear war planning[363] without providing Australians with any indication that their views or the views of their elected parliaments would be sought. This disclosed a propensity to make decisions that can have (and may already have had) the effect of ceding Australia's independent sovereignty to a foreign power and exposing us to nuclear attack, to defencelessness in any attacks (conventional and nuclear), and to the possibility of being complicit in nuclear attacks on other nations.

For considerable periods of its history, Australia's decisions on war have disregarded its commitments under international law. We hold discernible double standards on this matter. For instance, in 2003 Australia entered the illegal Iraq War ostensibly because of a claim that Iraq had weapons of mass destruction. The propagandist claim was revealed to be untrue and yet Australia's Prime Minister John Howard acted as though the potential presence of such weapons justified breaking international law by invading Iraq. But almost twenty years later, as if we had reached a point where our

---

December 2022. Tenth Japan-Australia 2+2 Foreign and Defence Ministerial Consultations Joint Statement | Defence Ministers. Australian Government, Prime Minister Anthony Albanese, "Australia and Japan Strengthen Security Cooperation", 20 October 2022. Australia and Japan Strengthen Security Cooperation | Prime Minister of Australia (pm.gov.au). Australian Government, Department of Foreign Affairs and Trade, "Australia-Japan Joint Declaration on Security Cooperation", 22 October 2022. Australia-Japan Joint Declaration on Security Cooperation | Australian Government Department of Foreign Affairs and Trade (dfat.gov.au)

363 See Mike Scrafton, "US National Defence Strategy reveals Australia's nuclear deterrence role", John Menadue's Pearls and Irritations, 9 November 2022, on the release in October 2022 of the US National Defence Strategy (NDS): "In the context of the basing of US aircraft at RAAF Tindal the initiative to 'Modernise the B-52H Stratofortress bomber fleet through 2050 as a nuclear stand-off platform with global reach' is revealing. In sum, the NDS effectively confirms Australia's role in American nuclear war planning. It declares 'The 2022 National Defence Strategy is a call to action for the defence enterprise to incorporate Allies and partners at every stage of defence planning', including nuclear. ... The NDS is the dreaming of a slipping hegemon but reveals the potential nightmare of nuclear war for Australia. A public debate on defence policy is now essential."

hypocrisy knew no bounds, Australia itself began contemplating the possibility of hosting weapons of mass destruction, signalling a potential preparedness to break the binding international law treaty we signed in 1970, the Treaty on the Non-Proliferation of Nuclear Weapons (NPT). This Treaty committed Australia not to acquire nuclear weapons and to adhere to strong non-proliferation obligations.

Australia was, at least until the 2020s, one of the NPT's strongest supporters and in 1995 succeeded with other signatories in ensuring the Treaty was extended indefinitely.[364] Nevertheless in the 2020s, without consultation with the Australian people, the government began contemplating breaking a law it has considered to be vital since World War II (by contemplating acquisition and/or hosting of submarines and B-52 aircraft capable of launching nuclear weapons). As we have seen, this is fairly typical of the way Australian governments fail to adhere to the treaties they sign and casually flout the so-called (in effect, fabricated) rules based order[365] they pretend to revere. But were a federal government to fail to adhere to this particular Treaty (on nuclear non-proliferation), that would represent a whole new order of willingness to defy international law and act contrary to the interests of the Australian people, interests that we know from research discussed in Chapter 5 lie in peace not war.

In 2020, Roy Morgan Research conducted a nationwide poll for Australians for War Powers Reform in which it was revealed that

> 83.3% of Australians want Parliament to decide whether our troops are sent into armed conflict abroad … and only 16.7% said they favour the current system whereby the Prime

---

[364] Australian Government, Department of Foreign Affairs and Trade, "Non-proliferation, disarmament and arms control" webpage, last accessed 10 November 2022. Nuclear Weapons | Australian Government Department of Foreign Affairs and Trade (dfat.gov.au)

[365] See Paul Keating, "Australia and China: A Conversation with Paul Keating", La Trobe University Ideas and Science, 12 October 2022: "There is no rules based order. I mean, walk into Iraq – what rule was that? Or Afghanistan – what rule was that?"

Minister and the executive alone decide if Australia goes to war.[366]

Bearing in mind the risk to life in such decisions, it should be evident that any decision which exposes Australians to war without consultation is far more offensive to Australians than the former Governor-General's disregard for their democracy in 1975. In the dismissal of the interests of Australians that is exhibited by the government's willingness to contemplate placement in Australia of weapons that do not relate to its defence and are useful only in offensive war postures,[367] we can see a drama in play that is, or should be, far more shocking than the dismissal of a prime minister and the appointment of a leader of the opposition as caretaker prime minister.

In 1975, the caretaker prime minister fortunately faced a new election and the system of government was therefore fairly quickly restored. But with the current Constitution, no similar restoration of the stability and safety of the nation would be reliably attainable if a prime minister were to make a decision on a war that was contrary to the interests and wishes of Australians.

In general, the current Constitution is inadequate for purposes of protecting Australians from executive abuse of power, and not just on war. As I have shown in Chapter 6, we are exposed in relation to our human rights as well. To some extent the introduction of a people's constitution would help us overcome these risks, but if such a reform is not accompanied by constitutional amendments to some

---

366 Australians for War Powers Reform Media Release, "Huge majority of Australians support war powers reform", 2020. Microsoft Word - AWPR Release 26 Nov.doc (warpowersreform.org.au)

367 Bruce Haigh, "God save Australia because America will not", John Menadue's Pearls and Irritations, 10 November 2022: "These are offensive weapons of war and do not relate to the defence of Australia. ... Basing nuclear capable B52's in the Northern Territory with the express aim of targeting China puts Australia on a war footing. In fact, it amounts to an act of war. ... It will be Australia that pays the price. America will slink away whilst we will be hostage to war reparations and possible occupation. ... Sycophantic until jilted. A vassal state which neither China nor the US respects." https://johnmenadue.com/god-save-australia-because-america-will-not/

executive powers, we will not be able to escape the particular risk presented by the fact that the prime minister is not accountable to the Australian people on decisions about war – a risk which these days can quickly escalate to an existential one.

Amendments to curb executive power in relation to decisions on war have featured on the agendas of some political parties and the community based advocacy group Australians for War Powers Reform[368] has campaigned on the issue for more than a decade, as have groups such as the 2017 Nobel Peace Prize winner, ICAN Australia[369] and the Independent and Peaceful Australia Network, IPAN.[370] At the same time, though, advocates of a republic do not seem to have recognised a need to place any limits on executive power where abuse would present extreme risk to Australians. In seeking to obtain the consent of Australians to transform the nation into a republic, the proponents have not fully comprehended the breadth of the risk associated with unlimited executive power in the Constitution.

At present, unlimited "prerogative" power is vested in the queen or king and is exercisable under section 61 of the Constitution by the governor-general as her or his representative.[371] By convention these "prerogative powers are historically discretionary powers, not exercised on advice, although in practice they typically are".[372] This means they are typically authorised and therefore exercised by the prime minister. In convention, it is the prime minister who effectively exercises the prerogative power to declare war and peace. However,

---

[368] Australians for War Powers Reform, https://warpowersreform.org.au/

[369] International Campaign to Abolish Nuclear Weapons, ICAN Australia, https://icanw.org.au/

[370] Independent and Peaceful Australia Network, IPAN, https://ipan.org.au/

[371] Australian Government Solicitor, *Australia's Constitution with Overview and Notes by the Australian Government Solicitor*, page 18, Section 61: "The executive power of the Commonwealth is vested in the Queen and is exercisable by the Governor-General as the Queen's representative, and extends to the execution and maintenance of this Constitution, and of the laws of the Commonwealth." foi-2021-017.pdf (pmc.gov.au).

[372] Australian Republican Movement, The Australian Choice Model: Proposed Amendments to the Australian Constitution, January 2022, page vi, Op. Cit.

in their suggestions for amendments to the Constitution for the Australian Republican Movement, legal experts on their Constitutional Advisory Body did not recommend any change to section 61, stating instead that

> The prerogatives are mostly a matter of historical convention, and are in practice left unspecified. In the Constitution, they are included by implication in section 61, and our view is that they remain there.[373]

From this inaction on reform of prerogative powers, we can only infer that, even for proponents of a republic, it is not apparent that some sort of check and balance on the executive power to declare war and peace is a necessity. This may be due to views that minimal change to executive powers would be more likely to smooth the passage of a referendum on a republic. Executive governments are more likely to support such a referendum if it changes nothing about their power. However, this pragmatic approach, while politically astute, still leaves Australia with a constitutional model that will do nothing more than take the crown off the head of a king and put it on a head of state who in turn is likely to be permitted to act no otherwise than in accordance with whatever is permitted by the real power behind the new throne – the prime minister. Because of its silence on who has what prerogative power, the Constitution effectively leaves war powers in the hands of the prime minister. While a governor-general may be the nominal head of the army, there is no way she or he could actually mobilise or demobilise it. In all practicability, only the prime minister holds this power and nothing short of a *coup d'état* could negate it.

This means that if section 61 remains unamended, the prime minister will have more power than the queen or king, which might be relatively tolerable in lower risk situations. But it would not be tolerable when it comes to the power to mount a nuclear war. Nothing can fix a mistake on that matter and as such it is time for republicans and monarchists alike to come to grips with the life and

---

[373] Australian Republican Movement, The Australian Choice Model: Proposed Amendments to the Australian Constitution, January 2022, page vi, Ibid.

death necessity of checks and balances on that particular executive power.

Any government accustomed to keeping a grip on executive power will of course advocate for the status quo on this vital matter. They will mount any argument, no matter how false, to hone down the possibility of Australians' having a say on whether it is in their interests to go to war – false arguments like this one in 2022 from Andrew Wallace, the Liberal MP who was then the deputy chair of the defence subcommittee of the parliamentary Joint Standing Committee on Foreign Affairs, Defence and Trade:

> If we had a situation where the Greens are holding the balance of power in the Senate, or maybe even independents are holding the balance of power in the House of Representatives, someone who could be ideologically opposed to any conflict could act in a way which is significantly contrary to our national interests. ... The executive has got to be given the power to govern the country and particularly in relation to national security issues. I don't care whether it's Labor or Liberal – they can't be hamstrung by the parliament.[374]

This implies that advocacy for peace is contrary to the national interest. But it is actually Mr Wallace's argument that is contrary to the national interest. While he was inveighing here against the possibility of a single person – like an Independent or a member of a minority party – capturing the power to make a decision on war or peace, he was simply suggesting that we should retain the system where a single person is able to make the decision. It should be obvious that a single person should not make this decision. The whole country, or at least its elected parliament, should make the decision and make it based not on ideology but on a full and proper assessment of what is and is not in the national interest. Moreover,

---

[374] Liberal MP Andrew Wallace quoted by Daniel Hurst, "Coalition warns against requiring parliamentary vote to commit Australia to war", The Guardian, 5 October 2022.

Wallace's argument is utterly specious in that the single person he imagines would be able to block the war initiative would only have the power do so if an entire half of both houses of the parliament was already opposed to it. In a parliamentary vote, no one person could block a war, or start one for that matter.

It may be acceptable in Wallace's view of how a democratically elected executive government should work to say that "the executive has got to be given the power to govern the country". But the one instance where the executive should not be given that power is in relation to war, or more particularly, offensive war (war which is not in response to an imminent or actual attack on Australia). Wallace dressed up his assertions about executive decisions on war by renaming them as decisions on "national security", although this was nothing but a species of Orwellian doublespeak, given that nothing risks our national security more than a war. But the ultimate insult to the Australian people was that Wallace blithely asserted that executive power "can't be hamstrung by the parliament". If executive power can't be controlled by the parliament, why do we even have a parliament? Why don't we just become a totalitarian state? Wallace's argument should be regarded as a total insult to the Australian people inasmuch as it constitutes a complete rejection of the principle of responsible government whereunder the executive government is accountable to the parliament and through them to the people.

There is only one instance where it would probably not be in the national interest to have the executive power controlled by the parliament. That instance would be in the event of an imminent direct attack on Australia. In every other matter of our lives (vital and non-vital) it is absolutely in the national interest to have executive power hamstrung, or to put it more correctly, *confirmed* by the parliament as legitimate and consistent with the national interest. The parliament is there to ensure the executive government acts in the national interest. At present, however, Australia operates on a system where the national interest is determined (ad hoc and mostly in secret) by the executive without reference to the people. This is a system suited more to embedding Australia in wars, regardless of whether they are in Australia's interests and regardless of whether they secure the nation.

It is of little comfort that both major parties in Australia have preferred that what is essentially a form of totalitarian power be retained in relation to decisions on war. In letters on the considerations of the defence subcommittee mentioned above, Deputy Prime Minister Richard Marles did not even give the committee a chance to consider the issue before he stated firmly that the existing arrangements whereby governments can commit Australia to war without parliamentary authorisation should "not be disturbed". As The Guardian reported:

> Marles told the committee conducting the review that under the existing system, decisions about the deployment of the Australian defence force into international armed conflicts were 'within the prerogative powers of the executive'. ... 'I am firmly of the view that these arrangements are appropriate and should not be disturbed,' he wrote.[375]

This means nothing more than that this particular Deputy Prime Minister wishes to retain full capacity to act contrary to the will of the people. And given that at the time of his statement, 76% of Australians had clearly expressed a preference for Australia to sign and ratify the United Nations Treaty on the Prohibition of Nuclear Weapons (TPNW),[376] Marles could not have misunderstood that will. His statement unmasks the fact that the terms "executive power" and "prerogative power", terms that lawyers and politicians use so casually in their arguments for the marginalisation or disregard of parliament, are nothing more than pseudonyms for "absolute power" – absolute power to disregard opposition from the people and their duly elected representatives. Marles' disregard of the will of the people might be tolerable, were it not about their life and death.

---

[375] Daniel Hurst, "Australia's defence minister advises against giving parliament veto over military deployments", The Guardian, 10 October 2022.

[376] Ipsos Poll for ICAN Australia, 13 May 2022, New poll results - ICAN Australia (icanw.org.au)

As it stands in 2022, this issue of war powers is at the heart of the much broader issue about executive power and who should hold it. The common reading of the Constitution is that there are separations between the parliament, the executive government, the governor-general and the judicature which should help moderate the possibility of abuse of power and contraventions of the national interest. But in relation to war these assumed checks and balances have always been discarded. This should not be surprising since the whole basis of the modern state is that executive power is created for the purpose of autocratic determinations on whether a nation shall go to war or not. In effect, the modern state, with its centralisation of executive power in a single person, was conceived with no other particular purpose in mind. Although it has been adapted for purposes of promoting the common welfare of the people to the extent that might suit governments from time to time, the main purpose of the modern state as it originally took shape was to centralise decisions on war and vest the power to make them in one person, and this persists today in our case, with that power vested in a person who has done nothing more than take an oath to be loyal to a dead foreigner and her heirs and successors, not the people of Australia. Nothing in the Constitution limits the prime minister in decisions on the sacrifice of our lives in war, not even the national interest.

But in a world where war now means potential annihilation, particularly if it is a war between nuclear-armed superpowers, it is evident that it is no longer efficacious (if it ever was) to confine executive power on war or any other matter to a single person or even to a small council (especially a small council of politically motivated people subject to the will of corporate donors and foreign purveyors of weapons of mass destruction). What point is there in an executive power that is unconstrained on decisions that have the potential to annihilate the people who trusted it with that power? This is not the 17th century. Wars are more likely to work out very badly for all parties – and much worse than they did in the small wars that could be afforded by a few monarchs whose treasuries were built on plunder and murder of less wealthy peoples.

In the 21st century we have better options available than in the 17th and a far greater need to choose them. Accordingly, amendments to the Constitution to oblige the prime minister to consult the Australian people, or in an emergency to at least consult their elected parliaments, on all matters of defence, defence posture and military planning, and all declarations of war and peace, are essential amendments, given the risk of annihilation that may be faced by Australians and anyone else caught up in the catastrophe of war.

Essential No. 4d – Elimination of racism in Australian law

There are many ways in which the culture, demography and political arrangements of 21st century Australia bear no resemblance to the idea of the nation its founders attempted to establish by formulating the Constitution in 1901. But the most obvious mismatch is between the original idea of Australia as a white colony subject to a Victorian era monarch and the post-war multicultural nation that we became.

The drafters of the Constitution could hardly have foreseen that their racist attitudes and the laws that underpinned them would become as irrelevant as they did to modern Australia, especially to the economic prosperity we came to enjoy by opening our doors to immigration. Nevertheless, the racist provisions in the Constitution have lingered and continue to cast a shadow over law in Australia that has held Indigenous nations back from achieving equality in health, wellbeing, and political influence. Those provisions also threaten the political and economic equality of non-Indigenous people but this is more a theoretical threat since constitutional lawyers have found that

> there are no laws on the federal statute book, nor is it apparent that there have ever been, that apply the races power to groups other than Aboriginal and Torres Strait Islander peoples.[377]

---

[377] Megan Davis and George Williams, *Everything You Need to Know About the Uluru Statement from the Heart*, UNSW Press, 2021, page 114.

As such, it seems Australian lawmakers have thus far reserved their practical application of discrimination in law uniquely for Aborigines and Torres Strait Islanders. Since Federation, at least 35 pieces of legislation have been enacted nationwide which affect Indigenous Australians.[378]

The racist provisions in the Constitution are mainly located in sections 25 and 51 as follows:

> Section 25. Provisions as to races disqualified from voting
>
> > For the purposes of the last section, if by the law of any State all persons of any race are disqualified from voting at elections for the more numerous House of the Parliament of the State, then, in reckoning the number of the people of the State or of the Commonwealth, persons of that race resident in that State shall not be counted.
>
> Section 51. Legislative powers of the Parliament
>
> > The Parliament shall, subject to this Constitution, have power to make laws for the peace, order, and good government of the Commonwealth with respect to: ...
> >
> > > (xxvi) the people of any race for whom it is deemed necessary to make special laws.[379]

The presence of these sections in the Constitution means that

> Australia is now the only nation in the world with a Constitution that contains a clause that empowers a national Parliament to discriminate against a group on the basis of race.[380]

---

[378] Wikipedia: (Incomplete) List of laws concerning Indigenous Australians, last accessed 14 November 2022.

[379] Australian Government Solicitor, *Australia's Constitution with Overview and Notes by the Australian Government Solicitor*, pages 11 and 18. foi-2021-017.pdf (pmc.gov.au)

[380] Megan Davis and George Williams, *Everything You Need to Know About the Uluru Statement from the Heart*, UNSW Press, 2021, page 110.

Decades of debate on this matter have resulted in broad acceptance of the need to remove the racist provisions but the debate has not resolved the issue of how to remove them so that we do not end up reintroducing the possibility of adverse discrimination or cutting off access by Indigenous peoples to direct, positive assistance from the federal government. Attempts to solve this problem culminated in 2012 in a proposal from an Expert Panel on the Recognition of Aboriginal and Torres Strait Islander Peoples in the Constitution, established by the Gillard government, to insert a new section 116A as follows:

> Section 116A. Prohibition of Racial Discrimination
>
> 1. The Commonwealth, a State or Territory shall not discriminate on the grounds of race, colour or ethnic or national origin.
> 2. Subsection (1) does not preclude the making of laws or measures for the purpose of overcoming disadvantage, ameliorating the effects of past discrimination, or protecting the cultures, language or heritage of any group.[381]

However, the views of the Indigenous community on the utility of this provision shifted after the High Court in the case of Maloney vs The Queen ruled that a Queensland law prohibiting Indigenous people from possessing alcohol was discriminatory but nevertheless permissible under the Racial Discrimination Act.[382] Given the High Court's unwillingness to challenge the parliament's primacy in determining what can justify racial discrimination (and that there can be a justification), it should therefore not be surprising that those who attended the First Nations Regional Dialogues for the Uluru law reforms did not consider it worth prioritising the repeal or replacement of the races power. According to Megan Davis and George Williams,

---

[381] Megan Davis and George Williams, *Everything You Need to Know About the Uluru Statement from the Heart*, UNSW Press, 2021, page 118.

[382] High Court of Australia, Maloney vs the Queen, [2013] HCA 28; 252 CLR 168; 87 ALJR 755; 298 ALR 308.

> This was because the alternative forms of wording can never prevent racially discriminatory adverse laws. Whether it is a 'peoples' power or 'subject matter' power or whether there is a preambular statement that seeks to confine the power to beneficial laws using words such as 'advancement' or 'for the betterment', there is no iron-clad guarantee that can be made that the power cannot be used for adverse purposes. Consequently, at Uluru it was determined that for the races power, the change [a new section 116A] is no better than the status quo. As a result, Indigenous peoples did not prioritise amending or repealing the races power as a meaningful form of constitutional recognition.[383]

In short, Indigenous nations were left high and dry again, this time by the frame of mind of the High Court and its apparent inability under the current Constitution to protect them from racial discrimination.

However, if we come back to the fact that there is broad acceptance that the racist provisions should be removed,[384] it is incumbent on Australians to find a way to safely remove them, particularly given the high likelihood that there would be advantages for Indigenes and non-Indigenes alike. To remove the races powers safely, it is likely that we would have to question the above contention by Davis and Williams that

> there is no iron-clad guarantee that can be made that the power [of new beneficially expressed laws] cannot be used for adverse purposes.

---

[383] Megan Davis and George Williams, *Everything You Need to Know About the Uluru Statement from the Heart*, UNSW Press, 2021, page 116.

[384] Megan Davis and George Williams, *Everything You Need to Know About the Uluru Statement from the Heart*, UNSW Press, 2021, page 112: "The Expert Panel recorded overwhelming community support for deleting sections 25 and 51(xxvi). Of the submissions it received that referred to these provisions, 97.5 per cent supported the repeal of section 25, while 94 per cent supported change to the races power. Independent polling conducted by the Expert Panel of the community at large also found that 73 per cent of respondents were in favour of removing these provisions."

I will leave aside any scepticism that iron clad guarantees may be provided by laws, being hitherto of the same persuasion as Samuel Butler that "in law, nothing is certain but the expense",[385] especially when the laws are made under a Constitution which provides little or no guidance on some matters for those required to issue judgements on what a particular law might or might not legitimately "guarantee" for an affected race. However, if the objective in making amendments to the Constitution is to seek out the safest course of action for protection of the people to whom the laws made under it shall apply, then we might contemplate the possibility that a statement of human rights might offer judges a basis for their judgements – a basis that guides them on what could or would be adverse to the interests of the people for whom a law is made. First Nations people in the Regional Dialogues for the Uluru Statement did not warm to the idea of judges deciding what is and isn't in their interests. For them, the Maloney case

> elevated concerns that the scope of section 116A would be determined entirely by the justices of the High Court. Attendees raised the issue that a non-discrimination clause deferred decision-making to justices who may have never set foot in an Indigenous community and yet would determine what is in the best interests of Indigenous women and children. It was also thought that if justices were going to defer to democratically elected representatives as they did in Maloney, then section 116A did not amount to a sufficient protection of Indigenous peoples from racial discrimination.

This is a valid objection but it nevertheless provides a clue as to how the problem might be solved. If the problem is that it is dangerous to delete the races provisions from the Constitution without inserting a clause like section 116A to prohibit adverse racial discrimination, and if there is a desire to avoid any downsides of a clause along those lines that may arise from judges (or a parliament for that matter) taking it upon themselves to determine what is in the best interests of Indigenous people, then conferral of a right of self-

---

[385] Samuel Butler, *Life and Habit*, 1878, Cambridge University Press 2009.

determination on Indigenous and non-Indigenous people alike would be likely to provide a means by which judges could limit the risk of discrimination either by the courts or parliaments against any particular set of people in the population (Indigenous and non-Indigenous). In other words, any law made by a parliament that denies what Indigenous people determine for themselves as being in their best interests is not in their best interests and should be disallowed by the courts.

The approach here would change the basis on which courts may seek to provide protection to First Nations people from discrimination by a parliament, such as the discrimination that occurred in the Northern Territory Intervention or in the Maloney case mentioned above. At present the courts would appear to assume that they have no basis in law that they can rely on to protect Indigenous peoples from adverse discrimination by a parliament. But a right of the Australian people to self-determination in the Constitution may provide that basis, inasmuch as people of a particular race who are adversely affected by a discriminatory law would (if necessary) be able to argue that the law is abusive of that right. Conversely, they could argue that a law may only be proved lawfully discriminatory if the racial community affected by it decided for themselves that it was in their best interests. Such an arrangement for this degree of self-determination could be facilitated if a First Nations Voice were enshrined in the Constitution and if local Indigenous Voice vehicles were established according to a design satisfactory to First Nations peoples.

This machinery of an Indigenous Voice, established alongside an enshrined right to self-determination for all, would create an avenue by which the courts may at the very least refer any adversely discriminatory law back to the parliament for review via a democratic Voice process. This in itself would create a new framework which would appropriately limit the capacity of *both* the parliament and the judiciary to decide what is in the best interests of Indigenous people. It would provide a means by which the courts could justify their decisions consistent with fundamental human rights laws. By this means we could finally put away the long outdated and now plainly preposterous notion that authorities like parliaments or courts have a right to decide what is in the interests of any peoples on the basis of race. Under the Universal Declaration of Human Rights and its attendant Covenants, neither parliaments nor courts have that right, although they have both carried on as if they do for decades in their debates as to which one of them is more entitled than the other to paternalistically determine the interests of Indigenous peoples. The preferable course from this point, given that there is now little if any support for racism in lawmaking, is to set Indigenous groups up so that they can organise themselves as they see fit to determine their best interests.

The above suggestion for safe deletion of the racist provisions in the Constitution may not (initially, at least) satisfy First Nations that the federal government would still be able to make laws that positively benefit them so that past injustices can be redressed and the adverse discrimination they have experienced can be eliminated in future. However, were we to contemplate inserting a national agreement on human rights and obligations into the Constitution in the form proposed in Chapter 6, that would confer on the parliament a constitutional obligation to uphold the rights of Indigenous peoples by making beneficial laws that advance their interests sufficiently to address inequalities and past injustices. For instance, Article 1 of the International Convention on the Elimination of All Forms of Racial Discrimination makes such positive discrimination lawful as follows:

> 4. Special measures taken for the sole purpose of securing adequate advancement of certain racial or ethnic groups or individuals requiring such protection as may be necessary in order to ensure such groups or individuals equal enjoyment or exercise of human rights and fundamental freedoms shall not be deemed racial discrimination, provided, however, that such measures do not, as a consequence, lead to the maintenance of separate rights for different racial groups and that they

> shall not be continued after the objectives for which they were taken have been achieved.[386]

And, of course, the United Nations Declaration on the Rights of Indigenous Peoples (UNDRIP) confers on governments and Indigenous peoples a capacity to devise laws which benefit the Indigenous members of the nation. In particular, Articles 21, 22, 23 and 46 and make it clear that positive discrimination to ameliorate the inequalities and injustices Indigenous peoples have suffered from colonisation and dispossession of their lands, territories and resources is a legitimate form of human rights protection and is not discriminatory. Indeed, had Articles 21 and 22 been adhered to at the time of the Northern Territory Intervention (although Australia had not signed the UNDRIP at that time), a far better culturally attuned remedy could have been developed simply because it would have required the government to work with the Indigenous community to determine the best way for the state to fulfil its obligation under the Declaration to take "special measures to ensure continuing improvement of their economic and social conditions" and to ensure that "Indigenous women and children enjoy the full protection and guarantees against all forms of violence and discrimination."[387]

In short, if Australians were to choose to grant themselves the benefit of their human rights under the national agreement on human rights and obligations suggested in Chapter 6, a solid basis could be provided in the Constitution that would enable the High Court to be sure that in its judgements it was acting in the legitimately declared interests of Aborigines and Torres Strait Islanders and that it was furthermore well positioned to counsel the parliament to confer with Indigenous peoples respectfully in the making of laws that affect them. If the Constitution obliges the parliament to do that – by enshrining both an Indigenous Voice and the right of self-determination – then all quandaries about whether a law is actually

---

[386] International Convention on the Elimination of All Forms of Racial Discrimination, Article 1. International Convention on the Elimination of all Forms of Racial Discrimination [1975] ATS 40 (austlii.edu.au)

[387] United Nations Declaration on the Rights of Indigenous Peoples, 2007, Articles 21 and 22, Op. Cit.

in the best interests of Aborigines and Torres Strait Islanders should be easily resolved. More than that, they should be resolvable in a manner that ensures that the making of a law for Indigenous protection or advantage is not discriminatory to *any* group (Indigenous or non-Indigenous) and is a balanced reflection of the rights of groups engaged in furthering the nation's interests as a whole. Such an adjustment of the Constitution would also provide for a peaceful coexistence of sovereignties.

The Labor government's first commitment on winning office in the 2022 federal election was to implement the Uluru Statement from the Heart in full.[388] It followed up swiftly with a proposed wording for enshrining an Indigenous Voice in the Constitution.[389] This was not, however, accompanied by an acknowledgement of the need to delete the races powers in the Constitution. It is obvious that if the Voice is enshrined but the races powers persist – and persist in a form that hamstrings the High Court into decisions that allow discrimination to persist – then this will significantly slow the pace by which Aborigines and Torres Strait Islanders will be able to access the benefits of the Voice. The Voice will allow Indigenous Australians a greater measure of self-determination than they have had to date but not as much as they need if they are to overcome the disadvantage they currently suffer. There is no doubt that the enshrined Voice is a vital step but the Constitution itself will hamstring the Voice of First Nations if it is not revised holistically so that it enshrines human rights for all. In that context, an enshrined Indigenous Voice should be considered as the first of many steps in Constitutional reform and a steady program for this reform should be established. I will talk more about this in Chapter 9, but for the moment all Australians would benefit if we focussed on the elimination of racism in our laws. Clearly these laws provide a platform for parliaments to behave in a racially discriminatory manner.

---

[388] Anthony Albanese acceptance speech on attaining government, 21 May 2022, ABC News, https://www.abc.net.au/news/2022-05-22/anthony-albanese-acceptance-speech-full-transcript/101088736

[389] Lorena Allam, "Anthony Albanese reveals 'simple and clear' wording of referendum question on Indigenous voice", The Guardian, 30 July 2022.

Escaping racism by embracing self-determination

It is fundamental to Australia's future as a cohesive, fair and prosperous society that the racist provisions in the Constitution should be repealed. But to ensure a safe repeal, Australian parliaments and executive governments will need to release some part of their grip on the paternalistic power they have enjoyed and, sadly, often misused under the current Constitution. The part of their grip on power that needs to be released is the part that prevents Australians from exploring what they can do for their communities with self-determination. Australian governments need to let go of their paternalism here. This does not mean that they would lose legislative power or the final word on laws. But it would immensely enhance their wisdom and in fact would release them from their own enslavement to a system that has proved sclerotic for purposes of the changes and progress Australians have called for.

From the perspective of the electors, refusal by the elected to countenance self-determination as a positive feature of our democracy is regrettable, to say the least. It would be different if governments were doing a better job. But on too many measures they are not,[390] and it is entirely foolhardy for them to assume that they could continue to use that system of government – in its current form, without the benefit of coherent guidance from Australians – and expect that things would turn out as Australians wish. Overcoming this will entail an accommodation on the part of elected federal parliamentarians – they will need to stop viewing self-determination as a threat.

Self-determination is not a threat either to stable governance or to the power of the elected, although as a distributed system of power it does challenge the centralised system of concentrated power (power gravitating away from local communities towards the Commonwealth) within which federal politicians typically prefer to

---

[390] For a comprehensive insight into the plight of Australia and our performance on measures of wellbeing, view Australian Community Futures Planning, The State of Australia 2022: End of Term Report, 46th Parliament of Australia, March 2022. https://www.austcfp.com.au/state-of-australia

define themselves as superior and successful. But leaving that threat to their egos aside, self-determination may be viewed in an entirely positive light as a straightforward reform that has more capacity than any other to enhance the effective functioning of the state. As such, it is time that politicians and Australians both began exploring what it can do for them.

Self-determination is mystifying to those who prefer more authoritative and controlling power systems but it is nothing more than a simple capacity that we all want and need. It is nothing more than the right to exercise at least some authority over policy development and service delivery. And to give effect to an appropriate quantum of that authority, it merely requires some simple institutional arrangements at all levels of government, (federal, state and local) as they interact with communities, and at all levels of regional cohesion (such as the boundary of an Indigenous Nation's traditional lands or an assembled community's interest). These simple institutions are not mystifying and to the extent that they already exist, we use them every day for the purpose of securing wellbeing. However, they could be better organised to facilitate orderly and more effective self-determination by distinct communities of interest and distinct cultures. A good example of the simplicity of this approach is the New Zealand social policy measure, Whānau Ora. Launched in 2010, it has developed:

> a form of self-determination in which *whānau* (families) can:
>
> - be self-managing
> - live healthy lifestyles
> - participate fully in society
> - confidently participate in Te Ao Māori [the Maori world]
> - enjoy economic security and successful involvement in wealth creation
> - be cohesive, resilient and nurturing

- be responsible stewards of their living and natural environments.[391]

This institutional model of distributed power demystifies self-determination entirely. It displays the fact that self-determination is not a threat to power at all, it is merely a capacity enhancement mechanism. But it is one that

> emphasises progressive advancement rather than the management of adversity, and focuses on functional capacities.[392]

In that vein, self-determination emerges quite obviously as the missing ingredient in the national project. It makes space for us to look forward and plan, rather than to react. This is the ideal basis for a National People's Voice along the lines of that proposed in Chapter 7, a voice – or rather a panoply of voices – that can be spread out and enabled at all levels of community engagement across the country to work within a nationally agreed project implementing the sovereign will of the people of a vast nation.

It is also a voice that politicians need to hear if they are to succeed. There is absolutely no way politicians will succeed unless they acknowledge the people's fundamental right to self-determination and thereby give us the capacity to organise ourselves to lead the lives we choose. Of course, to bring about that necessary acknowledgement, those who seek political office will need to shuffle off the mindset of their own superiority. This, however, need not entail a destabilisation of the state. It will simply require an adaptation by the federal government to the fact that the people of Australia do have a will of their own, both as individuals and as a collective, and that this will is a force for realisation of the common aspirations we hold for the future. The task for a federal government,

---

[391] Dominic O'Sullivan, *We are All Here To Stay: Citizenship, Sovereignty and the Universal Declaration of Human Rights*, Australian National University Press, 2020, pages 119-120, Op. Cit.

[392] Dominic O'Sullivan, *We are All Here To Stay: Citizenship, Sovereignty and the Universal Declaration of Human Rights*, Australian National University Press, 2020, page 120, Ibid.

if they can acknowledge this, then becomes a very simple one. They simply need to seek out the genuine will of the nation and then adapt their sphere of power to ensure that will is realised. This is only likely to be as difficult as federal governments choose to make it. Smart governments will grab the opportunity to reorganise their relationship with Australians. Or they can choose to impose their will as they did in 1901. Readers may judge for themselves which of those courses is futile and which will open the road to the full democracy to which Australians are entitled.

Moving towards a people's constitution

Throughout this book I have tried to simplify a path to empowerment of Australians in their own democracy. I have focussed on suggestions for a new Constitution which would facilitate inclusion of the people as the source of the sovereign will but with a view to increasing the stability of the state rather than destabilising it. This has resulted in proposals for the three major alterations described in Chapters 5, 6 and 7 and discussion in this Chapter 8 about the need for reform in another four areas – reforms that would be the minimum necessary to ensure that the three major additions to the Constitution will actually provide Australians with a reasonable share of power alongside the parliaments they elect. The objective has been to create a space where all those empowered under the Constitution are invested with a reasonable share of power – a share sufficient to ensure that the nation's project for the future, whatever it is, can be advanced in the interests of all, not just some, and that each empowered entity can play their full and, more importantly, their rightful part in democracy without abusing the power vested in them or the rights of another empowered party.

In developing the suggested reforms I have assumed a broadened structure of the current Constitution:

1. A Statement of Australian Values along the lines of the draft proposed for consultation in Chapter 5 would be the centrepiece of a new preamble to the Constitution. This could be built upon by community engagement and added to

if constitutional lawyers thought more was needed in terms of clauses to create a proper legal foundation for the new state that would be built by this Constitution – the Australian people's sovereign state. A special feature of this Statement would be that because it adds Indigenes into the centre of the Constitution, it would provide a full recognition of First Nations peoples, creating a basis for their equality with all Australians in political, civil, economic, social and cultural rights, and thereby creating the basis for reconciliation (treaty), a coexistence of sovereignties and a sufficiently powerful Indigenous Voice.

2. A National Agreement on Human Rights and Obligations and a National People's Voice along the lines of the drafts proposed for consultation in Chapters 6 and 7 respectively would form a new Chapter I in the Constitution, an addition which would effectively push back all the remaining chapters in their current order in the Constitution, changing the current Chapter I to Chapter II, Chapter II to Chapter III, and so on. The new chapter would be titled "Chapter I – The People", or preferably, "Chapter I – The Australian Sovereign People". As with the new preamble, the draft content of the people's chapter could be built upon by community engagement and added to if constitutional lawyers thought more was needed in terms of clauses to create a proper legal foundation for the people's sovereignty of the new state that would be built by this Constitution. The new Chapter I would also be the ideal place for the Aboriginal and Torres Strait Islander Voice, should the people of Australia support that in a referendum. Any other statements of recognition for First Nations in the Constitution would also be likely to find their most appropriate home in either the people's chapter or the new preamble.

3. Amendments to the existing chapters in the Constitution, including in the four areas I have suggested in this Chapter 8,

should be the subject of a new program for ongoing constitutional reform.

It may appear that insertion of a preamble and new chapter into the Constitution which offers power to the people of Australia is a threat to those who have enjoyed exclusive power under it since Federation. Specifically, the additions may appear as a threat to the federal parliament and executive government, the states and the governor-general. But in fact, while the proposals may specify some limits to the powers of the prime minister and the governor-general, they take nothing away from the powers of the elected Commonwealth parliaments, executive governments or the states. They simply offer the full share of a new type of power to the people – a power that is not being exercised by anyone at the moment and which, in any case, no-one is lawfully authorised to exercise. In this proposed new constitutional arrangement the people are accorded the power to voice their aspirations – the power to say what they want to become as a nation. They can fill a gap in power with something that is absolutely necessary to democracy – the rightful power of the people to express their sovereign will.

Moreover, so far from being a threat to elected parties, a people's constitution would enhance and properly legitimise the power of all parties to that old Constitution, compared to the power they can legitimately exercise now. It would enhance the way power can be used to effect the outcomes that all Australians want and to accelerate the speed with which they can reach those desired outcomes. Put simply, there is a very strong argument that a people's constitution would enhance the capacity of Australia's democracy to deliver a stable future for the nation. Any country that wishes to be a democracy needs to call on and politically enable the full capacity of all its members. Otherwise it isn't a democracy at all.

That said, the practicalities of shifting from a 19th century constitution for a colonial monarchy to a 21st century constitution for a people's sovereign state will present a logistical challenge. By this I do not mean some sort of challenge in legal drafting. Lawyerly quibbles about the feasibility of a people's constitution in law will be expected, but lawyers know full well that we can draft any laws we allow ourselves to draft and if we accept that the Constitution is the property of the Australian people and can only be approved by them, then “law” or “legality” have no place as a valid obstruction to the people’s right to craft the central law that shall govern how all other laws may be validly made.

The real logistical challenge is in development of a program for open and orderly engagement of the Australian community on revision of the Constitution for purposes of creating the arrangements of state that they want. This challenge, however, need not be insurmountable. With a degree of good will and genuine commitment to community engagement it can be managed with decency and even create great excitement about the nation we can become. In the next chapter I will sketch a possible program to smooth the path to empowerment of the Australian people by respectful engagement with them.

Part 3 – The path to empowerment of the Australian people

Chapter 9 – Processes for engagement on and adoption of The Australian People's Constitution

The time has come for Australians to engage with the possibility of establishing and affirming their own rightful share of power in the Constitution. More than that, it is time to claim that rightful share before our democracy is weakened any further, particularly by corporate influence and loss of political and civil rights. However, the processes by which Australians might alter their Constitution are fraught with obstructions. Some of these obstructions are legal in nature but these can be overcome more easily than the obstructions that will arise from politics.

On the face of it, Australians appear to be in control of their Constitution, since they are the only ones who can confirm a change to it. Nevertheless, the fact remains that they are the last to get the opportunity to do that because the Constitution itself provides the basis for political obstruction. To achieve a constitutional change, enfranchised voters must exercise their obligation under section 128 to vote in a referendum. But while section 128 of the Constitution offers them a deciding role with one hand, it takes it back again with the other by interpolating a process by which parliament must first come to majority agreement on any proposal to be put to the people.

As I have already mentioned, Geoffrey Sawer once declared that, constitutionally speaking, Australia is the frozen continent. And since only eight referendum questions have succeeded since 1901, he would appear to have opined correctly. Robert Menzies, in his best patrician manner, laid the blame for this at the foot of the Australian people by remarking that, "to get an affirmative vote from the Australian people on a referendum proposal is one of the labours of

Hercules." But it is much more likely that the fault for this long freeze lies with politicians themselves who either fail to develop proposals which do something other than enhance their own power relative to the people or fail to come to any agreement at all on proposals that should be put to the people. It is almost as if the minute a proposal comes forward which looks like it might be something that would create a more inclusive and democratic Australia, the politicians themselves lose all concern for anything but their own overweening share of power. It is politicians and not the people who will hoard in their clans to scuttle inclusive reforms, and section 128 aids and abets them in this obstruction.

However, the Constitution does not prohibit Australians from developing other procedures for constitutional reform. It does not prohibit the formation of citizen-led revision processes. A proposal by a parliament for an amendment need not be the sole starting place for change. Nor, as Helen Irving has pointed out, does section 128 limit Australians to piecemeal amendments. It is only politicians that are doing that. As Irving has said,

> The reality is, and has been for a good while, that Australians alone own their Constitution – all of it. They wrote it. Section 128 permits them to alter it.[393]

And Irving is not alone in this view. As far back as 1983, former Attorney-General Gareth Evans and others stated that,

> There is the possibility ... of simply making a fresh start with a brand new 'We the people ...' constitution, one having no continuity with its predecessor and owing nothing to the ultimate [and now defunct] authority of the British Parliament. Although amounting to a 'legal revolution', this sort of thing has happened in too many countries around the world for it to be dismissed as wildly implausible.[394]

---

[393] Helen Irving, *Five Things to Know About the Australian Constitution*, Cambridge University Press, New York, 2004, page 116.

[394] John McMillan, Gareth Evans and Haddon Storey, *Australia's Constitution: Time for Change?*, Law Foundation of New South Wales, Allen and Unwin Australia, 1983, page 358.

At the same time, Evans *et al.* envisaged that a referendum could achieve what amounts to an instant severing of all constitutional ties with Britain,

> by inserting into the Constitution new provisions which stated simply that UK laws ceased thereafter to apply in Australia, and that sovereignty was vested in the Australian people.[395]

So there it is. With referendums permissible under section 128 we can even go so far as to vest sovereignty in the Australian people. Fundamental reforms are possible if the Australian public wishes and quite feasible legally if politicians can bring themselves to get out of the way of the type of constitutional reforms that would be in the public interest – as well as their own. As I have already said, politicians would benefit in terms of their own conscience, their standing in the community, the legitimacy of their agendas, and their potential for longevity in office if they were to champion a re-balancing of power in democracy that would arise from the introduction of a specified share of power for Australians in their own governance. They would benefit if they paid more than lip service to the Australian people as the true source of sovereignty.

That said, it must be acknowledged that the likelihood that parliaments will come to agreement on a referendum proposal which might give electors the chance to consider whether they wish to *specifically* vest sovereignty in the Australian people is low. Many politicians find mere talk about a republic (where sovereignty would transfer from the British monarch to the parliament or the head of state, *not* to the people) unsettling enough, and so those who are more seriously discomforted by the thought of shuffling off the monarchical form of state would probably suffer apoplexy if asked to contemplate the possibility of the people being specifically acknowledged as the rightful source of sovereignty in Australia's democracy.

---

[395] John McMillan, Gareth Evans and Haddon Storey, *Australia's Constitution: Time for Change?*, Law Foundation of New South Wales, Allen and Unwin Australia, 1983, page 359.

But this does not mean that Australians themselves cannot *initiate* reform proposals along those lines. They can do that already under the Constitution and have done so to some extent, for instance, by the formation of groups like the Australian Republican Movement, Citizens for Democratic Renewal,[396] #OurDemocracy,[397] and the Australian Democracy Network.[398] In other words they can establish their own citizens' assembly to initiate constitutional reform, with or without the endorsement of parliament, and can set out a wide program of reform (wider than, say, amendments to create a republic). In fact, in the case of a comprehensive program of constitutional reform it is arguable that it would be better if they established such a forum without the endorsement of parliament, inasmuch as the independence would lend credibility to the apolitical nature of its deliberations. Nevertheless, were a parliament to willingly endorse an independent assembly of citizens to facilitate – that is, *to lead themselves* in – their own nation-wide conversation on options for a constitution for a 21st century Australian sovereign people's state, there is no reason why Australians should knock back the offer. It would be an unlikely offer but it should nevertheless be welcomed, as long as it does not politicise deliberations (or expose them to corporate interference).

Evans *et al.* envisaged that legislation could easily be established for this purpose in that the Commonwealth has the power in that regard. The "legal revolution" cited above for a completely new constitution could apparently be realised by

> the Commonwealth legislating – with or without the consent of the states – to create a new constituent assembly (perhaps in the form of a people's Convention) that would draft and then either ratify itself, or put to a referendum to be ratified, a new Australian constitution.[399]

---

[396] Citizens for Democratic Renewal, https://www.democraticrenewal.org.au/

[397] #OurDemocracy, https://www.ourdemocracy.com.au/

[398] Australian Democracy Network, https://australiandemocracy.org.au/

[399] John McMillan, Gareth Evans and Haddon Storey, *Australia's Constitution: Time for Change?*, Law Foundation of New South Wales, Allen and Unwin Australia, 1983, page 364.

But while this option is therefore legally feasible, it is also politically unlikely. And even if it were suddenly adopted as a political preference, a people's constitutional convention along one of the lines described above – that is, with power to ratify the terms of a new constitution *without a referendum* – would be entirely at odds with democracy. It would overturn the whole principle of section 128 which offers Australians the only power they have to define the parameters of law and policy – the power to have the last word on what shall and shall not be in their Constitution. Constitutional change without a referendum would also be out of kilter with the whole concept of vesting sovereignty in the Australian people and would therefore be unsuitable as a means of legitimately facilitating a transition to a full democracy. If anything, it might risk reinvesting sovereignty in a quasi-monarchical state (like America – a monarchy without a monarch) which makes no place for the voice of the people and gives them no greater power as shapers of their own future. It underestimates the scope of such a project and the ongoing involvement that will be necessary for those who, if they succeed in establishing a people's constitution, will find themselves to be members of probably the first western nation to be asked to take on both the power and the responsibility that comes with being a member of a full and sincerely inclusive democracy.

Obviously when Evans and Irving suggested the Constitution could be remade, they were thinking of a rather smaller concept of democracy and a narrower project of reform. Irving for instance assumed that the people are already sovereign inasmuch as the Constitution at least rests on a notion (albeit unspoken) that they are, and that this is evidenced by the fact that governments cannot be formed otherwise than by their consent.[400] But this does nothing to lift our perceptions and understanding of what sovereignty means in a full democracy. It shows what sovereignty means in a constitutional monarchy where once a government is elected all control is lost by

---

[400] Helen Irving, *Five Things to Know About the Australian Constitution*, Cambridge University Press, New York, 2004, page 89. "The Constitution rests upon the sovereignty of the people … their consent is the ultimate authority for government …"

the electors. In a full democracy, however, sovereignty entails much more in terms of opportunity and responsibility for involvement on policy and the direction of the nation. It entails the exercise of a voice beyond a vote. This makes it vitally important at the outset of any 21st century constitutional reform for Australians to be given the space to understand what could be achieved by a democracy that rests on an inclusive people's sovereignty rather than on a monarchical form of government. Australians should be given a neutral space in which to consider what life might be like in a system of governance in which the legitimate form of sovereignty is acknowledged as the people – and, specifically, the people acting in a form of state that is recognisable and understood as *the many in the one* rather than the one over the many.

In the 21st century, the whole concept of sovereignty has been undergoing a transformation. It has been shifting, slowly but steadily, from a *supposition* that sovereignty is something granted to a government (in whatever form) by the consent of a willingly submissive people, to a *proposition* that it is something to be shared by people who can exercise self-determination in political equality. This shift is not yet widely discussed, much less recognised as the paradigm shift that it is, but it has been brewing in the growing calls for citizen collaboration on decision-making[401] and, most importantly, has also been brought into clarity by the debates held internationally that resulted in the formation of the United Nations Declaration of the Rights of Indigenous Peoples.

Since the Uluru Statement was released in 2017, Australia has moved into a position where it is occupying the centre of the stage on which the next major scene is being played out in the debate about what sovereignty has meant in the past and what it can come to mean in the future. Australia's First Nations have led the way by grappling not just with what sovereignty should mean but also with what it can do for them if a *coexistence* of sovereignties can be achieved. In effect, a coexistence of sovereignties – where the power of self-

---

[401] Parliament of Australia, "Citizens' engagement in policymaking and the design of public services", Research Paper no. 1 2011–12. Last accessed December 2022.

determination is considered the equal right of all – can save lives and help Aborigines and Torres Strait Islanders "walk in two worlds",[402] as they must if they are to survive with a level of wellbeing that offers recognition and dignity. As Professor Dominic O'Sullivan has observed, the United Nations Declaration on the Rights of Indigenous Peoples

> helps societies to conceptualise what further capacities and powers shared sovereignty might entail and offers protections against the uncertainties of majoritarian democratic exclusion. Shared sovereignty is present when Indigenous values substantively influence public policy.[403]

The Declaration has certainly helped Indigenous Australians conceptualise what shared power in public policy can offer them. But it can do just as much for non-Indigenous Australians, not so that they could "walk in two worlds" of course, but because they would be able to accept in good conscience and with joy the fact that Aboriginal and Torres Strait Islander culture is "a gift to their country".[404] Not for nothing did Anthony Albanese celebrate the privilege that it is to live alongside the oldest continuing civilisation in the world, as he did in his acceptance speech on winning office in the federal election of 2022:

> Together we can be a self-reliant, resilient nation, confident in our values and in our place in the world. And together we can embrace the Uluru Statement from the Heart. We can answer its patient, gracious call for a voice enshrined in our constitution. Because all of us ought to be proud that amongst our great multicultural society we count the oldest living continuous culture in the world.[405]

---

[402] Uluru Statement from the Heart, Appendix 1.

[403] Dominic O'Sullivan, *We are All Here To Stay: Citizenship, Sovereignty and the Universal Declaration of Human Rights*, Australian National University Press, 2020, page 110, Op. Cit.

[404] Uluru Statement from the Heart, Appendix 1.

[405] Prime Minister of Australia, Anthony Albanese, ABC News, "Read incoming prime minister Anthony Albanese's full speech after Labor wins federal election", 21 May 2022, Op. Cit.

But to capitalise on this gift, Australians will need space to come to understand it for what it is. The gift is a form of sovereignty that we may conceptualise as the opposite of the Hobbesian concept of sovereignty, in that its whole focus is on inclusive decision-making but within a stable and efficient democratic process. In that new conceptualisation, it is not a radical overthrow of our current governance arrangements. It is not a displacement of representative democracy. Nor is it disruptive or discontinuous with the form of state which has thus far empowered parliaments, governments and the judicature. Instead it may be viewed simply as an augmentation of the sphere of power, achieving order by inclusion rather than exclusion. And it may also be viewed as a significant increase in the efficiency of the processes of democracy. If viewed in this way, it might be apparent that the opportunity to create an inclusive, fully democratic governance system is likely to be more attractive to Australians in a referendum process than piecemeal amendments, such as a republic, that have not been integrated with a wider reform program that makes sense of them.

The fact that Australians remain lukewarm about a republic more than two decades after they rejected the form proposed by the Howard government might be explained (although only in part) by the Australian Republican Movement's assessment that it is the model of how a head of state should be selected that is the sticking point for Australians, rather than whether we should have an Australian head of state. The ARM has stated that

> Polling and research have consistently shown that more of us are for a republic than against it, but when voters are asked to support a general proposition about a republic it achieves a bare majority. We know the model is the main variable because when asked about specific proposals, support varies dramatically: varying between one third and two-thirds in favour. 92% of Australians are open to the idea of a republic, with only 8% opposed to any form of change.[406]

---

[406] Australian Republican Movement, "The Australian Choice Model", January 2022, page 1. "ARM polling Dec 2021. Only 8.3% of respondents indicated

Staunch monarchists, of course, see no reason why we need disavow the British monarch and they will accordingly assert that there is no need to change anything about our colonial constitution. But it is likely that time and tide are against them and if a way can be found to put the decision about who shall be appointed as Australia's head of state into the hands of Australians, this is likely to improve the chances of success in a referendum on a republic. That said, it would be wise to recognise that the idea of a republic has not yet excited Australians much and it would be worth exploring why – because it may not be that that the model of how the head of state may be selected is the only problem.

Why has the broader idea of an Australian republic failed to inspire people? One possible answer is that, in the forms offered so far, a republic has not offered them much more in terms of power and control than they already have. And for as long as it is framed as a project which is about selecting our own governor, it is not likely to be perceived as offering much beyond symbolism. In that form, it amounts to nothing more than an offer to replace a figurehead in the existing exclusive system of government with another figurehead in the existing exclusive system of government.

Of course, this ignores the fact that the Australian Republican Movement is actually proposing more than that by way of reforms because it is suggesting amendments to scope down the power of the new head of state. And there is no denying that the symbolism itself would be very valuable to Australia, inasmuch as the change would enhance our capacity to project an image of Australia and its people as independent and self-reliant. For these purposes, a republic is an essential reform. But for those who are not up for the challenge of independence and self-reliance and for those who will gain nothing in terms of inclusive power, something more will be needed to attract them to enthusiastic support for a republic. That something should be the prospect of more control over their own lives and a greater sense that they will have at least some power to help create a nation

---

universal opposition to all model options presented." The Australian Choice Model - Detailed Policy 2022 (squarespace.com)

that they and their children will actually wish to identify with, a nation in which their unique life will have meaning, a nation to which they will always wish to belong.

The forms of a republic along any of the various lines proposed to date do not offer that sense. And if we wish to engender a greater enthusiasm for a republic and for the mature, self-reliant, independent state it implies, then the whole republican project needs to be contextualised as part of a reform designed not just to strengthen the existing system of power (so that a governor-general cannot exceed or abuse her or his reasonable share of power), but also to establish a share for those who shall eventually be governed by whomever they elect to represent them. If a constitution could be established that allows Australians to attain a share of power sufficient to guide those that they permit to govern, then that would give them a reason for greater enthusiasm about a republic, a reason to consider it less risky or less dull, and a reason to think that a project of national independence – like a fully democratic republic – would be worth the effort. It would give them a reason to hope that they would no longer be confined simply to having the first and last word on who shall govern them for good or ill but would also be able to organise themselves to have the first and last word on what constitutes governing for the good.

Obviously, what I am saying here is that if Australians are to be asked whether they wish their country to become a republic and if a government wants an answer in the affirmative, then the question should ideally be couched in a wider question of whether they wish to become a people's sovereign nation and whether within that they wish to accept a greater share of power than they currently have. In other words they should be asked if they wish to become a full democracy. These are vital questions because there is no doubt that in determining whether they wish Australia to become a republic, Australians will look to the experience of other nations that have made the transition from a colony to an independent state and will not wish to repeat their mistakes. Most notably they will look to America and its mistakes. They will sift through the strengths and weaknesses of the American system, especially because it is the most widely publicised and easily assessable system of democracy in the world, and it has been in place long enough for everyone to see which parts of it no longer work well for the purposes of a liberal democracy and which, by contrast, have endured the test of time in terms of their capacity to protect the freedoms and liberty for which the whole project of American independence was fought in the first place.

With America's experience of democracy being so openly played out, many Australians will recognise that a republic may offer them the chance to shuffle off colonialism but they will be naturally shy of reforms which appear to do little more than make them jump out of the frying pan into the fire. For very good reasons, caution will be as evident in a referendum on a republic as it has been in every other referendum. To assume otherwise would be to mistake the Australian people as unthinking in such processes, when in fact they give serious thought to each of these choices, as their engagement in both voting and opinion polling shows. Politically disengaged they are not when the issue at hand is actually about their prospects for the future, including the future of their democracy. Often this caution is mistaken for apathy when it is more likely to be the result of a failure by political leaders to excite the people about what the reform offers them. If it offers them a greater and fairer share of power in their democracy, it is very likely to excite them. By contrast, if it offers nothing more than a centralisation of power it is very likely to result in reactions ranging from boredom to deep suspicion.

If politicians need any proof for this, they need only examine the tenor of referendum questions they have put to Australians since 1901 and the success rates they have achieved. Of the 44 referendums held in Australia, 13 were merely technical in nature but 26 were little other than attempts to centralise power and only five could be classed as amendments offering the possibility of greater inclusion in the political system.[407] Of the 26 that would centralise power, only two were approved by referendum. These two were the referendums in 1946 to extend to the Commonwealth power to

---

[407] For a breakdown of national referendum questions see "Referendums in Australia", Wikipedia. Last accessed 18 November 2022.

provide social service benefits and in 1967 to extend the power of the Commonwealth to make laws for Aborigines and Torres Strait Islanders and count them in the census. In short, they proposed to centralise power but for the purpose of increasing inclusion and wellbeing; they did not simply centralise it for its own sake. Australians could see the democratic value of these two amendments and unambiguously signed off on them. The failure of the other 24 questions strongly indicates that Australians are not enamoured of further centralisation of power.

Of the five questions offering a more inclusive political system, only one which enabled ACT and Northern Territory electors to vote in referendums was carried. None of the five were offered before 1974 and it is deeply regrettable that from the late 1980s onward, Australians appear to have become so disenchanted with their leaders that even when they are offered something that might improve their parity with those they elect they have simply felt unable to trust the offer. Obviously, Australians are not likely to agree to constitutional changes with governments they don't trust. Trust is the first prerequisite to constitutional change and Australian governments have a long way to go before they establish a sufficient stock of it.

These reactions from Australians in referendums suggest strongly that:

- unless parliaments and governments can acknowledge the likely failure of piecemeal proposals which simply centralise power and/or offer no benefit in terms of sharing power more democratically, ***and***
- unless they can establish their credentials as trustworthy,

they will continue their record of failure in referendums. On the other hand, if governments choose to inspire Australians with an agenda offering the prospect of an inclusive democracy – one in which their participation will be not just tokenistically welcomed but practicably worthwhile – then they can significantly improve the prospect of success in referendums. This potential increase in the success rate would be likely to apply to any referendum question which offers the prospect of greater political equality. Questions that fit that description would include any that facilitate recognition of First Nations, statements of national values, agreements on human rights and obligations, and voices for all Australians. Questions about a republic may or may not fit well with an agenda for a full democracy. It would depend, as I have said, on whether they admit Australians into a fairer share of power. This suggests that if constitutional reform to strengthen Australia as a full democracy is to be a success, it is important to get the order of the questions right first. It will be important to scope a logical program of considerations for the establishment of a people's sovereign state.

To consider this wider reform agenda about whether we want a "We the people" constitution – whether we wish as a nation to become a full democracy where the people are sincerely acknowledged as sovereign – the community of Australia will need space. Such a wide ranging reform, whether it comes before a referendum on a republic or after it, will require a machinery for well-informed community engagement that is open to all, is efficient, and is comfortably distanced from political and corporate interference. In other words, Australians will need to be confident that such a process is independent and fully accessible and that the sequence of reforms is taking them along an orderly path to a place *they* want to go. Practical approaches to that sort of engagement are discussed below.

Practical approaches to community engagement on a people's constitution

The most useful and essentially democratic mechanism in Australia's constitution for its alteration is the referendum, and this should be the means by which we continue to confirm all alterations. But with a people's constitution we are not talking about piecemeal amendments. We are talking about a systematic review for which a logical and holistic program of review should be scoped *before* consultation begins and well before we reach the stage of referendums. Some options for organising that program include establishment of:

- a constitutional commission (something that could be done by the federal government or parliament), or
- a community-driven people's constitutional convention (not originated by the government or parliament but also not sponsored through corporate donations).

The former would benefit from the imprimatur of government; the latter would benefit from the distance it can maintain from governments. The former would benefit from an obviously secure source of funding but suffer from the taint of political interference whereas the latter would probably suffer from unreliable funding but would benefit from the sense of its being a project the community owns.

Bearing in mind that these benefits and disbenefits are pretty well evenly balanced, the least risk option is probably to seek a kind of hybrid model where the facilitation of national engagement is reliably funded (namely, by the federal government) but independently chartered to organise and transparently report on the deliberations of independent citizens' assemblies, each of which can be charged with considering whatever reforms have been programmed for establishment of a people's constitution.

This would suggest that a charter could be issued, perhaps by the Senate, to a group of suitably independent facilitators of a national collaborative process for design of a new Constitution. This group could start the process by scoping what the project of constitutional reform can be about – in other words the priority items for consideration by the citizens' assemblies. An efficient way to do that would be for the group to develop an issues paper which sets out the key factors in the Constitution that are affecting the capacity of Australians to use their democracy to its fullest potential to build the nation they want and to ensure their wellbeing and security into the future. This paper could also include examples of the benefits that may be obtained from a constitution designed *by* the people *for* the people – benefits which include but are not limited to the chance to establish:

- agreed national values;

- agreements on human rights and obligations;
- a voice for First Nations, a voice for all Australians and a collaborative mechanism for building a future together;
- a fairer distribution of powers;
- a safer system of decision-making on national security;
- an abandonment of racism and discrimination;
- an expression of what constitutes the permissible use of power in the public interest – the terms of trust on which power is granted by the people to those they elect; and
- a social contract which expresses what level of wellbeing and security electors and elected alike have agreed to work towards together.

From this sort of paper it is likely to emerge that Australians have two main choices about the shape of their democracy. Those choices are fairly simple to isolate because the country is at a pivotal point in terms of which direction we might want to take our democracy. We can choose to:

a) support the current form where sovereignty is handed to a government in elections without terms of trust; or
b) seek a new form where the people are openly acknowledged and participate as the source of sovereignty and increase their role in democracy by describing the purposes for which power will be exercised by those they elect.

In other words we can choose to stick with a merely representative democracy where the people have no voice beyond voting, or we can add in a new participatory capacity combining systems of a national voice and voting. This is a national conversation that must precede all others about reforms of the Constitution. And if as a result of that conversation there is discernible support for the second path **b)**, then the next logical step would be to commence an Australia-wide round of conversations to build a people's constitution. The above-mentioned group of independent facilitators could then be charged with organising what we might call the National Collaborative Process for Development of the Australian People's Constitution. They could scope a program of conversations about reforms in a logical sequence.

The National Collaborative Process for Development of the Australian People's Constitution

In determining the level of support for the second path (path **b)**) that might be necessary at the outset, we need not and should not restrict ourselves to a requirement for majority support. Were we to do that we would simply be taking our democratic process back towards the limits imposed by the current section 128 and back towards a system of exclusion. It would be to give up on strengthening democracy before we even start. It would cancel the process of democracy itself.

In any case, given the number of groups and organisations that have been established since 1975 in attempts to strengthen democracy and curb abuses of power, it would be a surprise if there were no support at all for a process to explore options for a people's constitution or wholesale rejection of the idea as a waste of money. Support for exploring the option of a people's constitution is most likely to come from groups who have suffered from the exclusive power structures of the current Constitution or who fear that they will suffer in the future if they do not find a way to exercise a greater share of power or political influence. But even if this initial conversation does not inspire the majority of Australians about the possibilities of an inclusive democracy, there is no reason in democracy to shelve the conversation. After all, the whole idea is to introduce some measure of protection for everyone from abuse and discrimination, and this is not a project that can be justifiably shirked by any government claiming to be democratic. In a democracy, majority support need only be required to confirm the final wording of that nation's constitution, not to start a debate about that form. As such, unless large numbers from all sectors of the community (male, female, LGBTIQ+, Indigenous, non-Indigenous, disabled, immigrant, employed, unemployed, carer, etc.) put forward compelling reasons as to why such a conversation should not be had at all, we would be justified as a nation in insisting that the process proceed to the next stage.

One other reason for establishing a National Collaborative Process for Development of the Australian People's Constitution is that such a process has proved successful in the past – in the case of the Referendum Council which was established by former Prime Minister Malcolm Turnbull and Opposition Leader Bill Shorten in 2015. This Council ran thirteen Regional Dialogues to discuss options for constitutional reform for recognition of First Nations and was designed to ensure that Aboriginal and Torres Strait Islander decision-making was at the heart of the process. The Dialogues functioned openly and very efficiently and culminated in 2017 in the development of the Uluru Statement from the Heart – a statement which no doubt will prove to be a historic moment in Australia's transition from a colonial outpost to an internationally respected, inclusive democracy. Based on the Uluru Statement, the government established a co-design process for the Aboriginal and Torres Strait Islander Voice, which in turn led to the announcement by the newly elected Labor Government in 2022 of an intention to hold a referendum seeking the support of Australians. The Referendum Council's process for the Regional Dialogues and the co-design process can serve as a model for this much wider process of collaboration on the design of an Australian people's constitution.

To sum up, Australia's current Constitution is not a barrier to development of a new constitution by the people for the people. Nor do we lack examples of models which would assist Australians to efficiently collaborate on its design. We have the means and the know-how. It is to be hoped therefore that were the people to put it to their federal parliament that there is an opportunity for this sort of reform and that it would vastly benefit electors and the elected alike, this would be received positively by the parliament. Any government proposing referendums on a constitutional Voice for First Nations and a republic should see that they can increase the chances of success in such referendums if they take up this sort of collaboration with Australians. We can stop the big freeze if we work together. We can be that "self-reliant, resilient nation, confident in our values and in our place in the world" that Anthony Albanese spoke of. We can start again and make Australia anything we want it to be. But if there is a will to do that, we will need to start soon.

The time for constitutional reform

The time for constitutional reform is now. In fact we are running a little late for the purpose, if lateness is defined by the point at which our time is running out.

In the same way that time is running out for the peoples of the world on climate change, time is running out for democracies of the world on the rights and freedoms they must be able to access in law if they are to secure permission to keep their democracies and strengthen them. Australians in the 21st century have shifted from being able to take it for granted that our governments would accord us rights and freedoms in good faith to a position where such faith is no longer justified by the evidence. Too many rights and freedoms have been wound back, particularly rights to protest. And too much state secrecy has been permitted – so that it now shields governments from exposure on the extent to which they have become beholden to unelected corporate power. It might be different if this corporate power – in its composition as a military, industrial, financial and resources sector complex – were not operating so wholly against the public interest and propelling the world to a level of exploitation, destruction and consumption that is far in excess of planetary capacity. But the excesses of multinational corporations are already well past the point of safety for humanity.

It is possible that these excesses may yet be wound back and perhaps even wound back in time to avert some of the wars and the higher degrees of global heating we might otherwise expect. But this will depend on whether governance systems can be developed which can control the destructive influence of these inhuman corporations.

Governance systems which enable as many of us as possible to responsibly exercise power for the good of all will be the single-most effective instrument we can devise to stem the massive human and environmental impacts of corporations. But the trend in the 21st century has been towards disempowerment. In that regard we have lost quite a lot in terms of human rights. But we have not yet lost too much of one of the great privileges of living in a democracy – the privilege of taking responsibility for ourselves and participating actively in building a community in which each of us can safely attain an acceptable degree of wellbeing and a reasonable share of national prosperity. Freedom in that particular privilege is still available.

That said, we need to get a move on before it too is gone. It is more than 25 years since one of Australia's most thoughtful leaders, Paul Keating, warned of the need to take more control in our democracy when on Remembrance Day 1996 he addressed the University of New South Wales and said:

> After all, what does democracy mean if not the right, the privilege, the chance to take responsibility? And when you've got a democracy like we have, why settle for anything less than taking it? For remember this – if we lose momentum, if we drift or retreat, if we begin to let fear, ignorance or prejudice govern us – it won't be me or my generation who pays the greatest price. We'll drop off the back of the cart. It will be young Australians who will have to ride it into the 21st century – and just now I reckon they should be seriously planning the means by which they can get hold of the reins.[408]

Decades have passed and it appears we did lose the momentum, we did drift. But in that period we can also observe the rise of very well-organised activist groups, community-based research groups, interlocking networks for community cohesion on particular issues, online communications instruments for connection and shared knowledge, and even the development of a means of planning a better future for a diverse nation – one in which they can "get hold of the reins" as Keating might say. Many in his generation have since dropped off the back of the cart but the young of Australia are actually better equipped than in the 1990s in the technical knowledge – in science and the humanities – that they can freely access and

[408] PJ Keating, "For the New Australia", *After Words: The Post-Prime Ministerial Speeches*, Allen and Unwin, Sydney, 2011, page 156.

share, and in the means of forming connections with each other that are necessary to increase their impact on our increasingly secretive and exclusive governments.

It is not too late for Australia's democracy, but it will be if the current generation does not seize every opportunity to reform it. A people's constitution is one of those opportunities not to be missed. So it is to be hoped that those members of the older generations who have not yet dropped off the back of the cart can join with young Australians and ensure their democracy is designed to enable them to take hold of the reins.

Chapter 10 – The possibilities of a new democracy under a people's constitution

Sydney, December 2022

Australia can establish a safe and prosperous future for all its peoples but only if it reconstitutes itself as an inclusive, full democracy – one in which the people have their rightful share of power and can establish a much better relationship of trust and productive collaboration with those they elect to represent them in parliament. The current Constitution cannot make that possible simply because it excludes the people from their essential share of power – the power of self-determination – and from the agency that can only be exercised if they and their will are fully and respectfully acknowledged as the source of the sovereignty.

General opinion is that the Constitution is based on an idea that representative democracy, if combined with adherence to a principle of "responsible government", will somehow be sufficient to safeguard the public interest and protect the people from abuse of power by the elected (and by any unelected head of state). But in reality the Australian Constitution is silent on democracy (representative or otherwise) and on responsible government, and is equally silent on the public interest and obligations of parliaments and governments to the people. Opportunities for disregard of the national interest and abuse of power abound under the current Constitution.

In its silence about the people of the nation – except in reference to the fact that their consent is periodically needed in elections for a handover of power and their consent is needed in referendums for a change to the Constitution itself – the current Australian Constitution does nothing more and nothing less than reduce the Australian people to subjection to a sovereignty that has no reciprocal obligation to them. Power as it is arranged in the Constitution is for their subjection, not their self-determination, and when this is combined with the fact that the public interest features nowhere in the Constitution (it is not described in any terms and isn't even mentioned as something to be respected) we have the makings of a distribution of power that amounts to little more than the tyranny of the few – a very tiny few.

On the surface, our representative democracy appears to be among the stronger and more advanced in the world but not only does the Constitution fail to underpin that strength, it also opens our democracy to threat. Over the decades since 1901 the Constitution has been easily undermined by a series of laws and court cases that have left it seriously weakened in terms of the protections it should provide against abuse of power. I have recorded in earlier chapters no less than five major High Court rulings where it has become apparent that the judicature – which is supposed to be able to ensure that the parliaments and executive governments operate in accordance with the Constitution and do not abuse their powers – has found itself unable to protect Australians from racism, human rights abuses, breaches of international law, and political exclusion, particularly by federal governments that have been able to force through laws that legitimise their power to behave in a manner most 21st century Australians would consider to be abhorrent. In short, the Constitution allows the making of laws which undermine political equality in our democracy. As such Australia does not have a structure in its polity capable of controlling the abuse of power. Nor does it have a democracy capable of supporting Australians as they attempt to chart a safe course to a better future.

Australia's future prospects depend on whether it can mobilise the full capacity of its population. And to succeed in this regard we will need as a minimum to ensure that every single one of us is included in society with full and equal political, civil, economic, social and cultural rights. As it is worded now, the Constitution does not facilitate that inclusion. And until such time as it:

- affirms our most sincerely held values as an indissoluble nation (the values that hold us together and define what we stand for);
- enshrines our human rights as equals;
- transparently sets out the government's obligations to the people in observance of those rights; and
- provides a guarantee that any and all of us shall be able to have a voice in how the nation should chart a course to a better future,

the Constitution will not be an enabling instrument for Australia's advancement either as an economically fortunate or democratically advanced country.

Throughout this book I have asserted that if our democracy is to be strengthened to the extent necessary to release the full potential of our social capital, Australians will need to be able to establish terms of trust with those they elect. A key objective in this has been to improve the quality of relationships between those who currently have no power under the Constitution (once they have voted) and the tiny few who currently have it all. Those relationships cannot be improved unless terms of trust between the electors and the elected are specified – and specified in a manner that grants the people a reasonable share of power as a player, or preferably as an acknowledged rightful and equal partner with other essential players in our representative democracy. By this I do not mean that the people should be accorded an overweening share of power. That would result in an obviation of representative democracy. It may risk replacing the tyranny of the few, under which we currently suffer, with the tyranny of the many – and if the many have no efficient way of organising themselves it is likely that Australians would be no happier under that arrangement.

Fortunately, though, it is not necessary to introduce a new tyranny to the structure and workings of our democracy. There is no need to destabilise representative democracy itself. We simply need to add a deliberative capacity into it so that we can overcome the worst shortcomings of a purely representative system. We need to add our voices to our votes. We need to build a representative democratic framework in which our consent to be governed by a parliament can still be freely and willingly granted, but on terms of trust that specify what for us counts as decency and fairness in both the relationship between the electors and the elected and in the national project itself. This has led me to suggest that it is a necessity for everyday Australians to be able to assemble themselves so that they can develop those terms of trust into what should amount to a coherent statement about the sovereign will of the people.

This statement should contain two different types of expression of the sovereign will – that is, it should enshrine:

- some constants – things that are likely to be constant through time; and
- an acknowledgment that aspirations – things which are likely to change through time – are also central to the will of the people and should therefore be expressed and taken seriously enough to form the basis of the agendas of the parliaments we elect.

In relation to the constants, the Constitution should contain commitments that the Australian people and those they elect are both willing to affirm as central to the sovereign will of the people because they are fundamental to our humanity. Our human rights and obligations to each other fall into that category if we accept that they are the natural birthright of all. And since we know that it is the Australian government's official policy that human rights are indeed universal, indivisible, inherent (as the birthright of all human beings, enjoyed by all simply by reason of their humanity rather than granted or bestowed), and inalienable (in the sense that they cannot be given up or taken away), we should be able to expect that no elected member of parliament will have difficulty in joining with the Australian people in affirmation of those rights and obligations. In fact the Constitution should enshrine our right to demand that affirmation.

Our values as members of the Australian nation also fall into this category of things that are likely to be fairly constant through time.

For instance, we might assume that peace is an enduring value, as is democracy. However, regardless of which values Australians finally settle on, they too should be affirmed by both electors and the elected and oaths of office should be developed which reflect commitment to those values.

In relation to aspirations, the important thing is to ensure that the Constitution enables us to express them and express them in a manner that enables parliaments and governments to scope policies and legislation that will maximise our chances of realising those aspirations. In short, the Constitution should enshrine what I have called a process for expression of a national people's voice, in addition to an Indigenous Voice. Both these voices must be enshrined if parliaments are to have the best chance of comprehending the full character of the new nation that would emerge under a people's constitution and the full significance of its expressed sovereign will.

That will, once it is expressed, is likely to paint a picture of Australia's future as a post-colonial, post-monarchical nation where political equality is the foundation of stability in the democracy. This should pertain particularly if the sovereign will is enshrined as a combination of national values, human rights and obligations, a national voice and an Indigenous Voice. With that combination of empowering commitments, Australians can give themselves the best chance to overcome the limitations and destructive aspects of representative democracy inasmuch as they will have the potential to install a fuller system of responsible government than we have now.

At present, Australians may take it for granted that we have a system of responsible government because as the Australian Government Solicitor has said:

> Under this principle, the Crown (represented by the Governor-General) acts on the advice of its Ministers who are in turn members of, and responsible to, the Parliament.[409]

---

[409] Australian Government Solicitor, *Australia's Constitution with Overview and Notes by the Australian Government Solicitor*, page v. foi-2021-017.pdf (pmc.gov.au)

But it is an unfortunate feature of this description of our system for responsible exercise of power that the responsibility appears to stop at the parliament. There is no mention of accountability extending through from the parliament to the people. They may as well not exist once they have voted. However, if we can find a way to add the people into the picture, creating a loop of accountability which ensures that not only is power shared but is shared responsibly, then the basis for collaboration and mutual respect between partners to that collaboration can be established. This will jettison our current form of state – the Hobbesian, unitary sovereign state – but not in such a way as to rob the society of an orderly form of governance. The combination of values, rights, obligations and voices, once enshrined, can circumvent the problems that may arise from more disruptive – shall I say, revolutionary or incendiary – approaches to reform of governance because it expands the power of a player who currently has none and makes that player integral to the deliberations of those who in the end must make the decisions on laws and policies. In that arrangement, disorder – with all its implications of turmoil, inequality, discrimination, and the demise of democracy – is avoided. The effect can only be to strengthen Australia's democracy.

Champions of constitutional reform have for decades called for the inclusion of a statement of Australian values and an affirmation of human rights in the Constitution. But the suggestion that the people – Indigenous and non-Indigenous – be given the power to voice their aspirations in a coherent statement of their preferred national project, *and* to have their values, rights and voices acknowledged by those they elect as the sovereign will, is a step the nation may take that is well beyond previous ideas of how democracy may be strengthened. It might be regarded as a quantum leap in the evolution of democracy and as the final confirmation that it is the form of government most likely to be truly of the people, by the people, for the people.

This extra step will be essential to Australians and to those they elect for a number of reasons, not least of which is the fact that time is running out for Australians to protect themselves from further loss of rights, further threats to their security in times of international conflict, and further disasters due to climate change. But it is also likely to be essential if Australians are to be able to restore their health and wellbeing to levels enjoyed prior to the attacks on our social security system sponsored by governments and corporations touting neoliberal policies of privatisation and deregulation. Those policies have been designed to systematically reduce – possibly to zero – any obligation governments have accepted in the past to provide for the economic, social and cultural wellbeing of Australians. However, in what might be reasonably taken to indicate a rejection of governments that seek to evade obligations to people, Australians happened to elect a new federal government in 2022 which campaigned on a policy of building wellbeing. And true to its word, that government began to speak of the need for a national conversation on wellbeing and how it might be secured. As the Labor government's Treasurer Jim Chalmers signalled on the introduction of his first budget in 2022:

> I am hoping that the Australian people are up for a serious conversation about how we pay for the services that they need and deserve and have a right to expect.[410]

Mr Chalmers was speaking in the context of needing to make decisions about the extent to which Australians should fund these services by taxation and in that context the conversation that might be expected is likely to be much narrower than the conversations necessary to develop a more secure future for Australia. But unless a national conversation on wellbeing can be conducted in the context of what wellbeing actually means for Australians, then a Treasurer is not likely to achieve much more than a grudging acceptance by taxpayers that they will be required to foot the bill for whatever services the government is prepared to include in what will probably be dressed up as a "wellbeing budget" but which may not deliver the sort of wellbeing Australians actually want. By contrast, conversations which start from the point where Australians are asked

---

[410] Federal Treasurer, Jim Chalmers, Press conference, Blue Room, Canberra, 11 October 2022. Press conference, Blue Room, Canberra | Treasury Ministers

what they want in terms of wellbeing are far more likely to result in a specification of a standard of living that can be financed with the willing consent of Australians. As such, if the Constitution includes a requirement for governments to enable those sorts of conversations on an ongoing basis, as though they are part of a normal cyclical dialogue about how to best fund the whole national project at the lowest long run cost, then those governments are more likely to position themselves to realise the aspirations of Australians and everyone is likely to get more value for their money. Everyone is also more likely to protect the interests of future generations. This implies that the sort of national conversation desired by Mr Chalmers will be more likely to benefit Australians (and governments themselves) if it is preceded by a process of collaborative development of a national long term integrated plan – a planning process that may only be securely established if it too is preceded by an acknowledgement in the Constitution of the value of the voices of Australians.

Aside from the potential of a people's constitution to offer Australians the benefit of a safer passage to a sustainable future where wellbeing and security are reliably available for all, there is of course one other major benefit that can accrue. We can achieve a coexistence of sovereignties based on self-determination. With a people's constitution power can be distributed to enable diverse people and groups of people to find a way to live and prosper together. For those who prefer the monarchical form of a sovereign state this is likely to be very challenging. But this is where the privilege of living alongside the oldest continuing culture in the world comes to our aid. Their tragic experience of dispossession has led First Nations peoples to a deep understanding of the value of self-determination – an understanding that is both intellectual and visceral. As Dominic O'Sullivan has observed, the Indigenous peoples of Australia know that it is essential to their survival that they be able to count on their right to self-determination. Constant and free exercise of that right is fundamental to their political capacity to "contribute equally to working out the terms of their membership of the nation-state".[411] They must also "have the capacity to exercise self-determination within their own political structures." Those structures, which are likely to be organised at the level of local Indigenous communities, can easily and productively sit alongside the political structures of the nation state to deliver a level of wellbeing to Aborigines and Torres Strait Islanders that they have hitherto been denied in their subjection to a state which simply has not recognised them at all.

Non-Indigenous Australians can learn much from this. They can learn, for instance, that self-determination is an enabling, even invigorating right, and they are as much in need of it as Indigenous people. It empowers individuals and peoples but without denying their absolutely essential dependency on each other. As Professor O'Sullivan has said, "Self-determination is not absolute autonomy." It "constitutes reconciliation" as a "politics of possibility":

> One knows that self-determination is occurring when indigenous peoples find that there is a reconfiguration of state power opening new and meaningful spaces of political opportunity. Those spaces are opened when public sovereignty is truly the people's authority and when all people—not just some—share that authority and have a meaningful say in determining what it means to be a citizen—what it means to be one who deliberates.[412]

In this rendition of Indigenous knowing, we can gain an insight into what it means to live in a democracy, the privileges it showers on us and the responsibilities it simultaneously imposes. For those politicians of the future who aspire to the privileges of democracy it should be evident that all they need to do to attain and hold the privilege of elected office is to be willing to share both power and responsibility with the people who elect them and to share it in a

---

[411] Dominic O'Sullivan, *We are All Here To Stay: Citizenship, Sovereignty and the Universal Declaration of Human Rights*, Australian National University Press, 2020, page 128, Op. Cit.

[412] Dominic O'Sullivan, *We are All Here To Stay: Citizenship, Sovereignty and the Universal Declaration of Human Rights*, Australian National University Press, 2020, page 128, Op. Cit.

deliberative framework – a framework in which rational discourse is made possible by the accessibility of collaborative planning processes and simple respect for the voices that are exercised within those processes.

Contemplating this framework, we may imagine a new democracy – one which offers the possibility of living our values to the fullest. With a people's constitution that enshrines values, rights, obligations (or call them responsibilities if you will), and voices – Australians can set themselves on a path to empowerment that will enable them to secure the future they actually want, a future of wellbeing, safety, security, connection and love – in other words, a truly indissoluble commonwealth. Realisation of this commonwealth is vital to our survival in the face of global heating, violence and economic disruption. But that realisation will require Australians – the electors and the elected alike – to identify with their constitution, to see themselves in it, and most importantly to recognise the coexistence of their sovereignties – the sovereignty of the peoples who sprang from the ancient heart of the land alongside the sovereignty of the people who came from elsewhere to make their home here – the sovereignty of the many in the one.

That sort of coexistence can only be achieved if the people are written indelibly into their own Constitution and until they are, until they own it, until they are acknowledged and acknowledge themselves as the source of sovereignty, the oath that those elected to parliament may take will be as hollow, unreliable and faithless as the oath they swear now to Queen Victoria, her heirs and successors. Australians need those they elect to take an oath to be loyal to them and to their Constitution, just as the Australian Republican Movement has suggested.[413] But until we are ready to *own* a people's constitution, until we can see that we are the centre of it, that *we* and those we love are the purpose of the nation and of its formation as a diverse indissoluble whole, the elected will be taking an oath that is as false as the one they are required to faithlessly mouth now.

---

[413] Australian Republican Movement, The Australian Choice Model: Proposed Amendments to the Australian Constitution, January 2022, page iii, Op. Cit.

If as a nation we wish to start again, and this time give ourselves the best chance that *all* our children and *all* those we love will flourish, there is no better time to accept the gracious invitation from First Nations to walk with them towards a better future. Our willing assent to a people's constitution which enshrines our political equality by means of enshrining our values, rights, obligations and voices is the key to that better future. We are limited in taking up this invitation to empower all our selves only by the extent of our imagination. We are not limited by any lack of means, practical incapacity, or legal strictures. We are not even limited by political short-sightedness. That will always be present but it need not obscure the truth for us – the truth that our nation is what we make it.

Our constitution makes the nation. It makes us as a unified "we". But that does not mean it governs us. Instead, we govern it. We are its masters and in re-writing it we can make it and the nation into whatever we want – at the behest of our own sovereign will. And we can keep re-making it in whatever shape we think necessary.

Manning Clark may have imagined and hoped in 1977 that the bitter experience of Australia's First Nations may by the 2020s have culminated in the realisation by Indigenes and non-Indigenes that it is time to walk around the "brick wall" of "that anachronism of contemporary Australia, the federal Constitution". But he might not have imagined how easy it now can be to walk around it. Such an invitation as First Nations have issued is easy to accept once it is clear that there are ways to give all Australians a voice and rights of self-determination that support a diverse collective – a polity of the many in the one. Manning Clark longed for a time when the Australian people might re-draft their constitution as their own – not as a "British or Yankee Constitution". He longed for the time when

> having at last liberated themselves from their own barbaric past, having shed the last vestiges of colonialism, and

provincialism, they will at long last have the faith in their power to make their own history.[414]

A people's constitution structured to enshrine their values, rights and voices can enable Australians to build that necessary faith in themselves – the power to make their own history. It is to be hoped, then, that they will accept the invitation to take rightful positions of power within their democracy by means that can only be offered under a people's constitution.

---

[414] Manning Clark, Essay on "The People and the Constitution" in Sol Encel, Donald Horne and Elaine Thompson (eds.), *Change the Rules: Towards a democratic constitution*, Penguin, Ringwood Victoria, 1977, pages 19-20.

Appendix 1 – The Uluru Statement from the Heart

We, gathered at the 2017 National Constitutional Convention, coming from all points of the southern sky, make this statement from the heart:

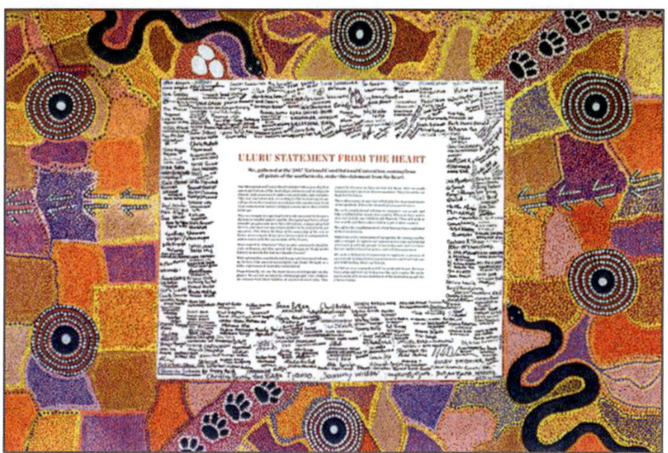
ULURU STATEMENT FROM THE HEART

Our Aboriginal and Torres Strait Islander tribes were the first sovereign Nations of the Australian continent and its adjacent islands, and possessed it under our own laws and customs. This our ancestors did, according to the reckoning of our culture, from the Creation, according to the common law from 'time immemorial', and according to science more than 60,000 years ago.

This sovereignty is a spiritual notion: the ancestral tie between the land, or 'mother nature', and the Aboriginal and Torres Strait Islander peoples who were born therefrom, remain attached thereto, and must one day return thither to be united with our ancestors. This link is the basis of the ownership of the soil, or better, of sovereignty. It has never been ceded or extinguished, and co-exists with the sovereignty of the Crown.

How could it be otherwise? That peoples possessed a land for sixty millennia and this sacred link disappears from world history in merely the last two hundred years?

With substantive constitutional change and structural reform, we believe this ancient sovereignty can shine through as a fuller expression of Australia's nationhood.

Proportionally, we are the most incarcerated people on the planet. We are not an innately criminal people. Our children are alienated from their families at unprecedented rates. This cannot be because we have no love for them. And our youth languish in detention in obscene numbers. They should be our hope for the future.

These dimensions of our crisis tell plainly the structural nature of our problem. This is the torment of our powerlessness.

We seek constitutional reforms to empower our people and take a rightful place in our own country. When we have power over our destiny our children will flourish. They will walk in two worlds and their culture will be a gift to their country.

We call for the establishment of a First Nations Voice enshrined in the Constitution.

Makarrata is the culmination of our agenda: the coming together after a struggle. It captures our aspirations for a fair and truthful relationship with the people of Australia and a better future for our children based on justice and self-determination.

We seek a Makarrata Commission to supervise a process of agreement-making between governments and First Nations and truth-telling about our history.

In 1967 we were counted, in 2017 we seek to be heard. We leave base camp and start our trek across this vast country. We invite you to walk with us in a movement of the Australian people for a better future.

Appendix 2 – Frontispiece of *Leviathan*

The conception of the modern state conceived by Thomas Hobbes in 1651 in *Leviathan: or the matter forme and power of a commonwealth ecclesiastical and civil* was depicted in this frontispiece by Abraham Bosse with creative input from Hobbes. The quote at the top, from the Bible's Book of Job, "Non est potestas Super Terram quae Comparetur ei" translates as "There is no power on earth to be compared with him".

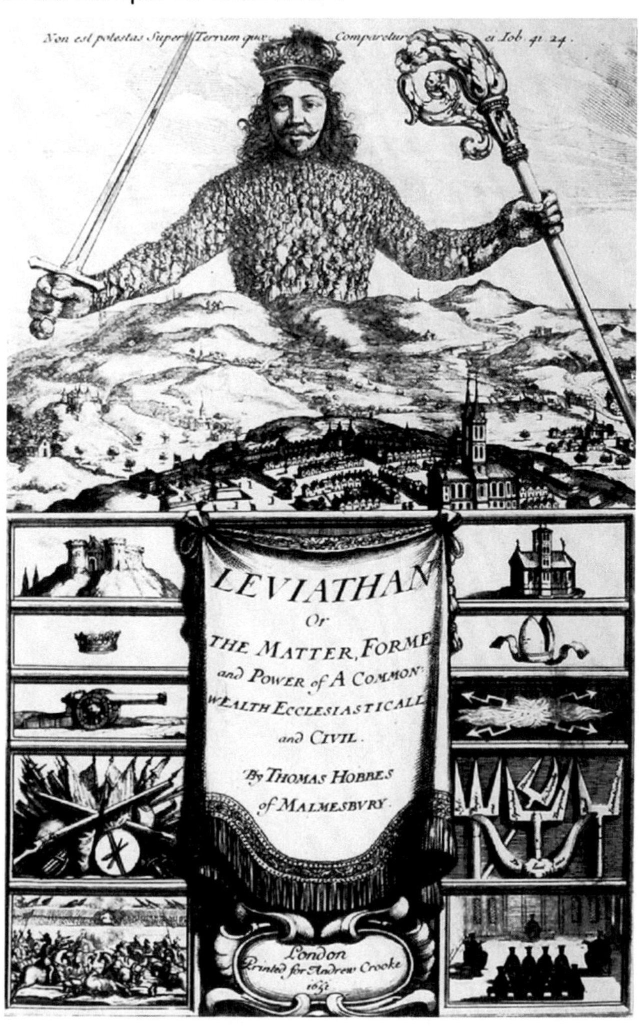

Appendix 3 – Summary of human rights and obligations under international treaties

The following tables provide a summary of rights and responsibilities conferred under core international treaties on human rights. These lists of rights and obligations of both citizens and their governments are provided to assist readers to examine for themselves whether enshrining the rights already conferred in the treaties directly into the Australian Constitution would impose unacceptable risks to the liberties of individuals or the security of the nation. They are designed to assist Australians to decide if they want these rights on an equal basis with all other people in the country and are prepared to accept the attendant responsibilities.

Readers are urged to consider each of the Covenants in full if concerns arise as to the wisdom of extension of any of these rights to people in Australia.

The tables below do not list the obligations of States Parties in reporting on compliance to any Human Rights Committee provided for under each Covenant.

International Covenant on Civil and Political Rights (ICCPR)

Summary of rights and responsibilities – International Covenant on Civil and Political Rights (ICCPR)[415]	
Rights and responsibilities	**Government obligations**
Article 1 • Right of self-determination. • Right of all humans to freely determine their political status and freely pursue their economic, social and cultural development.	• To promote the realisation of self-determination.
Article 2 • All rights to be applied without discrimination.	• To protect and ensure rights without discrimination. • To adopt laws to give effect to rights. • To ensure a competent judicial system and effective remedies for breaches of rights and enforcement of judicial remedies.
Article 3 • Rights are equal for all. • Rights are for the equal enjoyment of all.	• To undertake to ensure the equal right of all to the enjoyment of all civil and political rights.
Article 4 • Right to protection from loss of rights in certain circumstances. • Responsibility to accept government's ability to curtail rights in emergencies which threaten the life of the nation.	• To ensure no derogation from Articles, 6, 7, 8 (paragraphs 1 and 2), 11, 15, 16 and 18 under this provision. • No derogation is permissible if such measures are inconsistent with other obligations under international law. • Governments may take measures to derogate from these rights in times of public emergencies which threaten the life of the nation but may derogate only to the extent strictly required by the exigencies of the situation.

[415] International Covenant on Civil and Political Rights- external site

Summary of rights and responsibilities – International Covenant on Civil and Political Rights (ICCPR)[415]	
Rights and responsibilities	**Government obligations**
	• Governments may not derogate on a discriminatory basis.
Article 5 • Right of any state, group or person not to have a right or freedom (that is recognised in the Covenant) destroyed by any state, group or person or limited to a greater extent than is provided for in the Covenant.	• To ensure no restriction on rights already available in a country by reason of the possibility that the Covenant does not recognise the right or recognises it to a lesser extent.
Article 6 • Right to life.	• To ensure capital punishment is not permitted. • To ensure that the crime of genocide is not committed. • To ensure anyone sentenced to death has the right to seek and may be granted pardon or commutation of sentence in all cases. • To ensure sentence of death is not imposed for crimes committed by persons below the age of 18.
Article 7 • Right not to be subjected to torture or cruel, inhuman or degrading treatment or medical or scientific experimentation.	
Article 8 • Right not to be held in slavery, servitude or forced/compulsory labour.	• To prohibit all forms of slavery. • Compulsory labour does not preclude imprisonment with hard labour if it is lawful, military service, any national service required by conscientious objectors, or any service required in emergencies threatening the life of the nation.
Article 9 • Right to liberty and security of person.	• To ensure that anyone who is arrested or detained shall be

Summary of rights and responsibilities – International Covenant on Civil and Political Rights (ICCPR)[415]	
Rights and responsibilities	**Government obligations**
• Right not to be subjected to arbitrary detention. • Right not to be deprived of liberty except on grounds established by law. • Right in criminal cases to a trial within a reasonable time or to release. • Right to take proceedings in order that a court, without delay may decide the lawfulness of detention. • Right to compensation for unlawful arrest or detention.	brought promptly before an authorised judicial power. • To ensure persons awaiting trial shall not generally be detained in custody but release may be subject to guarantees to appear for trial and/or for sentencing.
Article 10 • Right of accused persons to be segregated from convicted persons. • Right of accused and convicted juvenile persons to be separated from adults in the detention system. • Right to speedy justice for juveniles.	• To treat all persons deprived of their liberty with humanity and respect for the inherent dignity of the human person. • To ensure the essential aim of the penitentiary system is reformation and social rehabilitation.
Article 11 • Right not to be imprisoned for failure to fulfil a contractual obligation.	
Article 12 • Right and freedom to choose a place of residence. • Right to freedom of movement. • Right to leave a country. • Right of citizens to enter their own country.	• To apply no restrictions except lawful measures to "protect national security, public order (*ordre public*), public health or morals or the rights and freedoms of others", consistent with the rights in the Covenant.
Article 13 • Right of lawful aliens not to be expelled unlawfully.	• To ensure a lawful alien can submit reasons against his/her expulsion before a competent authority.

Summary of rights and responsibilities – International Covenant on Civil and Political Rights (ICCPR)[415]	
Rights and responsibilities	**Government obligations**
	• Governments may derogate when there are compelling reasons of national security.
Article 14 • Right to equality before the law. • Right to a fair and public hearing by a competent, independent and impartial tribunal established by law. • Right of presumption of innocence until proved guilty. • Right to be informed fully and promptly of the detail of charges. • Right to adequate time to prepare a defence and communicate with counsel of choice. • Right to be tried without undue delay. • Right of defendants to be present at their trial and to defend themselves or through their chosen counsel. • Right to legal aid and interpreter services. • Right to examine witnesses. • Right of defendants not to testify against themselves or to confess guilt. • Right to have criminal convictions reviewed. • Right to compensation for wrongful conviction. • Right not to be tried more than once for an offence.	• To ensure any judgement rendered in a criminal case or in a suit at law shall be made public except where the interest of juvenile persons otherwise requires or the proceedings concern matrimonial disputes or the guardianship of children. • The press and the public may be excluded from all or part of a trial for reasons of morals, public order (*ordre public*) or national security in a democratic society, or when the interest of the private lives of the parties so requires, or to the extent strictly necessary in the opinion of the court in special circumstances where publicity would prejudice the interests of justice.
Article 15 • Right not to be held guilty for an offence which was not a crime when the offence was committed.	

Summary of rights and responsibilities – International Covenant on Civil and Political Rights (ICCPR)[415]	
Rights and responsibilities	**Government obligations**
• Right not to have a penalty imposed beyond that applicable at the time of the offence.	
Article 16 • Right to recognition everywhere as a person before the law.	
Article 17 • Right to privacy. • Right to reputation and to protection from attacks on privacy and reputation.	
Article 18 • Right to freedom of thought, conscience and religion. • Right to manifest one's religion and beliefs.	• To ensure no coercion that would impair freedom to adopt a religion or belief of choice. • To have respect for the liberty of parents in choosing the religion and education of their children. • Freedom to manifest one's religion or beliefs may be subject only to such limitations as are prescribed by law and are necessary to protect public safety, order, health, or morals or the fundamental rights and freedoms of others.
Article 19 • Right to hold opinions without interference. • Right to freedom of expression. • Right to seek, receive and impart information and ideas of all kinds. • These rights carry special responsibilities and may be subject to restrictions.	• These rights may be subject to certain restrictions, but these shall only be such as are provided by law and are necessary: (a) for respect of the rights or reputations of others; (b) for the protection of national security or of public order (*ordre public*), or of public health or morals.
Article 20 • Right to peace.[416]	• To prohibit by law any propaganda for war.

[416] The right to peace is implied rather than explicit in this Article. The right to peace may be reasonably inferred by the imperative in Article 20 to outlaw war propaganda and incitement to racial hatred, hostility and violence. It is also

Summary of rights and responsibilities – International Covenant on Civil and Political Rights (ICCPR)[415]	
Rights and responsibilities	**Government obligations**
• Right to protection from and prevention of racial hatred, hostility and violence.	• To prohibit by law any advocacy of national, racial or religious hatred that constitutes incitement to discrimination.
Article 21 • Right to peaceful assembly.	• To ensure no restrictions are placed on the exercise of this right other than those imposed in conformity with the law and which are necessary in a democratic society in the interests of national security or public safety, public order (*ordre public*), the protection of public health or morals or the protection of the rights and freedoms of others.
Article 22 • Right to freedom of association with others. • Right to form trade unions.	• To ensure no restrictions are placed on the exercise of this right other than those imposed in conformity with the law and which are necessary in a democratic society in the interests of national security or public safety, public order (*ordre public*), the protection of public health or morals or the protection of the rights and freedoms of others.
Article 23 • Right to marriage by men and women of marriageable age. • Right to no forced marriage.	• To acknowledge that the family is the natural and fundamental group unit of society and is entitled to protection by society and the state. • To take appropriate steps to ensure equality of rights and responsibilities of spouses as to

reasonably inferred from the objects of the Convention which state, among other things that the "equal and inalienable rights of all members of the human family [are] the foundation of freedom, justice and peace in the world".

Summary of rights and responsibilities – International Covenant on Civil and Political Rights (ICCPR)[415]	
Rights and responsibilities	**Government obligations**
	marriage, during marriage and at its dissolution. In the case of dissolution, provision shall be made for the necessary protection of any children.
Article 24 • Right of every child to protection of the state. • Right of every child to be registered and to have a name. • Right of every child to acquire a nationality.	
Article 25 • Right of every citizen to take part in the conduct of public affairs directly or through freely chosen representatives. • Right of every citizen to vote and be elected in elections of universal and equal suffrage and with secret ballot. • Right of every citizen to access, on general terms of equality, to public service.	• To ensure elections with universal and equal suffrage and with secret ballot. • To guarantee the free expression of the will of the electors.
Article 26 • Right to be equal before the law. • Right to equal protection of the law.	• To prohibit by law any discrimination and guarantee to all persons equal and effective protection against discrimination on any ground such as race, colour, sex, language, religion, political or other opinion, national or social origin, property, birth or other status.
Article 27 • Right of everyone to enjoy their own culture and religion. • Right of minorities to use their own language.	

International Covenant on Economic, Social and Cultural Rights (ICESCR)

Summary of rights and responsibilities – International Covenant on Economic, Social and Cultural Rights (ICESCR)[417]	
Rights and responsibilities	**Government obligations**
Article 1 • Right of self-determination. • Right of all humans to freely determine their political status and freely pursue their economic, social and cultural development.	• To promote the realisation of self-determination.
Article 2 • All rights to be applied without discrimination. • All rights to be applied to the fullest extent possible.	• To protect and ensure rights without discrimination. • To take steps, individually and through international assistance and co-operation, especially economic and technical, to the maximum of its available resources, with a view to achieving progressively the full realisation of the rights recognized in the present Covenant by all appropriate means, including particularly the adoption of legislative measures.
Article 3 • Rights are equal for all. • Rights are for the equal enjoyment of all.	• To undertake to ensure the equal right of all to the enjoyment of all economic, social and cultural rights.
Article 4 • Right to protection from limitation of rights.	• To recognize that, in the enjoyment of those rights provided by the state in conformity with the Covenant, the state may subject such rights only to such limitations as are determined by law only in so far as this may be compatible with the nature of these rights and

[417] International Covenant on Economic, Social and Cultural Rights- external site

Summary of rights and responsibilities – International Covenant on Economic, Social and Cultural Rights (ICESCR)[417]	
Rights and responsibilities	**Government obligations**
	solely for the purpose of promoting the general welfare in a democratic society. • The government may derogate from the obligations in the Covenant solely for the purpose of, and only to the extent necessary for, promoting the general welfare in a democratic society. [In other words limiting economic, social and cultural rights would only be lawful if it could be lawfully argued that the rights did not promote their general welfare.]
Article 5 • Right of any state, group or person not to have a right or freedom (that is recognised in the Covenant) destroyed by any state, group or person or limited to a greater extent than is provided for in the Covenant.	• To ensure no restriction on rights already available in a country by reason of the possibility that the Covenant does not recognise the right or recognises it to a lesser extent.
Article 6 • Right to work. • Right to free choice of work.	• To take steps that shall include technical and vocational guidance and training programmes, policies and techniques to achieve full realisation of the right to steady economic, social and cultural development and full and productive employment under conditions safeguarding fundamental political and economic freedoms to the individual.
Article 7 • Right of all workers to just and favourable conditions of work. • Right of all workers to fair remuneration which provides as a	• To ensure laws consistent with these rights.

Summary of rights and responsibilities – International Covenant on Economic, Social and Cultural Rights (ICESCR)[417]	
Rights and responsibilities	**Government obligations**
minimum a decent living for workers and their families. • Right of all workers to equal pay for work of equal value. • Right to safe and healthy working conditions. • Right to equal opportunity for promotion. • Right to rest, leisure, reasonable limitation of working hours, and periodic holidays with pay.	
Article 8 • Right to form and join trade unions. • Right of trade unions to federate and join international unions. • Right of trade unions to function freely subject to no limitations other than laws necessary in a free and democratic society. • Right to strike provided that it is exercised in conformity with the law.	• To ensure no restrictions are placed on the exercise of this right other than those prescribed by law and which are necessary in a democratic society in the interests of national security or public order or for the protection of the rights and freedoms of others. • These rights may be subject to certain restrictions, but these shall only be such as are provided by law and are necessary in a democratic society in the interests of national security or public order or for the protection of the rights and freedoms of others.
Article 9 • Right of everyone to social security including social insurance.	
Article 10 • Right to marriage by free consent. • Right to no forced marriage. • Right of mothers to special protection during a reasonable	• To acknowledge that the family is the natural and fundamental group unit of society and is entitled to protection by society and the state. • To ensure the employment of children and young adults in work

Summary of rights and responsibilities – International Covenant on Economic, Social and Cultural Rights (ICESCR)[417]	
Rights and responsibilities	**Government obligations**
period before and after childbirth. • Right to paid maternity leave with adequate social security benefits. • Right of children and young persons to freedom from economic or social exploitation. • Right of children and young persons to protection from employment in work harmful to their morals or health or dangerous to life or likely to hamper their normal development.	harmful to their morals or health or dangerous to life or likely to hamper their normal development is punishable by law. • To ensure age limits are set below which the paid employment of child labour should be prohibited and punishable by law.
Article 11 • Right of everyone to an adequate standard of living for themselves and their family, including adequate food, clothing and housing. • Right to the continuous improvement of living conditions. • Right of everyone to freedom from hunger.	• To take appropriate steps to ensure the realisation of this right, recognizing to this effect the essential importance of international cooperation based on free consent. • To improve methods of production, conservation and distribution of food by making full use of technical and scientific knowledge, by disseminating knowledge of the principles of nutrition and by developing or reforming agrarian systems in such a way as to achieve the most efficient development and utilization of natural resources. • Taking into account the problems of both food-importing and food-exporting countries, to ensure an equitable distribution of world food supplies in relation to need.
Article 12 • Right of everyone to enjoyment of the highest attainable standard of physical and mental health.	• To achieve the full realisation of this right by provisions for: o the reduction of the stillbirth-rate and of infant mortality

Summary of rights and responsibilities – International Covenant on Economic, Social and Cultural Rights (ICESCR)[417]	
Rights and responsibilities	**Government obligations**
	and for the healthy development of the child; o the improvement of all aspects of environmental and industrial hygiene; o the prevention, treatment and control of epidemic, endemic, occupational and other diseases; and o the creation of conditions which would assure to all medical service and medical attention in the event of sickness.
Article 13 • Right of everyone to education. • Right of free primary and secondary education. • Right of equal access to higher education on the basis of capacity.	• To ensure that education shall be directed to the full development of the human personality and the sense of its dignity, and shall strengthen the respect for human rights and fundamental freedoms. • To ensure that education shall enable all persons to participate effectively in a free society, promote understanding, tolerance and friendship among all nations and all racial, ethnic or religious groups, and further the activities of the United Nations for the maintenance of peace. • To provide free primary and secondary education. • To ensure equal access to higher education and progressively introduce free higher education. • To develop a system of schools. • To continuously improve the conditions of teachers. • To have respect for the liberty of parents in choosing schools for

Summary of rights and responsibilities – International Covenant on Economic, Social and Cultural Rights (ICESCR)[417]	
Rights and responsibilities	**Government obligations**
	the education of their children and any religious teaching.
Article 14 [No additional right is conferred under this clause.]	• To ensure provision of primary education free of charge.
Article 15 • Right of everyone to take part in cultural life. • Right of everyone to enjoy the benefits of scientific progress and its applications. • Right of authors to the benefit of the moral and material interests of their scientific, literary or artistic productions.	• The steps to be taken by the States Parties to the present Covenant to achieve the full realisation of this right shall include those necessary for the conservation, the development and the diffusion of science and culture. • To undertake to respect the freedom indispensable for scientific research and creative activity.

International Convention on the Elimination of All Forms of Racial Discrimination (CERD)

Summary of rights and responsibilities – International Convention the Elimination of All Forms of Racial Discrimination (CERD)[418]	
Rights and responsibilities	**Government obligations**
Article 1 • Right to protection from discrimination on the grounds of race, colour, descent, or national or ethnic origin. • Also contains definitions.	• To ensure no discrimination against a particular nationality in matters of citizenship and naturalisation. • To ensure enjoyment of everyone on an equal footing of human rights, fundamental freedoms in political, economic, social, cultural or any other field of life, regardless of race, colour, descent, and national or ethnic origin. • Special measures taken for the sole purpose of securing adequate advancement of certain racial or ethnic groups or individuals requiring such protection as may be necessary in order to ensure such groups or individuals equal enjoyment or exercise of human rights and fundamental freedoms shall not be deemed racial discrimination, provided, however, that such measures do not, as a consequence, lead to the maintenance of separate rights for different racial groups and that they shall not be continued after the objectives for which they were taken have been achieved.

[418] International Convention on the Elimination of All Forms of Racial Discrimination- external site

Summary of rights and responsibilities – International Convention the Elimination of All Forms of Racial Discrimination (CERD)[418]	
Rights and responsibilities	**Government obligations**
Article 2 • Right to protection from discrimination on the grounds of race, colour, descent, or national or ethnic origin.	• To condemn racial discrimination. • To pursue by all appropriate means and without delay a policy of eliminating racial discrimination in all its forms. • To promote understanding among all races. • To engage in no act or practice of racial discrimination against persons, groups of persons or institutions. • To ensure that all public authorities and public institutions, national and local, shall act in conformity with this obligation. • To not sponsor, defend or support racial discrimination by any persons or organizations. • To review governmental, national and local policies. • To amend, rescind or nullify any laws and regulations which have the effect of creating or perpetuating racial discrimination wherever it exists. • To prohibit and bring to an end, by all appropriate means, including legislation as required by circumstances, racial discrimination by any persons, group or organization. • To encourage, where appropriate, integrationist multiracial organizations and movements and other means of eliminating barriers between races.

Summary of rights and responsibilities – International Convention the Elimination of All Forms of Racial Discrimination (CERD)[418]	
Rights and responsibilities	**Government obligations**
	• To discourage anything which tends to strengthen racial division.
Article 3 • Right to protection from discrimination on the grounds of race, colour, descent, or national or ethnic origin.	• To condemn racial segregation and apartheid. • To prevent, prohibit and eradicate racial segregation and apartheid.

Article 4
• Right to protection from discrimination on the grounds of race, colour, descent, or national or ethnic origin.
	• To condemn all propaganda and all organizations which are based on ideas or theories of superiority of one race or group of persons of one colour or ethnic origin, or which attempt to justify or promote racial hatred and discrimination in any form.
	• To adopt immediate and positive measures designed to eradicate all incitement to, or acts of, such discrimination.
	• To declare the following an offence punishable by law:
	  o all dissemination of ideas based on racial superiority or hatred, incitement to racial discrimination,
	  o all acts of violence or incitement to such acts against any race or group of persons of another colour or ethnic origin,
	  o provision of any assistance to racist activities, including the financing thereof.
	• To declare illegal and prohibit organizations, and also organized and all other propaganda activities, which promote and incite racial discrimination and to recognize participation in such

Summary of rights and responsibilities – International Convention the Elimination of All Forms of Racial Discrimination (CERD)[418]	
Rights and responsibilities	**Government obligations**
	organizations or activities as an offence punishable by law. • To not permit public authorities or public institutions, national or local, to promote or incite racial discrimination.
Article 5 • Right to equal treatment before the tribunals and all other organs administering justice. • Right to security of person and protection by the State against violence or bodily harm, whether inflicted by government officials or by any individual group or institution. • Political rights, in particular the right to participate in elections-to vote and to stand for election-on the basis of universal and equal suffrage. • Right to take part in the Government as well as in the conduct of public affairs at any level and to have equal access to public service. • Other civil rights. • Right to freedom of movement and residence within the border of the State. • Right to leave any country, including one's own, and to return to one's country. • Right to nationality. • Right to marriage and choice of spouse. • Right to own property alone as well as in association with others. • Right to inherit.	• To prohibit and eliminate racial discrimination in all its forms. • To guarantee these rights without discrimination.

Summary of rights and responsibilities – International Convention the Elimination of All Forms of Racial Discrimination (CERD)[418]	
Rights and responsibilities	**Government obligations**
• Right to freedom of thought, conscience and religion. • Right to freedom of opinion and expression. • Right to freedom of peaceful assembly and association. • Economic, social and cultural rights. • Rights to work, to free choice of employment. • Right to just and favourable conditions of work. • Right to protection against unemployment. • Right to equal pay for equal work. • Right to just and favourable remuneration. • Right to form and join trade unions. • Right to housing. • Right to public health, medical care, social security and social services. • Right to education and training. Right to equal participation in cultural activities. • Right of access to any place or service intended for use by the general public, such as transport hotels, restaurants, cafes, theatres and parks.	
Article 6 • Right to protection from discrimination on the grounds of race, colour, descent, or national or ethnic origin.	• To assure to everyone within their jurisdiction effective protection and remedies, through the competent national tribunals and other State institutions, against any acts of racial discrimination which violate human rights and fundamental freedoms contrary to this

Summary of rights and responsibilities – International Convention the Elimination of All Forms of Racial Discrimination (CERD)[418]	
Rights and responsibilities	**Government obligations**
	Convention, as well as the right to seek from such tribunals just and adequate reparation or satisfaction for any damage suffered as a result of such discrimination.
Article 7 • Right to protection from discrimination on the grounds of race, colour, descent, or national or ethnic origin.	• To adopt immediate and effective measures, particularly in the fields of teaching, education, culture and information, with a view to combating prejudices which lead to racial discrimination and to promoting understanding, tolerance and friendship among nations and racial or ethnical groups, as well as to propagating the purposes and principles of the Charter of the United Nations, the Universal Declaration of Human Rights, the United Nations Declaration on the Elimination of All Forms of Racial Discrimination, and this Convention.

International Convention on the Elimination of All Forms of Discrimination Against Women (CEDAW)

Summary of rights and responsibilities – International Convention the Elimination of All Forms of Discrimination Against Women (CEDAW)[419]	
Rights and responsibilities	**Government obligations**
Article 1 • Right of all women to protection from discrimination on the grounds of sex. • Right of all women to protection from any distinction, exclusion or restriction which has the effect or purpose of impairing on nullifying the recognition, enjoyment or exercise by women – irrespective of their marital status, on a basis of equality of men and women – of human rights and fundamental freedoms in the political, economic, social, cultural, civil or any other field. • Also contains definitions.	• To ensure enjoyment of all women, on an equal footing with men, of human rights, fundamental freedoms in political, economic, social, cultural or any other field of life.
Article 2 • Right of all women to protection from discrimination on the grounds of sex. • Right of all women to enjoyment of human rights and fundamental freedoms on a basis of equality with men.	• To condemn discrimination against women in all its forms. • To embody the principle of the equality of men and women in their national constitutions or other appropriate legislation. • To adopt appropriate legislative and other measures, including sanctions where appropriate, prohibiting all discrimination against women. • To establish legal protection of the rights of women on an equal basis with men and to ensure through competent national

[419] Convention on the Elimination of All Forms of Discrimination against Women- external site

Summary of rights and responsibilities – International Convention the Elimination of All Forms of Discrimination Against Women (CEDAW)[419]	
Rights and responsibilities	**Government obligations**
	tribunals and other public institutions the effective protection of women against any act of discrimination. • To refrain from engaging in any act or practice of discrimination against women and to ensure that public authorities and institutions shall act in conformity with this obligation. • To take all appropriate measures to eliminate discrimination against women by any person, organization or enterprise. • To take all appropriate measures, including legislation, to modify or abolish existing laws, regulations, customs and practices which constitute discrimination against women. • To repeal all national penal provisions which constitute discrimination against women.
Article 3 • Right of all women to protection from discrimination on the grounds of sex. • Right of all women to enjoyment of human rights and fundamental freedoms on a basis of equality with men.	• To take in all fields, in particular in the political, social, economic and cultural fields, all appropriate measures, including legislation, to ensure the full development and advancement of women, for the purpose of guaranteeing them the exercise and enjoyment of human rights and fundamental freedoms on a basis of equality with men.
Article 4 • Right of all women to protection from discrimination on the grounds of sex. • Right of all women to enjoyment of human rights and fundamental	• To ensure enjoyment of all women, on an equal footing with men, of human rights, fundamental freedoms in political, economic, social, cultural or any other field of life.

Summary of rights and responsibilities – International Convention the Elimination of All Forms of Discrimination Against Women (CEDAW)[419]	
Rights and responsibilities	**Government obligations**
freedoms on a basis of equality with men.	• Temporary special measures aimed at accelerating de facto equality between men and women shall not be considered discrimination as defined in the Convention, but shall in no way entail as a consequence the maintenance of unequal or separate standards. • These measures shall be discontinued when the objectives of equality of opportunity and treatment have been achieved. • Adoption of special measures, including those measures contained in the Convention, aimed at protecting maternity shall not be considered discriminatory.
Article 5 • Right of all women to protection from discrimination on the grounds of sex. • Right of all women to enjoyment of human rights and fundamental freedoms on a basis of equality with men.	• To modify the social and cultural patterns of conduct of men and women, with a view to achieving the elimination of prejudices and customary and all other practices which are based on the idea of the inferiority or the superiority of either of the sexes or on stereotyped roles for men and women. • To ensure that family education includes a proper understanding of maternity as a social function and the recognition of the common responsibility of men and women in the upbringing and development of their children, it being understood that the interest of the children is the primordial consideration in all cases.

Summary of rights and responsibilities – International Convention the Elimination of All Forms of Discrimination Against Women (CEDAW)[419]	
Rights and responsibilities	**Government obligations**
Article 6 • Right of all women to protection from human trafficking, exploitation and prostitution.	• To take appropriate measures to protect all women from human trafficking, exploitation and prostitution.
Article 7 • Right of all women to participate in the public life of the country on equal terms with men. • Right to vote in all elections and public referenda and to be eligible for election to all publicly elected bodies. • Right to participate in the formulation of government policy and the implementation thereof and to hold public office and perform all public functions at all levels of government. • Right to participate in non-governmental organizations and associations concerned with the public and political life of the country.	• To take all appropriate measures to eliminate discrimination against women in the political and public life of the country and, to ensure enjoyment of these rights by women on equal terms with men.
Article 8 • Right of all women to the opportunity to represent their governments at the international level and to participate in the work of international organizations.	• To take all appropriate measures to ensure to women, on equal terms with men and without any discrimination, the opportunity to represent their governments at the international level and to participate in the work of international organizations.
Article 9 • Right of all women to acquire, change or retain their nationality. • Right of all women to retain nationality. • Right of all women equal with men with respect to the nationality of their children.	• To grant women equal rights with men to acquire, change or retain their nationality. • To ensure in particular that neither marriage to an alien nor change of nationality by the husband during marriage shall automatically change the nationality of the wife, render her

Summary of rights and responsibilities – International Convention the Elimination of All Forms of Discrimination Against Women (CEDAW)[419]	
Rights and responsibilities	**Government obligations**
	stateless or force upon her the nationality of the husband. • To grant women equal rights with men with respect to the nationality of their children.
Article 10 • Right of all women to education on an equal basis with men. • Right of all women on an equal basis with men to the same conditions for career and vocational guidance, for access to studies and for the achievement of diplomas in educational establishments of all categories in rural as well as in urban areas. • Right to equality in pre-school, general, technical, professional and higher technical education, as well as in all types of vocational training. • Right of all women to access to the same curricula, the same examinations, teaching staff with qualifications of the same standard and school premises and equipment of the same quality. • Right to the elimination of any stereotyped concept of the roles of men and women at all levels and in all forms of education. • Right of all women on an equal basis with men to the same opportunities to benefit from scholarships and other study grants, the same opportunities for access to programmes of continuing education, and the same opportunities to participate	• To take all appropriate measures to eliminate discrimination against women in order to ensure to them equal rights with men in the field of education. • To ensure women the same conditions for career and vocational guidance as men. • To ensure women, on an equal basis with men, access to studies and for the achievement of diplomas in educational establishments of all categories in rural as well as in urban areas; this equality shall be ensured in pre-school, general, technical, professional and higher technical education, as well as in all types of vocational training. • To ensure women, on an equal basis with men, have access to the same curricula, the same examinations, teaching staff with qualifications of the same standard and school premises and equipment of the same quality. • To eliminate any stereotyped concept of the roles of men and women at all levels and in all forms of education by encouraging coeducation and other types of education which will help to achieve this aim and, in particular, by the revision of

Summary of rights and responsibilities – International Convention the Elimination of All Forms of Discrimination Against Women (CEDAW)[419]	
Rights and responsibilities	**Government obligations**
actively in sports and physical education. • Right of all women to specific educational information to help to ensure the health and wellbeing of families, including information and advice on family planning.	textbooks and school programmes and the adaptation of teaching methods. • To ensure that women on an equal basis with men have the same opportunities to benefit from scholarships and other study grants, the same opportunities for access to programmes of continuing education, including adult and functional literacy programmes. • To ensure the reduction of female student drop-out rates and the organization of programmes for girls and women who have left school prematurely. • To provide women, on an equal basis with men, the same opportunities to participate actively in sports and physical education. • To provide women with access to specific educational information to help to ensure the health and wellbeing of families, including information and advice on family planning.
Article 11 • Right to employment on a basis of equality of men and women. • Right to work as an inalienable right of all human beings. • Right to the same employment opportunities, including the application of the same criteria for selection in matters of employment.	• To take all appropriate measures to eliminate discrimination against women in the field of employment in order to ensure, on a basis of equality of men and women, the same rights. • To ensure the right to work as an inalienable right of all human beings.

Summary of rights and responsibilities – International Convention the Elimination of All Forms of Discrimination Against Women (CEDAW)[419]	
Rights and responsibilities	**Government obligations**
• Right to free choice of profession and employment. • Right to promotion, job security and all benefits and conditions of service. • Right to receive vocational training and retraining, including apprenticeships, advanced vocational training and recurrent training. • Right to equal remuneration, including benefits. • Right to equal pay and treatment in respect of work of equal value. • Right to equality of treatment in the evaluation of the quality of work. • Right to social security, particularly in cases of retirement, unemployment, sickness, invalidity and old age and other incapacity to work. • Right to paid leave. • Right to protection of health and to safety in working conditions, including the safeguarding of the function of reproduction. • Right of all women to protection from discrimination on the grounds of marriage or maternity and to ensure their effective right to work. • Right to protection from the imposition of sanctions, dismissal on the grounds of pregnancy or of maternity leave and discrimination in dismissals on the basis of marital status. • Right to maternity leave with pay or with comparable social	• To ensure access to and the opportunity for realisation of all rights under this Article. • To prohibit, subject to the imposition of sanctions, dismissal on the grounds of pregnancy or of maternity leave and discrimination in dismissals on the basis of marital status. • To introduce maternity leave with pay or with comparable social benefits without loss of former employment, seniority or social allowances. • To encourage the provision of the necessary supporting social services to enable parents to combine family obligations with work responsibilities and participation in public life, in particular through promoting the establishment and development of a network of child-care facilities. • To provide special protection to women during pregnancy in types of work proved to be harmful to them • To institute protective legislation relating to matters covered in this article and to reviewed it periodically in the light of scientific and technological knowledge and to revise, repeal or extend this legislation as necessary.

Summary of rights and responsibilities – International Convention the Elimination of All Forms of Discrimination Against Women (CEDAW)[419]	
Rights and responsibilities	**Government obligations**
benefits without loss of former employment, seniority or social allowances. • Right to the necessary supporting social services to enable parents to combine family obligations with work responsibilities and participation in public life. • Right to special protection to women during pregnancy in types of work proved to be harmful to them.	
Article 12 • Right to health care appropriate to women, including care and services in family planning, pregnancy, confinement, post-natal periods and nutrition. • Right to free services in this area where necessary.	• To take all appropriate measures to eliminate discrimination against women in the field of health care in order to ensure, on a basis of equality of men and women, access to health care services, including those related to family planning. • To ensure to women appropriate services in connection with pregnancy, confinement and the post-natal period, granting free services where necessary, as well as adequate nutrition during pregnancy and lactation.
Article 13 • Right of all women on an equal basis with men to family benefits, bank loans, mortgages and other forms of financial credit. • Right of all women to participate in recreational activities, sports and all aspects of cultural life.	• To take all appropriate measures to eliminate discrimination against women in other areas of economic and social life in order to ensure, on a basis of equality of men and women, the same rights.
Article 14 • Right of women in rural areas, on a basis of equality of men and women, to participate in and benefit from rural development.	• To take into account the particular problems faced by rural women and the significant roles which rural women play in the economic survival of their

Summary of rights and responsibilities – International Convention the Elimination of All Forms of Discrimination Against Women (CEDAW)[419]	
Rights and responsibilities	**Government obligations**
• Right of rural women to participate in the elaboration and implementation of development planning at all levels. • Right of rural women to have access to adequate health care facilities, including information, counselling and services in family planning. • Right of rural women to benefit directly from social security programmes. • Right of rural women to obtain all types of training and education. • Right of rural women to organize self-help groups and co-operatives in order to obtain equal access to economic opportunities through employment or self-employment. Right of rural women to participate in all community activities. • Right of rural women to have access to agricultural credit and loans, marketing facilities, appropriate technology and equal treatment in land and agrarian reform as well as in land resettlement schemes. • Right of rural women to enjoy adequate living conditions, particularly in relation to housing, sanitation, electricity and water supply, transport and communications.	families, including their work in the non-monetized sectors of the economy. • To take all appropriate measures to ensure the application of the provisions of the Convention to women in rural areas.
Article 15 • Right of all women to equality with men before the law.	• To accord to women, in civil matters, a legal capacity identical to that of men and the same

Summary of rights and responsibilities – International Convention the Elimination of All Forms of Discrimination Against Women (CEDAW)[419]	
Rights and responsibilities	**Government obligations**
• Right of women on an equal basis with men to conclude contracts and to administer property. • Right of women to equal treatment in all stages of procedure in courts and tribunals. • Right, on an equal basis with men, to movement and to freedom of choice in their residence or domicile.	opportunities to exercise that capacity. • To treat women equally in all stages of procedure in courts and tribunals. • To ensure that all contracts and all other private instruments of any kind with a legal effect which is directed at restricting the legal capacity of women shall be deemed null and void. • To accord to men and women the same rights with regard to the law relating to the movement of persons and the freedom to choose their residence and domicile.
Article 16 • Right of women, on a basis of equality with men to: o the same right to enter into marriage; o the same right freely to choose a spouse and to enter into marriage only with their free and full consent; o the same rights and responsibilities during marriage and at its dissolution; o the same rights and responsibilities as parents, irrespective of their marital status, in matters relating to their children (in all cases the interests of the children shall be paramount); o the same rights to decide freely and responsibly on the number and spacing of their	• To take all appropriate measures to eliminate discrimination against women in all matters relating to marriage and family relations and in particular to ensure, on a basis of equality of men and women, all the rights conferred in this Convention.

Summary of rights and responsibilities – International Convention the Elimination of All Forms of Discrimination Against Women (CEDAW)[419]	
Rights and responsibilities	**Government obligations**
children and to have access to the information, education and means to enable them to exercise these rights; ○ the same rights and responsibilities with regard to guardianship, wardship, trusteeship and adoption of children, or similar institutions where these concepts exist in national legislation (in all cases the interests of the children shall be paramount); ○ the same personal rights as husband and wife, including the right to choose a family name, a profession and an occupation.	

International Convention Against Torture and Other Cruel, Inhuman or Degrading Treatment or Punishment (CAT)

Summary of rights and responsibilities – International Convention on Torture and Other Cruel, Inhuman or Degrading Treatment or Punishment (CAT)[420]	
Rights and responsibilities	**Government obligations**
Article 1 • Right (implied) to protection from torture by a public official or any person acting in an official capacity. • Includes definitions.	
Article 2 • Right (implied) to protection from torture by a public official or any person acting in an official capacity.	• To take effective legislative, administrative, judicial or other measures to prevent acts of torture in any territory under its jurisdiction. • No exceptional circumstances whatsoever, whether a state of war or a threat of war, internal political instability or any other public emergency, may be invoked as a justification of torture. • An order from a superior officer or a public authority may not be invoked as a justification of torture.
Article 3 • Right (implied) of any person not to be refouled to another State where there are substantial grounds for believing that he would be in danger of being subjected to torture.	• To ensure that a person is not expelled, returned ("refouled") or extradited to another State where there are substantial grounds for believing that he would be in danger of being subjected to torture.

[420] Convention against Torture and Other Cruel, Inhuman or Degrading Treatment or Punishment- external site

Summary of rights and responsibilities – International Convention on Torture and Other Cruel, Inhuman or Degrading Treatment or Punishment (CAT)[420]	
Rights and responsibilities	**Government obligations**
	• To take into account all relevant considerations including, where applicable, the existence in the State concerned of a consistent pattern of gross, flagrant or mass violations of human rights.
Article 4 • Right (implied) of all persons to the benefit of laws protecting them from torture.	• To ensure that all acts of torture are offences under criminal law. The same shall apply to an attempt to commit torture and to an act by any person which constitutes complicity or participation in torture. • To make these offences punishable by appropriate penalties which take into account their grave nature.
Article 5 • Right (implied) of all persons to the benefit of laws protecting them from torture.	• To take such measures as may be necessary to establish its jurisdiction over the offences referred to in Article 4 in the following cases: o when the offences are committed in any territory under its jurisdiction or on board a ship or aircraft registered in that State; o when the alleged offender is a national of the state; o when the victim is a national of the state. • To take such measures as may be necessary to establish jurisdiction over such offences in cases where the alleged offender is present in any territory under its jurisdiction and it does not extradite him pursuant to Article 8 to any of the

Summary of rights and responsibilities – International Convention on Torture and Other Cruel, Inhuman or Degrading Treatment or Punishment (CAT)[420]	
Rights and responsibilities	**Government obligations**
	states mentioned in paragraph 1 of this article.
Article 6 • Right (implied) of all persons to the benefit of laws protecting them from torture. • Right of any person charged with an offence under Article 4 to be guaranteed fair treatment at all stages of legal proceedings.	• To take into custody a person alleged to have committed any offence referred to in article 4, (upon being satisfied after an examination of information available to it, that the circumstances so warrant), or take other legal measures to ensure the person's presence. • To ensure that the custody and other legal measures shall be as provided in the law of the state but may be continued only for such time as is necessary to enable any criminal or extradition proceedings to be instituted. • To immediately make a preliminary inquiry into the facts. • To ensure any person in custody pursuant to paragraph 1 of this article shall be assisted in communicating immediately with the nearest appropriate representative of the state of which he is a national, or, if he is a stateless person, with the representative of the state where he usually resides. • To immediately notify the states referred to in article 5, paragraph 1, of the fact that such person is in custody and of the circumstances which warrant his detention. • To promptly report its findings to the said states and shall indicate

Summary of rights and responsibilities – International Convention on Torture and Other Cruel, Inhuman or Degrading Treatment or Punishment (CAT)[420]	
Rights and responsibilities	**Government obligations**
	whether it intends to exercise jurisdiction.
Article 7 • Right (implied) of all persons to the benefit of laws protecting them from torture. • Right of any person charged with an offence under Article 4 to be guaranteed fair treatment at all stages of legal proceedings.	• To ensure that anyone alleged to have committed any offence referred to in article 4 shall in the cases contemplated in article 5 (if it does not extradite him) submit the case to its competent authorities for the purpose of prosecution. • To ensure these authorities take their decision in the same manner as in the case of any ordinary offence of a serious nature under the law of that State. To ensure the standards of evidence required for prosecution and conviction shall in no way be less stringent than those which apply in the cases referred to in article 5, paragraph 1.
Article 8 • Right (implied) of all persons to the benefit of laws protecting them from torture. • Right of any person charged with an offence under Article 4 to be guaranteed fair treatment at all stages of legal proceedings.	• To ensure extradition treaties include offences in article 4 as extraditable offences in any extradition treaty existing between States Parties.
Article 9 • Right (implied) of all persons to the benefit of laws protecting them from torture. • Right of any person charged with an offence under Article 4 to be guaranteed fair treatment at all stages of legal proceedings.	• To afford other states the greatest measure of assistance in connection with criminal proceedings brought in respect of any of the offences referred to in article 4, including the supply of all evidence at their disposal necessary for the proceedings.

Summary of rights and responsibilities – International Convention on Torture and Other Cruel, Inhuman or Degrading Treatment or Punishment (CAT)[420]	
Rights and responsibilities	**Government obligations**
Article 10 • Right (implied) to protection from torture by a public official or any person acting in an official capacity.	• To ensure that education and information regarding the prohibition against torture are fully included in the training of law enforcement personnel, civil or military, medical personnel, public officials and other persons who may be involved in the custody, interrogation or treatment of any individual subjected to any form of arrest, detention or imprisonment. • To prohibit torture in the rules or instructions issued in regard to the duties and functions of any such person.
Article 11 • Right (implied) to protection from torture by a public official or any person acting in an official capacity.	• To keep under systematic review interrogation rules, instructions, methods and practices as well as arrangements for the custody and treatment of persons subjected to any form of arrest, detention or imprisonment in any territory under its jurisdiction, with a view to preventing any cases of torture.
Article 12 • Right (implied) to protection from torture by a public official or any person acting in an official capacity.	• To ensure that its competent authorities proceed to a prompt and impartial investigation, wherever there is reasonable ground to believe that an act of torture has been committed in any territory under its jurisdiction.
Article 13 • Right (implied) to protection from torture by a public official or any person acting in an official capacity.	• To ensure that any individual who alleges he has been subjected to torture in any territory under its jurisdiction has the right to complain to, and to have his case

Summary of rights and responsibilities – International Convention on Torture and Other Cruel, Inhuman or Degrading Treatment or Punishment (CAT)[420]	
Rights and responsibilities	**Government obligations**
• Right to complain of torture. • Right to have complaints promptly and impartially examined by competent authorities. • Right to protection for complainants and witnesses against all ill-treatment or intimidation as a consequence of the complaint or any evidence given.	promptly and impartially examined by competent authorities. • To ensure that the complainant and witnesses are protected against all ill-treatment or intimidation as a consequence of his complaint or any evidence given.
Article 14 • Right of victims of torture to redress and compensation. • Right of families of victims of torture to redress and compensation when torture has resulted in the death of the victim.	• Each State Party shall ensure in its legal system that the victim of an act of torture obtains redress and has an enforceable right to fair and adequate compensation, including the means for as full rehabilitation as possible. In the event of the death of the victim as a result of an act of torture, his dependants shall be entitled to compensation.
Article 15 • Right of torture victims that a statement made by them under torture cannot be used in evidence against them in any proceedings.	• To ensure that any statement which is established to have been made as a result of torture shall not be invoked as evidence in any proceedings, except against a person accused of torture as evidence that the statement was made.
Article 16 • Right (implied) to protection from acts of cruel, inhuman or degrading treatment or punishment by a public official or any person acting in an official capacity.	• To ensure prevention of other acts of cruel, inhuman or degrading treatment or punishment which do not amount to torture as defined in Article 1, when such acts are committed by or at the instigation of or with the consent or acquiescence of a public official or other person

Summary of rights and responsibilities – International Convention on Torture and Other Cruel, Inhuman or Degrading Treatment or Punishment (CAT)[420]	
Rights and responsibilities	**Government obligations**
	acting in an official capacity. In particular, the obligations contained in articles 10, 11, 12 and 13 shall apply with the substitution for references to torture of references to other forms of cruel, inhuman or degrading treatment or punishment.

International Convention on the Rights of the Child (CRC)

Summary of rights and responsibilities – International Convention on the Rights of the Child (CRC)[421]	
Rights and responsibilities	**Government obligations**
Article 1 • Includes definition of "child" as every human being below the age of 18 years unless under the law applicable to the child, majority is attained earlier. • [In Australia a child becomes an adult at the age of 18.]	
Article 2 • Right of any child to all protections of the Convention without discrimination of any kind, irrespective of the child's or his or her parent's or legal guardian's race, colour, sex, language, religion, political or other opinion, national, ethnic or social origin, property, disability, birth or other status.	• To respect and ensure the rights in the Convention to each child without discrimination of any kind, irrespective of the child's or his or her parent's or legal guardian's race, colour, sex, language, religion, political or other opinion, national, ethnic or social origin, property, disability, birth or other status. • To take all appropriate measures to ensure that the child is protected against all forms of discrimination or punishment on the basis of the status, activities, expressed opinions, or beliefs of the child's parents, legal guardians, or family members.
Article 3 • Right of all children to be protected as the primary human interest in legal actions – i.e., the rights, best interests and wellbeing of the child are paramount.	• To ensure that in all actions concerning children, whether undertaken by public or private social welfare institutions, courts of law, administrative authorities or legislative bodies, the best

421 Convention on the Rights of the Child- external site

Summary of rights and responsibilities – International Convention on the Rights of the Child (CRC)[421]	
Rights and responsibilities	**Government obligations**
	interests of the child shall be a primary consideration. • To ensure the child such protection and care as is necessary for his or her wellbeing, taking into account the rights and duties of his or her parents, legal guardians, or other individuals legally responsible for him or her, and, to this end, to take all appropriate legislative and administrative measures. • To ensure that the institutions, services and facilities responsible for the care or protection of children shall conform with the standards established by competent authorities, particularly in the areas of safety, health, in the number and suitability of their staff, as well as competent supervision.
Article 4 • Right of any child to all protections of the Convention without discrimination of any kind, irrespective of the child's or his or her parent's or legal guardian's race, colour, sex, language, religion, political or other opinion, national, ethnic or social origin, property, disability, birth or other status.	• To undertake all appropriate legislative, administrative, and other measures for the implementation of the rights recognized in the Convention. • To undertake, with regard to economic, social and cultural rights such measures to the maximum extent of their available resources and, where needed, within the framework of international co-operation.
Article 5 • Right of any child to all protections of the Convention without discrimination of any kind, irrespective of the child's or his or her parent's or legal	• To respect the responsibilities, rights and duties of parents or, where applicable, the members of the extended family or community as provided for by local custom, legal guardians or

Summary of rights and responsibilities – International Convention on the Rights of the Child (CRC)[421]	
Rights and responsibilities	**Government obligations**
guardian's race, colour, sex, language, religion, political or other opinion, national, ethnic or social origin, property, disability, birth or other status.	other persons legally responsible for the child, to provide, in a manner consistent with the evolving capacities of the child, appropriate direction and guidance in the exercise by the child of the rights recognized in the Convention.
Article 6 • Right to life of every child.	• To ensure to the maximum extent possible the survival and development of the child.
Article 7 • Right of every child to protection of the state. • Right of every child to be registered immediately after birth and to have a name. • Right of every child to acquire a nationality. • Right of every child (as far as possible) to know and be cared for by his or her parents.	• To ensure the implementation of these rights in accordance with their national law and their obligations under the relevant international instruments in this field, in particular where the child would otherwise be stateless.
Article 8 • Right of every child to the preservation of his or her identity, including nationality, name and family relations as recognized by law without unlawful interference.	• To respect the right of the child to preserve his or her identity, including nationality, name and family relations as recognized by law without unlawful interference. • To ensure, where a child is illegally deprived of some or all of the elements of his or her identity, that he or she shall be provided appropriate assistance and protection, with a view to re-establishing speedily his or her identity.
Article 9 • Right of a child not to be separated from his or her parents against their will (except when a	• To ensure that a child shall not be separated from his or her parents against their will, except when competent authorities subject to

Summary of rights and responsibilities – International Convention on the Rights of the Child (CRC)[421]	
Rights and responsibilities	**Government obligations**
competent judicial authority determines that the separation is in the best interests of the child).	judicial review determine, in accordance with applicable law and procedures, that such separation is necessary for the best interests of the child. • To ensure all interested parties shall be given an opportunity to participate in proceedings and make their views known. • To respect the right of the child who is separated from one or both parents to maintain personal relations and direct contact with both parents on a regular basis, except if it is contrary to the child's best interests.
Article 10 • Right of a child whose parents reside in different states to maintain on a regular basis, save in exceptional circumstances personal relations and direct contacts with both parents. • Right of a child and his or her parents to leave any country, including their own, and to enter their own country.	• To ensure applications by a child or his or her parents to enter or leave a State Party for the purpose of family reunification shall be dealt with by States Parties in a positive, humane and expeditious manner. • To respect the right of the child and his or her parents to leave any country, including their own, and to enter their own country. • The right to leave any country shall be subject only to such restrictions as are prescribed by law and which are necessary to protect the national security, public order (*ordre public*), public health or morals or the rights and freedoms of others and are consistent with the other rights recognised in the Convention.
Article 11	• To take measures to combat the illicit transfer and non-return of

Summary of rights and responsibilities – International Convention on the Rights of the Child (CRC)[421]	
Rights and responsibilities	**Government obligations**
• Right of every child to be protected from illicit transfer abroad.	children abroad. To this end, States Parties shall promote the conclusion of bilateral or multilateral agreements or accession to existing agreements.
Article 12 • Right of a child to express his or her views freely in all matters affecting the child.	• To assure to the child who is capable of forming his or her own views the right to express those views freely in all matters affecting the child, the views of the child being given due weight in accordance with the age and maturity of the child. • To provide a child the opportunity to be heard in any judicial and administrative proceedings affecting the child, either directly, or through a representative or an appropriate body, in a manner consistent with the procedural rules of national law.
Article 13 • Right of all children to freedom of expression, including freedom to seek, receive and impart information and ideas of all kinds, regardless of frontiers, either orally, in writing or in print, in the form of art, or through any other media of the child's choice.	• To respect the right of the child to freedom of expression. • The exercise of this right may be subject to certain restrictions, but these shall only be such as are provided by law and are necessary: (a) for respect of the rights or reputations of others; or (b) for the protection of national security or of public order (*ordre public*), or of public health or morals.
Article 14 • Right of the child to freedom of thought, conscience and religion.	• To respect the right of the child to freedom of thought, conscience and religion. • To respect the rights and duties of the parents and, when applicable, legal guardians, to

Summary of rights and responsibilities – International Convention on the Rights of the Child (CRC)[421]	
Rights and responsibilities	**Government obligations**
	provide direction to the child in the exercise of his or her right in a manner consistent with the evolving capacities of the child. • Freedom to manifest one's religion or beliefs may be subject only to such limitations as are prescribed by law and are necessary to protect public safety, order, health or morals, or the fundamental rights and freedoms of others.
Article 15 • Right of the child to freedom of association and to freedom of peaceful assembly.	• To recognize the rights of the child to freedom of association and to freedom of peaceful assembly. • No restrictions may be placed on the exercise of these rights other than those imposed in conformity with the law and which are necessary in a democratic society in the interests of national security or public safety, public order (*ordre public*), the protection of public health or morals or the protection of the rights and freedoms of others.
Article 16 • Right of the child not to be subjected to arbitrary or unlawful interference with his or her privacy, family, home or correspondence, nor to unlawful attacks on his or her honour and reputation.	• To ensure the child has the right to the protection of the law against such interference or attacks.
Article 17 • Right (implied) of the child to information.	• To recognize the important function performed by the mass media and to ensure the child has access to information and material from a diversity of

Summary of rights and responsibilities – International Convention on the Rights of the Child (CRC)[421]	
Rights and responsibilities	**Government obligations**
	national and international sources, especially those aimed at the promotion of his or her social, spiritual and moral wellbeing and physical and mental health. • To encourage the mass media to disseminate information and material of social and cultural benefit to the child and in accordance with the spirit of Article 29. • To encourage international co-operation in the production, exchange and dissemination of such information and material from a diversity of cultural, national and international sources. • To encourage the production and dissemination of children's books. • To encourage the mass media to have particular regard to the linguistic needs of the child who belongs to a minority group or who is Indigenous. • To encourage the development of appropriate guidelines for the protection of the child from information and material injurious to his or her wellbeing, bearing in mind the provisions of Articles 13 and 18.
Article 18 • Right of children to the benefit of their parents' care. • Right of children to benefit from childcare facilities.	• To use best efforts to ensure recognition of the principle that both parents have common responsibilities for the upbringing and development of the child. • To ensure, for the purpose of guaranteeing and promoting the rights set forth in the Convention,

Summary of rights and responsibilities – International Convention on the Rights of the Child (CRC)[421]	
Rights and responsibilities	**Government obligations**
	that all appropriate assistance is rendered to parents and legal guardians in the performance of their child-rearing responsibilities and to ensure the development of institutions, facilities and services for the care of children. • To take all appropriate measures to ensure that children of working parents have the right to benefit from child-care services and facilities for which they are eligible.
Article 19 • Right of all children to protection from all forms of physical or mental violence, injury or abuse, neglect or negligent treatment, maltreatment or exploitation, including sexual abuse, while in the care of parent(s), legal guardian(s) or any other person who has the care of the child.	• To take all appropriate legislative, administrative, social and educational measures to protect the child from all forms of physical or mental violence, injury or abuse, neglect or negligent treatment, maltreatment or exploitation, including sexual abuse, while in the care of parent(s), legal guardian(s) or any other person who has the care of the child.
Article 20 • Right of a child deprived of family to special protection and assistance provided by the State.	• To ensure alternative care for such a child. Such care could include, inter alia, foster placement, kafalah of Islamic law, adoption or if necessary placement in suitable institutions for the care of children. When considering solutions, due regard shall be paid to the desirability of continuity in a child's upbringing and to the child's ethnic, religious, cultural and linguistic background.
Article 21	• To recognize and/or permit a system of adoption that shall

Summary of rights and responsibilities – International Convention on the Rights of the Child (CRC)[421]	
Rights and responsibilities	**Government obligations**
• Right of a child in adoption to protection in their best interests.	ensure that the best interests of the child shall be the paramount consideration. • To ensure that the adoption of a child is authorized only by competent authorities who determine, in accordance with applicable law and procedures and on the basis of all pertinent and reliable information, that the adoption is permissible in view of the child's status concerning parents, relatives and legal guardians and that, if required, the persons concerned have given their informed consent to the adoption on the basis of such counselling as may be necessary. • To ensure that the child concerned by inter-country adoption enjoys safeguards and standards equivalent to those existing in the case of national adoption. • To take all appropriate measures to ensure that, in inter-country adoption, the placement does not result in improper financial gain for those involved in it. • To promote, where appropriate, the objectives of the present article by concluding bilateral or multilateral arrangements or agreements, and endeavour, within this framework, to ensure that the placement of the child in another country is carried out by competent authorities or organs.
Article 22	• States Parties shall take appropriate measures to ensure

Summary of rights and responsibilities – International Convention on the Rights of the Child (CRC)[421]	
Rights and responsibilities	**Government obligations**
• Right of child refugees to protection and humanitarian assistance. • Right of child refugees to all rights in the Convention and all other human rights instruments.	that a child who is seeking refugee status or who is considered a refugee in accordance with applicable international or domestic law and procedures shall, whether unaccompanied or accompanied by his or her parents or by any other person, receive appropriate protection and humanitarian assistance in the enjoyment of applicable rights set forth in the Convention and in other international human rights or humanitarian instruments to which the said States are Parties. • To provide, as they consider appropriate, co-operation in any efforts by the United Nations and other competent intergovernmental organisations or non-governmental organizations co-operating with the United Nations to protect and assist such a child and to trace the parents or other members of the family of any refugee child in order to obtain information necessary for reunification with his or her family. In cases where no parents or other members of the family can be found, the child shall be accorded the same protection as any other child permanently or temporarily deprived of his or her family environment for any reason, as set forth in the Convention.
Article 23	• To recognize the right of the disabled child to special care and

Summary of rights and responsibilities – International Convention on the Rights of the Child (CRC)[421]	
Rights and responsibilities	**Government obligations**
• Right of a mentally or physically disabled child to enjoy a full and decent life in conditions which ensure dignity, promote self-reliance and facilitate the child's active participation in the community.	encourage and ensure the extension, subject to available resources, to the eligible child and those responsible for his or her care, of assistance for which application is made and which is appropriate to the child's condition and to the circumstances of the parents or others caring for the child. • To recognize the special needs of a disabled child, assistance extended in accordance with paragraph 2 of the present article shall be provided free of charge, whenever possible, taking into account the financial resources of the parents or others caring for the child, and shall be designed to ensure that the disabled child has effective access to and receives education, training, health care services, rehabilitation services, preparation for employment and recreation opportunities in a manner conducive to the child's achieving the fullest possible social integration and individual development, including his or her cultural and spiritual development.
Article 24 • Right of the child to the enjoyment of the highest attainable standard of health and to facilities for the treatment of illness and rehabilitation of health.	• To strive to ensure that no child is deprived of his or her right of access to such health care services. • To pursue full implementation of this right and, in particular, to take appropriate measures to: o diminish infant and child mortality;

Summary of rights and responsibilities – International Convention on the Rights of the Child (CRC)[421]	
Rights and responsibilities	**Government obligations**
	○ ensure the provision of necessary medical assistance and health care to all children with emphasis on the development of primary health care; ○ combat disease and malnutrition, including within the framework of primary health care, through, inter alia, the application of readily available technology and through the provision of adequate nutritious foods and clean drinking-water, taking into consideration the dangers and risks of environmental pollution; ○ ensure appropriate pre-natal and post-natal health care for mothers; ○ ensure that all segments of society, in particular parents and children, are informed, have access to education and are supported in the use of basic knowledge of child health and nutrition, the advantages of breastfeeding, hygiene and environmental sanitation and the prevention of accidents; ○ develop preventive health care, guidance for parents and family planning education and services. • To take all effective and appropriate measures with a view to abolishing traditional practices

Summary of rights and responsibilities – International Convention on the Rights of the Child (CRC)[421]	
Rights and responsibilities	**Government obligations**
	prejudicial to the health of children.
Article 25 • Right of a child who has been placed by the competent authorities for the purposes of care, protection or treatment of his or her physical or mental health, to a periodic review of the treatment provided to the child and all other circumstances relevant to his or her placement.	• To recognise the right of a child who has been placed by the competent authorities for the purposes of care, protection or treatment of his or her physical or mental health, to a periodic review of the treatment provided to the child and all other circumstances relevant to his or her placement.
Article 26 • Right of every child to benefit from social security, including social insurance.	• To recognize for every child the right to benefit from social security, including social insurance. • To take the necessary measures to achieve the full realization of this right in accordance with their national law.
Article 27 • Right of every child to a standard of living adequate for the child's physical, mental, spiritual, moral and social development. • Obligation of parents or others responsible for the child to take primary responsibility to secure, within their abilities and financial capacities, the conditions of living necessary for the child's development.	• To recognize the right of every child to a standard of living adequate for the child's physical, mental, spiritual, moral and social development. • To take, in accordance with national conditions and within their means, appropriate measures to assist parents and others responsible for the child to implement this right and to, in case of need, provide material assistance and support programmes, particularly with regard to nutrition, clothing and housing. • To take all appropriate measures to secure the recovery of maintenance for the child from the parents or other persons

Summary of rights and responsibilities – International Convention on the Rights of the Child (CRC)[421]	
Rights and responsibilities	**Government obligations**
	having financial responsibility for the child.
Article 28 • Right of every child to education.	• To recognize the right of the child to education with a view to achieving this right progressively and on the basis of equal opportunity. • To make primary education compulsory and available free to all. • To encourage the development of different forms of secondary education, including general and vocational education, make them available and accessible to every child, and take appropriate measures such as the introduction of free education and offering financial assistance in case of need. • To make higher education accessible to all on the basis of capacity by every appropriate means. • To make educational and vocational information and guidance available and accessible to all children. • To take measures to encourage regular attendance at schools and the reduction of drop-out rates. • To take all appropriate measures to ensure that school discipline is administered in a manner consistent with the child's human dignity and in conformity with the Convention. • To promote and encourage international cooperation in matters relating to education, in

Summary of rights and responsibilities – International Convention on the Rights of the Child (CRC)[421]	
Rights and responsibilities	**Government obligations**
	particular with a view to contributing to the elimination of ignorance and illiteracy throughout the world and facilitating access to scientific and technical knowledge and modern teaching methods.
Article 29 • Right of the child to education likely to ensure their development to their fullest potential within their society and culture.	• To ensure that the education of the child shall be directed to: (a) The development of the child's personality, talents and mental and physical abilities to their fullest potential; (b) The development of respect for human rights and fundamental freedoms, and for the principles enshrined in the Charter of the United Nations; (c) The development of respect for the child's parents, his or her own cultural identity, language and values, for the national values of the country in which the child is living, the country from which he or she may originate, and for civilizations different from his or her own; (d) The preparation of the child for responsible life in a free society, in the spirit of understanding, peace, tolerance, equality of sexes, and friendship among all peoples, ethnic, national and religious groups and persons of Indigenous origin; (e) The development of respect for the natural environment. • No part of the present article or Article 28 shall be construed so as to interfere with the liberty of individuals and bodies to

Summary of rights and responsibilities – International Convention on the Rights of the Child (CRC)[421]	
Rights and responsibilities	**Government obligations**
	establish and direct educational institutions, subject always to the observance of the principle set forth in paragraph 1 of the present Article and to the requirements that the education given in such institutions shall conform to such minimum standards as may be laid down by the state.
Article 30 • Right of the child to enjoy his or her own culture.	• To ensure that no child shall be denied the right, in community with other members of his or her group, to enjoy his or her own culture, to profess and practise his or her own religion, or to use his or her own language.
Article 31 • Right of the child to rest and leisure, to engage in play and recreational activities appropriate to the age of the child and to participate freely in cultural life and the arts.	• To respect and promote the right of the child to participate fully in cultural and artistic life and to encourage the provision of appropriate and equal opportunities for cultural, artistic, recreational and leisure activity.
Article 32 • Right of the child to be protected from economic exploitation and from performing any work that is likely to be hazardous or to interfere with the child's education, or to be harmful to the child's health or physical, mental, spiritual, moral or social development.	• To take legislative, administrative, social and educational measures to ensure the implementation of the present article. • To provide for a minimum age or minimum ages for admission to employment. • To provide for appropriate regulation of the hours and conditions of employment. • To provide for appropriate penalties or other sanctions to ensure the effective enforcement of the present Article.

Summary of rights and responsibilities – International Convention on the Rights of the Child (CRC)[421]	
Rights and responsibilities	**Government obligations**
Article 33 • Right of all children to protection from the illicit use of narcotic drugs and psychotropic substances as defined in the relevant international treaties.	• To take all appropriate measures, including legislative, administrative, social and educational measures, to protect children from the illicit use of narcotic drugs and psychotropic substances as defined in the relevant international treaties, and to prevent the use of children in the illicit production and trafficking of such substances.
Article 34 • Right of all children to protection from all forms of sexual exploitation and sexual abuse.	• To protect the child from all forms of sexual exploitation and sexual abuse. • To take all appropriate national, bilateral and multilateral measures to prevent: (a) The inducement or coercion of a child to engage in any unlawful sexual activity; (b) The exploitative use of children in prostitution or other unlawful sexual practices; (c) The exploitative use of children in pornographic performances and materials.
Article 35 • Right of all children to protection from human trafficking, exploitation and prostitution. • Right of all children to protection from abduction and sale.	• To take all appropriate national, bilateral and multilateral measures to prevent the abduction of, the sale of or traffic in children for any purpose or in any form.
Article 36 • Right of all children to protection against all other forms of exploitation prejudicial to any aspects of the child's welfare.	• To protect the child against all other forms of exploitation prejudicial to any aspects of the child's welfare.
Article 37 • Right of all children to protection from torture or other cruel,	• To ensure that no child shall be subjected to torture or other cruel, inhuman or degrading treatment or punishment.

Summary of rights and responsibilities – International Convention on the Rights of the Child (CRC)[421]	
Rights and responsibilities	**Government obligations**
inhuman or degrading treatment or punishment. • Right of all children not to be imprisoned for life and not to receive capital punishment. • Right of all children not to be deprived of liberty unlawfully or arbitrarily. • Right of a child lawfully deprived of liberty to be treated with humanity and respect for the inherent dignity of the human person, and in a manner which takes into account the needs of persons of his or her age. • Right of every child deprived of liberty not to be imprisoned with adults unless it is in the child's best interests. • Right of every child deprived of liberty to maintain contact with his or her family. • Right of every child deprived of his or her liberty to prompt access to legal and other appropriate assistance, as well as the right to challenge the legality of the deprivation of his or her liberty before a court or other competent, independent and impartial authority, and to a prompt decision on any such action.	Neither capital punishment nor life imprisonment without possibility of release shall be imposed for offences committed by persons below eighteen years of age. • To ensure that no child shall be deprived of his or her liberty unlawfully or arbitrarily. The arrest, detention or imprisonment of a child shall be in conformity with the law and shall be used only as a measure of last resort and for the shortest appropriate period of time. • To ensure that every child deprived of liberty shall be treated with humanity and respect for the inherent dignity of the human person, and in a manner which takes into account the needs of persons of his or her age. • To ensure that every child deprived of liberty shall be separated from adults unless it is considered in the child's best interest not to do so and shall have the right to maintain contact with his or her family through correspondence and visits, save in exceptional circumstances. • To ensure every child deprived of his or her liberty shall have the right to prompt access to legal and other appropriate assistance, as well as the right to challenge the legality of the deprivation of his or her liberty before a court or

Summary of rights and responsibilities – International Convention on the Rights of the Child (CRC)[421]	
Rights and responsibilities	**Government obligations**
	other competent, independent and impartial authority, and to a prompt decision on any such action.
Article 38 • Right of every child under the age of 15 not to take part in armed conflicts. • Right of all children to care and protection in an armed conflict.	• To ensure that persons who have not attained the age of fifteen years do not take a direct part in hostilities in an armed conflict. • To refrain from recruiting any person who has not attained the age of fifteen years into their armed forces. • To take all feasible measures to ensure protection and care of children who are affected by an armed conflict.
Article 39 • Right of the child to recovery and reintegration after abuse.	• To take all appropriate measures to promote physical and psychological recovery and social reintegration of a child victim of: any form of neglect, exploitation, or abuse; torture or any other form of cruel, inhuman or degrading treatment or punishment; or armed conflicts. Such recovery and reintegration shall take place in an environment which fosters the health, self-respect and dignity of the child.
Article 40 • Right of every child alleged as, accused of, or recognized as having infringed the penal law to be treated in a manner consistent with the promotion of the child's sense of dignity and worth, which reinforces the child's respect for the human rights and fundamental freedoms of others	• To ensure that no child shall be alleged as, be accused of, or recognized as having infringed the penal law by reason of acts or omissions that were not prohibited by national or international law at the time they were committed. • To promote the establishment of laws, procedures, authorities and

Summary of rights and responsibilities – International Convention on the Rights of the Child (CRC)[421]	
Rights and responsibilities	**Government obligations**
and which takes into account the child's age and the desirability of promoting the child's reintegration and the child's assuming a constructive role in society. • Right of the child to be presumed innocent until proven guilty according to law. • Right of the child to be informed promptly and directly of the charges against him or her, and, if appropriate, through his or her parents or legal guardians, and to have legal or other appropriate assistance in the preparation and presentation of his or her defence. • Right of the child to have the matter determined without delay by a competent, independent and impartial authority or judicial body in a fair hearing according to law, in the presence of legal or other appropriate assistance and, unless it is considered not to be in the best interest of the child, in particular, taking into account his or her age or situation, his or her parents or legal guardians. • Right of the child not to be compelled to give testimony or to confess guilt. • Right of the child to examine or have examined adverse witnesses and to obtain the participation and examination of witnesses on his or her behalf under conditions of equality.	institutions specifically applicable to children alleged as, accused of, or recognized as having infringed the penal law. • To establish a minimum age below which children shall be presumed not to have the capacity to infringe the penal law. • To ensure, whenever appropriate and desirable, provision of measures for dealing with such children without resorting to judicial proceedings, providing that human rights and legal safeguards are fully respected. • To provide that a variety of dispositions, such as care, guidance and supervision orders; counselling; probation; foster care; education and vocational training programmes and other alternatives to institutional care shall be available to ensure that children are dealt with in a manner appropriate to their wellbeing and proportionate both to their circumstances and the offence.

Summary of rights and responsibilities – International Convention on the Rights of the Child (CRC)[421]	
Rights and responsibilities	**Government obligations**
• Right of the child, if considered to have infringed the penal law, to have this decision and any measures imposed in consequence thereof reviewed by a higher competent, independent and impartial authority or judicial body according to law. • Right of the child to have the free assistance of an interpreter if the child cannot understand or speak the language used. • Right of the child to have his or her privacy fully respected at all stages of the proceedings.	

International Convention on the Rights of Persons with Disabilities (CRPD)

Summary of rights and responsibilities – International Convention on the Rights of Persons with Disabilities (CRPD)[422]	
Rights and responsibilities	**Government obligations**
Article 1 • Right of full and equal enjoyment of all human rights and fundamental freedoms by all persons with disabilities. • Includes definitions.	• To promote respect for the inherent dignity of persons with disabilities.
Article 2 • Miscellaneous definitions.	
Article 3 • Rights for all persons with disabilities in accordance with principles of: o respect for inherent dignity, individual autonomy including the freedom to make one's own choices, and independence of persons; o non-discrimination; o full and effective participation and inclusion in society; o respect for difference and acceptance of persons with disabilities as part of human diversity and humanity; o equality of opportunity; o accessibility; o equality between men and women; o respect for the evolving capacities of children with disabilities; and	• To observe principles of the Convention.

[422] Convention on the Rights of Persons with Disabilities- external site

Summary of rights and responsibilities – International Convention on the Rights of Persons with Disabilities (CRPD)[422]	
Rights and responsibilities	**Government obligations**
o respect for the right of children with disabilities to preserve their identities.	
Article 4 • Right of persons with disabilities to full realisation of all human rights and fundamental freedoms without discrimination of any kind on the basis of disability.	• To adopt all appropriate legislative, administrative and other measures for the implementation of the rights recognized in the Convention. • To take all appropriate measures, including legislation, to modify or abolish existing laws, regulations, customs and practices that constitute discrimination against persons with disabilities. • To take into account the protection and promotion of the human rights of persons with disabilities in all policies and programmes. • To refrain from engaging in any act or practice that is inconsistent with the Convention and to ensure that public authorities and institutions act in conformity with the Convention. • To take all appropriate measures to eliminate discrimination on the basis of disability by any person, organization or private enterprise. • To undertake or promote research and development of universally designed goods, services, equipment and facilities, as defined in Article 2 of the Convention, which should require the minimum possible adaptation and the least cost to meet the specific needs of a person with disabilities, to promote their

Summary of rights and responsibilities – International Convention on the Rights of Persons with Disabilities (CRPD)[422]	
Rights and responsibilities	**Government obligations**
	availability and use, and to promote universal design in the development of standards and guidelines. • To undertake or promote research and development of, and to promote the availability and use of new technologies, including information and communications technologies, mobility aids, devices and assistive technologies, suitable for persons with disabilities, giving priority to technologies at an affordable cost. • To provide accessible information to persons with disabilities about mobility aids, devices and assistive technologies, including new technologies, as well as other forms of assistance, support services and facilities. • To promote the training of professionals and staff working with persons with disabilities in the rights recognized in the Convention so as to better provide the assistance and services guaranteed by those rights. • To take measures to the maximum of its available resources and, where needed, within the framework of international cooperation, with a view to achieving progressively the full realization of these rights, without prejudice to those obligations contained in the Convention that are immediately

Summary of rights and responsibilities – International Convention on the Rights of Persons with Disabilities (CRPD)[422]	
Rights and responsibilities	**Government obligations**
	applicable according to international law. • To closely consult with and actively involve persons with disabilities, including children with disabilities, through their representative organizations. • Nothing in the Convention shall affect any provisions which are more conducive to the realization of the rights of persons with disabilities and which may be contained in the law of a State Party or international law in force for that State. There shall be no restriction upon or derogation from any of the human rights and fundamental freedoms recognized or existing in any State Party to the Convention pursuant to law, conventions, regulation or custom on the pretext that the Convention does not recognize such rights or freedoms or that it recognizes them to a lesser extent. • The provisions of the Convention shall extend to all parts of federal States without any limitations or exceptions.
Article 5 • Right of all persons with disabilities to equality before and under the law. • Right of all persons with disabilities to equal protection and equal benefit of the law. • Right to protection from discrimination on the basis of disability.	• To recognize that all persons are equal before and under the law and are entitled without any discrimination to the equal protection and equal benefit of the law. • To prohibit all discrimination on the basis of disability and guarantee to persons with disabilities equal and effective

Summary of rights and responsibilities – International Convention on the Rights of Persons with Disabilities (CRPD)[422]	
Rights and responsibilities	**Government obligations**
• Right of all persons with disabilities to effective legal protection against discrimination of all kinds.	legal protection against discrimination on all grounds. • Specific measures which are necessary to accelerate or achieve de facto equality of persons with disabilities shall not be considered discrimination under the terms of the Convention.
Article 6 • Right of all women and girls with disabilities to the full and equal enjoyment of all human rights and fundamental freedoms without discrimination.	• To take all appropriate measures to ensure the full development, advancement and empowerment of women, for the purpose of guaranteeing them the exercise and enjoyment of the human rights and fundamental freedoms set out in the Convention.
Article 7 • Right of all children with disabilities to the full and equal enjoyment of all human rights and fundamental freedoms without discrimination, on an equal basis with other children. • Right of all children with disabilities to express their views freely on all matters affecting them, on an equal basis with other children.	• To ensure that in all actions concerning children with disabilities, the best interests of the child shall be a primary consideration. • To ensure that children with disabilities have the right to express their views freely on all matters affecting them, their views being given due weight in accordance with their age and maturity, on an equal basis with other children, and to be provided with disability and age-appropriate assistance to realise that right.
Article 8 • Right of persons with disabilities to full realisation of all human rights and fundamental freedoms without discrimination of any kind, including discrimination based on sex and age.	• To raise awareness throughout society, including at the family level, regarding persons with disabilities, and to foster respect for the rights and dignity of persons with disabilities,

Summary of rights and responsibilities – International Convention on the Rights of Persons with Disabilities (CRPD)[422]	
Rights and responsibilities	**Government obligations**
	• To combat stereotypes, prejudices and harmful practices relating to persons with disabilities, including those based on sex and age, in all areas of life. • To promote awareness of the capabilities and contributions of persons with disabilities.
Article 9 • Right of persons with disabilities to live independently. • Right of persons with disabilities to participate fully in all aspects of life. • Right of persons with disabilities on an equal basis with others to access to the physical environment, to transportation, to information and communications, including information and communications technologies and systems, and to other facilities and services open or provided to the public, both in urban and in rural areas.	• To take measures which shall include the identification and elimination of obstacles and barriers to accessibility, shall apply to, inter alia: (a) buildings, roads, transportation and other indoor and outdoor facilities, including schools, housing, medical facilities and workplaces; (b) Information, communications and other services, including electronic services and emergency services. • To develop, promulgate and monitor the implementation of minimum standards and guidelines for the accessibility of facilities and services open or provided to the public. • To ensure that private entities that offer facilities and services which are open or provided to the public take into account all aspects of accessibility for persons with disabilities. • To provide training for stakeholders on accessibility issues facing persons with disabilities. • To provide in buildings and other facilities open to the public

Summary of rights and responsibilities – International Convention on the Rights of Persons with Disabilities (CRPD)[422]	
Rights and responsibilities	**Government obligations**
	signage in Braille and in easy to read and understand forms. • To provide forms of live assistance and intermediaries, including guides, readers and professional sign language interpreters, to facilitate accessibility to buildings and other facilities open to the public. • To promote other appropriate forms of assistance and support to persons with disabilities to ensure their access to information. • To promote access for persons with disabilities to new information and communications technologies and systems, including the Internet. • To promote the design, development, production and distribution of accessible information and communications technologies and systems at an early stage, so that these technologies and systems become accessible at minimum cost.
Article 10 • Right to life of persons with disabilities.	• To affirm that every human being has the inherent right to life and shall take all necessary measures to ensure its effective enjoyment by persons with disabilities on an equal basis with others.
Article 11 • Right to protection and safety of persons with disabilities in situations of risk, including situations of armed conflict, humanitarian emergencies and	• To take, in accordance with their obligations under international law, including international humanitarian law and international human rights law, all necessary measures to ensure

Summary of rights and responsibilities – International Convention on the Rights of Persons with Disabilities (CRPD)[422]	
Rights and responsibilities	**Government obligations**
the occurrence of natural disasters.	the protection and safety of persons with disabilities in situations of risk, including situations of armed conflict, humanitarian emergencies and the occurrence of natural disasters.
Article 12 • Right of persons with disabilities to equality before the law. • Right of persons with disabilities to enjoy legal capacity on an equal basis with others in all aspects of life. • Right of persons with disabilities to own or inherit property, to control their own financial affairs and to have equal access to bank loans, mortgages and other forms of financial credit. • Right of persons with disabilities not to be arbitrarily deprived of their property.	• To take appropriate measures to provide access by persons with disabilities to the support they may require in exercising their legal capacity. • To ensure that all measures that relate to the exercise of legal capacity provide for appropriate and effective safeguards to prevent abuse in accordance with international human rights law. • To take all appropriate and effective measures to ensure the equal right of persons with disabilities to own or inherit property, to control their own financial affairs and to have equal access to bank loans, mortgages and other forms of financial credit. • To ensure that persons with disabilities are not arbitrarily deprived of their property.
Article 13 • Right of persons with disabilities to justice on an equal basis with others.	• To ensure effective access to justice for persons with disabilities on an equal basis with others, including through the provision of procedural and age-appropriate accommodations, in order to facilitate their effective role as direct and indirect participants, including as witnesses, in all legal

Summary of rights and responsibilities – International Convention on the Rights of Persons with Disabilities (CRPD)[422]	
Rights and responsibilities	**Government obligations**
	proceedings, including at investigative and other preliminary stages.
Article 14 • Right of persons with disabilities, on an equal basis with others, to liberty and security of person. • Right of persons with disabilities, on an equal basis with others, not to be deprived of their liberty unlawfully or arbitrarily.	• To ensure that persons with disabilities, on an equal basis with others: (a) Enjoy the right to liberty and security of person; (b) Are not deprived of their liberty unlawfully or arbitrarily, and that any deprivation of liberty is in conformity with the law, and that the existence of a disability shall in no case justify a deprivation of liberty. • To ensure that if persons with disabilities are deprived of their liberty through any process, they are, on an equal basis with others, entitled to guarantees in accordance with international human rights law and shall be treated in compliance with the objectives and principles of the Convention, including by provision of reasonable accommodation.
Article 15 • Right of persons with disabilities not to be subjected to cruel, inhuman or degrading treatment or punishment. • Right of persons with disabilities not to be subjected to medical or scientific experimentation.	• To take all effective legislative, administrative, judicial or other measures to prevent persons with disabilities, on an equal basis with others, from being subjected to torture or cruel, inhuman or degrading treatment or punishment.
Article 16 • Right of persons with disabilities to freedom from exploitation, violence and abuse.	• To take all appropriate measures to prevent all forms of exploitation, violence and abuse by ensuring, inter alia, appropriate forms of gender- and age-sensitive assistance and

Summary of rights and responsibilities – International Convention on the Rights of Persons with Disabilities (CRPD)[422]	
Rights and responsibilities	**Government obligations**
• Right of persons with disabilities to recovery and reintegration after abuse.	support for persons with disabilities and their families and caregivers, including through the provision of information and education on how to avoid, recognize and report instances of exploitation, violence and abuse. • To ensure that protection services are age-, gender- and disability-sensitive. • To ensure that all facilities and programmes designed to serve persons with disabilities are effectively monitored by independent authorities. • To take all appropriate measures to promote the physical, cognitive and psychological recovery, rehabilitation and social reintegration of persons with disabilities who become victims of any form of exploitation, violence or abuse, including through the provision of protection services. • To put in place effective legislation and policies, including women- and child-focused legislation and policies, to ensure that instances of exploitation, violence and abuse against persons with disabilities are identified, investigated and, where appropriate, prosecuted.
Article 17 • Right of persons with disabilities to right respect for his or her physical and mental integrity on an equal basis with others.	

<table>
<tr><th colspan="2">Summary of rights and responsibilities – International Convention on the Rights of Persons with Disabilities (CRPD)[422]</th></tr>
<tr><th>Rights and responsibilities</th><th>Government obligations</th></tr>
<tr><td>Article 18
• Right of persons with disabilities, on an equal basis with others:
o to liberty of movement;
o to freedom to choose their residence and to a nationality;
o to acquire and change a nationality;
o to not be deprived of their nationality arbitrarily or on the basis of disability;
o to not be deprived, on the basis of disability, of their ability to obtain, possess and utilize documentation of their nationality or other documentation of identification, or to utilize relevant processes such as immigration proceedings;
o to leave any country, including their own;
o to not be deprived, arbitrarily or on the basis of disability, of the right to enter their own country.
• Right of children with disabilities to be registered immediately after birth.
• Right of children with disabilities to a name.
• Right of children with disabilities to acquire a nationality and, as far as possible, the right to know and be cared for by their parents.</td><td>• To recognize the rights of persons with disabilities that may be needed to facilitate exercise of all these rights.</td></tr>
<tr><td>Article 19
• Right of persons with disabilities to live independently and be included in the community.</td><td>• To recognize the equal right of all persons with disabilities to these rights.</td></tr>
</table>

Summary of rights and responsibilities – International Convention on the Rights of Persons with Disabilities (CRPD)[422]	
Rights and responsibilities	**Government obligations**
	• To take all effective and appropriate measures to facilitate full enjoyment by persons with disabilities of these rights. • To ensure that persons with disabilities have the opportunity to choose their place of residence and where and with whom they live on an equal basis with others and are not obliged to live in a particular living arrangement. • To ensure access to a range of in-home, residential and other community support services, including personal assistance necessary to support living and inclusion in the community, and to prevent isolation or segregation from the community, • To ensure community services and facilities for the general population are available on an equal basis to persons with disabilities and are responsive to their needs.
Article 20 • Right of person with disabilities to mobility.	• To take effective measures to ensure personal mobility with the greatest possible independence for persons with disabilities.
Article 21 • Right of persons with disabilities to freedom of expression and opinion, and access to information.	• To take all appropriate measures to ensure that persons with disabilities can exercise the right to freedom of expression and opinion, including the freedom to seek, receive and impart information and ideas on an equal basis with others and through all forms of communication of their choice, as

Summary of rights and responsibilities – International Convention on the Rights of Persons with Disabilities (CRPD)[422]	
Rights and responsibilities	**Government obligations**
	defined in Article 2 of the Convention.
Article 22 • Right of persons with disabilities to privacy.	• To ensure persons with disabilities have the right to the protection of the law against interference in or attacks on their privacy on an equal basis with others.
Article 23 • Right of persons with disabilities, on a basis of equality with all others: o to be protected from discrimination in all matters relating to marriage, family, parenthood and relationships; o to found a family; o to decide freely and responsibly on the number and spacing of their children and to have access to age-appropriate information, reproductive and family planning education. • Right of persons with disabilities, including children, to retain their fertility on an equal basis with others. • Right of children with disabilities to enjoy family life.	• To take effective and appropriate measures to eliminate discrimination against persons with disabilities in all matters relating to marriage, family, parenthood and relationships, on an equal basis with others. • To take the means necessary to enable them to exercise these rights. • To ensure the rights and responsibilities of persons with disabilities, with regard to guardianship, wardship, trusteeship, adoption of children or similar institutions, where these concepts exist in national legislation; in all cases the best interests of the child shall be paramount. • To render appropriate assistance to persons with disabilities in the performance of their child-rearing responsibilities. • To ensure that children with disabilities have equal rights with respect to family life. With a view to realizing these rights, and to prevent concealment, abandonment, neglect and segregation of children with disabilities, to undertake to

Summary of rights and responsibilities – International Convention on the Rights of Persons with Disabilities (CRPD)[422]	
Rights and responsibilities	**Government obligations**
	provide early and comprehensive information, services and support to children with disabilities and their families. • To ensure that a child shall not be separated from his or her parents against their will, except when competent authorities subject to judicial review determine, in accordance with applicable law and procedures, that such separation is necessary for the best interests of the child. In no case shall a child be separated from parents on the basis of a disability of either the child or one or both of the parents. • To undertake, where the immediate family is unable to care for a child with disabilities, every effort to provide alternative care within the wider family, and failing that, within the community in a family setting.
Article 24 • Right of persons with disabilities, on an equal basis with others, to education likely to ensure their development to their fullest potential within their society and culture, the sense of dignity and self-worth.	• To recognize the right of persons with disabilities to education. • To ensure that persons with disabilities are not excluded from the general education system on the basis of disability, and that children with disabilities are not excluded from free and compulsory primary education, or from secondary education, on the basis of disability. • To ensure persons with disabilities can access an inclusive, quality and free primary education and secondary education on an equal basis with

Summary of rights and responsibilities – International Convention on the Rights of Persons with Disabilities (CRPD)[422]	
Rights and responsibilities	**Government obligations**
	others in the communities in which they live. • To ensure reasonable accommodation of the individual's requirements is provided and persons with disabilities receive the support required, within the general education system, to facilitate their effective education. • To ensure that persons with disabilities are able to access general tertiary education, vocational training, adult education and lifelong learning without discrimination and on an equal basis with others.
Article 25 • Right of persons with disabilities to enjoyment of the highest attainable standard of health without discrimination on the basis of disability.	• To take all appropriate measures to ensure access for persons with disabilities to health services that are gender-sensitive, including health-related rehabilitation.
Article 26 • Right of persons with disabilities to attain and maintain maximum independence, full physical, mental, social and vocational ability, and full inclusion and participation in all aspects of life.	• To organize, strengthen and extend comprehensive habilitation and rehabilitation services and programmes, particularly in the areas of health, employment, education and social services.
Article 27 • Right of persons with disabilities to work, on an equal basis with others. • Right of persons with disabilities to be protected from discrimination in relation to work and all matters of employment. • Rights of persons with disabilities, on an equal basis with others, to	• To recognize the right of persons with disabilities to work, on an equal basis with others; this includes the right to the opportunity to gain a living by work freely chosen or accepted in a labour market and work environment that is open, inclusive and accessible to persons with disabilities.

Summary of rights and responsibilities – International Convention on the Rights of Persons with Disabilities (CRPD)[422]	
Rights and responsibilities	**Government obligations**
just and favourable conditions of work, including equal opportunities and equal remuneration for work of equal value, safe and healthy working conditions, including protection from harassment, and the redress of grievances. • Right of all persons with disabilities not to be held in slavery, servitude or forced/compulsory labour.	• To safeguard and promote the realization of the right to work, including for those who acquire a disability during the course of employment. • To prohibit discrimination on the basis of disability with regard to all matters concerning all forms of employment, including conditions of recruitment, hiring and employment, continuance of employment, career advancement and safe and healthy working conditions. • To ensure that persons with disabilities are not held in slavery or in servitude, and are protected, on an equal basis with others, from forced or compulsory labour.
Article 28 • Right of persons with disabilities to an adequate standard of living for themselves and their families, including adequate food, clothing and housing, and to the continuous improvement of living conditions.	• To take appropriate steps to safeguard and promote the realization of this right without discrimination on the basis of disability. • To recognize the right of persons with disabilities to social protection and to the enjoyment of that right without discrimination on the basis of disability, and to take appropriate steps to safeguard and promote the realization of this right.
Article 29 • Right of persons with disabilities to political rights and the opportunity to enjoy them on an equal basis with others.	• To ensure that persons with disabilities can effectively and fully participate in political and public life on an equal basis with others, directly or through freely chosen representatives, including the right and opportunity for

Summary of rights and responsibilities – International Convention on the Rights of Persons with Disabilities (CRPD)[422]	
Rights and responsibilities	**Government obligations**
	persons with disabilities to vote and be elected.
Article 30 • Right of persons with disabilities to take part on an equal basis with others in cultural life. • Right of persons with disabilities to participate on an equal basis with others in recreational, leisure and sporting activities.	• To take appropriate measures to enable persons with disabilities to have the opportunity to develop and utilize their creative, artistic and intellectual potential, not only for their own benefit, but also for the enrichment of society. • To encourage and promote the participation, to the fullest extent possible, of persons with disabilities in mainstream sporting activities at all levels.

United Nations Declaration on the Rights of Indigenous Peoples (UNDRIP).

Summary of rights and responsibilities – United Nations Declaration on the Rights of Indigenous Peoples (UNDRIP)[423]	
Rights and responsibilities	**Government obligations**
Article 1 • Right of Indigenous peoples to the full enjoyment, as a collective or as individuals, of all human rights and fundamental freedoms as recognized in the Charter of the United Nations, the Universal Declaration of Human Rights and international human rights law.	
Article 2 • Right of Indigenous peoples and individuals, on a basis of equality with all other peoples and individuals, to be free from any kind of discrimination in the exercise of their rights and in particular that based on their Indigenous origin or identity.	
Article 3 • Right of Indigenous peoples to self-determination. • Right of Indigenous peoples to freely determine their political status and freely pursue their economic, social and cultural development.	
Article 4 • Right of Indigenous peoples, in exercising their right to self-determination, to autonomy or self-government in matters relating to their internal and local	

[423] United Nations Declaration on the Rights of Indigenous Peoples, 2007. DRIPS_en.pdf (un.org)

Summary of rights and responsibilities – United Nations Declaration on the Rights of Indigenous Peoples (UNDRIP)[423]	
Rights and responsibilities	**Government obligations**
affairs, as well as ways and means for financing their autonomous functions.	
Article 5 • Right of Indigenous peoples to maintain and strengthen their distinct political, legal, economic, social and cultural institutions, while retaining their right to participate fully, if they so choose, in the political, economic, social and cultural life of the State.	
Article 6 • Right of Indigenous peoples to a nationality.	
Article 7 • Right of Indigenous individuals to life, physical and mental integrity, liberty and security of person. • Right of Indigenous peoples collectively to live in freedom, peace and security as distinct peoples. • Right of Indigenous peoples not to be subjected to any act of genocide or any other act of violence, including forcibly removing children of the group to another group.	
Article 8 • Right of Indigenous peoples and individuals not to be subjected to forced assimilation or destruction of their culture.	• To provide effective mechanisms for prevention of, and redress for: ○ any action which has the aim or effect of depriving them of their integrity as distinct peoples, or of their cultural values or ethnic identities; ○ any action which has the aim or effect of dispossessing

Summary of rights and responsibilities – United Nations Declaration on the Rights of Indigenous Peoples (UNDRIP)[423]	
Rights and responsibilities	**Government obligations**
	them of their lands, territories or resources; ○ any form of forced population transfer which has the aim or effect of violating or undermining any of their rights; ○ any form of forced assimilation or integration; ○ any form of propaganda designed to promote or incite racial or ethnic discrimination directed against them.
Article 9 • Right of Indigenous peoples and individuals to belong to an Indigenous community or nation, in accordance with the traditions and customs of the community or nation concerned.	• To ensure in law that no discrimination of any kind may arise from the exercise of this right.
Article 10 • Right of Indigenous peoples to not be forcibly removed from their lands or territories.	• To ensure no relocation shall take place without the free, prior and informed consent of the Indigenous peoples concerned and after agreement on just and fair compensation and, where possible, with the option of return.
Article 11 • Right of Indigenous peoples to practise and revitalize their cultural traditions and customs, including the right to maintain, protect and develop the past, present and future manifestations of their cultures, such as archaeological and historical sites, artefacts, designs, ceremonies, technologies and	• To provide redress through effective mechanisms, which may include restitution, developed in conjunction with Indigenous peoples, with respect to their cultural, intellectual, religious and spiritual property taken without their free, prior and informed consent or in violation of their laws, traditions and customs.

Summary of rights and responsibilities – United Nations Declaration on the Rights of Indigenous Peoples (UNDRIP)[423]	
Rights and responsibilities	**Government obligations**
visual and performing arts and literature.	
Article 12 • Right of Indigenous peoples to manifest, practise, develop and teach their spiritual and religious traditions, customs and ceremonies. • Right of Indigenous peoples to maintain, protect, and have access in privacy to their religious and cultural sites. • Right of Indigenous peoples to the use and control of their ceremonial objects. • Right of Indigenous peoples to the repatriation of their human remains.	• To enable the access and/or repatriation of ceremonial objects and human remains in their possession through fair, transparent and effective mechanisms developed in conjunction with Indigenous peoples concerned.
Article 13 • Right of Indigenous peoples to revitalize, use, develop and transmit to future generations their histories, languages, oral traditions, philosophies, writing systems and literatures, and to designate and retain their own names for communities, places and persons.	• To take effective measures to ensure that this right is protected and also to ensure that Indigenous peoples can understand and be understood in political, legal and administrative proceedings, where necessary through the provision of interpretation or by other appropriate means.
Article 14 • Right of Indigenous peoples to establish and control their educational systems and institutions providing education in their own languages, in a manner appropriate to their cultural methods of teaching and learning. • Right of Indigenous individuals, particularly children, to all levels	• To, in conjunction with Indigenous peoples, take effective measures, in order for Indigenous individuals, particularly children, including those living outside their communities, to have access, when possible, to an education in their own culture and provided in their own language.

Summary of rights and responsibilities – United Nations Declaration on the Rights of Indigenous Peoples (UNDRIP)[423]	
Rights and responsibilities	**Government obligations**
and forms of education of the State without discrimination.	
Article 15 • Right of Indigenous peoples to the dignity and diversity of their cultures, traditions, histories and aspirations which shall be appropriately reflected in education and public information.	• To take effective measures, in consultation and cooperation with the Indigenous peoples concerned, to combat prejudice and eliminate discrimination and to promote tolerance, understanding and good relations among Indigenous peoples and all other segments of society.
Article 16 • Right of Indigenous peoples to establish their own media in their own languages and to have access to all forms of non-Indigenous media without discrimination.	• To take effective measures to ensure that State-owned media duly reflect Indigenous cultural diversity. • To encourage, without prejudice to ensuring full freedom of expression, privately owned media to adequately reflect Indigenous cultural diversity.
Article 17 • Right of Indigenous individuals and peoples to enjoy fully all rights established under applicable international and domestic labour law. • Right of Indigenous individuals not to be subjected to any discriminatory conditions of labour and, inter alia, employment or salary.	• To take specific measures, in consultation and cooperation with Indigenous peoples, to protect Indigenous children from economic exploitation and from performing any work that is likely to be hazardous or to interfere with the child's education, or to be harmful to the child's health or physical, mental, spiritual, moral or social development, taking into account their special vulnerability and the importance of education for their empowerment.
Article 18 • Right of Indigenous peoples to participate in decision-making in matters which would affect their rights, through representatives	

Summary of rights and responsibilities – United Nations Declaration on the Rights of Indigenous Peoples (UNDRIP)[423]	
Rights and responsibilities	**Government obligations**
chosen by themselves in accordance with their own procedures, as well as to maintain and develop their own Indigenous decision-making institutions.	
Article 19 • Right (implied) to an Indigenous Voice in the Constitution.	• To consult and cooperate in good faith with the Indigenous peoples concerned through their own representative institutions in order to obtain their free, prior and informed consent before adopting and implementing legislative or administrative measures that may affect them.
Article 20 • Right of Indigenous peoples to maintain and develop their political, economic and social systems or institutions, to be secure in the enjoyment of their own means of subsistence and development, and to engage freely in all their traditional and other economic activities. • Right of Indigenous peoples deprived of their means of subsistence and development, to just and fair redress.	• To recognise and ensure Indigenous peoples deprived of their means of subsistence and development are entitled to just and fair redress.
Article 21 • Right of Indigenous peoples, without discrimination, to the improvement of their economic and social conditions, including, inter alia, in the areas of education, employment, vocational training and retraining, housing, sanitation, health and social security.	• To take effective measures and, where appropriate, special measures to ensure continuing improvement of their economic and social conditions. Particular attention shall be paid to the rights and special needs of Indigenous elders, women, youth, children and persons with disabilities.

Summary of rights and responsibilities – United Nations Declaration on the Rights of Indigenous Peoples (UNDRIP)[423]	
Rights and responsibilities	**Government obligations**
Article 22	• To ensure particular attention is paid to the rights and special needs of Indigenous elders, women, youth, children and persons with disabilities in the implementation of this Declaration. • To take measures, in conjunction with Indigenous peoples, to ensure that Indigenous women and children enjoy the full protection and guarantees against all forms of violence and discrimination.
Article 23 • Right of Indigenous peoples to determine and develop priorities and strategies for exercising their right to development. • Right of Indigenous peoples to be actively involved in developing and determining health, housing and other economic and social programmes affecting them and, as far as possible, to administer such programmes through their own institutions.	• To recognise and ensure Indigenous peoples have the right to be actively involved in developing and determining health, housing and other economic and social programmes affecting them and, as far as possible, to administer such programmes through their own institutions.
Article 24 • Right of Indigenous peoples to their traditional medicines and to maintain their health practices, including the conservation of their vital medicinal plants, animals and minerals. • Right of Indigenous individuals to access, without any discrimination, all social and health services. • Right of Indigenous individuals, on an equal basis with non-	• To take the necessary steps with a view to achieving progressively the full realization of this right.

Summary of rights and responsibilities – United Nations Declaration on the Rights of Indigenous Peoples (UNDRIP)[423]	
Rights and responsibilities	**Government obligations**
Indigenes, to the enjoyment of the highest attainable standard of physical and mental health.	
Article 25 • Right of Indigenous peoples to maintain and strengthen their distinctive spiritual relationship with their traditionally owned or otherwise occupied and used lands, territories, waters and coastal seas and other resources and to uphold their responsibilities to future generations in this regard.	
Article 26 • Right of Indigenous peoples to the lands, territories and resources which they have traditionally owned, occupied or otherwise used or acquired. • Right of Indigenous peoples to own, use, develop and control the lands, territories and resources that they possess by reason of traditional ownership or other traditional occupation or use, as well as those which they have otherwise acquired.	• To give legal recognition and protection to these lands, territories and resources. Such recognition shall be conducted with due respect to the customs, traditions and land tenure systems of the Indigenous peoples concerned.
Article 27 • Right of Indigenous peoples to participate in a fair, independent, impartial, open and transparent process, giving due recognition to Indigenous peoples' laws, traditions, customs and land tenure systems.	• To establish and implement, in conjunction with Indigenous peoples concerned, a fair, independent, impartial, open and transparent process, giving due recognition to Indigenous peoples' laws, traditions, customs and land tenure systems, to recognize and adjudicate the rights of Indigenous peoples pertaining to their lands, territories and resources,

Summary of rights and responsibilities – United Nations Declaration on the Rights of Indigenous Peoples (UNDRIP)[423]	
Rights and responsibilities	**Government obligations**
	including those which were traditionally owned or otherwise occupied or used.
Article 28 • Right of Indigenous peoples to redress, by means that can include restitution or, when this is not possible, just, fair and equitable compensation, for the lands, territories and resources which they have traditionally owned or otherwise occupied or used, and which have been confiscated, taken, occupied, used or damaged without their free, prior and informed consent.	• To provide, unless otherwise freely agreed upon by the peoples concerned, compensation in the form of lands, territories and resources equal in quality, size and legal status or of monetary compensation or other appropriate redress.
Article 29 • Right of Indigenous peoples to the conservation and protection of the environment and the productive capacity of their lands or territories and resources.	• To establish and implement assistance programmes for Indigenous peoples for such conservation and protection, without discrimination. • To take effective measures to ensure that no storage or disposal of hazardous materials shall take place in the lands or territories of Indigenous peoples without their free, prior and informed consent. • To take effective measures to ensure, as needed, that programmes for monitoring, maintaining and restoring the health of Indigenous peoples, as developed and implemented by the peoples affected by such materials, are duly implemented.
Article 30 • Right of Indigenous peoples not to have military activities take place in their lands or territories,	• To ensure military activities shall not take place in the lands or territories of Indigenous peoples, unless justified by a relevant

Summary of rights and responsibilities – United Nations Declaration on the Rights of Indigenous Peoples (UNDRIP)[423]	
Rights and responsibilities	**Government obligations**
unless justified by a relevant public interest or otherwise freely agreed with or requested by the Indigenous peoples concerned.	public interest or otherwise freely agreed with or requested by the Indigenous peoples concerned. • To undertake effective consultations with the Indigenous peoples concerned, through appropriate procedures and in particular through their representative institutions, prior to using their lands or territories for military activities.
Article 31 • Right of Indigenous peoples to maintain, control, protect and develop their cultural heritage, traditional knowledge and traditional cultural expressions, as well as the manifestations of their sciences, technologies and cultures, including human and genetic resources, seeds, medicines, knowledge of the properties of fauna and flora, oral traditions, literatures, designs, sports and traditional games and visual and performing arts. • Right of Indigenous peoples to maintain, control, protect and develop their intellectual property over such cultural heritage, traditional knowledge, and traditional cultural expressions.	• To, in conjunction with Indigenous peoples, take effective measures to recognize and protect the exercise of these rights.
Article 32 • Right of Indigenous peoples to determine and develop priorities and strategies for the development or use of their lands or territories and other resources.	• To consult and cooperate in good faith with the Indigenous peoples concerned through their own representative institutions in order to obtain their free and informed consent prior to the approval of any project affecting

Summary of rights and responsibilities – United Nations Declaration on the Rights of Indigenous Peoples (UNDRIP)[423]	
Rights and responsibilities	**Government obligations**
	their lands or territories and other resources, particularly in connection with the development, utilization or exploitation of mineral, water or other resources. • To provide effective mechanisms for just and fair redress for any such activities. • To ensure appropriate measures shall be taken to mitigate adverse environmental, economic, social, cultural or spiritual impact.
Article 33 • Right of Indigenous peoples to determine their own identity or membership in accordance with their customs and traditions. This does not impair the right of Indigenous individuals to obtain citizenship of the States in which they live. • Right of Indigenous peoples to determine the structures and to select the membership of their institutions in accordance with their own procedures.	•
Article 34 • Right of Indigenous peoples to promote, develop and maintain their institutional structures and their distinctive customs, spirituality, traditions, procedures, practices and, in the cases where they exist, juridical systems or customs, in accordance with international human rights standards.	• To ensure that Indigenous peoples can promote, develop and maintain their institutional structures and their distinctive customs, spirituality, traditions, procedures, practices and, in the cases where they exist, juridical systems or customs, in accordance with international human rights standards.
Article 35	

Summary of rights and responsibilities – United Nations Declaration on the Rights of Indigenous Peoples (UNDRIP)[423]	
Rights and responsibilities	**Government obligations**
• Right of Indigenous peoples to determine the responsibilities of individuals to their communities.	
Article 36 • Right of Indigenous peoples, in particular those divided by international borders, to maintain and develop contacts, relations and cooperation, including activities for spiritual, cultural, political, economic and social purposes, with their own members as well as other peoples across borders.	• To, in consultation and cooperation with Indigenous peoples, take effective measures to facilitate the exercise and ensure the implementation of this right.
Article 37 • Right of Indigenous peoples to the recognition, observance and enforcement of treaties, agreements and other constructive arrangements concluded with States or their successors and to have States honour and respect such treaties, agreements and other constructive arrangements. Nothing in this Declaration may be interpreted as diminishing or eliminating the rights of Indigenous peoples contained in treaties, agreements and other constructive arrangements.	• To ensure the establishment, recognition, observance and enforcement of treaties, agreements and other constructive arrangements concluded with Indigenous people or their successors and honour and respect such treaties, agreements and other constructive arrangements.
Article 38	• To, in consultation and cooperation with Indigenous peoples, take the appropriate measures, including legislative measures, to achieve the ends of this Declaration.
Article 39 • Right of Indigenous peoples to have access to financial and	• To ensure provision of financial and technical assistance for the

Summary of rights and responsibilities – United Nations Declaration on the Rights of Indigenous Peoples (UNDRIP)[423]	
Rights and responsibilities	**Government obligations**
technical assistance from States and through international cooperation, for the enjoyment of the rights contained in this Declaration.	enjoyment of the rights contained in this Declaration.
Article 40 • Right of Indigenous peoples to access to and prompt decision through just and fair procedures for the resolution of conflicts and disputes with States or other parties, as well as to effective remedies for all infringements of their individual and collective rights. Such a decision shall give due consideration to the customs, traditions, rules and legal systems of the Indigenous peoples concerned and international human rights.	• To ensure Indigenous peoples have the right to access to and prompt decision through just and fair procedures for the resolution of conflicts and disputes with States or other parties, as well as to effective remedies for all infringements of their individual and collective rights. Such a decision shall give due consideration to the customs, traditions, rules and legal systems of the Indigenous peoples concerned and international human rights.

Appendix 4 – Civil and political rights protected or at risk in Australia

The following table is provided to assist in assessment of the number of civil and political rights in the International Covenant on Civil and Political Rights that are:

- available to natural persons in Australia with some reliability because they have some legislative basis and/or are underpinned by the Constitution;
- not reliably available to natural persons in Australia because they are not fully provided for in the Australian Constitution; and/or
- at risk in their availability to natural persons based on evidence of abuse of these rights by Australian authorities, reservations held in regard to those rights by the Australian government, or legislative action by the parliament which has had the effect of reducing these rights.

The table is for indicative purposes only, inasmuch as an exhaustive legislative review has not been undertaken by the author. Some rights marked as "not reliably available" may be available in state legislation; but because state legislation can be overridden by the Commonwealth it is assumed here that these rights are not reliably secured.

Summary of rights – International Covenant on Civil and Political Rights (ICCPR)[424]				
Article	**Rights and responsibilities**	**Available for all with some reliability**	**Not reliably available**	**At risk – under clear threat**
Article 1	• Right of self-determination. • Right of all humans to freely determine their political status and freely pursue their economic, social and cultural development.		**1**	
Article 2	• All rights to be applied without discrimination.		**1**	
Article 3	• Rights are equal for all. • Rights are for the equal enjoyment of all.		**1**	**1**
Article 4	• Right to protection from loss of rights in certain circumstances. • Responsibility to accept government's ability to curtail rights in emergencies which threaten the life of the nation.		**1**	**1**
Article 5	• Right of any state, group or person not to have a right or freedom (that is recognised in the Covenant) destroyed by any state, group or person or limited to a greater extent than is provided for in the Covenant.		**1**	**1**
Article 6	• Right to life.		**1**	

424 International Covenant on Civil and Political Rights- external site

Summary of rights – International Covenant on Civil and Political Rights (ICCPR)[424]				
Article	**Rights and responsibilities**	**Available for all with some reliability**	**Not reliably available**	**At risk – under clear threat**
Article 7	• Right not to be subjected to torture or cruel, inhuman or degrading treatment or medical or scientific experimentation.		**1**	**1**
Article 8	• Right not to be held in slavery, servitude or forced/compulsory labour.		**1**	
Article 9	• Right to liberty and security of person.		**1**	
	• Right not to be subjected to arbitrary detention.		**1**	
	• Right not to be deprived of liberty except on grounds established by law.		**1**	
	• Right in criminal cases to a trial within a reasonable time or to release.		**1**	
	• Right to take proceedings in order that a court, without delay may decide the lawfulness of detention.		**1**	
	• Right to compensation for unlawful arrest or detention.		**1**	
Article 10	• Right of accused persons to be segregated from convicted persons.		**1**	**1**
	• Right of accused and convicted juvenile persons to be separated from adults in the detention system.		**1**	**1**
	• Right to speedy justice for juveniles.		**1**	**1**

Summary of rights – International Covenant on Civil and Political Rights (ICCPR)[424]				
Article	**Rights and responsibilities**	**Available for all with some reliability**	**Not reliably available**	**At risk – under clear threat**
Article 11	• Right not to be imprisoned for failure to fulfil a contractual obligation.		**1**	
Article 12	• Right and freedom to choose a place of residence.	**1**		
	• Right to freedom of movement.	**1**		**1**
	• Right to leave a country.		**1**	**1**
	• Right of citizens to enter their own country.		**1**	**1**
Article 13	• Right of lawful aliens not to be expelled unlawfully.			
Article 14	• Right to equality before the law.		**1**	**1**
	• Right to a fair and public hearing by a competent, independent and impartial tribunal established by law.		**1**	
	• Right of presumption of innocence until proved guilty.		**1**	**1**
	• Right to be informed fully and promptly of the detail of charges.		**1**	**1**
	• Right to adequate time to prepare a defence and communicate with counsel of choice.		**1**	**1**
	• Right to be tried without undue delay.		**1**	**1**
	• Right of defendants to be present at their trial and to defend themselves or		**1**	**1**

Summary of rights – International Covenant on Civil and Political Rights (ICCPR)[424]				
Article	**Rights and responsibilities**	**Available for all with some reliability**	**Not reliably available**	**At risk – under clear threat**
	through their chosen counsel.			
	• Right to legal aid and interpreter services.		1	1
	• Right to examine witnesses.		1	1
	• Right of defendants not to testify against themselves or to confess guilt.		1	
	• Right to have criminal convictions reviewed.		1	
	• Right to compensation for wrongful conviction.		1	1
	• Right not to be tried more than once for an offence.		1	
Article 15	• Right not to be held guilty for an offence which was not a crime when the offence was committed.		1	
	• Right not to have a penalty imposed beyond that applicable at the time of the offence.		1	
Article 16	• Right to recognition everywhere as a person before the law.		1	1
Article 17	• Right to privacy.		1	1
	• Right to reputation and to protection from attacks on privacy and reputation.		1	1
Article 18	• Right to freedom of thought, conscience and religion.	1		
	• Right to manifest one's religion and beliefs.	1		

Summary of rights – International Covenant on Civil and Political Rights (ICCPR)[424]				
Article	**Rights and responsibilities**	**Available for all with some reliability**	**Not reliably available**	**At risk – under clear threat**
Article 19	• Right to hold opinions without interference.		**1**	**1**
	• Right to freedom of expression.		**1**	**1**
	• Right to seek, receive and impart information and ideas of all kinds.		**1**	**1**
Article 20	• Implied right to peace		**1**	**1**
	• Right to protection from and prevention of racial hatred, hostility and violence.	**1**		**1**
Article 21	• Right to peaceful assembly.		**1**	**1**
Article 22	• Right to freedom of association with others.		**1**	**1**
	• Right to form trade unions.	**1**		
Article 23	• Right to marriage by men and women of marriageable age.	**1**		
	• Right to no forced marriage.	**1**		
Article 24	• Right of every child to protection of the state.		**1**	**1**
	• Right of every child to be registered and to have a name.		**1**	
	• Right of every child to acquire a nationality.		**1**	
Article 25	• Right of every citizen to take part in the conduct of public affairs directly or through freely chosen representatives.		**1**	**1**

Summary of rights – International Covenant on Civil and Political Rights (ICCPR)[424]				
Article	**Rights and responsibilities**	**Available for all with some reliability**	**Not reliably available**	**At risk – under clear threat**
	• Right of every citizen to vote and be elected in elections of universal and equal suffrage and with secret ballot.		1	1
	• Right of every citizen to access, on general terms of equality, to public service.		1	1
Article 26	• Right to be equal before the law.		1	1
	• Right to equal protection of the law.		1	1
Article 27	• Right of everyone to enjoy their own culture and religion.	1		
	• Right of minorities to use their own language.		1	1
	Total	**9**	**53**	**36**